Greater Shanghai
(CENTRAL PORTION)

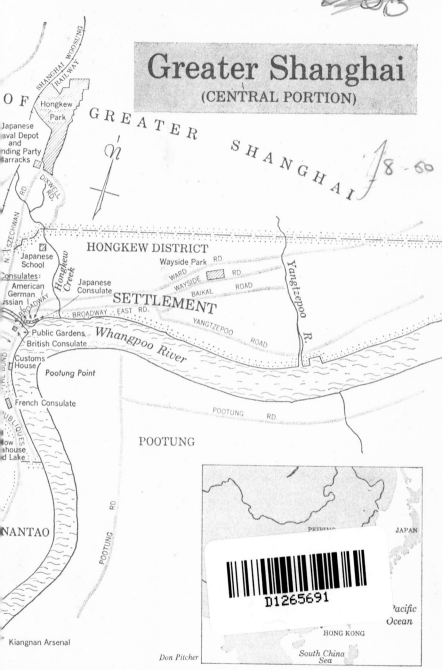

£2-50

A PLACE IN TIME

A Place in Time

Georges Spunt

LONDON

MICHAEL JOSEPH

First published in Great Britain by
MICHAEL JOSEPH LTD
26 Bloomsbury Street
*London, W.C.*1
1969

7181 0679 2

Printed in Great Britain by
Western Printing Services Ltd, Bristol

For Mama, Papa, Sascha, and Aristide
Wherever you are, that's nice . . .

J'ai plus de souvenirs que si J'avais mille ans

BAUDELAIRE

A PLACE IN TIME

1

THOUGH lacking in formal education, Mama would have considered herself most admirably suited to the task of writing this book. For, like the compulsively epistolary French ladies of previous centuries, Mama wrote endlessly. This can be attested to by cartons of ribbon-bound letters, sporadically filled diaries (actually bound in purple leather), and even scraps of brown paper sacking. The letters Mama wrote were full of trifling details correctly spelled, as though ever conscious of her untutored state she was writing with an eye for grades in posterity. What she failed to understand, but what her letters show all too clearly, is that the minute one interrupts passion for the sake of accuracy, the product is aborted. However, the entries in her diaries made in honest haste and without the support of dictionaries give some clue to the true essence of Mama's spirit. Here is one item where Mama describes a visit made to the Pitti Palace in Florence during a trip there in the late twenties: 'We sore a paneting by sumbuddy calld Rubens. I think he was Jewish. Such fat nakid wimen. Who needs reminders?'

But as precise and possibly sterile as her carefully worked-over book might have been, there is a chance that you would have gleaned from Mama the answers to a number of things I will never know and which now remain unanswerable. For instance, the Italian prince: Was he her lover *before* Papa died? And that nasty business in Alexandria. Were the facts she finally submitted the real ones? And above all, there is the simple question of her attitude towards the Chinese people among whom she lived from the age of fourteen. As I sift through years of accumulated correspondence I can find no inkling of her feelings on the subject. Conceivably it may be assumed that like most of the foreign residents in that evanescent port Shanghai, Mama was little concerned with the fate of China itself. But my own observations of her compel me to indicate otherwise. That is why in spite of the restraint she would have shown, I cannot help wishing that Mama had been able to write this book.

For once she might have committed to pen and paper all that she had hesitated to say in her lifetime and more than she was willing to disclose to me, her youngest son.

I would gladly have left this telling to my brothers, Sascha and Aristide, but this is impossible since they too are dead. Anyway, Sascha, who was already ten years old when I was born, had utterly traditional views, blinding himself to anything except a socially acceptable framework. His dedication to the fact that we were French citizens and the sons of the wealthiest foreign cotton merchant in Shanghai eliminated for him the necessity to delve into ghetto origins.

Aristide was two years old when I was born, and I am sorry his interpretation of our family is lost. It would be exciting and pungent but, regrettably, mostly untrue since this fanciful brother was never one to sacrifice a pithy story for mere facts. At a certain point in his life, during an infatuation with monarchy, he actually had me believing Mama was a Russian grand duchess, and when in exasperation Mama brought evidence to the contrary, he regarded it as malice.

It remains then for me to tell this story. Maybe rightly so, since in my brothers' lifetime I existed in a state of polarity, attracted to one and repelled by the other, leaving me with little else but their happenings to record.

I learned the truth of my mother's family background from my grandmother, Raizil, whose parents were Russian Jews of modest means. Orphaned early, Raizil had been reared by her grandmother, Miriam, in Berdichev some fifty kilometres southwest of Kiev. Miriam was of sufficient substance and learning to hold a position at the temple. It was her job to marshal the women in the upper tiers and translate into Yiddish the Hebrew prayers intoned by the rabbi. At given points Miriam would announce, '*Hier ist zu weinen!*'. Whereupon the women would respond at once with loud wailing and rending of clothes. Although Miriam treated her granddaughter like a menial, Raizil dutifully accompanied her on visits to Kiev, where Miriam went to take the waters. I loved to hear Grandmama tell of the time in that city when kindly Catholic Poles hid them from rampaging Cossacks during a pogrom. When Raizil was nearly thirty and Miriam was too old to travel, she arranged a match for her granddaughter with Abram Savine. Abram was born in Odessa at the time of the Crimean War which made him roughly six years older than Raizil. He was a childless widower with no outward signs of economic success. Even at the time I first remember Grandpapa, when he was already quite old, his handsomeness was extraordinary. He had large, fearlessly blue eyes with the hard sparkle of corundum. His brows were heavy but well defined and black like ermine tails. Most exceptional was his complexion. There was to it none of the boiled look or the peppering of freckles which make all redheads seem like members of one family. His skin, though pale, was not waxen but finely translucent, on his arms and legs as well. How his mouth was shaped remained a mystery always, for under a large but straight nose rested a walrus moustache. To hear Grandmama carry on about her husband's striking looks, one might never have guessed that she was at the beginning averse to the idea of marriage with him. She had pleaded with Miriam to let her stay on as her helper.

'Listen to me, my child,' Miriam had said. 'God knows best about these matters, and it's his decree that children obey their elders.' Then she told Raizil about the legend of the Roman lady who asked Rabbi Akiba what his God had been doing since he completed the work of the creation. 'He's been arranging marriages,' the rabbi replied. But when Grandmama was not consoled by this, Miriam grew testy and told Grandmama that Abram was the best bargain she could hope to make: 'After all, you are not such a *mihtseeah*.'

When Grandmama spoke of Miriam's uncharitable appraisal, she did so with a hesitant laugh as though she really were in concurrence. The first photographs of Grandmama which I saw were tinted, taken when Grandmama was in her early forties. Even then it is clear that Miriam had underestimated her granddaughter's assets. Raizil was delicately built. Under a sable-coloured pompadour with a topknot was a fine oval face. Her features were not Slavic or Semitic, or even a recognizable mixture of both. Her eyes had the blue freshness of field flowers, and while they were deeply set and not particularly large, they had a liveliness quite unlike the piscine look of Russian eyes. Without being hooked, her nose had a royal curve perfectly balanced in proportion to her other features. It was her smile that was most charming, however, for it seemed to set her face alive with delight.

Miriam settled a small dowry on Abram, and in 1889 he married

13

Raizil. Mama was born the following year and at the age of a hundred and three, Miriam died in her sleep, having bequeathed her solid gold samovar and a fine string of pearls to the synagogue.

After the assassination of the liberal Alexander the Second and the ascension to the throne of his son in 1881, life had become intolerable for Jews in Russia. My grandparents told of villages razed, Cossacks who slashed breasts off Jewish women and skewered babies on their bayonets. When it became evident upon the death of Alexander the Third in 1894 that his son Nicholas the Second intended to continue persecuting the Jews, Grandpapa knew that the time had come to prepare for leaving Russia.

Two years later, Abram, Raizil, and Mama, who was six, left for Alexandria. Abram had heard stories of great settlements of Jews living among a variety of nationalities and faiths, who were able to follow their own beliefs and who could exist without becoming usurers or running vodka shops, the only vocations Imperial edicts had allowed Jews in Russia. But in Alexandria, Abram found an altered and perplexing set of circumstances. Although Egypt was under British occupation with an Egyptian khedive, or viceroy, the influence of the former French conquest was still much in evidence. True enough, Jews of Spanish descent, the *Sephardim*, had become wealthy merchants and were respected members of the community, but the newer arrivals from Rumania and Russia were for the most part engaged in being *sarrafs* or street money-changers.

Abram settled his wife and daughter in the Arab district near the western harbour. The single-story building was little more than a hovel with cracked plaster walls and an earth floor. Grandmama set about to spruce it up as much as she was able and began making confections which she displayed on trays lined with fresh linen. Since her customers were mainly Arabs, Greeks, Armenians, and Syrians, she specialized in delicacies which would appeal to them.

Mama was sent to a convent run by an order of nuns from Turin. While this decision must have been arrived at with considerable soul-searching on the part of my grandparents, convent schooling was free, and the sisters, eager for converts, accepted all faiths. Besides a natural facility for languages common to most Russians and a fine penmanship, Mama was, with the exception of one other subject, a poor student. She idled away so much of her time making ink rings on her fingers that the distracted nuns thrashed her with their wooden pointers. They let her remain only because of Mama's fascination with the pageantry of Catholicism. As a result she was a star pupil in catechism and knew the legend of every saint. She won a number of prizes, lead images, and enamelled medals which she carefully hid from view at home. But beyond her curiosity and a desire for trappings, Mama remained impervious to the blandishments of the sisters, and they eventually had to content themselves with changing only her name. Instead of calling Mama by her Hebrew name of Malke, or queen, they called her Regina. Both French and Italian were taught at the convent; Mama immediately embraced the latter and became fluent in it. She did her best to look like the Italian students, copied their manner of dress, and parted her long hair in the centre, pinning it away from her temples with barrettes the way the Italian girls did. She was ecstatic when Grandmama robbed the cigar box, in which Abram cached the store's sales, to purchase a tiny pair of gold hoops for her ears.

Sometimes on holidays the nuns took their students to open-air operas in the Champs Elysées Park. Mama soon learned the principal arias of Verdi's and Puccini's heroines and sang constantly in her curious toasty voice. The sisters also arranged train excursions to Mex, Ramleh, and San Stefano. Best of all Mama liked the suburb of Ramleh which was on the eastern shore about sixteen miles from Alexandria on an unbroken stretch of coast.

Under the guidance of Arab donkey boys, the girls rode along the beaches. Mama infuriated the sisters by riding astride like the native women, instead of sidesaddle which was proper for European young ladies. One late afternoon as she dallied behind her group astride a donkey, singing happily away, she became aware of being watched. A boy of sixteen or so, by his style obviously an Italian, was sitting above the beach on a dune. Around his neck hung a mandolin on which he strummed a salute. Fearful the sisters would notice, Mama snatched the stick out of the surprised donkey-boy's hand and tapped the animal on the head, racing to catch up with the rest of her party. The next weekend Mama returned to Ramleh by herself, filching the necessary eight piastres from Grandpapa's change box to get her there and back. The Italian youth, whose name was Vittorio Barrometti, was waiting for her.

Every Sabbath when the shop was closed, Mama was permitted to assist the nuns at the convent. Of course, she went straight to meet

15

the Italian boy. Each time she told him that this had to be the last, that if her father ever found out he would flay her alive. But when another week had passed, thoughts of strolling by the fringe of the Mediterranean, of eating *amardeen*—sun-dried apricots flattened into sheets like leather—or sitting closely in the gardens of the Variety Theatre, overcame any fear, and Mama knew that what she felt for Vittorio was love.

Like the Arab girls of her age, Mama was well developed, and Abram decided that it was time for her to help in the shop. Once when I was able to penetrate the loyalty she had to her parents, Mama confessed that she had pleaded against leaving the convent and had cried all night in the lap of her mother, but they both knew that Grandpapa's word was law.

Soon after Mama began to work in the shop there was a substantial increase in the male clientele, interested in the one delicacy which was ostensibly not for sale. Grandmama kept her daughter's hair combed in long tresses to signify that Mama was still a child, and Grandpapa brandished a nâbût, the thick stick watchmen carried, made of Caramanian ash.

Although I can attribute to my mother almost everything I know of her life in Alexandria, it was characteristic of her total lack of vanity that the following information came from Grandmama. Along with her French and Italian, Mama had acquired more than a smattering of other languages. Customers from the European section and outlying areas began to patronize the shop. Sometimes a Levantine merchant or an officer from the British garrison at Camp Moustapha, in an effort to curry favour, would buy Mama confections from the counters, which under Grandpapa's ferret-eyed stare she would return to the trays when the customers had gone. Mama's beauty became so well known that the wife of a European consul-general sought her out. The woman was an accomplished portraitist and she persuaded Mama to sit for her. When the painting was awarded the first prize at an exhibition in London, the artist's gift to Mama was the purchase price of a dozen photographs. I suppose this is the reason why there are so many pictures of Mama and her parents at this period. I learned too from Grandmama that during the painting sessions a relative of the Khedive had called on the artist.

The first time the glistening victoria with its liveried groom and

16

coachman stopped by the store there was considerable excitement. Sherif Pasha was stout, nattily dressed in a Western suit, and given to such finery as gold watch chains, a large ruby fob, and cuff links. Mama said that he smelled like a combination of jasmine and mutton, and she did not like him.

When Grandmama and her daughter were invited to the palace of the Khedive's mother in Ramleh and when two emissaries began returning almost daily, it became clear that the Pasha was paying court. Grandmama told me of many discussions, between the emissaries and Abram in the little back room, which often lasted until gas had to be lit in the lamps. Each time the men arrived, they brought gifts, flaçons of perfumed oil for Grandmama and Mama, and choice comestibles for Grandpapa. They were always accompanied by two boys, slaves possibly, who carried Damascus rugs which they spread on the earthen floor of the shop. Grandmama related these episodes with great pride, stressing Mama's loveliness and Grandpapa's vigilance over her. She implied that while the idea of courtship from a member of the Viceroy's family with its attendant benefits was as it should be, marriage to a Moslem was unthinkable. Unaccountably, when Grandmama was telling of these times, she would lose a year. No matter how often Grandmama and her daughter discussed Mama's thirteenth year, they never went beyond the flattering interest of customers and the prize-winning painting. The business about the Pasha's attentions was briefly touched upon, and then looks were exchanged and the conversation was abruptly switched. When I was older and nourished on the elaborate details of their storytelling, I sensed something amiss. There were those photographs for instance. In one of them my grandparents are standing behind Mama, who is seated upon what appears to be a piano bench. Grandpapa, whose vest shows between his parted jacket, is sporting a fairly massive gold chain. Grandmama is wearing an afternoon gown of silk surah and a tricorne of ostrich feathers, the hand holding a matching feather boa at the waist is mittened, and there is a substantial marquise-shaped diamond on one of the fingers. In this particular photograph, Mama looks little more than a child in an empire-waisted dress which comes just above the knee. She is wearing high, laced, white leather boots. From the brow, her hair is swept up, caught with a large satin bow at the back, while the remainder falls to her waist. Even then her eyes were fixed in that gentle expression of looking above and beyond, like a madonna. Around her neck is a gold locket lavaliere.

There are several others, but the notable thing about all of them is the quality of clothing and the jewellery. Having seen these pictures from infancy, I did not question the inconsistency of my grandparents' circumstances with the opulence of the photographs until much later.

Barrometti, the Italian youth, appears to have been lost in the shuffle of that year as well. Mama seemed reluctant to discuss him, and when she did it was as though she were expunging a loss.

The reason my grandparents suddenly decided to leave Alexandria was a mystery to me for a long time. I only know that when I was little and the discussion came up Grandmama would murmur, 'By my life—' and, clasping both her ears with her hands, would shake her head from side to side. Once only did I hear her mention *skandal*. This much I was sure of: Barrometti could not have been instrumental in a scandal. The story of their departure, as Grandmama told it to me, was simply that a Jewish merchant who had befriended Abram convinced him that Shanghai was the new city of opportunity, citing as an example the fact that his brother had gone there only four years earlier and already owned the finest hotel in the International Settlement.

On a humid night in April, 1904, my grandparents and Mama boarded a Russian cargo boat, where they were led to their quarters, which turned out to be a portion of the lower deck sheltered only by oilcloths.

When they discussed this voyage, there was always some little discourse between Grandmama and her daughter that set them to laughing: Grandmama shaking her head, one finger pressed against her nose, and Mama as though the memory were fresh, covering her face with both hands. 'That Abram and his *zekl*,' Grandmama would say at last. Because he trusted no one, Grandpapa had persuaded his wife to knit him a pouch in which to place his currency, which he then tied securely over his testicles.

2

EARLY one morning, a day or so after they had left Alexandria, the freighter steamed into the inner harbour at Port Said and docked at the *Bassin Commerciale*. Abram and Raizil, standing on the upper deck, noted little to justify the newfound prosperity of this port, which had only come into being upon the opening of the Suez Canal. Port Said was not old, it was not modern; it was not Alexandria. The dock itself teemed with hawkers, and the ubiquitous carpet sellers followed by their Nubian boys were already beating a path to the gangway.

Raizil touched her husband's arm. 'Look,' she said, pointing to a kiosk at the entrance of the dock. Peering through the eye-watering humidity, Abram saw a group of very young girls standing behind a woman who seemed to be in charge. The girls were dressed alike in middies and dark skirts. Some of them had wound flowers in their hair, and one or two wore beads and earrings. The woman was dressed in white cotton. A sun veil was tied around the straw boater on her head. She carried what looked like a book in her hands.

'*Nahvkas*,' Grandpapa said. This Hebrew term for prostitutes is derived from the verb *nahv*, meaning to pant. With their passion for both phonetic and descriptive literalness, the Jews describe a woman who pants as a *nahvka*.

'What are you saying? They're church ladies,' Grandmama replied.

As the woman herded the girls towards the freighter, a swarm of female visitors broke through the crowd and raced past the officials at the kiosk towards the group now waiting to board. These new girls were much the same age as the prospective passengers and to a degree resembled them, but for the fact that they wore bright dresses and held coloured silk parasols and spangled fans. They were heavily rouged, and in the Egyptian manner all of them had painted antimony around their eyes. The smell of perfumed oils was wafted up to the deck.

'I told you,' Abram said. 'Street women.'

Grandmama pointed to the woman in white. 'You are trying to tell me *that* is a madam?'

'You are both correct,' a voice said in Russian. At my grandparents' elbows stood the skipper watching the scene below through field glasses. He was a portly man whose uniform was dusty with wear and age but whose buttons shined with a mirror polish. Although there was a scant total of twenty passengers, the skipper made no obvious class distinctions and my grandparents felt quite comfortable on the upper deck in his presence.

'Those waiting to board are *former* prostitutes,' he said, 'and the tall woman is an English missionary. With the Cairo–Port Said Railway this year, there has been an enormous population influx. Enormous prosperity too, and with prosperity comes prostitution.'

'Then why are they leaving with the church lady?' ever-practical Abram asked.

The skipper crossed himself. 'Respectable citizens, Christ should save us from them. After the café-concerts, the Quai François Joseph has become so crowded with these girls that the city officials have been forced to take action. Every day shiploads are deported to Smyrna, Palermo, and Marseille.'

'What about those?' Abram asked, indicating the visitors.

'As you can see, they are all native girls,' the skipper said. 'Where could they be deported?'

At this point the gangplanks were cleared for the passengers to board. The visiting girls thronged closer to their departing sisters. Some clapped their hands and some cast flowers and all of them seemed to be shrilling with the cheerless intensity of the condemned. The dozen girls who were leaving barely reacted. A couple of them seemed embarrassed, one wept, and one of those wearing a brilliant scarf made a finger at the visitors. The English woman formed her group in rows of two. The hand holding the book was pressed against her chest. She raised the other in signal. The skipper sighed, 'Now they sing about lambs and Jesus and salvation.' But they did not sing. They just went up the gangplank.

The missionary, whose name was Miss Skipworth, had been given cabin accommodation of sorts while the girls were relegated to the lower deck where my grandparents and Mama were settled. Although the girls were placed at the other extreme of the deck, their presence had a disconcerting effect on Grandmama. However, when Grandpapa conversed with the girls, they said that they were musicians and had been part of the female orchestra of the Concert Khedivial. Having created this aura of respectability for themselves, the girls did what they could to uphold it. They were generally well behaved and, with one or two exceptions, fairly quiet. In the course of Grandpapa's conversation with them, some light was shed on Miss Skipworth. They explained that the jealousy of other 'musicians' had caused them to be jailed pending deportation proceedings. Miss Skipworth had visited them with an offer of a new way of life in China. She had told them that they could learn a craft, help the needy, or, if they should lean towards it, teach His word.

'And what about all the time you have put into being musicians?' Abram asked.

'An instrument doesn't last forever,' one of the girls replied. Reassured that under their present circumstances the girls did not represent a source of moral contamination to her own daughter, Grandmama got busy. By the time the freighter left the Suez Canal she had persuaded Miss Skipworth to tutor Mama. 'You will learn English, a very important language. Everywhere we go, English are the masters. It will be so in our new home, *avoda*, Abram?' And Grandpapa agreed.

Miss Skipworth's authority made her seem older to Mama than her twenty-three years. She was a tall woman with autumn colourings. Her hair was drawn unfashionably over her ears into a tight back-knot. She had pale dry lips, although she moistened them often. When she was being firm, they would clamp down over big clergical teeth.

Classes were held in the dining saloon, between meals. Miss Skipworth set up a blackboard and distributed pens with G nibs, inkwells, and copybooks. She compartmentalized her teaching so that not a moment was unaccounted for. The day began with Bible class, reading, and a study of the scriptures. These were conducted in French, the one language the girls had in common. This was followed by a general history of their future home. Mama liked these accounts of China best.

While Miss Skipworth seemed to Mama far less steeped in religious dogma than the Alexandria nuns, and while her relationship to the girls was on a human and practical basis rather than a divine and remote one, the drawn-out sessions of Bible class bored

21

Mama. 'It's the same old New Testament that I had with the nuns,' she complained to Abram.

At Grandmama's subtle intervention, Miss Skipworth agreed to let Mama off Bible class. 'She can use the time to copy out the first and second epistles to the Thessalonians,' said Miss Skipworth, marking the pages on a note. 'That will improve both her English and her script.'

They had been at sea for about a week and were leaving the Gulf of Aden when an incident occurred in the classes that revealed to Mama that for all Miss Skipworth's apparent casualness she could be as much of a disciplinarian as the nuns with their pointers. It was at an afternoon session on how the foreigners came to establish trade between the West and China. She told her class that for several centuries the overland silk routes had been the only mercantile links between China and Europe. With the emergence of trade through steamships in the last century, the Western world became anxious for the increased revenue which could be obtained from China via sea routes. Aside from a restricted quarter in Canton, the Chinese government refused access to any other ports. China looked upon the West as barbaric and scarcely capable of providing an ancient culture with anything of real value, and the overland routes were adequate for the relatively small amounts of British imports. From their point of view, the British with their growing markets for tea, and the constant demand for silk, found it more desirable to barter with goods than to purchase outright in silver. During her discussion Miss Skipworth noticed that the girls appeared to be taking turns at opening and shutting the same porthole on the pretext that they needed air. She observed too that this action was followed by much giggling in the class. Miss Skipworth went to the porthole and looked out. From where she sat Mama saw the missionary's upper lip clamp firmly down, and in a second Miss Skipworth was out of the saloon. Lelia, a Syrian girl, was missing from the class. In the noisy speculation which ensued during the English woman's absence, Mama learned that Lelia had fallen in with a Russian seaman and that she was getting thoroughly fed up with the restrictions imposed on her. The door of the saloon burst open. Miss Skipworth held onto the Syrian girl's wrists like a vice. Lelia was wearing a sheer blouse pulled below her shoulders. The embroidered basque of her flame-coloured dirndl was cinched so tightly it was no wonder that she could not wrench herself from Miss Skipworth's grasp. By now every porthole to the saloon framed the eager faces of sailors. Lelia pulled one hand free and then the other. Before Miss Skipworth could move, Lelia ripped her blouse so that one breast was exposed. With her thumb and forefinger she manipulated her nipple so that the teat disappeared from view. Miss Skipworth stood absolutely still. Then Lelia turned to the class with her exposed breast and the winking effect she had achieved with her nipple. The girls in the class stamped and screamed their approval. Finally, with a big carmined grin, Lelia turned to the portholes and there was an explosion of cheering from the sailors. Miss Skipworth pressed her Bible to her chest with one hand and raised the other as though in search of divine guidance. Then deciding all at once not to wait for it, she ran to the portholes and drew the curtains. Next she turned to Lelia and struck her repeatedly, using her book as a clout. When the girl begged her to stop, Miss Skipworth could scarcely breathe. 'Forbearance be damned,' she gasped.

Being assured that the girl was genuinely contrite, Miss Skipworth dismissed the episode. There were no more digressions from her charges and the classes progressed without incident.

In her next discourse on the establishment of the treaty ports, Miss Skipworth told about the causes and effects of the war between England and China. Opium, she said, was the bloom of evil, by which the Western powers were able to achieve their ends. Originally imported in small amounts for medicinal purposes, opium became valued for its narcotic effect, and sales grew rapidly. Ministers to the Emperor, alarmed at the outgo of cash for the imported drug as well as at its debilitating characteristics, urged the outlaw of opium. A smuggling boom for the forbidden product enriched many foreign importers and corrupt Chinese officials. Matters were brought to a head when the Emperor dispatched an Imperial commissioner, a man of imputrescible character, to destroy an entire cargo. The end result of this action brought about the Opium War in which the Chinese, hopelessly unequipped to fight either on land or sea against a power such as the British, were easily defeated.

The treaty of Nanking, signed in 1842, established the British aim of five treaty ports and extraterritorial advantages for its citizens. Other Western powers such as America and France moved in at once with demands for settlements, and individual treaties were signed.

The group's studies were affected again almost two weeks later, after the boat had stopped at Colombo for refuelling and was crossing the Indian Ocean. Malaria and dysentery broke out on board and most of the girls were stricken. Miss Skipworth continued in her duties as teacher to those who could go on with their lessons and stayed up nights tending to the ill. She took it as most natural that Mama should attend her classes and perform as nurse's helper at night.

On the night before they were due to arrive at Singapore, the English woman suggested a stroll on the deck with Mama. It was during these moments that Mama learned Miss Skipworth's true purpose. She spoke of the position of missionaries as being poised precariously between the indifference and contempt of the profit-minded merchants, both foreign and Chinese. Her chapter of the mission was the Gates of Grace, whose object it was to rehabilitate girls and women who were abandoned, who were sold into white slavery, or who sought the aid of the mission. 'We teach them crafts as well as the word of the Lord,' she concluded. But she made it patently clear that it was towards the aim of self-reliance, rather than spiritual salvation, that she was directing her energies.

But for these interludes, it was an uneventful journey sparked only by one moment of excitement when news was relayed aboard the ship that the Japanese were gaining in their war with Russia. On a mid-afternoon early in June the ship tied up at the Woosung Bar, some twelve miles from Shanghai.

Miss Skipworth was standing beside Mama and her parents on the tender which cut a swathe through the yellow billows of the Whangpoo River. The shoreline, like a full smile, came into view. The missionary described the sight before them. From north to south was a stretch of river frontage; the portion of it beyond the jetties paved with grassy promenades was known as the International Settlement Bund. An impressive array of classic-style buildings rose behind the jetties. To the south, Mama saw another quay which Miss Skipworth said was the French Bund. Instead of trim tenders and light craft, these jetties were crowded with ferryboats, barges, and junks. Miss Skipworth shuddered slightly, for the junks moored at these pontoons were opium hulks. The buildings which crested the waterfront of the Quai de France were mainly godowns and offices of not very inspirational quality. Still farther south, somewhat lower on the shoreline, was the Chinese Bund, and it was on this waterfront that the walled city of Shanghai was located. The shores of this section were crowded with hundreds of mat-covered little boats, which Miss Skipworth called sampans and which were moored to the jetties, like a mobile village. The contrast between the native Shanghai and the Western civilization which had seized this port was etched most sharply for Mama when the English woman urged her to look at a tung-stained junk with eyes painted on its bow sailing grandly past a British gunboat lying in the harbour.

Miss Skipworth proved an asset in helping Mama and her parents through the customs shed, which, but for Grandpapa's determination not to have his luggage disturbed, would have been a simple enough matter in view of their meagre belongings. On the promenade they were beset by offers of transportation from cabriolet drivers and rickshaw coolies. The English lady settled each of the members of the family into a rickshaw with some of their possessions and obtained a fourth rickshaw to carry the remaining baggage. Grandpapa, taking the Alexandria merchant at his word, told Miss Skipworth to direct the coolies to the finest hotel in the city. She embraced Mama and told her that the mission was quite close to the Astor House and that she would inquire for her in a day or so.

3

THE skipper had exchanged some of Grandpapa's pounds for the local currency, and as the coolies jogged northward along the broad roadway of the Bund, Mama could hear the jingling of the silver dollars and coins that bulged from Grandpapa's pockets. Mama stared around her, marvelling as the coolies dodged wheelbarrows, handcarts, carriages, and pedestrians. On the river side of the Bund where they had landed, the walks were uncluttered stretches of green but on the left, across the wide road, mercantile structures made a solid facing. It was strange to think that these buildings towered on what Miss Skipworth had said was once a marshy towpath for the hauling of tribute junks.

Mama watched the rickshaw coolies with their queues flying

straight behind them, their bodies streaming sweat in the dying sun of the subtropical heat. They wore nothing more than ragged breeches rolled up over their knees and on their feet were straw sandals. Padding alongside were four coolies bearing a sedan chair. The Chinese gentleman seated in it was clothed in silks.

As the rickshaw coolies proceeded farther north, they came to a widening of the promenade on the riverside which led into what was obviously a park. This was Mama's first glimpse of the Public Gardens, and she could see beyond the shelter of giant magnolias to the bandstand. Miss Skipworth had told her that the British Consulate was opposite the gardens.

A carriage was coming out of the consulate's gates, and Mama noticed that the women in it were Europeans. She watched as they chatted easily, their gloved hands busy with parasols or folding fans; she absorbed the details of their clothing from the eyelet organdies of their dresses to the great flowered and beribboned hats like overturned washbaskets shading porcelain-white faces, and she looked in dismay at her wrinkled taffeta skirt and her soiled shirtwaist. If Grandmama, sitting erectly in her travelling suit and cloak, had noticed the women or was suffering by the comparison, she gave no sign of it. Mama looked at her mother's tired face and saw that the strands of greying hair were neatly brushed into a pompadour over which her feather tricorne fluttered like ragged pennants, and she tried to emulate her mother's air of self-possession.

The pullers arrived at a slight rise in the normally flat road, and as they headed towards the approach of a bridge they strained their muscles and groaned in a singsong chant. Soochow Creek, over which the bridge was spanned, seemed like a floating compression of human life. Here were the omnipresent sampans, and barges piled high with produce. On some, fish lay in glittering heaps, stark-eyed and uncovered, while old women with palm-frond fans waved desultorily at the gathering swarms of flies. Many of the river barges were controlled by sinewy women or girls younger than Mama, who manoeuvred through the water traffic by means of long poles while naked little boys ran about chewing sugar cane or unconcernedly urinated in the creek. The men balanced what seemed to be the heaviest of cargo by means of rope and bamboo poles. On a few of the larger craft, tables were set as for a festival with fat red candles and metal incense holders. Red banners with Chinese characters in black hung from the masts. In this cluttered stretch of water, refuse and human excrement made a pattern between the hulls of each craft, and the hot stench borne by the gentle river breeze assailed them from all sides.

The pullers leaned back against the shafts of the rickshaws as they began the downhill run at the other end of the bridge. They were now entering Broadway in the Hongkew district, which had been the main street of the American Concession before their amalgamation with the British into the International Settlement. The coolies made a sharp right as they came off the bridge and, heedless of oncoming traffic, cut across the street to a building which occupied the entire corner of Whangpoo Road and Broadway. Paying off the rickshaw coolies, Abram picked up as much luggage as he could carry and, indicating to his wife and daughter that they should do likewise, entered the hotel.

Inside the burled wood and marble interior of the Astor House, none of the desk clerks had ever heard of the merchant's brother, whom Grandpapa demanded to see. The impression of that moment on Mama, who was not quite fourteen, was indelible. She recalled Abram mopping at his brow with a wrinkled handkerchief and pressing his carefully treasured letter on the desk as he repeated the name he had been given, again and again. By the impatient manner in which Grandmama clacked her large tortoiseshell fan and the hauteur of her demeanour, which she undoubtedly felt was in keeping with her surroundings, no one would have ever guessed that she was entirely unfamiliar with such opulence.

Finally a young accountant appeared from the inner offices. He was a dapper fellow, Mama remembered, his hair slicked with vaseline, and he wore an opal stickpin in his cravat. He said that he knew the Russian Jew by name and, with considerable sideplay to his confreres and after a long unveiling look at Mama, proceeded to give Grandpapa directions.

The city was bathed in the rose-gold light of crepuscule when Mama and her parents arrived at Wayside. This district, reached by continuing along Broadway, then turning west, had already fallen into disfavour. Saloons and river-type hostelries catering to sailors, chandlers, and merchant seamen had replaced most of the original villas.

Segalsky, for that was the name of the man Grandpapa was seeking, owned a ramshackle rooming house with a saloon on the main floor. Mama and her mother waited in the tiny lobby while Grandpapa presented his letter. There was considerable exchange between Abram and the owner. When Segalsky smiled in the direction of the women, Mama saw that his teeth were uneven and stained brown, and his chin reminded her of the heel of a loaf of bread. Finally Grandpapa shrugged, and coming over to the two women, he gave Mama a key to their quarters, telling her that Grandmama would join her presently.

The room in which all three were to stay contained two white-painted iron cots, a dresser with its mirror cracked, and a creaky wardrobe. A single bulb shone unremittingly from the ceiling. Mama was in the process of hanging their clothes when Grandmama returned, closing the door behind her. As she twisted at the strings of her silk purse, she no longer was the self-contained grande dame who had stood in the lobby of the Astor House.

Grandmama's normal conversation was a blend of Russian laced with any other language which best emphasized what she wanted to say, but when she was upset, she reverted entirely to Yiddish. 'We can stay here,' she said in that tongue. 'Only you will have to help, that's all.'

Mama sat slowly on one of the beds, with her back to her mother. Grandmama came up to her and placed a hand gently on Mama's head. She drew a large bone comb out of her purse and began combing her daughter's hair, in upward sweeps. Mama shuddered. 'It will not be for long, my *kindela*,' Raizil said.

Segalsky had suggested that Abram would be wiser to let Mama support her parents by waiting on his customers rather than to deplete his meagre finances while he sought a suitable occupation. But Segalsky assured Grandpapa his customers were well behaved and that Mama's job would be perfectly *laytish*. To be *laytish*, whatever the outward appearance might seem, was the key, the promise of an ultimately profitable match. Since most Jewish families who came from Russia had become adapted to the limitations of profession allowed them, it was comparatively respectable to work in a bar. Of course, it was much more *laytish* to be proprietor of one's own saloon, but failing that, if a girl was properly chaperoned in the course of her work, she could in the stern eyes of the community be considered reasonably respectable. To that end, Grandpapa posted

28

himself behind the bar, his trusty nâbût handy, while Mama brought drinks to the tables. Within the week that she worked there, Mama attracted many customers and Segalsky was delighted. Had it not been for a British sailor, how long Mama might have had to continue in this work is speculative. Feeling pleasantly high on rum, the sailor leaned over the bar and asked Abram how much money he wanted to permit the tar to take Mama out. Down came the nâbût on the sailor's head and a brawl ensued, causing considerable damage. Reluctantly, Segalsky fired Mama, explaining that he owed much of his business to the men of the British Navy. Grandpapa was obliged to dip into his funds to keep them at the hotel.

I recall that once, when Mama was telling of this experience, Aristide had said, 'But why did Grandpapa make you work in a bar, when you had all those jewels and things?'

'What jewels?' Mama said.

'You know in the photographs, all those gold chains and that big diamond on Grandmama's finger,' Aristide said.

'They were lost, stolen—and we had to pay for our passage,' Mama said. 'Besides, I did what my father told me. Not like today's children.'

Meanwhile, Grandmama had made a friend. Madame Liebgold was a pleasant woman who owned a dressmaking establishment. Like every Jewish woman, she was an irrepressible matchmaker at heart, and she approached her role of *unterfuhrka* with a hardheaded practicality. 'Never mind, she has no dowry. For such a jewel, who needs a setting?' She told Abram and Raizil that they were insane to permit Mama to work when there was a crying need for marriageable girls. There were over eleven thousand foreigners in the International Settlement and the French Concession, she said, and not nearly enough young women for the bachelors. 'If you don't think of your daughter, think of those poor young men, wasting themselves on Kiangsi Road *nahvkas*.' Madame Liebgold threw herself into the project with both skill and zest. She outfitted Mama completely and called daily to take Mama for drives in her carriage.

Mama found the older woman a pleasant enough guide and was grateful for the attention. Madame Liebgold paraded her down the Maloo, or Great Horse, Road, which the foreigners called Nanking Road. This stretch of fine Western and Chinese silk, silver, and curio shops was second only in importance to the Bund. Nanking Road continued into a poplar-lined avenue called Bubbling Well Road, and Mama saw for the first time the handsome mansions with porticos and verandahs in the colonial style of the first foreign business leaders or taipans, as the Chinese called them. She was fascinated most by the ancient Zing Ang Sze Temple and the well with its water charged by carbonic gas. This sojourn continued to a point called St. George's, the farthest point west in the Settlement that had been developed. Much of it was still countrylike, with graves cluttering the open fields. Madame Liebgold's itinerary did not include crossing the Yangking Pang, a canal which separated the French Concession from the International Settlement. The entire French Concession was then only three hundred and sixty acres. Besides its Bund and a few avenues laid out straight from end to end in the French manner, it was mostly given over to some consular residences and commercial buildings. Mama's mentor also declined to visit the Chinese city, which bordered the French Concession to the south.

'But it has a wall four hundred years old,' Mama protested. For centuries China had only been as strong as its walls, Miss Skipworth had told Mama.

'You want to see old walls, sit in your room,' the Jewish woman replied. But she did take Mama to all the fashionable places to which she had access. They had ices at Sweet Meat Castle and afternoon tea at the Astor House. She took Mama to matinee concerts at the Town Hall and they attended the races.

It has been said that the two things an Englishman must have is a king and a racecourse. As early as 1850, before the organization of a municipal council, grounds were secured for a race park, and to the foreign residents of Shanghai, horse-racing was as much a social as a sporting event.

For the race meeting held on a Saturday afternoon, Madame Liebgold dressed Mama in Alençon lace. Over a hat of leghorn straw, plumes in the shades of beige and grey and black nestled. Upon their return, Madame Liebgold was ecstatic. She told Abram and Raizil, 'When our carriage entered the driveway with that queen of yours, there was a dead silence in the pavilion, and even the horses stopped to look at her.' Predictably Madame Liebgold had been right, for in less than two weeks the suitors began to call.

Although our oldest brother, Sascha, would take no part in such

30

childish fantasy, nothing delighted Aristide and me more than when Mama told us of these courtships. The setting for these accounts was always her carved oaken bed where she sat propped up with innumerable cushions. Then Mama would instruct either Aristide or me to fetch one of her jewel boxes from the large standup safe. This safe was never secured even though everything else, particularly the storeroom, was kept firmly under lock and key. The jewel boxes were of tooled Venetian leather, and each contained a separate collection of valuables. The bronze leather case, for instance, held gold jewellery. The black leather contained important pieces. The olive-coloured box held what Mama called her sports jewellery, and in these were unset cabochons and faceted stones. Among them was a chamois bag in which she kept the gifts of the men who had courted her on her fourteenth birthday. While I have long forgotten who gave them or what stories accompanied the enamelled pillbox or the gold brooch set with Persian turquoises which spelled out Remembrance, there is in my mind's eye a clear picture of Mama's meeting with the Spunt brothers.

There were five suitors paying court to Mama, and encouraged by the attentions of these young men to their daughter, my grand-parents decided to give Mama a party on her fourteenth birthday. It was the middle of July. The day before, excited by the prepara-tions, Mama was standing on the balcony of the hotel to get some air. Madame Liebgold, well pleased with the turn of events, was sharing the view with her. A smart black victoria with groom and footman drove slowly by. One of the occupants, an agreeably homely young man, looked out of the carriage window. Mama's companion chuckled.

'Do you know him?' Mama asked.

'There are two. Maximilian and Jeremiah Spunt. They were originally Austrians. Now they are French protégés and very success-ful. They have two sisters, but one, Annie, is a *soldat*.' She put her hand on Mama's as though to restrain an impossible ambition. 'Those men are the best catches in the city, my dear; forget it.'

'Invite them to my party,' Mama said.

I had heard the details of this episode so many times that, were it not impossible, I should insist on having been present. I can, for instance, quite sharply smell the fragrance of sandalwood mingled with the melting tar odour of the streets. I can see Mama's hair, the

31

mahogany shade ablaze with sunlight, caught up with an amber comb and contrasting with the opalescent whiteness of her skin. (Much later Papa told her that she had appeared to him as a shimmering vision of the Pre-Raphaelites, and although Mama repeated the compliment meticulously, when Aristide questioned her on the Pre-Raphaelites she hazarded a guess that they must be an early tribe of the Jews.)

Although he had heard this story as often as I, Aristide always relished hearing it again, asking in his exasperating manner for more details and for this or that passage to be repeated. Mama lifted a silk sack which she untied, and onto the bed spilled an assortment of glittering coloured gems. These were for the most part Ural Mountain stones, rubelite tourmalines, pink, mauve, and yellow sapphires, and purple amethysts. They had been Aunt Annie's wedding present to Mama, and when she let us play with these gems, she would sometimes recount her first meeting with Papa's sisters.

Aunt Annie was the oldest of the Spunts. The sides of her forehead were close in, as though the accoucheuse presiding at her birth had been obliged to use forceps. Lacking was the nobility of brow which characterized her two brothers and her sister Rose. Her features were round to the point of being indistinguishable. Bifocals attached to a black soutache ribbon which she wore around her neck were an inseparable part of that face. She was married to a meek little gentleman of British naturalization who worked as a minor official for the customs.

Grandpapa took no more time than was necessary to check Rosenstock's directory of Shanghai to decide on Maximilian Spunt for his son-in-law, but it was only when Papa announced his engagement to Mama that Aunt Annie extended an invitation to tea.

However, it was Aunt Rose who came to fetch her in Papa's victoria. Aunt Rose was as round as a pincushion and in her middle twenties. Her hair, which was a powdery grey, gave her the appearance of one of the good-natured court ladies of the eighteenth century. She had a fine complexion with high colouring, which particularly marked her pigeon chest and the outer palms of her hands. Her eyes were dark, but unlike Aunt Annie's implacable stare, they were candid and capable of light and laughter.

Aunt Annie greeted Mama while presiding over her silver teakettle. She wore black as usual, with scroll designs on her dress. She was generally over-filigreed and wore rings on practically every finger.

Aunt Annie surveyed Mama blankly from behind the windows of her bifocals. The quivering of the suspended black ribbon was the only indication of her emotion, and it wasn't love. She got down to business at once. As she handed Mama a cup of tea, she said, 'Why do you want to marry Maximilian instead of Jeremiah?' As Mama told us the story, she always said, 'I never thought of saying that I loved him, because I didn't. I couldn't say my mother said to marry the cripple because he would be kinder, so I said, "Because he is younger."' Aunt Annie accepted that as reason enough. It had not occurred to her either that love might be a factor.

'You know, of course,' Aunt Annie had continued, 'that my brother is very successful and could have his pick of Shanghai society. I don't suppose you have a dowry.'

'I have no *dot*,' Mama said.

'You will amount to nothing in this city, unless you speak English,' Aunt Annie said. 'It's all very well that you can get along in French and Italian——'

'And Russian, Arabic, and Greek,' Rose said, pushing for Mama.

'To be upper crust, it's English,' Aunt Annie continued, ignoring her sister. 'Maximilian wanted desperately to be naturalized British, but that's a distinction that's not so easily come by. However, to be a French protégé is not too bad.' She turned to Rose. 'Bring in the kugelhopf, will you?'

When Aunt Rose was out of the room, she said, 'Anything is better than being a Hun. Rose is married to one. The family is excellent stock, but they "*shprech*", if you know what I mean; they don't speak and who are they?'

Aunt Rose's marriage had been a love match. Her husband, Wolfgang, was a handsome and amiable fellow, fonder of living than of providing a livelihood. Aunt Rose was a skilful homemaker, able to transform the bleakest four walls into a warmly lived-in atmosphere. Wolfgang was the less fortunate member of an illustrious family. His brother was a general and his sister was a famous actress in Berlin.

Aunt Rose returned with the kugelhopf which *she* had baked. Aunt Annie served it sparingly with chilled balls of butter. It was clear to Mama that Aunt Annie considered Rose an indisputable

33

failure when Rose, tasting the butter, marvelled at its flavour and asked Aunt Annie for the brand name.

'It's Daisy butter,' Aunt Annie said. 'Twenty cents a pound, and decidedly *not* for your pocket.' The tea party continued in silence, and when she considered it was over, Aunt Annie got up to signify the fact. She had difficulty rising, and when Mama tried to assist her, she explained her problem: 'Piles—big as figs.'

Just as Mama was leaving, Aunt Annie looked at her fixedly, 'Tell me, are you a girl?'

Since *maydl*, girl in Yiddish, generally refers to a virgin, Mama thought she understood what Aunt Annie was getting at. If only from her exposure to Miss Skipworth's charges, she knew that there were good girls—*maydls*—and bad girls—*nahvkas* and *kourvas*—and that the latter permitted men, in some cryptic way, to take liberties with their bodies. Offended by Annie's implication, she determined to give her no satisfaction. Returning the older woman's stare, she replied, 'Well, I'm not a man.'

'That's not what I mean,' Aunt Annie said.

Aunt Rose pressed her hands to her chest, which had turned a flaming pink. 'Please, Annie, please,' she implored.

Mama replied after a moment, 'If I marry your brother, you can ask him, and if I don't, he can thank you.'

Looking back on it now, I find it strange that Mama would have told us these details when we were at an age where she would have known that we surely could not have understood the implications. I have come to the conclusion that Mama, with intuitive accuracy of aim, fired off these confessions, trusting that her sons would understand all that they needed to and would be unconcerned about what they didn't. And she was right, for even when I overheard to what lengths Aunt Annie went to satisfy her curiosity, it was many years later before I fully understood.

4

WHEN it became clear that my grandparents favoured Maximilian, Uncle Jeremiah, who was ten years older, bowed out by going on an extended trip. Grandpapa was set up with a monthly income and a house in the Settlement. Madame Liebgold, amply rewarded by Papa, had undertaken Mama's trousseau. A gown of Brussels lace was ordered from Paris and the wedding was set for September.

In the group photograph taken in the gardens of the Astor House, where the reception was held, Mama and Papa are seated in the centre foreground. Mama appears quite stiff, as she undoubtedly was, encased in the boned health corset which gave the desired S shape to her figure. On top of her high-piled hair there is ruching of tulle from where the veil flows to the ground. Her face is set in repose. Mama's features might have been the prototype of the Gibson beauty then fashionable, with large candid eyes and bud mouth set between a firm nose and chin. There is naturally no hint of the luminous complexion, contrasting with ocean-blue eyes and the winewood shade of her hair. What is most lacking in the image is the *suddenness* of her beauty. She is, as represented, the ultimate pearl, but the woman I was to know had nuances and shades and brilliance like the infinitely more alive nacre on the inside of the shell. Papa's joy at his acquisition, of love truly, is obvious. He sits very close, a hand resting on each knee, the ovoid face accentuated by hair parted in the middle and slicked down to his ears. The tight-fitting cutaway and the collar like a cangue of bone around his neck seem of no concern. Abram and Raizil are standing behind the couple. Abram has the coolly detached expression of one used to besting others in business deals. In Grandmama's face there is a mixture of complacency and pride and just a hint, I feel, of concern. Papa's sisters are there, of course, with their respective husbands. Aunt Rose, the matron of honour, is beaming, and Aunt Annie is staring at the camera and looks as if she has just eaten something disagreeable.

What I know of my father's family is only what Mama was able to cull from Papa and Aunt Rose. To listen to Aunt Annie, Mama said, you would have thought that the Spunts were descended from the Hapsburgs. Alta Spunt (most likely spelled Shpunt, then) fled from Vienna when Jews became eligible for military conscription. Under the Austro-Hungarian Empire the Jew's lot was no better than it was in Russia, and the conscript was badgered into the meanest of duties. Like so many Jews of that generation, Alta and his wife, Chaya, yielded to the glowing promises of security held by the Far East. They settled in Yokohama where Alta opened a saloon. Papa, the youngest of four children and a cripple, was born in 1884. In time, the saloon prospered moderately and Alta enlisted the services of his children. Aunt Annie, the eldest, whom Papa described as a *gezunt* or stalwart girl, handled the disorderly customers; Aunt Rose played the piano while Uncle Jeremiah waited on customers. Papa, who as a mere child had shown an uncanny aptitude for cards, played whist with the sailors to keep them amused. It was, according to Papa, as sedate and *laytish* as could be hoped for under the circumstances.

In spite of Aunt Rose's and Papa's euphemisms, Alta emerges as a cruel man, ready with a clout and a whip, and his frail wife and children were terrified of him. Only Aunt Annie is on record for stating her feelings. In a letter to Papa sometime after the wedding, making one of her endless requests for money, she wrote, 'How we suffered under that evil man, may he burn in hell. Remember that I was like a mother to you. Remember the *clops* I took in the face when you ran away to Shanghai. . . .'

Actually, it was Aunt Rose who had taken the drubbing for Papa's escape. It was she who had helped him to pack a few belongings and who had crept out of the house before dawn to see him off. Uncle Jeremiah had left a few years earlier and was working at the mills in Shanghai as a clerk. He had sent Papa his passage money. Papa was twelve years old when he entered the Richard Ashbury School for boys. Upon graduation at the age of sixteen, he was employed by an elderly Swiss importer, and in three years had risen to general manager of the small firm. Upon the death of the proprietor he inherited the business.

Around the turn of the century the French had offered protection to any nationals who wished eventually to become citizens. People who applied for this became French protégés. Avid Anglophiles, Papa and his brother nevertheless accepted French protection, grateful for the chance of bearing a passport without the distinguishing word *Juden* stamped across it.

I have mentioned earlier that there were many facets of Mama's character that Sascha preferred to ignore. For instance, I am sure that he would never have dreamed of telling you what Mama asked for, and got, as her wedding present.

There was, in the first decade of the century in Shanghai, a very successful brothel keeper whose name was Belleanna Duval. Madame Duval was a Negro from Martinique whose house was famed both for the sumptuousness of its appointments and for the quality of its stock of English and American girls. Madame Duval's carriage with its pair of patent-leather-black Arabs was the talk and, I suspect, the envy of Shanghai society. Each sundown Belleanna and one or two of her girls would drive slowly along the Bund towards the Garden Bridge. Well, what do you think Mama requested? Of course, the carriage and pair!

'But everyone will think you're one of Duval's girls,' Papa said.

'Let them,' replied Mama.

In spite of his reluctance to tell these episodes, if it had not been for Sascha's eagerness at the age of sixteen to unburden himself of his virginity, I might never have quite understood my parents' early relationship. Naturally Mama's confidences, which took place shortly after Papa's death, were made directly to Sascha. Aristide and I overheard the discussion in her bedroom as we listened outside, taking turns to peep through the keyhole.

Sascha was seated in the brocade wing chair facing Mama's bed. Mama lay with her cologne-soaked handkerchief tied low around her forehead, so that she could pull it over her eyes if she became embarrassed. 'I am telling you this, Sascha,' she said, 'because now you have no father, I have to be father and mother. Nothing is worse than not knowing what is expected of you. . . .'

Then she went on to tell Sascha that, after the ceremony, the newlyweds moved into a house in the Hongkew district. On their wedding night Papa went to their room and tried the door. It was locked.

'Regina, darling, it's me,' he said softly.

'What do you want?' Mama replied.

'It's *me*, Maximilian, your *husband*,' Papa said.

'Oh, good night, dear,' Mama said. Confused, Papa decided that this was maidenly modesty and that certainly by the next night Mama would come around. She did not, nor for the rest of the week, at which time Papa decided to confide in his sister Rose.

One afternoon shortly after, Aunt Rose came to call on her new sister-in-law. She complimented Mama on the attractiveness of the upstairs sitting-room where Mama received her, and then she produced a large bottle of brandy.

'We'll have a little schnapps, just we two girls,' Aunt Rose said, pouring.

'I don't drink,' Mama replied, 'but just a drop to keep you company.' After several drinks Aunt Rose sighed heavily, and Mama waited for her to explain the reason for her call, watching as the fine crystals of perspiration formed at the silvery hairline and high on the bosom where the limewater solution Aunt Rose used for prickly heat had dried. She took an ivory brisé fan from her purse and began fanning herself.

'My dear child,' Aunt Rose began at last, 'marriage has so many responsibilities.' Mama agreed with her: there was laundry to collect, send out, and keep track of; she showed Aunt Rose a copybook in which she made her laundry entries.

Aunt Rose allowed as to how that was very nice, but she went on to say, 'A husband, Regina, a man—wants something besides a little starch in his shirts.' The sisters-in-law stared at each other, Aunt Rose's fan moving as nervously as the wings of a hummingbird. Then Mama thought she knew what Aunt Rose was getting at.

'What a man wants is good food,' said Mama. 'Dah Su is going to show me how to prepare all those wonderful dishes.' Dah Su was a former rickshaw boy whom Aunt Rose had taught the refinements of cooking.

Aunt Rose said that she would stay only long enough to have another drink, in which, still to be polite, Mama joined her. It was dusk and nearly time for Papa to return from work when Aunt Rose staggered down the steps and into her waiting carriage, and Mama, who thought she was quite composed, lurched into her bedroom and securely bolted the door.

At this point of the narrative Sascha snorted with laughter. Through the keyhole we saw Mama pull the handkerchief up over her eyes as she said, 'It's not funny, Sascha. That poor man, what he must have gone through.'

38

Nearly a month after the wedding, Grandmama came to see Mama. She twirled her silk umbrella impatiently and pointed it at Mama.

'By my life, what kind of a woman are you? Max wants a divorce,' she said.

Mama turned pale. 'Why, what have I done?'

Grandmama smote her head with a delicately gloved hand. 'Dommy, what have you *not* done?' Then she proceeded to give Mama a thumbnail course in a bride's duties other than housewifery.

Up to that moment it had not struck Mama that marriage vows constituted an endorsement of those physical liberties, which Grandmama had just graphically detailed and which Mama had thought only bad girls ever permitted.

'I won't do it,' Mama said, her face flaming. 'That's for *kourvas.*'

'*Zehr shayn,*' Grandmama said. 'Let that fat soldier Annie tell everybody what she always suspected is true.'

'What has she always suspected?' Mama asked.

'That you are not a *maydl.*'

Mama recalled the conversation at Aunt Annie's tea.

'All right,' she said to her mother, 'don't worry about Annie.' That night Mama unlocked the door. Ideally, I suppose I should stop at this point, but how Mama reacted to becoming a woman is something I feel should be told.

A happy Maximilian started down the stairway to work the next morning. All at once Mama stood at the top of the steps, her body firm with youth, and outrage clearly limned behind the long nightgown. In a second it was over her head and rolled into a ball.

'Maximilian,' she said. He looked up. Mama threw the nightgown into his face. 'Show that to your sister Annie,' she cried.

5

AT the time of Papa's marriage, China's cotton business was operated exclusively through the large mills. Uncle Jeremiah, who had become by then chief accountant of the Laou Kung Mao Mills, estimated that while a Chinese mill worker could be obtained for fifty percent less than a Lancashire hand, it required two unskilled Chinese to do the work of one foreigner. Papa reasoned that if the mills could be left to concentrate on training help and thus increase production at a minimum cost, there would be an enormous upswing in China's cotton market. With Uncle Jeremiah as a partner, he founded the first independent cotton brokerage business. In order to make certain of delivery, Papa's first years in this venture were spent in travelling the interior and northern and central China.

To be with her husband, Mama endured the hardships of rough accommodation and sedan travel. Her first child was stillborn in Wu-ch'ang. Two more children died in their infancy, and Mama swore that she would not bear another until she was settled in her own home.

The Chinese revolution of 1911 had little effect on the foreigners in China. They were used to insurrection of one sort or another, some of them having survived the Taiping Rebellion, the Ningpo Guild riots, and the Yangtze riots, and most of them having lived through the recent Boxer Uprising.

Papa, who was establishing an office in Hankow, was an eyewitness to the incident which led to the overthrow of the Manchus. An accidental explosion led to the discovery of an undercover bomb factory in the Russian Concession. Acting rapidly, the revolutionaries, backed by public approval, inspired the Imperial troops in Wu-ch'ang to mutiny.

In short order Wu-ch'ang and Hankow fell to the republic. City after city tore down the Manchu flag with its emblem of the Imperial Dragon and hoisted white banners. Soon these were replaced by flags of the Republic which had five horizontal stripes of colour, representing the five races of China. By the end of the year, fourteen out of the eighteen provinces declared against the Manchus. A provisional government was set up at Nanking, headed by the father of the revolution, Sun Yat-sen.

In February of the following year, the boy emperor P'u-i, who had succeeded the dowager Empress under the regency of his uncle, abdicated the throne, transferring the government to the Kuomintang or National People's Party. Yüan Shih-k'ai, an extremely powerful premier under the Manchu dynasty, negotiated for the changeover. In order to strengthen the northern position of the new government, Sun Yat-sen resigned in favour of the popular Yüan, and in April, 1912, the government was established in Peking.

The founding of the republic, however unstable for the Chinese, had a salutary effect on the foreign position in the treaty ports. In Shanghai, the hub of foreign trade was reinforced by greater controls allocated to the Municipal Council, such as expansion of authority over customs and salt revenues. The French municipality succeeded in their claim for more territory and were allocated two thousand or so acres west of their old boundaries.

When Yüan Shih-k'ai negotiated loans with six countries without Kuomintang or parliamentary approval, it became evident to the party that his aims were directed towards a dictatorship rather than a constitutional republic. The Chinese press urged the people to rise up against Yüan and overthrow his government. A second revolution broke out in the summer of 1913. Both foreigners and Chinese mercantile groups in Shanghai were disinterested in the revolt against Yüan's Peking government. He was in their eyes an able politician, and they could negotiate with him to their own ends. They looked upon the second revolution as a minor uprising. Within three months it was quelled.

Sascha was born that summer. By then regular shipments of raw materials were automatic, precluding the necessity for travelling the interior, and my parents moved into a penthouse on one of the new buildings on the Bund. Sascha had been a frail infant, weighing only four pounds at birth. Ironically, Mama was unable to breast-feed the child for whom she had waited so long. Chinese wet nurses were the solution for foreign women who either did not care to or could not feed their own children. These wet nurses were in a specially favoured position and were paid, fed, and housed in circumstances far more luxurious than the ordinary nursemaid or amah.

It was in this capacity that Min Hsia Tse came to work for us. She was in her thirties, with a very calm countenance belied by a ptosis of her left eye, which gave the impression of perpetual conspiracy. She was Catholic, which was all right with Mama, but she smoked endlessly and Mama was somewhat afraid of her. The doctor said that she was in excellent health, and she had recommendations from the nuns at St. Joseph's who had apparently cared for her during her pregnancy. She would not tell Mama either about herself or her husband, not in outright refusal but in catch-

41

phrases of evasion. For example, if she were asked where she came from, she would say, 'Shanghai, more far.' Actually she came from the village of Pootung, across the Whangpoo River. When Mama inquired about her child, she stared back blankly and Mama realized that the child was dead. For all her personal secrecy, the woman was a conscientious nurse, and by the time Aristide and I were born, Hoboo, or Great Aunt, as she chose to be called, was a fixture in our home.

The penthouse which Papa rented at the time of Sascha's birth included the top floor and roof garden of a six-story office building, which was considered a skyscraper, since this was at that time the maximum height which the subsoil of Shanghai could support.

The apartment consisted of twelve rooms and two enormous halls. On all sides the rooms opened onto verandahs with wrought-iron railings, like great continuous window boxes.

Papa's business flourished throughout the war, and he made large and anonymous contributions to the Allies. Faded office receipts show donations totalling one hundred thousand pounds to the Allied Red Cross, and there are files of grateful letters from Lady Roberts for the 'excessively generous gift to my father's field glass fund'.

In spite of his munificence to the British, it was Papa's loan of six million francs to the French Government at only two percent interest that secured for him the offer of a street named in his honour, which he declined. The French minister to China put in a petition for naturalization, which was approved, and my parents then became French citizens.

They were sociable, and the Bund apartment in the International Settlement was the scene of lavish hospitality. Musicians such as Elman, Moisevitsch, and Zimbalist were entertained at large soirees, and because of her grace and aptitude for languages, Mama became popular with the European diplomats.

As Papa's status rose and he was invited to become an honorary member of the best clubs in the city, Aunt Annie attempted to insinuate herself and her husband into these institutions. She was a determined climber who believed that her husband's nationality was a substantial enough wedge for her entrance into Shanghai society. On St. George's Day, her carriage, aflutter with tiny Union Jacks, could be seen parading along the Bund. On such occasions she liked to drop in unannounced to complain of the strain of attending affairs at the British Consulate, to which Mama pointed out that the Consul General was obliged to invite all British subjects on national holidays. She lived at the Astor House, which was then a significant label of affluence, and she borrowed heavily from Papa to maintain what she thought of as her position. The truth of the matter was that, in spite of her perseverance, Aunt Annie failed. Mama put it succinctly enough once when Aunt Annie was being discussed. She was a 'kike', and in that word was expressed the final and most damning judgment from one's own kind.

6

UPON the outbreak of World War I, China declared its neutrality. Disregarding China's stand, Japan attacked Germany's possessions in the Shantung province. With token assistance from the British, the Japanese were victorious. The following year, Japan then set forth twenty-one demands which assured its complete sovereignty over railways, mining, and other vital rights in Shantung. This proposal, made in secret to Yüan Shih-k'ai's government, was revealed by him to the foreign press, evoking enormous indignation from the Chinese people. But Japan pressed Yüan to an ultimatum, and he was forced to accept most of the Japanese demands.

By now Yüan had established his dictatorship and was in the process of setting up his own dynasty, with himself as Emperor. Rebellion broke out against him in Yünnan and in the provinces of the south, and his aims were thwarted. In 1916, Yüan Shih-k'ai died suddenly, and the next year Sun Yat-sen, who had opposed Yüan's dictatorship, founded a military government in Canton, which was not recognized by the foreign powers.

Meanwhile, upon the urging of the United States, China broke off relations with Germany and subsequently declared war. This measure was taken as a means of securing a place at the peace conference in order to thwart Japan's expansion plans, specifically in Shantung.

For the members of Shanghai's foreign colony there was a great deal of social activity, fund raising, bazaars, and Red Cross organization. Some of the military-age griffins, Britishers who came east to apprentice for large concerns, returned home to join up. But by and large the impact of war itself was not felt.

The signing of peace was attended by representatives of both the Peking and the Canton governments. It came to light that the British, French, and Italians had, in secret notes, promised to support Japan's claims on China, and in 1917 the United States had entered into an agreement with Japan by which it recognized that Japan had special interests in China because of territorial propinquity. A faction of the Peking government had concluded agreements with Japan for extensive construction of railroads in Shantung, Manchuria, and Mongolia and had borrowed heavily from Japan. The Treaty of Versailles upheld the Japanese demands. China's many other claims were discarded as not within the realm of the conference.

News of the Versailles Settlement precipitated a tremendous surge of nationalism in China, and throughout the country student demonstrations against the Peking government took place. It was the beginning of the long road to national emergence.

Compared to what it had hoped for, China's gains for participation in the war were few. It obtained membership in the League of Nations and saw the first break of extraterritorial rights when the Germans' settlement privileges were cancelled and the indemnity for the Boxer Rebellion was repealed.

In the treaty ports anti-German feeling ran high among the foreigners, particularly the British. At the end of the war they persuaded the Chinese Government to dispossess German citizens of their holdings and repatriate them.

More than patriotism was involved in the British campaign against the Germans, whose trade had increased to the point where Germany had become England's keenest competitor in China.

Aunt Annie, who waged her own separate war, had from the beginning ostracized Uncle Wolfgang and tolerated Aunt Rose on sufferance.

Prior to repatriation, all German nationals were turned out of their homes. Aunt Rose's family found shelter with another couple in a Chinese house in Yangtzepoo, the mill area east of Hongkew. The influenza epidemic which had blanketed most of the northern hemisphere in the previous year had spread in two more waves, and

44

in that spring felled thousands of people in Asia. Two days after Uncle Wolfgang was repatriated, Aunt Rose came down with the infection. Aunt Annie phoned Mama. Rose's amah had come to her pleading assistance for her mistress. Aunt Annie was most put out. 'A fine thing, that *sklektah hint* of a German gets shipped home and leaves his wife on *our* shoulders. . . .' Aunt Annie said that she could not under any circumstances contact a British doctor to aid a German citizen.

'Annie, the war is over,' Mama argued. 'I can't go in my condition, and Rose may be very sick.' Mama was in the last month of pregnancy. For some time she had wanted another child, but she had waited until Sascha was five years old and, by every indication, flourishing, before she permitted herself to conceive. In spite of the doctor's assurance that she was in magnificent health, the three fatalities before Sascha's birth haunted her. So she limited her activities, whiling away the time by transforming her bedroom into a pink lace confection in preparation for the infant she *knew* would be a girl.

'Listen,' Annie said. 'If I go, what happens to us? The wife of a customs official, giving comfort to a former enemy? If it wasn't for my husband's position, I swear by the child you're carrying. . . .'

It was clear that Aunt Annie could not be persuaded to visit her sister.

Mama found Aunt Rose stretched out on a bamboo bed. The woman who shared the Chinese house with Rose was of Russian birth and so was exempt from deportation, but her husband had been expatriated with Wolfgang. Her teen-age daughter was also a victim of the epidemic. The woman was seated on the floor next to the cot in which her child lay; she was tearing linen handkerchiefs into strips. Her amah brought a basin of steaming liquid which Mama recognized by its smell as *shaoshing*, the common wine of the Chinese, made from fermented rice or millet. Next the foreign woman began paring what seemed to Mama like ginger root. She soaked slivers of the ginger in the hot wine and made compresses with the linen strips which she then sponged over the body of her daughter.

Mama took Aunt Rose's hand. Her sister-in-law squeezed Mama's hand hard. 'He's gone, you know,' she said.

'I know,' Mama said.

45

'He didn't want to, but they made him go,' Rose said. Under the circumstances, Papa could have worked out at least a delay for Wolfgang, but the truth was that he had wanted to return to Germany.

'Rest,' Mama said. 'Don't talk.'

Prior to the war our family had been under the care of the German doctors. At this time we dealt with the 'J' firm of Drs. Jenkins, Jarvis, and Jordan, who were located on a lower floor in the same building in which we lived. Dr. Jarvis' relationship to our family was a close one. Tall and raw as a eucalyptus tree, the Scotsman diagnosed Aunt Rose's case as pneumonia. She had to have hospital care at once. As the stretcher-bearers carried Aunt Rose to the waiting ambulance, Mama turned to the woman who was applying the poultices to her daughter, but she did not look up from her work.

When Mama came home, she told Papa what had happened. He was appreciative but concerned as to how she had paid for his sister's admittance to the hospital. 'By cheque, of course,' Mama said. Papa handed her a fold of currency. 'Go at once to the receiving desk, and ask for your cheque back,' he said.

In two weeks Aunt Rose was dead. Mama, who was due at any moment, insisted on attending the funeral. Aunt Annie, who had never been to see her sister, was the loudest lamenter. She arrived heavily veiled and supported by her two brothers, her face shaking like a bowl of yeast dough; but when the officiating rabbi tried to cut the neckline of her dress, an ancient ritual called the *Kreah* signifying the severance of the dead from the living, Aunt Annie pushed him aside, protesting that the dress was new.

That night Mama went into labour. Dr. Jarvis was on a houseboating party. A younger member of the firm attended to what appeared to be a normal birth. As Papa bent over to wipe his wife's brow, he said, 'She's beautiful, like you, my love.' And the English nurse assigned for night duty placed the eight-pound girl in Mama's arms. During the night it seemed to Mama that the infant cried ceaselessly. 'Please look at the baby,' she said to the nurse.

'Nonsense,' the young woman replied on several occasions. 'It's good for her lungs.' Or, 'We don't want to spoil her.'

By morning the baby was dead, the result of a freak accident. Her umbilical had been cut too short, and she had bled to death. When Mama recovered from the shock, she remembered that Aunt Annie

46

had taken an oath by the child that Mama had been carrying, and she never forgave her sister-in-law.

Aristide was born on New Year's Day in 1921. With their unfortunate experiences in the loss of children, my parents had indulged Sascha, who was eight years old by then, to the point where he was completely secure in his position as heir apparent. As Aristide once put it glumly, 'All Sascha had to do was survive to be considered some kind of miracle.' But Mama was weary of lead soldiers, mechano sets, and Tiger Tim comics. She fussed over a pink bassinet, and even the coverlet and pillowslips for Aristide's double-size wicker carriage were fashioned of monogrammed lace.

It was as though Aristide knew that in order to compete with Sascha he must make his entry into the world spectacularly. From 1912, when Charles Kettering's self-started vehicle was marketed, my family had favoured Cadillacs. Just before Aristide's birth, Papa purchased a bottle-green Imperial Suburban.

Since it was considered 'common' for anyone to be born in a hospital, Mama was rushing back from a ladies' tea to give birth at home. Instead, she had Aristide with the assistance of the chauffeur right in the Imperial Suburban, stopping all the traffic on the Bund. Over the years, when anyone brought up the subject of cars even vaguely related to status, Aristide would say loftily, 'I was born in a Cadillac.'

Mama insisted that his name, too, must not be commonplace, and she ignored the Jewish tradition of naming children after deceased relatives. She insisted that they could be propitiated later, which is, of course, how I got my name.

Then there were the Yureff diamonds. These were a pair of twenty-six-carat stones set in gold mountings with silver claws. They were being sold by a Russian prince, and Papa had promised them to Mama if she produced another son. He was so delighted at the birth of Aristide that he presented the servants, twelve in all, with a hundred-dollar sweepstake ticket for the Spring Champions as the races were called. When their ticket drew the hundred-thousand-dollar first prize, there was great excitement at our house. Clearly, said the servants, this good fortune was due to the birth of the second son.

In Jewish families the rite of circumcision is performed with much ceremony. Typical of my parents' religious inconsistency,

Aristide was ministered to wearing a gown especially made for the occasion by the nuns of the Siccawei convent, and Mama had forgotten to remove the medal of madonna and child from around her neck, prompting Aunt Annie to remark, 'What a family—only in birth and in death are you Jews.'

Although the practice of employing wet nurses by foreigners had given way to canned milk formulas, Hoboo was thoroughly entrenched in her position as chief nursemaid.

After the guests had left, the servants assembled around Hoboo, who stood in the centre of the group. She lifted the child high, for the rest of the servants to see.

'*Dondee Neetsu*,' she said.

'*Dondee Neetsu*,' they agreed, for he was indeed to them the money son.

In a very short time all but four of the servants left, using their winnings for ventures of their own. There remained of the original staff only Zee, the number one boy; Dah Su (who had come to us on Rose's death); Pao-shing, the chauffeur; and, of course, Hoboo. Even in those days when she was provoked, her bronze kettle face would boil over darkly, the ptosis eye flicking wildly as the other popped wide open.

'I die dis house,' she would say whenever Mama, challenging her authority, told her that she could leave.

The legend of the money son was perpetuated each year on Aristide's birthday by the arrival, as at a divine pilgrimage, of all the retired servants and their families.

When Uncle Jeremiah, a teetotaller, succumbed to cirrhosis of the liver early in 1923, Aunt Annie, the self-acclaimed diagnostician, insisted that Jeremiah's predilection for pickled foods had led to his demise. But she was most eager for the reading of Jeremiah's will.

Upon the disclosure that the bulk of his estate from his fifteen percent partnership in Papa's business was bequeathed to Mama, Aunt Annie became choleric and threatened to contest the will, but Uncle Jeremiah had been as meticulous in financial matters as Papa was casual, and the will was airtight.

Papa's business had prospered so well that by the end of the war a number of American firms set up their own cotton brokerage companies in imitation of him. Even though he was now president of the Shanghai Cotton Exchange, Papa realized that if he was to consolidate his American trade he must establish branches in the United States. He made plans to leave for America in the summer. Meanwhile Mama was at last to visit Italy, where Papa would later join her. The information that she was again pregnant had a disastrous effect on these plans. Some ineffectual means were devised to rid Mama of the pregnancy, but I was born one autumn morning in 1923, practically strangled, my face indigo. There were no Yureff diamonds, no Champions sweepstakes, no dramatic issuance from the Imperial Suburban, with crowds watching as at a royal *levée*. Instead, Dr. Jarvis who had sat up all night with Papa playing poker, slapped me smartly on the rump and announced to Mama that she had a fine broth of a lad. Rhoda Cunningham, wife of the American Consul General, took one look at the flower-banked bedroom and said, 'My God, Regina, it's like a funeral parlour!'

Now, I can understand Mama's mixed emotions at the birth of another child, and a son at that, coinciding with her long-awaited trip to Europe. She was, after all, at the height of her beauty, in her early thirties, and restless with her role as hostess and mother.

It was not until the early summer of 1926 that, bolstered by the services of Hoboo and sixty pieces of luggage, Mama and her sons left for Europe.

7

WHILE my recollection of Italy is hazy, Mama's close friend Tila Golitsky stands out in my memory clearly. Of similar origins as my mother, Tila had emigrated to France as a child. She was studying voice in Paris when, at a party which Diaghilev gave in honour of Ravel, she met Baron Golitsky. The Russian aristocrat married Tila and they maintained an active salon for artists until the revolution, when, upon returning to Russia, the baron was assassinated. Heiress to a considerable fortune, Tila embarked on a concert tour which took her to Shanghai. Mama and Tila felt an affinity for each other at once. Their resemblance was extraordinary, the differences being so subtly drawn that Papa was prompted to say, 'They are as alike as two drops of water, one pure, one impure'.

49

Mama's essential femininity was an instant source of attraction to men. She inspired chivalry and was the object of mementos, sonnets, letters written in despairing love, and affairs which though lifelong were unconsummated. Tila, an iconoclast when it came to ideals or mere institutions like marriage, embodied challenge. Her peridot eyes would narrow languorously at the sight of a handsome male, and the slightest tug of a smile at her lips invariably suggested something carnal.

As children, we were dazzled by Tila's opulence and intimidated by her size, but we loved the laughter, the gregariousness, the mobility, and the sense that she was forever Christmas.

We had barely arrived in Venice and were not in Tila's suite for more than ten minutes when she snatched a shawl off the piano, tucked a rose behind her ear, and set the stage for *Carmen*. To conserve her energy, she enlisted Aristide's support by having him dance on the table while she kept time with her hand, singing the seguidilla, with her pair of Pekingese, Dixie and Ming, yapping excitedly at her feet.

Most else which I refer to in Italy has been dredged up from glimmerings of memory, what has been told to me by Mama herself, or what I have been able to deduce from her diaries. I remember the Palace Excelsior Hotel with its terrace and coloured lights. I remember the Lido beach dotted with cabanas, and the sun making a cauldron on the Adriatic. I can clearly see the identical tiger-striped black and orange bathing suits which my brothers and I wore and Tante Tila fastidiously covered with a voile to keep from getting sunburned. Mama spreading cocoa butter on her arms and legs, gradually became almost the same shade as her hair. On Sundays, Hoboo drove Mama to distraction by taking Aristide and me to early mass at Saint Mark's. Mama could be seen along the landings, anxiously questioning carabinieri as to whether they had seen her infants, whom she was positive each week had been kidnapped, only to have us chug up in a *motoscafo* with Hoboo complacently holding one heretic on each knee. No amount of berating from Mama had any effect on the amah, and we attended Sunday mass all the time we were in Italy.

I don't remember too much of Sascha except that he acted quite American, possibly because Papa, who was in New York, sent him clothing, books, and records. He wore knickers, chewed gum, strummed on a ukelele like Gus Edwards, and generally frustrated the staff at the hotel by demanding salt-water taffy and root beer.

Perhaps because I was so close to him in both years and spirit, I recall the Aristide of this period quite well. He willingly accepted Mama's choice of velvet and silk suits, making a great to-do over the feel of the fabric and holding the stuff to the light to examine the colour. I suspect that it was by Papa's decree that I was clothed in sailor outfits of linen and serge, but my underpants were batiste with fine lace trim, and we both wore Betsy Jane shoes. For summer we were given identical Milan straws with naval ribbons, and Aristide wore his with the jauntiness of an It Girl. His hair, styled in the Buster Brown fashion of that time, was a source of endless joy to him. He was forever in front of a mirror combing his bangs and twisting the side locks into spit curls.

In the afternoons, when we were supposed to be napping, Aristide would stroll out onto the terrace and spend hours practising the tango by himself. I suppose the sight of a pretty child in bloomers which were always half-way to the ground, dancing to the strains of the rehearsing orchestra, must have evoked some comment. Mama thought it amusing enough when it was reported that, in reply to the compliments of some French lady tourists, Aristide had winked archly and said, '*Tu sais ma chambre coco, vas y.*' She didn't think it was a bit funny when an Italian officer told her that Aristide had repeated the invitation to him.

'It's his hair,' Sascha protested.

'All boys wear their hair like that now,' Mama said.

'But all boys don't think that they are girls,' Sascha insisted. So Mama agreed that when we returned to Shanghai she would see that Aristide had his hair cut.

The day Mama met Francesco di Volfieri, we were on the beach. Tante Tila pointed him out. The man was lying on his stomach in front of a nearby cabana. The skin that showed from his one-piece knit swimsuit was ripely olive. He had long legs and his toes digging into the sand made them look like garden rakes.

'He's been staring at us for weeks,' Tante Tila said in her wonderful chest tones.

'Well, we're not a pair of chippies. Don't look,' Mama replied. The man looked up and smiled broadly. It was a smile of complicity which engaged his entire face. The wide lips were bracketed by deep lines, not dimples and not wrinkles either. His nose was long but somewhat flattened, much like Vasari's portrait of Lorenzo the Magnificent.

As Mama was, particularly by the flapper standards of the twenties, a large woman, she had commissioned a number of beach capes. It became Hoboo's job to accompany her to the fringe of the ocean, where, with a deft movement, Mama would cast off the garment and immediately submerge. After a few minutes of walking around while she assiduously spread her arms in the style of the breast stroke, she would come out to be hastily cloaked by Hoboo.

On this day, to Mama's consternation, she found Hoboo's place taken by the tall Italian. He was holding up the cape for her. Mama splashed around nervously, staring at the stranger. By now Aristide and I had meandered to the water's edge, with Aristide impractically pretending to build sand castles. Finally Mama said to the young man, '*Dov'e la mia serva?*'

He threw up his hands in an Italian gesture of despair. '*E sparito*, she's a go away.'

'Oh, she's a go away,' Mama repeated, and seeing that she had no alternative, she mustered all her dignity and walked into the outheld cape. The light of laughter came into the man's pale grey eyes as he wrapped the cape a little too solicitously around Mama.

'*Come la venere di Botticelli*,' he said.

Mama snatched the tie strings of the cape and, granting him the briefest smile, said, '*Grazie*.'

From the diaries I learned what followed this episode. That same night Mama and Tila were dining at the Chez Moi, which was the hotel restaurant. They saw the man again. With her attention to detail, Mama records that he was wearing an ivory silk suit, a pink shirt, and a black tie. He must be very much a man to combine such colours, she notes. When she saw him, Tante Tila said, 'I'll go to the ladies' room, and you see if he stares at me.'

When she returned, Mama said, 'He stared, but not at you.'

'Hah!' Tante Tila said. 'He must be one of those lousy Neapolitans who like fat ones.'

I must interject between these notations from Mama's diaries that the remark was not typical of Tante Tila. Indeed, it was she herself who always acknowledged Mama's priority when it came to men. I can only assume that she must have been momentarily disturbed at the repetition in pattern. Furthermore, as Mama put it in her diary, that remark coming from Tila is absurd. After all, she's no sylph (spelled silf).

An acquaintance whom Tante Tila knew through her operatic connections finally arranged an introduction for the man. As it turned out, Tante Tila was correct; Prince Francesco di Volfieri was from an ancient Neapolitan family.

At this point the entries in the diaries become spare, which always reveals to me that the writer is living more when writing less. Although as a widow Tante Tila could legitimately lay every snare, it was soon evident that Chicho, as he was called, had fallen in love with Mama.

I have a photograph of the three of them. Francesco is seated between Mama and Tante Tila. Mama is watching the photographer or, as was her habit, a little beyond him. Her stole appears to have slipped over one shoulder, for she would never contrive to let it fall. She is serene, almost unnaturally so. There is to her mouth only a secretive upturn of the lips.

Tante Tila is wearing a lamé headband under which undisciplined wisps of bobbed hair stick out like aigrettes. She is flourishing an ostrich-feather fan. She is quite charmingly arch, in spite of the dated posturing. Francesco's gaze is fixed on Mama.

Mama had wanted for many years to visit the Vatican. Christmas seemed to be an ideal time. In preparation, she bought an exquisite mantilla of white Venetian lace for which she paid twenty thousand lire. Chicho had agreed to accompany us.

We were in our suite awaiting what was sure to be a positive reply from Papa. Aristide, carried away by the exuberance and not being above impressing the Pope, had draped the white mantilla over his head. Somewhere he had found a candle and was making a big ceremony of genuflecting all the way across the room. Francesco and Tante Tila found his pious performance hilarious. I am not sure about Mama. At any rate, before there was a chance of ascertaining her feelings, the bell-boy arrived with Papa's return wire from New York. The contents read: 'Must return to Shanghai. Follow on first ship. Forget Vatican.' It was signed M.

Only then did Tante Tila confess that her trustees had been advising her return to Shanghai where she had invested heavily in real estate. 'It seems there's some damned antiforeign group, called

53

Nationalists, who want to take over.' Despondently, plans were made to return at once.

Both bedrooms, Mama's and the one my brothers and I shared with Hoboo, led into the living-room. I was awakened that night by voices: Francesco's low, pleading, and so urgent that at first I did not recognize it, and Mama's soft but very firm. They were, of course, speaking in Italian, and although I did not know what it was all about, I could always understand when Mama spoke a foreign language. She was saying, 'Chicho, I am married. Yes, I love my husband. What could any woman ask for more than I have? *Si, si, amo il mio marito.*'

8

BY his policy of terrorism and bribery, Yüan Shih-k'ai set the stage for warlordism in China. For ten years after his death various strong men used armed troops to gain power.

The warlords bartered their strength for party endorsement and seals of office. With this attained, they levied taxes and bled the villages. To gain their own ends, this venal group supported opposing political cliques so that under the republic China was in a perpetual state of conflict.

Besides the general deterioration of living conditions imposed by them, the warlords were responsible for the regeneration of the opium trade. To stimulate this handsome source of revenue, they raised land taxes to the point where nothing but the growing of poppy could meet the payments.

By 1926 Sun Yat-sen was dead. Two battles had been waged in the Shanghai-Nanking area by competing warlords. In the north Chang Tso-lin controlled Manchuria, the Peking-Tientsin area, and Shantung province. Chekiang and Fukien were in the grip of Sun Chuan-fang; Hupei, Honan, and the Peking–Hankow railway were under Wu P'ei-fu. There were three other positions held by less powerful but more stable warlords. To the world at large what was known as the Peking government, despite its cliques, continued to be recognized. But a storm was brewing in the south. While Papa was in the States and the rest of our family summered in Italy, Chiang Kai-shek, a disciple of Sun Yat-sen, marshalled the three minor warlords. Strongly tinged with antiforeign sentiments, a march from the south to the north began.

There comes a time with everyone, I think, where the kaleidoscope of memory stops its oscillating and each prismatic slide falls into sequence, so that memory is no longer fragmented but begins its life as a chain of events to which one may return for reference. Such a point in time for me was January 1, 1927. It was Aristide's sixth birthday and we had returned from Europe just the night before. I was not quite four at the time and Sascha was going on fourteen. Like all of Aristide's birthdays, this promised to be an event, and my second brother was highly excited.

It was mid-morning when I joined him in the alcove, where we children normally ate. This was in the second hall, an immense and gloomy chamber with its oak-panelled walls, and on the parquet floors were Axminster Persians woven at Papa's express order in the Scottish Hebrides. There were several bronze figurines about, mostly heroic men or women holding aloft some sort of beacon which doubled in most cases as a lamp. A fire was kept going in the tiled fireplace opposite the alcove, and on the carved oak mantel stood silver-framed portraits of family members, mostly Papa's, who had not made it on the mantels of the drawing-room. Tante Tila, whose tastes ran to the rococo, once described the halls as 'a fruitcake stew'.

Anxious to receive his offerings, Aristide had not permitted Hoboo to dress him, and he was wearing a chemise and a pair of baggy bloomers. Around his neck, suspended on a black velvet ribbon like a miniature miner's lamp, was one of the Yureff diamonds. I can only surmise that he had cajoled Mama into letting him play with the gem and, banking on her casualness about such things, had simply not returned it. At any rate there it was, gleaming in the semi-dark like the jewel of a temple god.

Then Mama came in from the front hall where she had been unpacking. Even with her loosely pinned-up hair and dressed in a peignor, she was at once regal yet warmly approachable. With a swiftness that belied her size, she walked to the alcove. As she embraced us both, I saw her glance at the diamond around Aristide's neck, but she did not remark on it.

At the end of the hall near the kitchen there was the sound of rustling and of children being hushed. The retired servants come to pay homage to the second son were assembling. Aristide set his face into an expression of judicial patience.

I can see again the reedlike wives trembling as they stood in line, their delicate scent of jasmine pervading the hall. The boys ranged in age from one to seven years, the older ones in their long gowns and brocaded jackets and some of the smaller ones so heavily rouged that they looked artificially bright-eyed, as though they were intoxicated. The girls, most of them plump in their satin pants and jackets lined with goat skin, had many bangles on their chubby wrists. The infants wore tiny gold earrings, the girls two loops, the boys one loop. Since evil spirits prefer boys, the earring, the opulent silks, and the rouge were devices to camouflage the male sex from the greedy devil eye. One or two of the retired menservants were in Western business suits, but the majority wore dark padded gowns and cloth slippers.

Slowly the line approached Aristide, the parents bowing and prodding their children to do likewise. They handed him gifts in the Chinese manner with both hands. Gravely Aristide accepted each gift with both hands, bowing in return. Mama asked many questions of the servants who had left to open their own businesses. As Aristide unwrapped his presents, Mama was able to gauge the success or failure of the donor's year. When a straw basket of loquats appeared with a scarlet slip of paper wishing good joss instead of the gold rice bowl or coral and silver chopsticks of previous years, there was an envelope waiting for that servant in the kitchen at the time of his departure.

A youth we had not seen previously stepped forward. 'Who is he?' Mama asked. 'Mastah hire,' Hoboo said. Then she went on to explain that the coolie, whose name was Lao Ni, came from the same village that she did. Aristide glared at the newcomer who did not bring him a gift. The first thing I noticed about the young man as he bowed to my brother was his bamboo leanness. The bones of his hips stuck out beneath the wrinkled apron someone in the kitchen had thrust on him to cover the shabby coolie cloth jacket and pants he was wearing. The broad cheekbones of his face curved to form concentric semi-circles with his long upturned lips when he smiled. His eyes, though direct, were of a softness not too often seen in eyes

56

of such darkness. 'Tell him,' Mama said to Hoboo, 'that I hope he will have long life in this house.' 'Long life' was one of Mama's standard phrases in regard to servants. Mama was in the habit of saying, when a servant had been added to the staff and failed to do things quite as she expected, 'I don't think that servant is going to have long life in this house.' But the fact remained that she never sacked one. When everyone had left, Mama told Hoboo to tidy us up since we were to lunch with Papa in the dining-room. Very lightly she lifted the diamond off Aristide's neck and stuffed it into her bosom.

There followed the usual, and what was for me always distasteful, business of a bath. This time Lao Ni assisted Hoboo with the ritual after which came a brisk rubdown with glycerine and rose water. Occasionally, when she did not dilute the mixture sufficiently, my skin would sting, but the taste of the glycerine was sweet and I liked it. I did not like the calloused feel of Lao Ni's country-crude hands on me. True, Hoboo's hands were gnarled and work-worn, but there was a familiar softness of touch. Aristide, however, did not seem to mind, and he made a great production of his bath scene, rolling in the suds and splashing wildly, much to Hoboo's exasperation. He made quite a point of covering his lower extremities when he got out of the tub, at which Hoboo cackled, but he responded with such sighs and grunts to the coolie's massaging that Hoboo snapped something in Chinese which I did not understand, and I don't remember Lao Ni's ever bathing us again.

After being dressed, we rejoined Mama, who was unpacking in the main hall. This gloomy replica of the second hall, from which it was separated by swinging glass doors, looked like the customs shed. The luggage, mostly Hartmann trunks with their mauve brocade innards exposed, spilled out the booty Mama had acquired on this trip. Scattered over the floor were the hundred pairs of a single style shoe which Mama had favoured and copied in different fabrics and shades. Two exquisite birds of paradise were perched rigidly atop one of the Morris chairs. 'I didn't buy one piece of jewellery,' Mama said proudly to no one in particular, as the next instant she was unwrapping sets of parures, earrings, and rings of angel skin and oxblood coral she had 'picked up' in Florence. Presumably, since these fell into the category of what Mama called sports jewellery, they didn't count.

57

As usual, Mama made much over Aristide with extravagant gestures of smoothing the hair out of his eyes, when it was nowhere near his eyes. Controlling his annoyance, Aristide expertly patted his locks back into place. As I look back on it and recall Aristide in his amber velvet suit with its starched collar and myself in Viyella shirt and shorts with a knitted tie, I can fully understand why no one took us for brothers. Let me say in all fairness that Aristide's magnificence was a natural thing. In sackcloth he would have outshone me, and anyway it was his birthday.

Sascha joined us. He was already stout and had assumed much of Papa's bearing. His hair was slicked down and his jaw slung out like a drawbridge. He wore the school blazer, but knickers instead of grey flannels, and although I expect he was clean enough, he always presented to me the appearance of a pillow after a pillow fight. He condescended to Aristide, shaking hands and saying, 'Well, well, six years old, eh, kid?'

'Kiss your brother,' Mama said. Sascha reluctantly walked over to Aristide, who stuck his face up, pursing his mouth distastefully, like our Grandmother when we kissed her.

Aristide said, 'He always stinks of cheese and oranges.' Sascha raised one hand as though to strike him.

'You brute,' Mama murmured nonchalantly, when she had assessed with a glance that Sascha did not intend to strike. To this day I'm not sure at whom she directed the remark. Mama was always one ahead for good measure. If she came upon the three of us in the same room, and Sascha and Aristide were wrecking it in battle, as they so often were, Mama would slap Sascha's face, then Aristide's, and although I was usually just a silent witness, mine too, 'just to be sure'.

Mama glanced at her wristwatch. 'I wonder where Papa is. He knows I have to take Aristide at one thirty.'

'Take me where?' Aristide asked.

'Out—to the photographer; you always have your picture taken on your birthday, don't you?' Mama said. There was an unpleasant grin on Sascha's face.

Papa came through the front door. He stood for a moment leaning on his fruitwood cane with its agate handle. Aristide ran to him and I followed, of course. I had completely forgotten Papa in the six months we were in Italy, but as he hugged me the mingled

58

essences of Crème Simon which he used after shaving, the stern fragrance of his Philippine cigar, even the boutonniere which he bought daily from the crippled vendor who waited for him, were the same I had always known. The whole authoritative image with respect and fear stitched together by guilt was recalled in that embrace.

The night before, although by the time we'd gone through customs I had been barely able to keep my eyes open, there had been for me a sense of something amiss: an indefinable thread of coolness between my parents; the kind of detached courtesy I was to see a great deal of between the parents of my English friends. But Mama and Papa. . . . I strive for a word to describe the vibration, the tremor, the passion that was evoked when they discussed even the weather. The best I can do is 'sanguine', and that quality was missing.

Now as he limped with great dignity towards Mama, his face was too calm. When he merely brushed her cheek with his lips, I knew something was wrong between them.

'Papa and I are going into the dining-room to talk for a few minutes,' Mama said. 'When you're called for lunch, come!' Feeling snubbed, Sascha walked off by himself to the smoking-room, from where in a few minutes came the deafening sounds of his marches on the Victrola. The favourite at the moment was 'Sombre et Meuse'.

As soon as my parents left the hall, Aristide began poking around in the drawers of the wardrobe trunks; he lifted the tops of packing cases and rifled through a number of suitcases. I knew what he was looking for. At last in a zinc-lined chest he found them, his collection of European dolls. His favourites were the Lenci dolls with their tinted skins and human hair. Aristide had had a difficult time in Italy, sheltering them from Sascha. At the summer school in which Mama had entered him, fencing was a favoured sport, and already Sascha had jabbed the sawdust out of one of Aristide's favourites. Assured that his treasures were safe, Aristide pulled out his portable phonograph and an album of records. He put on the one of Tito Schipa singing 'Valencia'. There was no volume control on Aristide's portable, and the musical schism between my brothers might have ended badly for Aristide but for the fact that Sascha, who was already at the doorway of the smoking-room glowering like a bull, was called into the dining-room. He made a loud announcement that he was going to get cleaned up before eating. Aristide and I started for the dining-room.

At the doorway Aristide stopped. Our parents were already seated and were talking in low tones. I started to go in, but Aristide held me back, his eyes like buttons of chrysoberyl, chatoyant in the dark. When I resisted, the eyes narrowed to buttonholes.

'Stop, cretin, I've got to listen.'

Mama was saying, 'Forty thousand troops to protect us from what? From whom?'

'The Nationalist revolution,' Papa replied.

Mama was fairly fluent in at least five languages. She could sing the entire score and with unerring ear supply instrumental background to the works of most Italian composers. She had read Dante without understanding much of the *Divina Comedia*, but she could quote D'Annunzio at length. Through travelling companies rather than by reading she had discovered Shakespeare and used his lines characteristically to suit her immediate purposes. For example, 'Many a truth is said *from the chest*'.

She could discourse on popular writers, particularly if they happened to be Elinor Glyn or Gertrude Atherton. As a person she had developed through observation, learning early to practise the social graces which came to her by instinct. But when it came to current events, political economy, or merely general history, Mama lived in a vacuum. Once I overheard her ask Sascha if Abraham Lincoln was Jewish.

'What's wrong with this government?' Mama said. 'I don't see how they can be so bad. They let us live.' To be let live was understandably a fundamental concern of Mama's. When it came down to survival Mama forgot the Italian image of herself, and archetypically she remembered Miriam and the pogroms at Kiev and tales of breast-slashing Cossacks.

'They let us live because they haven't the initiative to do anything about us. For the first time you hear about Chinese soldiers who do not act like brigands. Where shops used to close and people drew the shutters on their houses, people line the streets to cheer Chiang Kai-shek's troops on,' Papa said.

'This Chiang Kai-what's his name, is he antiforeign?' Mama asked.

'Nobody knows exactly where Chiang stands towards the foreigners. His armies are almost at Hankow; then we'll see. Anyway,' Papa went on, 'his propaganda is strictly against the treaties and foreign control in China.'

'Then he *is* antiforeign,' Mama said.

'Or maybe just pro-Chinese,' Papa replied.

As Aristide and I were listening at the doorway, I remembered Sascha's excitement at the sight of the foreign battleships at anchor in the Whangpoo River. He had counted American, British, French, Italian, and Japanese among the flags represented. Actually at that time there were no less than a hundred and fifty warships in and around Shanghai.

'We should *never* have come back,' Mama said.

'No,' Papa replied. 'I imagine gondolas in Venice are much more romantic than a garrison city with your husband.'

'I don't mean that. What I mean is that you should have come to Europe.'

'You, the Italian prince, and me, all in one gondola?' Papa said. From the great oak door which led into the room we could see Mama reach for the one Melachrino that Papa allowed her at the *end* of each meal. In Italy, she had smoked incessantly.

'Prince?' Mama said, exhaling a wide screen of smoke.

'You are fickle, Regina. Was there more than one?'

'What's fickle?' asked Mama in an effort to arrange her defence. 'You mean like *La Donna e mobile*?'

'*Si*,' said Papa.

'This is really rot, Maximilian. He's one of Tila's amours.' Mama ground out her cigarette furiously.

In their entire married life Papa never overcame a Victorian code of behaviour for Mama. Since he was a cripple and could not dance, it was tacitly agreed between them that Mama would never dance. If Mama happened to be at a club and a single man asked for a ride in her car, she was obliged to refuse even if another woman was along.

The tone changed at once as we entered the dining-room. We took our places on either side of Mama. Then Sascha joined us, seating himself beside Papa. He seemed to take this business of lunching with our parents very much in his stride. As for myself, I was paralysed with the ecstasy of such acceptance. Next to Aristide's plate and on the floor were stacks of presents which he immediately began unwrapping. There was a set of Chinese gold cuff links with the characters for good luck on one side and long life on the other. Aristide seemed quite pleased with these. There were building blocks and games like snakes and ladders and many toys. Papa said he had on order a toy bus big enough for Sascha to drive while the others sat on top. Aristide worked over the packages with flushed intensity and considerable restraint of expression. He had learned from experience not to express too much pleasure for fear that the supreme power of Sascha might wrest this joy from him. For any gift or toy which Sascha could not appropriate or at least share represented a threat to him. As far back as I can remember he oversaw all our presents. On Boxing Day, for instance, Sascha would be up first and have gathered all the gifts around him under the tree. He would then begin distribution in the manner of a potentate, taking not the usual tithe but most often the whole harvest.

As Aristide continued unwrapping, the excitement seemed to diminish in him and he was betrayed only by two points of colour in his cheeks. There were no dolls among the presents this year.

The meal progressed without much conversation. Mama barely touched her food, but I was not concerned about it, for I knew that she enjoyed eating at irregular times.

As the dessert plates were being set before us, Papa reached into his breast pocket and pulled out a narrow package wrapped in white paper. He tossed it to Mama, saying, 'For you if you don't cut.' Mama looked at it for what seemed to be a long moment. Then she unwrapped the package and opened a velvet box. We saw a bracelet about two inches in width.

'Emeralds and diamonds, my favourites,' Mama said. She closed the box and handing it to Aristide said, 'Give this back to your father.'

'You understand,' Papa said, 'you'll never see it again.'

'I understand,' Mama replied. 'I thought you did.'

Papa stood and leaned forward on his cane. For the first time Aristide spoke. 'What does Papa mean, if you don't cut?'

Mama bent towards him and placed one hand on his. With her free hand she worked dexterously in her hair. A variety of tortoise-shell combs, bone, and wire pins were soon assembled beside her, as the locks of mahogany-coloured hair cascaded over her shoulders to the floor.

'Aristide,' she said in that toasty voice of hers with its strong rolling *r*'s, 'it is now the fashion for women to wear bobbed hair, as it is the style for boys to have short hair. We are both, you and I, going to Antoine's to have our hair cut.'

The two spots of pink stood out like pinch marks against the white of Aristide's face. Papa raised his cane and pointed it deliberately at Aristide. 'Not a sound,' he said. 'I'm leaving and I don't want to hear a sound out of you.' With surprising speed, Papa left the room.

I looked at Sascha. He was unconcernedly making bread pellets. Aristide opened his mouth in an expression of dumb agony. Then he uttered a terrible cry, his mouth still wide open. Aiming carefully, Sascha tried to hurl a bread pellet into it, but missed. Mama patted Aristide's hand. 'Darling, don't cry.'

That of course was the signal, and I remember how uncontrollable was the need to reach my brother, and I began to cry also. Mama looked at me and then back at Aristide. 'Now stop,' she said, 'both of you, or I'll give you something to cry for.' By this time we were crying in counterpoint and the noise must have been terrible. '*Basta,*' Mama said, lapsing into Italian. '*Basta,* or I'll give you each a slap *in* the face. . . .'

I saw Aristide glance at Mama, and when he saw the tears running down her face, his screaming reached crescendo.

Suddenly I felt a stinging whack across my cheek. Stunned, I looked at Aristide who was holding one side of his face as his mouth opened and shut in shuddering surprise.

Mama smoothed the palms of her hands in a wiping-off gesture. 'Now cry for something,' she said.

At the doorway to the kitchen stood the number one boy with Hoboo behind him holding high a birthday cake with its lighted candles flickering.

9

WHEN Aristide returned from his shearing, Sascha and I met him at the front door. The cropped black thatch of hair seemed to bristle with violation. Sascha doubled over and shrieked with laughter. Looking at Aristide, I thought I had never seen anyone so foreign. He stared at us both for a moment, eyes filled with hurt and anger. Then he covered his face with both his hands and ran from the room.

Later in the day I found Aristide experimenting with a comb in front of our bedroom mirror. He coaxed the hair into various side and middle partings and settled finally for a combed-down effect, a sort of stiff fringe which he achieved with soap. Noticing me, he explained that the style was borrowed from some French actress then popular, Irene Bordoni or Fifi D'Orsay, I'm not sure which, but clearly neither of these ladies in his estimation came up to Clara Bow, and after a while he gave up in disgust.

Out of his hearing, Mama admitted that she felt naked without her long hair, but she didn't look any different to me; she was cheating, as Aristide put it, because she had had Antoine fashion two braids from the cut hair which she wore coiled over either ear, or twisted as a coronet on top of her head.

We were not home more than two days when I felt a strange sense of impermanence, as though since our return from Italy, something, or worse than that, someone, had been left behind. Life went on very much as it always had been, I imagine. Sascha returned to school. Papa went to work and came home for a long lunch period, at the end of which, when he was lighting his cigar or swallowing one of the innumerable pills he had begun to take, Aristide and I were brought in to visit with him. Now when we came to the table, there was an abrupt change in tone between him and Mama, the introduction of sudden harmony in a dissonant arrangement.

Mama seemed most natural on the surface. At once she fell into her routine of menu planning, supplying the servants with provisions from the storeroom or the linen room. There was the constant sound of jingling from her large bunch of keys suspended on a battered gold ring. The phone rang often and we could tell by the slightest change of inflection or accent whether the call was social or mercantile, from Grandmama or from Tante Tila. On the third day of our return Aristide pointed out that there was a change in Mama's procedure regarding the mail. Normally delivery was made after Papa had gone to work and just before Hoboo took Aristide and me to the Public Gardens across the street. Mama had opened the front door herself several times in order to meet the postman. I would have given this no thought but Aristide insisted that Mama had always been in the habit of having the mail brought to her bedroom with her morning coffee. Then Aristide revealed why Mama was so eager for the mail.

'See how she hunts for the square blue envelope with the crest on it? They're from *him*.'

By that evening I had forgotten Aristide's remark. Mama had ordered an early dinner to be served in the alcove, which meant she did not expect Papa to return. We had just seated ourselves when he appeared. He went straight to his room after asking that a servant be sent to assist him. Mama had let most of the servants go for the evening, and only Hoboo and the new coolie remained. Lao Ni was sent to help Papa change, while Hoboo served the dinner.

We ate in silence, and Papa came into the hall again dressed for the evening, his face smoothly oval, his hair parted in the middle and plastered down, the gold watch chains across his vest and the scent of Eau de Farina. He always made me think of a very elaborate Easter egg. Behind him, richly pleased with his handiwork, stood Lao Ni. Apparently Papa had made plans for himself and Mama for that evening and had either forgotten to consult her or had neglected to. It was as simple as that.

'Get dressed,' Papa said in a stranger's voice.

'It's too late. I don't want to go.'

'Wilden is giving this affair for the Mayor,' Papa said. Monsieur Wilden was the French Minister to China who had been responsible for our citizenship.

'You go. Make my apologies,' Mama said.

'You have to go.'

'I have to go nowhere.'

The fight which ensued was the most vivid and certainly the worst recollection of my childhood. I don't know who broke the first plate or threw what glass, but as with everything my parents did, this battle was on a grand scale. We ducked to avoid the flying cutlery and jumped up on the chairs as Papa ripped off the tablecloth. Sascha tried to come between Papa and the table and was pushed away. With a terrific heave Mama shoved the table almost directly on Papa's foot. He lifted his cane. Lao Ni thrust himself in front of Papa and tried to stave off his blow, and the cane fell hard on the servant's back. Lao Ni looked up at Papa as though he expected him to strike again. There was no expression on his face. Mama rose to her feet unsteadily, supporting herself against the wall of the alcove with both hands spread against it.

'You crippled dog,' she yelled.

Papa stood staring at her for several minutes. Then he limped to the door, stopped, and pointed his cane at Mama as though he were going to say something. Instead, he went out. Mama sank to the floor; she was moaning and sobbing, while blood from her cut fingers dripped slowly onto her peignoir. All at once she sprang to her feet and was at the front door. I began screaming and Sascha grabbed at the panels of Mama's robe. Mama fought like Boadicea, and she was gaining headway. Then Hoboo cried, 'Missy, Missy, look-see Aristide.'

My brother was sitting on the floor beside the upset table and the broken glass. His eyes were black against the paleness of his face. He just nodded up and down. Mama ran to him and held him to her. Finally Aristide began to sob, and when he could speak he said, 'Oh Mama, I know, I know. . . .'

Mama held him away to look into his face. For a moment I thought she was going to shake him. 'What do you know?' she asked. But Aristide just said, 'I know, Mama.' And that was all.

Early the next morning Hoboo took me to the Public Gardens. Aristide, she explained, had spent the night with Mama and it was better to let them sleep. I thoroughly enjoyed being alone with Hoboo, because when she didn't have to contend with Aristide she told me wonderful tales, and when I grew drowsy she would cover me with her curry-coloured shawl and sing me a lullaby in French which she had learned from the nuns of St. Joseph's:

> Do do, do do,
> Mama va acheter chocolat,
> Papa va acheter gâteau.

Hoboo was at once the weather vane and climate of our childhood. She was a substitute mother for whom one never needed to feel embarrassment. She peopled our lives with fantasies drawn from her Roman Catholic faith, myths of ancient China, and the personalities she had encountered while in the family's employ. I could listen for hours to her anecdotes told always in her native tongue, as she puffed on her cigarettes, allowing the ashes to grow long and fall in her lap.

As we crossed from the Gardens to the grass-covered promenade, Hoboo with a sudden switch of humour told he that as recently as Sascha's birth this walkway had been used for public executions. She had witnessed many, she confessed, the last being the torture of a young girl who had killed her mother in self-defence. The girl had been tied to a pole. Several lengths of catgut were tied around her waist. A large basket was suspended from the catgut, and passers-by tossed heavy stones into the basket. As the weight of the stones increased, the gut gradually cut the girl in half.

'Shame, shame on Chinese to be so cruel,' I cried.

Hoboo pointed to the front of the lawn. Then she said, 'Before, not so long ago, there was a sign, "Chinese and dogs not allowed in the Public Gardens"'.

I don't know what I expected when I saw Mama and Aristide in the smoking-room. Mama was fully dressed, and except for the large cologne-soaked handkerchief which was tied around her head and the fingers which were neatly bandaged in gauze, there was no sign of the previous night's havoc. I discounted the headband at once, as this was a sort of trademark. Aristide was doing the Charleston to 'Button Up Your Overcoat', which was blaring from the Victrola. The smoking-room was the least formal and, under any circumstances, the happiest room in the apartment.

Here it was in times of harmony that Papa sat at his marquetry desk after meals, untangling Mama's household budgets, while she, seated in one of the brown leather club chairs, strummed on a mandolin and sang Italian songs. In the middle of the room was a heavy oak game table with a green felt top at which my parents often lunched in warmer weather. French windows led to the verandahs overlooking the Bund and the river. Even with them closed, one could hear the shrill piping of tenders and the blast of funnels over the persistent chant of the wharf coolies.

Somehow the complete jolliness of the scene offended me. I had spent a troubled night, not having learned yet of the peculiar resilience which the very emotional and alcoholics share, that ability to emerge completely impervious to the trauma they have caused.

Sascha returned from school full of excitement. He told us that Hankow had fallen to the Nationalists. Truculent mobs had stormed the British Concession. Royal Marines trying to hold down the entrances to the concessions without firing had been forced to abandon their posts. Crowds then swarmed into the area led by Communist agitators and Nationalist troops who occupied it. Foreign residents had been obliged to get aboard ships for safety. 'They've destroyed the Cenotaph opposite the British Consulate,' Sascha said, and went to the window to see whether the duplicate war memorial on the Bund might have suffered a similar fate. Sascha went on to say that he had gone for a drive with Pao-shing, the chauffeur. 'There are sandbags and barbed wire all around the International Settlement and blockhouses on the boundaries of the French Concession. Everyone says the Nationalists are going to take Shanghai next.'

'Who's everyone?' Mama asked.

'Just everyone,' Sascha said. 'Mama, when can I join the volunteer corps?' The Shanghai Volunteer Corps was an international military organization established for the protection of foreigners at the time of the Taiping rebellion in 1853 and whose forces now exceeded two thousand nonprofessional but trained men of various nationalities.

Before Mama could reply we saw Zee going to the front door. Papa was talking with someone who had a distinctly British accent. Mama immediately snatched the handkerchief from her head and thrust her bandaged hand into her pocket; at a glance from her, Aristide turned off the Victrola. She was starting to leave the room when she was met by Papa and another man at the door. You would never have guessed from the way Papa introduced Inspector Burnham of the Central Police Station that there had been the least dissension in our family. Papa's suit was crumpled as though he had slept in it. The tiny fresh bud in his lapel, by contrast, looked surprised.

Zee brought in pink gins and plain water tinted with a drop of bitters for Papa, who had learned this device at the Shanghai Club where he negotiated many of his major transactions.

Inspector Burnham was a longtime resident of Shanghai, and he discussed the question of the Nationalist attitude towards extra-territorial rights with the complacency typical of an Old China hand. 'Nationalists, northerners, or Communists, they're all of a piece, really. They're Chinese who hate the white man.' He reminded us that the Chinese had taught their young that foreigners were barbarians and that to teach the Chinese language to these barbarians was a capital crime. As for the territories, in the first place the Chinese thought of them as ghettos, where the white devil could toy with the idea of drainage and macadamized roads. Secondly, they afforded an ideal sanctuary for the Chinese warlord who had fallen from favour. 'Now that we've built cities out of their mud flats, they want to chuck us out.'

'But,' Papa said, wagging his cigar lightly in the inspector's direction, 'with this revolution going on, it doesn't seem to be a matter of choice whether we keep our concessions or not.'

'If you can call these rabble-rousing tactics a revolution. They are not likely to get away with what they've done in Hankow, unless they're ready for a full-scale war. Perhaps the Peking government is corrupt, but they are better than these Nationalists and the Communist agitators behind them.'

'Do you think that Chiang endorses Communism?' Papa asked.

'Personally, I'm of the opinion that Chiang is faking a coalition in order to use Communist forces.' The inspector then told Papa of the struggle for power which was ensuing in the Central Executive Committee based in Hankow. Left-wing members of the Kuomintang and leaders of the Communist party openly accused Chiang of veering too far to the right. In an attempt to limit Chiang's power, the Central Executive Committee had recalled Wang Ching-wei, another of Sun Yat-sen's disciples, from exile in Europe.

Mama was silent. Like a vast majority of foreigners at the time, she had no idea of either the complexity of the issues or how serious the situation actually was. She complained that Jascha Heifetz was considering cancelling his concert in Shanghai.

'I daresay that is a bother,' the inspector said with a slight smile.

'I'm delighted by your visit, Inspector,' Papa said, 'but I must confess that I am curious as to why you have called on me.'

'Of course,' the Britisher said, draining his glass, which Zee promptly refilled. 'You've heard of Liu Yueh-sung,' he asked. Liu

Moh-bi, or Pockmarked Liu, as he was known to foreigners, had grown up in the back streets of Shanghai. The son of a hawker, he had become, before long, a mobster, extortionist, and head man of amusement and gambling syndicates throughout China. His greatest wealth was said to stem from the opium combines whose reaches extended to the United States and South America, with rebates on all dope transactions in China. Juxtaposed against the vast under-world which he ruled was Liu's position as director of several banks and financier of many civic and national construction projects. To the business world at large, he was known simply as the 'Shanghai Bankers'.

'Pockmarked Liu; I've heard of him,' Papa said.

'You have also undoubtedly heard of the secret societies?' the inspector pursued. Papa nodded.

'It is rumoured that Chiang belongs to one of the societies and that he may be able to enlist Liu's gangster army to help in the taking of Shanghai. As it stands, we in the settlement are not sure of which way Liu will turn. He might, if it suits his interests, even support the Communist faction.'

'What is my association with this?' Papa said.

'Liu naturally has many agents. They are well trained and as slippery as eels. The commissioner of defence has a lead to one of these men and he has asked our assistance.'

'I still don't understand,' Papa said.

'You have a servant, a woman from Liu's village.'

'Hoboo,' Mama said.

'What could Hoboo have to do with Liu or his agents? She is a peasant woman with no outside interests but this family,' Papa said.

'She's a Catholic,' Mama said.

The inspector turned to Mama and said, 'That is no guarantee she is not a revolutionary.' He explained that many of the poorer Chinese in the villages converted to Christianity because of the famines, and they were known as 'rice-bowl Christians.'

'She wouldn't,' Mama insisted. 'She's a *devoured* Catholic.'

'What is your connection with Hoboo and this possibility?' Papa asked.

'This woman of yours comes from Pootung, where the population is small. She is from the Koo family. Recently some other members of that family have moved to Shanghai. The commissioner is interested in one Koo Ah-ching, who works as a labourer and also attends the Shanghai University. He has not been able to locate him for questioning. We were hoping she could help.'

'Hoboo has been with our family for nearly fourteen years, Inspector. I have never heard her mention any relatives,' Papa said.

'Most likely your servant is quite innocent of any goings on, but you must realize that we are obliged to cooperate in any investigations,' the inspector said.

Papa acknowledged this, and the Britisher asked him to send for Hoboo. Meanwhile Inspector Burnham went to his car to fetch a northern army officer.

Hoboo entered the room, staring with her good eye at the inspector and the Chinese in his grey uniform. At the sight of the officer's hand resting idly on a mauser holstered at his waist, her other eye began its flickering.

The northern officer questioned Hoboo in proficient Shanghai dialect.

'I don't have any family. I am an orphan,' Hoboo said. 'I was brought to Shanghai as a child and the nuns took me. See, I had no parents to bind my feet.' She thrust her normal-size, slipper-shod foot at the officer for him to examine. He ignored the gesture.

'Where is Ah-ching?' he demanded.

'What Ah-ching? I know no one. I know only this family.' She pointed to Aristide and me. I saw the look exchanged by Mama and Aristide, and all at once I thought of Lao Ni, the new coolie. Lao Ni isn't a name really, it only means second oldest. I looked quickly at Sascha, but then I remembered that Sascha had not been present when Hoboo had introduced Lao Ni, saying that he was from her village.

'Old woman,' the officer said, 'we can make you talk or we can silence you forever by tearing your tongue out.'

Mama got up. 'Inspector, tell the officer that if Hoboo had any relatives, they would be hanging on her skirt.' She looked at Hoboo. 'On her pants.' She turned to Papa and said, 'Darling, you must change if we are to be ready when Sir Sidney arrives.'

At the mention of the British consul general's name, Inspector Burnham jumped to his feet, said something to the northern officer, and they started for the door. Sascha of course joined Papa in seeing the men out of the apartment.

The mask of pretence curled at the edges of Mama's face and dropped, leaving a cold expression. She placed one hand on Aristide's shoulder and the other on mine. 'I only want to know one thing. Is the new coolie Ah-ching?'

'He no Ah-ching,' Hoboo said, reverting to pidgin English as she always did when speaking with Mama.

'Remember what you told the police,' Mama warned. 'These boys are your family, but they are my children.' Her grip on our shoulders became hard as only Mama's hands could. 'If anything you do hurts them, I'll let the northerners kill you.'

Hoboo faced Mama without any expression. Then she said to me in Chinese, 'Little devil, it's time to wash.'

I looked at her, suddenly indignant. 'I washed yesterday.'

'And did you eat today?' the old woman replied.

10

I HAVE tried many times to understand why Mama chose not to reveal that Lao Ni came from Pootung. Was it because he had taken a blow aimed at her from Papa? Was she so thoroughly imbued with the foreigner's sense of inviolability that she thought the matter was not of too much consequence? I have never been sure. I was not surprised that Papa did not pursue the subject. He was very matter-of-fact about the hiring of servants. The coolie had been taken on because a new servant was needed, and there was no reason for him to connect Lao Ni with Hoboo or the inspector's quest.

In the Britisher's presence, my parents had put on a fine performance. Mama's remarks cut across Papa obliquely to the inspector. Papa was courtesy personified, even to the point of supporting Mama's barefaced lie about the British consul's coming for lunch.

A few days after the inspector's visit, Grandmama appeared without warning. While Grandpapa never stirred out of his house, Grandmama visited often, but not without advance notice, so that the car might be sent to fetch her. Mama, she, and I were seated in the smoking-room. Grandmama's smile was betrayed by her nostrils, which twitched impatiently as though eager to pick up the full scent of trouble. I knew for sure that her knowledge of my parents' fight was complete in detail. Her reporter of course was Aristide, who had by now discovered the telephone. But Grandmama was a past master at playing for time, and I watched, fascinated, as with ceremony she removed the hatpins and unfurled the veiling from her toque. In her sixties, Grandmama was still as well proportioned as a blanc de Chine figurine. Her eyes had not shrunk with age and were still of an inquisitive brilliance. But the years had sharpened the curves of her nose and chin, so that her profile resembled Punchinello. Her lips housed a perfect set of dentures, like pearls against the crinkled velvet of her skin, but her smile still had the extraordinary quality of catalysing her other features. With her aluminium-grey hair piled high and tiny snake curls clustering her forehead, she bore a striking resemblance to Queen Mary. In point of fact from the time of the English Queen's coronation in 1911, Grandmama identified with her completely. She too held herself erectly as though she had swallowed a cane, and when she was being chauffeured in the Imperial Suburban she would amaze the Chinese mobs in the streets by making noble salutations with her gloved hands, flicking them sharply from the wrist as though she were tightening a light bulb.

Grandmama spoke what I now think of as a sort of domestic blend. It was really a mixture of Yiddish and Russian larded with English and garnished with an occasional French word. With her it was not so much the pottage of language but rather how she stirred it. In the course of a discussion with her one could rarely escape a proverb that might easily be a thousand years old or an epithet uncomfortably close to home.

Quite early in her conversation, it became obvious that Grandmama knew about Mama's refusal of the bracelet, and in view of her background this rocked her sense of security. I shuddered to think of how she would have reacted if she knew that at this very moment Aristide was in the front hall using Mama's Ural Mountain gems as marbles. Mama's rationale was 'Why not? Marbles are a boy's game if there ever was one.' Actually Aristide was playing jacks with the unset cabochons, and Sascha, home from school for lunch, was doing his best to filch them away from him.

'Your friend Tila would have cut the hair, put on the artificial braids, *and* taken the bracelet. Remember, when you pick a *phlomm* from the tree, you have it,' Grandmama was saying.

73

'That's fine for Tila,' Mama said. 'Maybe she still needs plums.'

'But how does it look, you and Max fighting? And why? Why?' Grandmama persisted.

'We are not fighting. We are just not friends. When we go out together no one would ever guess anything is wrong. *I* even forget, to tell you the truth, Mama, because Max is so clever. Last night he corrected two Oxford graduates on a long quotation from Shakespeare.'

Although Grandmama had no idea who Shakespeare was, she pressed her fingers against her cheek and shook her head from side to side with true Semitic reverence for scholarship.

'But,' Mama continued, 'I remember again as soon as we get into the car. I go to my room, and he goes to his.' Papa had taken to eating his noonday meal at the Shanghai Club.

The telephone rang. As soon as Mama answered, I could tell that it was Tante Tila at the other end. By the sympathetic sounds Mama was making and the clue phrases she spoke, it was evident that a romance of Tante Tila's was foundering. Aboard ship she had met an attractive French count, who had indisputedly pursued her instead of Mama. It had seemed a promising situation; Michel de Raveur was a widower, and although he did not use his title, the Raveur family dated back to the eleventh century. Moreover, he had an excellent position locally. Apparently something had gone amiss. 'Don't worry, Tila, you'll meet another one better than him,' Mama consoled. Then Tante Tila must have suggested something, because Mama immediately countered with, 'Oh, no, I couldn't. You know what a fortune I spent in Italy.' There was the crackling sound of vocal pressure through the wires at Tila's end. Then Mama was saying, 'You know there's nothing I like better than a game.' The crackling picked up in volume. Mama said, 'What do you call small stakes? Ten thousand the most! Maximilian would throw me out.'

The sound on the other end of the receiver indicated that Tila took this as preposterous. Mama put her hand over the mouthpiece and said to Grandmama, 'Tila says that no man in his right mind would divorce me, never mind what I did.'

Grandmama sneered.

'Listen, Tila,' Mama said, 'I can't. You know how Max feels about me going out to strange places.'

Finally Tila was put off. As Mama hung up, she said, 'Tila wants me for a poker game. The way Maximilian gambles, I should have said sure, but two wrongs don't make one right, uh, Mama?'

Grandmama nodded. '*Avoda*, why spit in a well today, you may want to drink from it tomorrow.'

Since Papa was not expected, Mama called for Zee to set the game table in the smoking-room. Besides the service for a six-course repast, there were the inevitable symbols of a well-laid table of that time: silver napkin rings; a cruet stand; sterling place plates which remained throughout the meal; after the fish and meat courses, finger bowls with hot water and thin slices of lemon; and after the fruit, more finger bowls with iced orange-flower water. Although our storeroom was stocked with a complete selection of wines, liqueurs, and cognac, alcohol was not served unless company was present.

We were joined by Sascha and Aristide, whom Grandmama embraced, stretching the pleats of her neck as she thrust her face forward. Almost at once Aristide discovered some of his stones bulging out of Sascha's cardigan pocket.

They started a noisy wrangling, which Mama halted by sending Aristide off to wash his hands.

'What that child should have is an *ertsiherin*,' Grandmama said.

I don't know what Mama thought of a Jewish governess, but she said, 'He wouldn't stand for anyone but Hoboo.'

'Hoboo,' Grandmama sniffed. 'I know a very fine Jewish lady whose father was a rabbi.'

Aristide returned at that point, and Mama indicated that the conversation be dropped.

Tiffin was served. The first course was borscht, which Grandmama had taught the cook to prepare. After sipping her soup gingerly, Grandmama replaced her spoon and sat patiently silent. Well aware of this customary gambit, Mama tried to ignore her. Grandmama picked her water tumbler up and set it down an inch away from where it had been. Finally Mama succumbed. 'You don't like the borscht, Mama?'

'Very nice,' Grandmama said, with a fierce curling of her upper lip.

'What can be bad?' Mama said. 'It's just like you taught the

75

keha.' It was always apparent when Grandmama had succeeded in rattling Mama, because of what happened to Mama's English. She talked just like Grandmama, tossing in Yiddish words for emphasis and arranging her grammar so that communication was assured.

'Very nice,' Grandmama repeated. 'So you eat it.'

'It's du-licious, I don't know,' Mama said, choking.

Grandmama shrugged; what could you expect of children reared in a household which celebrated Christmas and not Chanukah? What could be said in defence of a man who denied his son the ritual of Bar Mitzvah? When, upon hearing the news that Sascha was to forgo his Bar Mitzvah, Grandmama had appealed to Mama, Mama had replied, 'Maximilian's only religion is fair play. On Sascha's last birthday his father asked him to remember one thing. A very hard thing. To be as good a man as he could.'

For the longest time I shared Grandmama's confusion, if not her frustration, at the laxity of my family's attitude towards religion. It was said we were Jews, but nothing—no rites, no prayers, no festivals —seemed to confirm that we were Jewish. And Aristide was always ready with some improvisation to prove the contrary.

'Why is it none of us look Jewish?' he had said. I remember scrutinizing my brother as he spoke. Although he cleaved to Mama's notion that he looked Latin, he alone of us children had Semitic features. His face with its gabled eyebrows was the quintessence of gentle persecution, a composite of all of Raphael's madonnas.

Once, primed with some credibility-stretching myth of Aristide's creation, I challenged Mama on the point. We had been alone in the lacey sanctuary of her bedroom. With some surprise at my question, Mama said that we were indeed Jews. I tugged lightly at the Catholic medal she was wearing around her neck. 'What's that?' I said. Mama was silent for a moment, then she said, 'Darling, listen to your Mama. You know the way a bee goes to a flower. He takes the honey, but does he take the thorn? What I mean is, in life take the honey from everything, from all religions and leave the thorns.'

'Is that why we have a Christmas tree and Easter eggs?'

'Sure, but do I ask you to eat fish on Friday and suffer through Lent?'

'And is that why we never fast on Yom Kippur?' (What a ruckus Grandmama had caused about that!)

76

'Bad enough when you haven't got the money for food. We show how grateful we are by eating twice as much,' Mama had concluded, delighted with her own reasonable credo.

It would be an exaggeration to say that the meal progressed, but the fish and meat courses came and went, and Grandmama scratched at each dish.

I am sure that no one paid particular attention to the fact that when Zee appeared with the dessert (presumably steamed pudding since it was brought in a closed serving dish), he seemed unusually nervous. He approached Mama tentatively. With a flourish of impatience, Mama lifted the lid of the dish and immediately slammed it down again. Not soon enough, however, for we all saw that what the dish contained was no dessert but a pile of torn scraps of blue letter paper and envelopes.

As I think back on this scene, I realize how remarkably well Mama behaved, conscious as she must have been of all of us staring at her, waiting for the eruption. In quite a controlled voice, hardly one she ever used to reproach the servants, she said, 'Master teach you to do this, Zee?' Without waiting for his reply, she got up and went to the telephone.

Grandmama said, 'My child, vot are you doing?'

'I am calling Tila,' Mama said, 'and I'm going to pick myself a plum.'

11

AROUND two o'clock Mama went down to Tila's waiting car after cautioning Hoboo to bring us home early from the Public Gardens. Sascha had gone back to school.

When Hoboo herded Aristide and me to the elevator, I noticed that she was wearing her Sunday outfit—silk jacket, pleated wool skirt, and a black satin headband; her rosary was not tied at the waist, so I knew we were not headed for church. When we got outside, to our surprise she hailed a rickshaw. As a group of coolies padded up to the entrance, Hoboo began the usual harangue over prices, proclaiming her contempt at fares she thought outrageous.

Finally she decided on one coolie and never letting go of our hands settled us in the rickshaw.

'Hoboo, where we go?' Aristide asked.

'Go see flends,' she said.

The coolie ran along Nanking Road, plunging headlong into the morass of automobiles, buses, and railless cars, dodging pedestrians who seemed to walk right into his rickshaw shafts. There were loud imprecations on all sides, and Chinese gentlemen with expert grace pulled at the hems of their long gowns to escape the splash of the gutters, while coolies manning the wheelbarrows spat and swore. Servicemen crowded the street. There were many Japanese and Italian sailors, Annamites with their brass-tipped helmets, British soldiers, and a few American Marines who were stationed in Shanghai. Sascha had commented this morning that a number of American troops were in port, but that they were not allowed to leave their ships since billeting was a problem.

Hoboo peeled a mandarin orange and fed us segments. The wind whipped around, and Hoboo spread her rough-knit shawl over our legs to warm us. Aristide's cheeks were like Korean apples. He was having a high time, for this was off the beaten path, and adventure for all of Aristide's days was the equation of life.

'Hoboo,' he said expansively, 'when I get rich, what you want?'

'You be good boy, dat's all,' she said.

'No, really, what you want?'

'Ten picul lice,' Hoboo said. A picul is a Chinese weight, approximately 130 pounds.

'Rice is not enough,' Aristide replied in disgust.

'Enough,' Hoboo said. Aristide was quiet. He had given up asking me what I wanted because apparently I had failed this test too. I had asked for warriors, having been much impressed by some Hollywood epic. I had thought that a few legions in breastplate and helmets with me at the lead naturally was the most wonderful prospect. I had battle theories too. One had to pretend to be dead very quickly and of course the enemy would overlook you. I wish I could say that the idea was that I could then mount my steed and rally my forces to victory, but all I could imagine was to wait until dark to creep back to safety.

'Warriors?' Aristide had snorted. He had seen Monsieur Beaucaire, and he wanted a château and lakes with black swans and

78

a wardrobe of brocaded jackets, jewelled vests, and powdered wigs. I was *finished* as far as he was concerned. Hoboo's request put a pall on him. It never entered his mind that he would be anything but Croesus rich, what with the birthday rites and all. The truth is that Hoboo went even further. When she bathed Aristide, she would turn him around and, like an expert poulterer, stretch his limbs and plump his flesh between her fingers. She had discovered a mole on his shoulder, and her excitement was compounded when she discovered another on one of the cheeks of his buttocks.

'Hai Yah, you after velly lich,' she announced. Then and there Aristide was all for rewarding her and magnanimously asked her to state her request. But Hoboo would not ask for anything. Once with a sudden blaze of anger she snapped, 'You same Sascha, alee same. Hoboo, I lich what you want?' she mimicked. 'Eat excrement,' she said in Chinese. 'That is what Sascha has to give me now.'

The rickshaw coolie had reached the point where Thibet and Nanking roads intersected. Although it was early afternoon, the street corners were already crowded with brightly painted prostitutes wearing Colleen Moore hair bobs and high-heeled shoes, their short cheongsans split up to the thigh. Aristide stared goggle-eyed, taking in every detail, but Hoboo abruptly shut out the view by drawing her shawl over our faces. 'No looksee wild chickens!' she said. Then we heard her chuckle, and when we were allowed to look again, the rickshaw coolie had turned on Thibet Road heading north. After a number of turns he slowed down. Hoboo gave him some instructions and he padded into an alley of Chinese dwellings. Here was bean curd sizzling in peanut oil and a carton of staring fish heads and the pickled odour of salted greens and the raw yellow soap smell of laundry water from a basin into the cobblestone alley.

Another odour, sweet and strange and salivating, hung over the narrow lane, where the sky could only be seen in an eyelet ribbon pattern over the closely pressed tiled rooftops. Here were China-blue garments hung up to dry and sausages and poultry and entrails. Here a cat crept stealthily towards the cut heads and a yellow tail yapped furiously behind a torn screen door. Hoboo paid the rickshaw coolie and instructed him to return, if he could, in a couple of hours. The doorway at which we had stopped had no more than a faded cloth nailed over it. We went into a dark room with a hardened earth floor. In one corner there were several planks nailed together to form what was supposed to be a cot. Some quilts of wadding and cloth were spread on other corners of the room. In the middle, there was a large round cherrywood table at which some rough stools were placed. I don't remember seeing any windows, but both cooking and heat were provided by charcoal, glowing dimly in used five-gallon kerosene tins.

As we entered we were met by a woman much younger than Hoboo, but who then seemed to me older. She was small and gnarled as a gingseng root. Her hair, brushed back from a balding forehead, fell in wisps by her ears. On one side of her face was a shiny black patch, which intrigued Aristide at once.

'Medicine,' Hoboo explained. The two women greeted each other with many pleasantries and Hoboo called the other one sister. 'Come,' the strange woman said. 'Come and see your brother-in-law.' She led us to the cot. The man lying in it looked up as though in searching reverie. In his quill-like fingers was the stem of a pipe the likes of which neither Aristide nor I had ever seen. Papa's were of burled wood and amber, but short of stem and not nearly so impressive. Through the grey gauze of the smoky room we could see the man's face. It was the colour of untanned leather. Sparse whiskers grew from cheeks that were deeply sunken. The eyes were placid like those of a dumb animal.

'Where is Ah-ching?' Hoboo asked.

'He has gone to find his father the "black rice". We have so much trouble with him. He has no respect, only ideas. I cannot break him, and his father is weak,' the woman said, her voice rising angrily.

'Every day I give thanks to the Holy Virgin for Lao Ni and the *siao* Didi, but the oldest one will bring shame and disaster to our home.'

'I must talk to him,' Hoboo said.

The woman ushered us to the round table. When we were seated she went to the entrance of the room and called for her youngest child. *Siao* Didi, littlest brother, stood at the doorway. He had been playing in the alley and he was covered with grime, but he smiled widely at the sight of Aristide and me. Didi was about my age, and all of his head was shaved with the exception of one tuft which was tied with a strand of red yarn. There is a Chinese superstition that a child must pass through many gates in his life. If he arrives at a gate with no hair, he dies an untimely death, for the gods will not let him pass. Didi sidled up to us, and we saw that he was wearing the padded split breeches common to children his age. Hoboo embraced the little one and drew him onto her lap. Aristide pressed jealously against her side. Hoboo told Aristide and me to take the stools on either side of her. The woman brought a large bowl of soup with noodles to the table. '*Tong,*' she said. Hoboo smacked her lips. A plate of *yi-ts'eh*, the salted mustard greens which were the mainstay of the coolie classes, was next. Bowls and spoons for each of us, chopsticks for the noodles, and that was all. To my brother and me food never tasted quite as good as it did from the servants' bowls. We ate greedily, accepting the treasured morsels of roast pork that Hoboo fed us with her chopsticks and never giving a second thought to the fact that we were eating the substance of weeks of savings and deprivation. Hoboo fed Didi too, and he chewed on a sliver of pork, his mouth wet with the juices, his eyes round and bright. Between munches he made happy sounds and pointed at Aristide or me, chuckling with pleasure. Aristide's early jealousy vanished and he responded to Didi, as he did to me, with tolerance, even affection.

A young man strode up to the table; he resembled Lao Ni, except that he was more heavily built and his eyes were not soft. He had the same curved cheekbones and wide flared lips, and his voice was loud.

'Did you get the stuff?' his mother asked anxiously.

Ah-ching, who was the *Lao Du* or number one or simply the oldest brother, hiked up his jacket, and I saw that he was wearing the blue peasant trousers, wide at the waist, folded over several times, and held in place by a broad leather belt with a big brass buckle. From the inner folds of the pleats under the belt he produced a small packet wrapped in white butcher paper. He cast it on the table.

'Let him dream into oblivion.'

The mother took the package quickly. 'Your father is a worthy man. He was a number one mill worker,' she cried.

'Now he is nothing but a number one corpse—breathing, but dead just the same.'

'Ah-ching,' Hoboo said, 'they came to look for you a few days ago, the northerners with the British police.'

'Why didn't Lao Ni come to warn me?' Ah-ching said.

'I was questioned about you. They suspect that we are of the same family. Since they seem to know nothing of Lao Ni it is better that he doesn't get mixed up in this business,' Hoboo replied.

'Better,' Ah-ching cried out in a laugh which sounded more like a cry of rage or pain. 'Better for whom? Do you want Lao Ni and Didi to end their lives as the whipped dogs of foreign imperialists?'

'Foreign imperialists,' Hoboo said. 'What does that mean? Do our people care about us? At least the foreigners pay us a living wage.'

'Until the foreign devils came, China was like a sponge drinking in her conquerors. But they have resisted and we must drive them out.'

'Why?' Hoboo asked. 'They have brought good as well as evil. They have given us churches and hospitals and rice.'

'And taken away your land, your husband, and your child,' the young man said. Hoboo extracted a cigarette from the pink and gold package of Ruby Queens which she produced from a pocket. When she spoke it seemed that she was caught up in a dream. Ah-ching and his mother exchanged glances quickly, for they knew what she was going to say. It was as if by repetition of it she might someday believe in its actuality.

'Yang-hsi was a good husband and provided well enough so I never questioned how he made his living. That summer of the second revolution he told me to come to the foreign settlement. There was to be a celebration, he said, near the race-course, and he was going to make a speech. When I got there, clinging onto my new baby, I found trouble in the streets. Crowds were pushing against foreign soldiers who joined hands to make a ring around the group of speakers, and some of them were standing on boxes throwing out leaflets. I saw Yang-hsi among them. Then an iron car of northern troops arrived and they began firing. I tried to get through to Yang-hsi, but with the baby in my arms and the crowds of people it was very difficult. I saw the soldiers take the baskets of leaflets and dump them over the bodies of Yang-hsi and the others. They sprinkled gasoline on them and made a fire. At last I pushed through the people and the cordon of soldiers and I tried to tell a northern officer that Yang-hsi was not a thief or a murderer but a good man. He looked at me as though he understood what I was saying, and then he pulled the baby from my arms and threw him on top of the flames.' Hoboo drew heavily on her cigarette and looked at Ah-

82

ching. 'It was not a *foreign* soldier who killed my husband and my baby.'

'But who supported the Peking government? Who refused to recognize Sun Yat-sen?'

Hoboo shook her head. 'I don't know anymore.'

'The foreigners,' Ah-ching said. 'They call these corrupt northern dogs their *allies*. This time we have a military leader to enforce our policy. Chiang Kai-shek will unify China by ridding us of the war-lords and their foreign supporters.'

'And what about the Communists?' Hoboo asked.

'They will fall into line with Nationalism or be crushed,' Ah-ching said.

'So then we will have a war with brothers,' Hoboo said.

'It will never come to that, old Auntie. The three party principles of Sun Yat-sen are not reconcilable to Marxism.'

'I don't understand party principles or Marxism, but I do know that it doesn't matter what name you give it, Ah-ching. Foreigners, Peking government, Communists, there will always be a ruling order of one sort or another, and we will have to pay our tribute.'

'Those who think that they serve just by living, like Lao Ni and you and my old parents, belong to the past, to the dead,' Ah-ching said.

I could see that Hoboo was very angry; her jowls began to shake. 'What kind of talk is that for a Christian?' she cried.

'As our little father once said,' Ah-ching replied, quoting Sun Yat-sen, 'I do not belong to the Christianity of churches but the Christianity of Jesus, who was a revolutionary.'

The mother was sifting rice with her hands in a large wicker tray. 'It's that university filling his head with dissatisfaction, ideas of liberation, and peoples' rights nonsense,' she said.

Ah-ching went to where his mother was seated. He picked up a handful of rice and let grains fall slowly back onto the tray. 'Sun Yat-sen said that China was like shifting sands. You cannot make a rope of sand and you cannot make a rope of rice. If we don't knot ourselves into a rope, if we don't become united in the cause to free China from the greater powers, we will always remain a semi-colony.'

'This kind of talk will feed you and your whole family to the tigers,' the mother cried. 'They will come, the police or these labourer troublemakers that you mix with, and they will cut our heads off one by one, *nema hao*, then you'll be satisfied.'

Ah-ching said, 'If I knew that it would be the end of foreigners trying us in their courts and not letting us try them in ours, if I knew that they would return the concessions and territories to our people, yes, I would be satisfied then.'

From the cot in the corner of the room there was a stirring. One scrawny hand like a small winter branch was extended quiveringly. The mother went to the cot and said something in a tone of voice that was different from that which she had used up to now. I watched from the table as she went to a carton and produced a small alcohol burner which she lit. Next she opened the packet Ah-ching had brought and carefully spread the contents into a shallow square cigarette tin. Then taking a metal wire, she dipped one end of it into the opium and twirled it around slowly to collect a blob of it on the end of the wire. She repeated the twirling process over the flame, but quite rapidly to prevent the ball of opium from catching fire. When smoke started emanating from the ball, I recognized the gorge-filling sweetness that I had smelled in the alley. The woman leaned over the man in the bunk and touched the wire with the ball of opium over the opening in the metal bowl of the man's pipe. I could see by the rising of his thin chest that the man was breathing in deeply. He did this a few times and then he fell back gently into a hypnotic sleep.

Hoboo began arranging her shawl. 'We must get back,' she said. Little Didi caught hold of Aristide's hand, and his fingers strayed to the cuffs of my brother's shirt. In the semidarkness the gold character cuff links which he had received on his birthday gleamed. On impulse Aristide worked at his cuffs, trying unsuccessfully to remove the links.

I judged by Hoboo's expression that she was about to protest, but before she had a chance, Ah-ching said, 'Sure, take them, little brother, small enough price for what the *Nahkuning* have taken from our people.' *Nahkuning* is a colloquialism meaning foreigner. Its contempt is measured by the literal translation, which implies foreigners are so different that their bones are outside of their bodies. 'Take them; by and by the white police will come with their black trucks and Hindu giants, and Gung! Gung! Gung!' He made gestures of rapid random firing over the room. Didi began to wail.

Then Hoboo eased the links from Aristide's cuffs and thrust them into the jacket pocket of the Chinese child, who wailed louder than ever. Ah-ching spread his hands on his hips and threw back his head in laughter. 'Thank you, good Auntie, for coming to warn me, but I have better protection than you think.' He made a thumbs-up gesture meaning number one. Hoboo ignored him. She said good-bye to the mother and herded us to the door.

Ah-ching said, 'What about those two?'

Hoboo's good eye widened. 'What do you mean?'

'Not very wise to have brought them. They might talk.'

'I had to bring them. They won't,' Hoboo said angrily.

'I can take care of it,' Ah-ching said lightly.

Hoboo turned to Ah-ching. 'I could have lived like Empress Tsu Hsi for the rest of my days on the money I turned over to this cause. Don't ever make me ashamed for having made a poor choice.' Her face was ashen as she pushed Aristide and me before her out the doorway.

As we got into our waiting rickshaw, a black Pierce-Arrow drove up to the alley. A Chinese man in a bulky-looking foreign suit and wearing a felt hat was at the driver's wheel. Through the crazed amber glass we could see the sole occupant in the back seat. He was an enormously stout man whose skin was pitted largely. It reminded me of a honeycomb. His head was shaved, which made the elephantine ears stand out prominently. One hand held a cigarette to his open lips. The nails of his fingers were long and the colour of tung oil stain. Hoboo snapped an order at the rickshaw coolie and we started for home.

It was getting dark when we reached the apartment on the Bund. As the iron-grilled elevator started its slow ascent, Hoboo said to Aristide, 'By'n by, you lich, you helpee Hoboo?'

'Oh, yes, Hoboo, when I rich you have plenty piculs of rice,' Aristide said.

'Hoboo no wanchee lice. You listen Hoboo. . . .' She paused until we were on our landing. Then she said in Chinese, 'You have soft ear roots, easily bent. You must not talk about where we went today.'

'I know, Hoboo,' he replied.

I tugged at the amah's jacket. 'I no talk.'

She smiled at me; her roughened fingers grazed the top of my head. 'Little urchin,' she said.

85

12

THE next morning Aristide was to start piano lessons. We were waiting in the main hall for the arrival of his teacher when Mama appeared dressed for shopping. We had not seen her on her return the evening before, and she was obviously in no mood to be trifled with. There was going to be a party, apparently something Papa had planned long in advance. Although she had most likely been informed by note only this morning, with Mama's ingrained sense of the politic this meant that there would be, for the time being at least, an extension of the armed truce.

My parents' ability to make surrenders conditional to their circumstances never ceased to amaze me. She called for the cook and Zee and began a shopping list. After the menu had been decided on and all orders for the dinner arrangements concluded, Mama sorted through the stacked mail, rifling expertly to separate the square blue envelopes from bills and other inconsequential matter. The envelopes were folded and they disappeared into the labyrinths of Mama's bosom. As she pulled on her kid gloves, she looked from Aristide to me. My brother and I both knew what that meant. Gearing myself for the struggle and protest over her choice, which would surely be Aristide (without stopping to think about the piano lessons any more than he did), I was in the middle of my openmouthed protest when I heard for a wonder Mama say, 'No, Aristide, you play the piano. I'm taking your brother.'

The antics Aristide went through with seemingly no effort were a marvel of determination. He used devices I had never seen before, jiggling his feet and cocking his head brokenly on one side and gasping for breath between screams, all of which Mama, collecting the sundry mail, ignored. Aristide was now wailing and choking and turning quite an effective blue, without actually shedding one tear. 'All right,' Mama said, 'I'll give you twenty cents.'

Without even a break in his wailing, Aristide looked icily at Mama. 'I want a dollar,' he said.

'Will you take twenty cents, or two slaps *in* the face?' Mama asked.

'A dollar, a dollar,' Aristide insisted.

Although Aristide didn't get anything, not even the slap in the face, the dazzling victory over him was short-lived and I learned a primary lesson in acceptance. From that time on when Aristide was chosen to go with Mama on her expeditions, I did not fight it.

I remember my elation in the car beside Mama, her personal musky fragrance blending with the faint patchouli of Egyptian cigarettes. We stopped at many stores. I got enormous excitement from the sight of Mama sailing empty-handed into a shop and seeing through the windows the flurry she stirred among the staffs and her return to the car with a retinue of salespeople in her wake. But today something was wrong, different in Mama's attitude. There was no graciousness in the way she dismissed the parcel-bearing assistants. There was no smile on her face, and her commands to Pao-shing were peremptory.

How natural, as I think back, it was to come across Tante Tila outside of the jewellers, Boyes Basset, holding up a gem to the light.

Tila saw us, and in the traffic stall she snaked her way through the congestion as though walking on knife blades, flouncing her fox fur piece imperiously at rickshaw coolies and buses which impeded her progress. She rapped on the car window.

Pao-shing went around to let her in. She pounced on Mama and kissed her on both cheeks and then she kissed and hugged me. Then she glanced around to see if there was anyone else upon whom to bestow her affection. Her gaze lighted on Pao-shing, but after the briefest pause, she shrugged and settled back in the car.

'*Dis, on peut parler devant le petit?*'

They're back at that again, I thought. It was always first, the question of whether one could talk in front of me safely, followed immediately by the insulting assumption that they could, and invariably they did. In fact, Mama looked around to see to whom Tila was referring.

'Oh, this one's as good as gold, never repeats anything,' she said. 'But listen, Tila, I knew we were going out for a game, but I didn't know your friend was taking us to the underworld.'

'Michel knows everyone,' Tila said proudly. 'Liu Yueh-sung is the boss of Shanghai.'

'Well, he's a gonif,' Mama said.

'How much did you lose?' Tila asked.

Mama looked at me nervously, then she said, 'Fifty thousand

taels.' Tila whistled and wrung one hand as though she had burned it. Judging by Mama's expression, she wished Tila had. 'Don't worry,' Mama continued. 'I called the bank and put a stop order on my cheque.'

'You cancelled the cheque?' Tila said. 'But you lost the money.'

'Like hell I lost the money,' Mama replied. She told Tila that halfway through the poker game she realized the cards were marked. She memorized them and shortly was ahead a considerable sum. 'Then this bandit has a servant pour tea, only he doesn't serve it at all, he upsets the tray over the cards, which have to be changed. Different markings that I couldn't remember, and I lose fifty thousand taels.'

'You've got to pay. When someone doesn't pay Pockmarked Liu they can expect a nice shiny coffin at the front door,' Tila said.

'He wouldn't dare,' Mama said.

Tila told Mama of an episode concerning the warlord. Several important officials in the French concession, among them a consul general, a judge, and a prominent barrister, had in Liu's opinion double-crossed him. On the pretence of a conciliation he invited them to a large banquet. Within twenty-four hours his enemies were dead. They had all suffered the same symptoms, perforated intestines. Rumour had it that the agent used was ground diamonds; however, nothing was revealed at the inquests. The story must have struck a note of remembrance for Mama because she seemed much less confident. She said, 'Tila, I don't feel well; is your car in town?' Tila said that it was and we dropped her off.

If Mama had been in a bad frame of mind when we started out, now she was furious. She snatched a bag of dragées which I had gotten into, casting the almonds over the floor of the car. When we reached the apartment, in my eagerness to get away from Mama, I opened the door of the car. At a word from her I slammed it shut, forgetting to remove my hand. I was more scared than hurt and began crying. I had never seen Mama so angered with me. 'Wait till I get you upstairs; I'll beat you with a brush, I'll beat you, you little idiot.'

Aristide was in the drawing-room, making a dreadful racket on the Steinway, but he didn't come out to welcome us home. Mama hauled me to our room and, true to her promise, went through the motions of tanning me with a hairbrush. More acutely than anything else, I remember the horrible sense of injustice I felt, and I screamed in outrage for the first time in my life. In those moments, I crossed the border of love into a cold and unknown hatred. Hoboo, muttering angrily in Chinese, cradled me in her arms, and still crying, I fell asleep.

Early that evening I awoke, and Hoboo had a tray of food from which she served me. Mama came to see me. She was dressed for dinner in gold metallic lace. She smiled warmly at me. 'Is Mama's *mizinik* sorry?' When I would occasionally protest that my mother preferred my brothers to me, Mama would say, 'If you have five fingers and you cut one, the whole hand hurts,' but when she felt more like compromising, she would say, 'You are Mama's *mizinik*. The youngest son is always special.' Since I never felt special and certainly felt far from it at this point, I kept resentfully silent.

The party my parents were giving this night was in honour of several Chinese business acquaintances. This was an unusual procedure for a foreign taipan. Apart from missionaries, the Americans were the first to make social concessions to the Chinese. Europeans, rankling at what was originally rejection by the Chinese, remained withdrawn, but Papa, having learned in his youth the values placed on honour and face by the Chinese, began to cultivate them as friends.

The rest of that evening was filled with the rush of the servants and the sound of people arriving, all of whom seemed to be talking at the tops of their voices. I remember Sascha and Aristide, who preferred to wait for their supper so that they could eat what the guests did, being delighted when some platter had only been slightly disturbed and being dismayed when the dessert returned in small ruins. I slept.

13

WHEN I awoke the next morning, it was earlier than usual. Not dark, but as a rule, lying on my bed, I could see sun motes by the light of the window, and although it was clear, this day there were none. A standard delicacy Mama bought for all her parties was marrons glacés. These expensive confections were kept in a supposedly secret hiding place in the dining-room. I sat up to make sure that Hoboo had gone to church, then I got out of bed and slipped on a kimono. Walking softly so as not to wake Aristide, I tiptoed out of the room.

Although in many ways Papa had risen above the commonplace attitude of foreigners towards Chinese, in his home there was little evidence of Chinese artistry. There was not a stick of teak or rosewood in the entire apartment. The dining-room was softly lighted through the lace mesh of Nottingham panels bordered by olive velvet drapes and could have been the banqueting room in any English ancestral home. In fact the wainscoting had been torn out of a manor in Worcestershire County, and for a long time I thought that Worcestershire sauce was extracted from these woods. The table, which opened out with leaves to seat forty-eight, was of oak, as were the high-backed Jacobean chairs and the massive wooden linked chandelier. On the buffet a wide array of Baccarat decanters, dishes, and bowls was prominently displayed. Doilies and runners covered the tops of occasional tables on which Limoges or hideously floral Gallé vases stood. On the mantel over the fireplace, concession had been allocated to the few Chinese art objects which had been given to my parents as wedding gifts. These were, in total, a Ming urn which had arrived at my parents' reception with four body-guards, a charming twelve-inch Chi'en Lung bud vase and some carved rose quartz. By the windows opposite the fireplace was a cabinet containing crystal stemware for forty-eight. There was at the base of the cabinet a panel, which slid open at the touch of a concealed button. The booty that I was seeking was hidden there.

The dining-table had not yet been cleared, and the shambles of the banquet were everywhere in evidence. I crept by the table towards the glass cabinet and hurriedly pressed the button. The panel slid sideways, revealing the large white and gold box of marrons. I had just grabbed a handful when the sound of voices at the door-way stopped me in my actions. I tried to stuff the candied chestnuts into my kimono, but realized soon enough that there were no pockets. Quickly I scrambled for cover under the table. I caught sight of Zee's long white gown as he began clearing the table. When he had done that, he set a place at the head of the table, where I was hiding. Then I heard Papa asking for the North China *Daily*, as he walked towards where I was hidden, his cane hitting the rug with an evenly spaced thud. I dared not move. One sound, I knew, would reveal me, and I had had enough in the last day. Papa eased himself into the chair, his feet slipping out from under him like anchors. I pressed myself away from them against the chair at his left and stared in abhorrence at the two shiny boots, one of which had a sole three inches thicker than the other. The marrons in their foil wrappings were beginning to melt from the heat of my palm. The smell of coffee, scones, and butter floated tantalizingly down to me. I put the marrons on the carpet and then cautiously began to peel the wrapper off one. Before I had finished that one, I had unwrapped another and popped it into my mouth. At that moment Papa shifted positions and kicked me squarely in the shins. In a split second of surprise and pain I yelled. There was no action from the upper deck. I sat very still, hardly daring to chew; the chestnut syrup trickled from the corners of my mouth. Then Papa said, 'Fee Fi Fo Fum, I smell the blood of my youngest son.' I shook my head negatively under the table. Another silence. Then a hand reached under the table and with complete sureness of aim found its mark. I must have been quite a sight with chestnut pureed all over my mouth and chin. Papa looked at me gravely. 'Raiding the marrons glacés?' He paused reflectively and drew on his cigar. 'Well, what penalty shall we exact? Marching the plank? The cat-o'-nine-tails? A ducking in Malmsey!' Papa had been rediscovering Robert Louis Stevenson with Sascha, and I expect the first two penalties were culled from that. As for the Malmsey, in spite of his omnivorous taste in literature, Papa could always be counted on to fall back on Shakespeare.

Since I rarely understood all that Papa said, I remained silent. He must have wondered at my inarticulateness compared to Sascha's force of character and Aristide's glib assurance.

Papa indicated that I was to sit next to him, and Zee brought me breakfast. From time to time I would catch Papa looking at me over the top of his newspaper.

'Papa,' I finally said, 'why are the Chinese so angry with foreigners?'

'What do you mean, son?' Papa said.

'Why they don't like us, we are *Nahkuning*.'

Papa put his paper down and looked intently at me. 'We have taken their land and made our own laws,' he said.

'Is that bad?'

'I don't know,' he said, 'but the Chinese don't feel that it's right.'

'Is it? Is it right, Papa?'

'I don't think so, son.'

'Do you love Sascha, Papa?'

'Of course.'

'And me and Aristide?'

'Naturally.'

'Do you love Mama?'

'Why do you ask me that?'

'Do you? Do you?'

'Yes, of course I love Mama.'

I gave a big sigh of relief. 'Papa, if a black shiny coffin came for Mama, would she be dead?' I knew all about coffins and graves and death. The countryside was covered with grave mounds, and the coffins of children who were fortunate enough to have been buried were encased in grey brick and had tiled roofs to resemble houses. I knew very well what a black lacquer coffin would look like.

'What are you talking about, my boy?' Papa seemed disturbed and I began stammering. Mama came into the dining-room with Aristide; Sascha was on an outing in Jessfield Park. Lao Ni, who had been promoted by Papa to a number two boy position, probably as a salve for his conscience, assisted Zee with the serving.

We ate in a silence broken only by Aristide's chatter: 'Miss Krantz says that I'm very talented. Miss Krantz says that in six months I'll be playing a concert with Henriette du Lac.' Since no one appeared to be paying him any attention he addressed me. 'Henriette is only six years old and already she's a *vee comtesse*, did you know that?' I didn't, so I just stared back stupidly.

The doorbell rang, and when Zee returned he said, 'Mastah, Chinese gentleman to see you.' Behind Zee the portly figure of a man dressed in a dark blue robe could be seen. He was accompanied by two men in foreign-style suits. As Zee stepped aside to let the man enter, I saw his face. It was the big Chinese that we had seen in the car outside Ah-ching's house. If Aristide made the same mental connection, you would never have guessed it by his behaviour.

'Monsieur, Madame Spunt,' the Chinese man said, '*vous m'excusez que je vous dérange.*'

Dérange was a good word for how Mama looked at that moment. She gave me a scolding glance, and I realized that she thought that

I had something to do with Liu Yueh-sung's presence. Papa invited the man to join us, which he did, glancing in a strange manner over both shoulders. His guards posted themselves behind him on either side of the warlord's seat. Close up, Liu's complexion looked even more like a large-celled honeycomb. His short flat nose with flaring nostrils made me think he should have a ring through them. The huge ears, considered a sign of generosity, were contradicted by a weal-like mouth. As he brushed aside Zee's offer of coffee, I noticed the two-inch brown nails of his fingers, and I thought of the hands of Ah-ching's father. Lao Ni came into the room carrying a tray. At the sight of Liu, his face turned very pale and the tray began to rattle. Then I knew that Aristide had recognized the man, because he didn't even glance around.

I expect that Pockmarked Liu had phoned before coming and that Papa had known in advance the purpose of the visit. All the same he kept up a noncommittal conversation with the warlord.

Then quite suddenly Liu directed his gaze across to the opposite end of the table where Mama was seated. Although his lips tipped into a smile, his eyes were those of a taxidermist's bird.

Mama fumbled in her purse, which of course was being uncooperative. Out came a tiny address book, a pocketbook, the bunch of keys, lipsticks, a rabbit's foot, a maze of hairnets, a tin of blackcurrant pastilles, and finally a chubby green bottle. She opened the smelling salts and inhaled deeply.

Mama put down her smelling salts. 'It was not a fair game, Mr. Liu.'

'How so, not fair?' he asked.

'The cards were marked,' Mama said.

Liu produced a deck of cards. They were elaborate French playing cards. He handed them to Papa to examine. Papa took them but did not look at them.

'Hah,' Mama said, 'what about the first pack? What about the ones your servant spilled the tea on?'

Liu undid the top frog of his gown, and as he did so, I caught a glimpse of what seemed to be a metal casing. Pockmarked Liu was like an enormous sausage in his bulletproof vest. He fumbled for a few seconds and then withdrew a small bundle of embroidered silk. He untied the corners and produced another pack of cards which he handed to Papa.

93

'Observe, Monsieur Spunt, still wet.'

Papa took the pack of cards, and by the way his fingers stuck to them it was pretty obvious that they were wet. Liu Yueh-sung never took his eyes off Papa. Still Papa did not examine the cards for markings. After a moment's silence, he said, 'Mr Liu, you are a most tolerant man, a forgiving soul, to take all this trouble.'

The warlord made a deprecating gesture.

Papa looked at Mama, who was beginning to show white around the lips. 'But,' he went on in a confiding voice, leaning closer to the Chinese, 'women have such imagination, their fancies sometimes play them tricks. Now I have an idea. . . .' Since it would be un-gallant to acknowledge that Mama was at fault and an unmitigated loss of face for her, and since obviously Mr. Liu's cards were very much in order, Papa's suggestion was a simple draw using either deck of Mr. Liu's cards, with the winner donating the money to the loser's prescribed charity.

Papa's mediation was a classic of Chinese compromise with face saved on either side and a gamble thrown in. The warlord was ham-strung by his own type of device. There was that crazy weal im-personating a smile again and those glassy dead eyes. Only the huge nostrils betrayed Liu's fury, and I expected them to spout fire at any second. Coldly he selected the deck of dry cards and began shuffling. He offered Papa the privilege of cutting, which Papa declined, say-ing as he did so, 'Mr. Liu, our servants have a superstition that my second son is favoured by the gods. With your permission I will let him draw for me.'

Aristide came bounding up to Papa and scrambled onto his lap. He was very excited and wet his lips and fussed with locks of hair he no longer possessed. Mr. Liu held out the deck to Aristide, who shut his eyes and reached blindly for a card; after some pinching and changing of his mind, he drew one. It was the four of spades. Mama sniffed on her salts and the warlord sighed heavily. It was now his turn to draw, and Aristide extended the deck of cards to him, muttering some incantation, which sounded familiarly like, 'son-ummmbitch-wishyoudie'. Papa shushed him. The warlord drew; his face as he looked at the card was impassive. He flipped it on the table. It was the two of diamonds. Papa's hand gently cupped Aristide's mouth.

'To whom shall I send the cheque?' the warlord said.

94

'You may make it out to the Society for Chinese Indigents,' Papa said, producing his own gold pen in a salesmanship manoeuvre to get the cheque written in front of him.

'I regret that I have not brought my chequebook,' the Chinese apologized, 'but I will mail the cheque in your name, Monsieur Spunt.' Mr. Liu had no intention of mailing a cheque in Papa's name or anyone else's. The contribution to the Society of Chinese Indigents made the whole gesture a double-edged sword. This group tended to addicts who were victims of the warlord's opium combines, giving them treatment where possible or decent burial in cases of death. Up to the time of its organization, narcotics victims were rounded up in trucks outside of dens where they had been cast and dumped into the river early in the morning at the outgoing tide. It was discovered that some of these unfortunates were not dead when they were thrown into the Whangpoo. Papa said, 'Mr. Liu, I am but a speck in the vast area of China, but your causes on behalf of mankind are known to one and all. Today my Chinese colleagues and I are lunching with the elders in charge of the society; I will announce the great news of your generosity to them and they will see that all of China hears of the open heart of Liu Yueh-sung, the Shanghai Bankers.'

The warlord got up, looking in that odd manner right and left behind him. He barked an order at his guards who came to attention at once.

'Monsieur Spunt, you do me *trop d'honneur*. Perhaps someday I can repay you.' He nodded to Mama and marched out of the room, his men following.

Mama looked across the table at her husband, and she smiled for the first time like she had in Europe. It was as though a thousand levers had suddenly been sprung and each feature was bathed in radiance.

'Maximilian,' she said, 'you are a—I don't know, a *man*.'

Papa held Mama's look in a long gentle moment. The deep claret brown of his eyes glowed softly. And all at once it was there again, as though it had never drifted away, the pounding sense of sanguine between them.

14

BY late January there had still been no settlement between the Nationalists and the leaders of the British concessions in Hankow. As precautionary measures against a similar overthrow in Shanghai, the British admiralty sent an additional flotilla to patrol the Yangtze.

Rather than cope with the high-handed labour union, Papa, like other foreign businessmen who had branches in Hankow, closed his offices there. This tactic concerned the Nationalists since it threatened an economic standstill which would affect the entire province. Early in February, encouraged by the turmoil in Hankow, the General Labour Union in Shanghai began plans for a massive strike. Leaflets were issued, students paraded, and workers gave antiforeign speeches, the gist of which were the timeworn demands for the return of concessions, an end to the unequal treaties, and death to the running dogs of imperialism. Papa, watching an agitator on the promenade in front of the Public Gardens, shook his head sadly. 'What they want is so right, and how they are going about it is so hopeless,' he said.

The commissioner of defence was fast to act. A proclamation was issued forbidding the distribution of inflammatory pamphlets; even the possession of them meant instant death. Northern soldiers under his orders raided the Shanghai University and arrested thirteen students, five of whom were girls. They were executed without trials. Sascha, returning from a school outing in Jessfield Park in the western section of the city, told of seeing an elderly Chinese man and woman holding leaflets. Although they were obviously peasants and could not read, they had been forced to their knees by the soldiers and beheaded in full view of the public. So the strike was quelled; the northern generals made positive announcements of stemming the Nationalist drive, and the city breathed easily again.

In our apartment the microcosm of a foreigner's life in China continued. Mama presided over gatherings to review the latest fashions from Paris at 'elevenses, when she served Möet Chandon, and Beluga caviar purchased in five-gallon tins from an enterprising Russian skipper. Papa went to his office daily and Sascha attended school. Although it had been decided that Aristide was to join Sascha at the Richard Ashbury, our parents now felt that this plan should be delayed because the school was situated near the Chinese suburb, Chapei, where there was heavy mobilization. It became clearer, however, as the days went by, that something had to be 'done' about the middle son.

The business of outdrawing the warlord seemed to have special significance for Aristide. Until then he had taken the matter of his being a symbol of good luck rather complacently. Now at the least provocation he was shrilling, 'I wish you die!' Or clapping his hands together as he had seen the Arab do in *Beau Geste*, crying, 'I blot you out of existence.'

Sascha was Aristide's chosen mark. Like most healthy, sports-minded people, Sascha showed little respect for the supernatural. Nevertheless, he protested vigorously when Aristide pointed a finger at him. It was eerie to watch as Sascha, hooting his ridicule at Aristide, pedalled the huge toy bus (which I might add he had commandeered since its arrival) right through the plate-glass doors that led from the entrance hall into the one beyond. Aside from a few contusions and a bad shaking-up, Sascha was not hurt, but he was very angry and complained to Papa.

Mama and Papa saw eye to eye on everything since their renewed compatibility. How Mama managed the blue letters, which still arrived in batches, I can only guess. As for Papa, I would assume he simply did not believe her capable of physical infidelity. At the family council held in the smoking-room, Papa warned Aristide that if he ever uttered another curse he would be 'thrashed within an inch of his life'. He was not allowed to go to the Gardens for a week and was obliged to sit for an hour daily in the wing chair in our parents' bedroom, where he was told to 'hold your tongue', an edict Aristide and I always took literally, to our own discomfort and Papa's well-controlled amusement.

What neither of our parents considered was the fact that Aristide was reacting to being pushed out of Mama's sphere of immediate attention, but I saw his face when he went to their bedroom in the morning and found the door locked to him.

In part, Grandmama's suggestion of a governess came up as the logical solution of what to do with Aristide. Since we were, after all, French citizens, what better time for him to begin studies in that language?

Chosen for this position was Madame du Change, who had the

97

square, strapped, and belted appearance of an upended sea chest. She had a long nose, broad at the base and dimpled at the tip. Her hair was done up in classical ringlets, which Aristide described as 'worms'. To Madame the simplest phrase was a challenge to her skill as an orator. She would stand by the velvet drapes in the dining-room with a book pressed against her bosom and one hand raised in entreaty. Whether she was reading *Le Chat et Le Rat, Contes et Legendes,* or *Le Tour de France par deux petits Enfants,* she was invariably in her own estimation no less than superb. *Le Chat et Le Rat* we could follow after a while, but it soon became obvious that Madame was oblivious to her audience when she began quoting from Racine and Sainte-Beuve.

In order to mitigate the dreariness of these sessions, Aristide began to devise means of unsettling the woman. For *Le Petit Goûter,* she had taught us to eat tartines of thickly buttered bread with a slab of chocolate on it. Once when she was reading from *Causeries du Lundi,* of all things, Aristide slipped a tartine which he had worked into an admirable chocolate butter glue onto her seat. As Madame pronounced the last lines of her recitation, she sank into the chair with a faintly tragic smile on her face, which in a matter of seconds changed to an expression of pure fury. Papa thoroughly approved of the caning Madame gave Aristide. Mama however was less than pleased. She pressed Aristide, who was screaming mightily, against her breast: 'If there is one thing I can't stand, it's for anyone else to touch my child.' Then, I suppose to prove that she was as good as her word, she shook Aristide thoroughly. When he began to yell again, she looked up and cried, 'Women who pray for children should be lined against a wall and shot.' As part of her terms for staying on, Madame insisted on complete control. It was obvious, she said crossing herself, that the child was possessed, and apparently only she could drive the devil out of him. This of course did not endear her to Hoboo.

The climax came when the Frenchwoman decided that she should take over our daily outing to the Public Gardens. Aristide overheard these plans and contrived with Hoboo to beat Madame to the punch. Loaded with a thermos of Horlicks malted milk and a Chefoo pear for each of us, Hoboo smuggled us out of the apartment early one morning, only to find Madame ready and waiting as we reached the main floor.

Naturally there was a tussle, for Aristide was not going to give in to this type of coercion readily. In the mêlée of tugging from Madame and pulling from Hoboo, Aristide's pear fell, rolled through the grating of the elevator cage, and dropped to the basement. He was determined to retrieve it. Madame stormed into the elevator after him and tried to drag him out. Aristide wrenched himself from her grip and ran out of the cage. Turning, he pointed a finger at her, '*Si ning*, I wish you die!' In rage Madame stamped her foot and opened her mouth to speak. All at once the elevator cage disappeared from view with Madame in it. We heard it crash some ten feet below on the basement landing. The facts were never made entirely clear. The regular lift man had been off duty, and Hoboo had run the elevator by herself. Somehow my parents took it for granted that Aristide had, as Mama said, 'opened his nasty mouth', and she was quite vexed with him. 'Never dig graves for others,' she said, quoting one of Grandmama's favourite proverbs, '—you might fall in one yourself.'

Papa kept in touch with the Sainte Marie Hospital where the governess had been sent, and presently he informed us that she had suffered a couple of broken ribs but that her condition was not serious. Aristide put on a grave face while Papa lectured to him on the sins of the evil eye and suggested that Aristide give thanks to God that Madame was alive and that her condition was one of discomfort and cost rather than one of tragedy.

In the privacy of our room, minutes later, I never saw anyone less concerned than Aristide, as he calmly dressed one of his dolls, crooning softly:

> Do do, do do,
> Mama va acheter chocolat,
> Papa va acheter gâteau.

For a few days after Madame's departure, Aristide behaved very well, and the amah was reinstated in her full capacity. Hoboo went through a nightly toilette, as complicated as any of Mama's rituals when she was going to an official function. She would begin by standing in front of the bureau mirror, stripped to the waist, her medals jiggling on their grey cord as she swung her arms. First she would comb a type of wood resin dye into her long hair where the few grey ones stood out coarsely, like bean threads. The comb she used was broad and had a double row of teeth into which she had forced cotton to absorb the excess colouring and collect the lifeless hair. After she had set her hair into its traditional knot, she would run a towel, wrung out in jasmine water, over her shoulders, under her armpits, and under each of her great gourdlike breasts, whose nipples made me think of the dried persimmons sold by street vendors. Once in a while, glancing in the mirror, she would catch us watching her and would cackle in amusement.

She had a rough brass ring from which was suspended an ear cleaner, an iron nail cutter, a nose swab that looked like a fluffy dandelion, and a number of other instruments which I never got a chance to investigate. By the time she was through with her brass ring cycle she was ready for her beads and bed.

One night, for some reason, Aristide and I chatted for what must have seemed an eternity to Hoboo. Ignoring us at first, she began chanting her rosary. When she had finished with that, and we were still talking and giggling, she invoked Jesus, then Mary, and all the apostles. When everything else failed she cried to Buddha to rid her of these two devils. By then we were laughing convulsively. Hoboo got out of bed and, kneeling on the floor, slapped herself soundly on each cheek over and over again. We stopped laughing at once, but Hoboo continued to slap herself and when she pounded her head against the wall we tumbled on our knees at her side, imploring her to stop; but she did not stop, and Aristide tried to seize her hands and pull her to bed. Then Hoboo turned on him and with her thumb and forefinger pinched the flesh between his shoulder blades until Aristide's face turned white. I thought when Aristide first began to scream that he would wreak vengeance on the old woman with a choice and final curse, and indeed Hoboo was now staring at him in a challenging fascination as though it was what she most expected too. For some reason Aristide did not curse Hoboo. Perhaps it was because he suspected that Hoboo might have a device or two of her own. At any rate all he did was scream at the top of his lungs. The light flicked on and there was Mama in the doorway.

'What is it? What's the matter?' Mama demanded, her eyes travelling over the entire scene. Aristide tapered his screams to a whimper but did not reply.

'What did she do to you?' Mama insisted. Hoboo looked at Mama; her expression was cold and empty.

'I—I hit my toe on the corner of the bed,' Aristide said. I nodded at Mama affirmatively. Mama stood in the doorway for some time; then she said, 'All right, you come and sleep with me, Aristide.'

Shortly after that night, Aristide overhead Mama telling Papa that Hoboo was responsible for Aristide's notion of his own supernatural powers: 'All that nonsense about *dondee neetsu*!' They discussed sending Hoboo away but dismissed the idea because of the possible effect it might have on us.

One day when February was still young, Papa brought E-ling to the house. She had come to his office and through one of his Chinese associates secured an interview. When Papa explained that there was little he could offer her in the way of secretarial work, she protested that her primary vocation was teaching; being a northerner she spoke Mandarin, and her greatest desire was to be a link, however small, in creating better understanding between the Chinese and the foreigners. Besides she had ageing parents who needed her financial help. . . .

Mama approved of E-ling. She remarked that with E-ling's shoulder-length hair caught neatly in a barrette, she was a refreshing change from all those impudently bobbed, short-skirted girls who exemplified the liberation movement in China. True enough, E-ling was exceptionally pretty, with wide cheekbones like altar bowls glowing with tiny lights. Her eyes were large but deepset, so that they appeared shadowy and never seemed to focus directly on you; the total effect was one of most appealing shyness. She spoke very slowly, thoughtfully, in a voice that was barely above a whisper.

It would be an understatement to say that E-ling was a class above Hoboo. To begin with, she had attended a Chinese municipal school and could read and write commendable English. Her position might have been awkward, since although she held the titular position of governess, she was not a foreigner and did not become part of the family; nor was she a servant and she was not expected to mix with them. It was her own unobtrusive handling of the lines of demarcation in the beginning that made my parents think that the choice had been a good one. E-ling was given a room adjacent to the one we shared with Hoboo, and she took her meals there. She did, however, sit with us in the alcove while we ate and tried to teach us some practical Mandarin. On her first evening at our house, E-ling picked up a bowl and said for us to repeat, '*cher fan*.'

'*Chu-veh*,' Hoboo said in a blatant Shanghai dialect.

'*Cher fan*,' Sascha parroted E-ling.

'*Veh dung*,' Hoboo snorted. Aristide and I giggled, and E-ling made an effort to control herself by placing a dainty hand across her mouth. Sascha was touchy about his weight, and being called a rice tub in front of someone he was obviously trying to impress maddened him.

Hoboo gathered Aristide and me in preparation for bed. Before leaving the table she turned to Sascha and said, 'Young potato has no eyes.' If the foreign governess had been an affront to Hoboo, the idea of another Chinese superseding her position was one of terrible loss of face, but when Aristide asked Hoboo why she disliked E-ling, the old woman had a ready reply: 'No likee northerner.' Dah Su was originally Cantonese; Pao-shing came from Szechwan in the southwest; the number one coolie was from the Wuhan provinces; and Zee, with whom she got on splendidly, was a northerner from Tientsin.

When E-ling was not trying to teach us to master the three tones, she would spend some time each day reading to us in English. Aristide had taken a copy of Oscar Wilde's fairy tales from the shelves in the smoking-room, and E-ling read us the story of why the rose was red and of the happy prince who allowed his sapphire eyes to be pecked out so that the match girl could have warmth. In our heated and fully provisioned home, Aristide and I were moved to tears by the stories, but E-ling read them flatly in her little voice as though if she understood sentiment she chose not to express it.

It soon became evident that Lao Ni was smitten with E-ling. He would pause midway between any chore to follow her with the flowered eyes of love as she walked across the halls, her dark cardigan stretched over breasts like two clenched fists. Once, when Sascha made a clumsy attempt at fondling her, Lao Ni betrayed himself by dropping a tray, but E-ling smoothed out the situation by calmly telling Sascha that he was after all very young so she would not mention this to our parents, but that he had better try to be a gentleman.

Until he had met E-ling, Lao Ni's life had been typically that of a lower-echelon servant. E-ling exposed him to other dimensions. I heard Lao Ni in the kitchen bragging about an excursion he had taken with the girl to the Great World. This amusement palace was unlike any other. Here Western forms of diversion, shooting galleries, distorted mirrors, and ferris wheels operated cheek by jowl with Chinese classic dramas, operas, and concerts. There were roof garden restaurants, aviaries, menageries, and a donkey course. As these outings in each other's company became frequent, there developed between the two a discernible bond of warmth, like the current between Mama and Papa. Hoboo sensed this too, and she began to hint that Lao Ni would bring shame to the house.

When E-ling had time off during the day, she would go to the servants' quarters at the rear of the kitchen, where Lao Ni's room was. E-ling claimed to be teaching the servant English, and they always left the door circumspectly open.

One rare afternoon when I was left to my own devices, I went into the kitchen, which was deserted. Dah Su was taking his customary nap and the other servants either were performing their duties or had the time off. After foraging around for a bit, I discovered a rather stale jelly roll under a net cover and was just about to slice off a piece when I felt a hand on my shoulder. On turning I found that it was only Hoboo. I suppose to anyone else the sight of her big wet grin, where the space from a newly missing front tooth gaped blankly, might have seemed sinister but to me she was a most welcome sight, the kitchen being strictly forbidden territory. All at once we heard voices coming from the direction of Lao Ni's room.

'Lovely day, isn't it?' we heard E-ling saying precisely.

'Luvahly day—don't you?' Lao Ni repeated hesitatingly. There was the rustling sound of intimacy and little squeals of laughter, and then the sound of a door being kicked shut. I pulled at Hoboo's sleeve, almost unable to contain my amusement, but when her face met mine it was dark with anger. Silently she took down a large tin of Jacob's cream crackers and put a few on a plate. She boiled some coffee, strained the grounds, added lots of milk, and assembled the snack on a tray; then because she never smoked in Mama's presence, she stabbed out her cigarette.

Mama was sitting up in bed brushing her hair. When she saw me she dropped the brush and extended her arms to lift me up beside her. Hoboo laid the tray of crackers and café au lait on her lap. When Mama had eaten, Hoboo told her of Lao Ni's affair with E-ling. 'Shame, Missy,' she said. 'No face. You got small boy,' she added with a reproachful look at me, as though instead of being a weighty instrument in her complaint I was a hindrance. Mama listened to Hoboo's story, probing womanishly for details. As she whispered each indiscretion, Hoboo stood back with an air of injury.

'Well,' Mama said, 'it's none of your business, and it's none of my business. What can I do?'

'Talkee mastah,' Hoboo said.

Mama told Hoboo to fetch her bottle of chypre from the dressing-table as she pondered her reply. She poured a quantity of the cologne from the crystal bottle into the palm of her hand and splashed it onto her neck and chest; then she reached over and rubbed some onto my forehead and almost blinded me, but although I squirmed miserably, I didn't say anything. Finally Mama said, 'No, I can't do that.'

'Wha for no can?' Hoboo said. Mama shrugged impatiently, and then as though to ensure communication between them, she lapsed into pidgin English: 'Just now all Chinese very angry foreign man; I no must mix up. E-ling no marry, Lao Ni no marry, can do as they bally well want, savee?'

'You have small boy,' Hoboo insisted.

'I don't want to hear *not* one word about it,' Mama said. Then she sighed heavily. I wonder now whether she was thinking of her own situation.

I don't know how far Hoboo would have pressed her case, but she was curtailed by the appearance of Zee at the door of Mama's room. He brought Mama what looked like a telegram. Mama tore the envelope nervously, and when she had read the contents, she leaned back against her pillows, one hand moving to her neck. 'My God,' she said.

'What's the matter, Mama?' I cried, tugging at her other hand, but Mama just patted my fingers and said nothing. Then Hoboo took me out of the room.

104

15

MAMA made no reference to the telegram, and any thought I might have given to it was lost in the happenings that immediately followed.

The strike which had been thwarted earlier in the month erupted on the nineteenth of February. Sascha excitedly told of seeing northern soldiers in armoured cars and a truckload of professional executioners headed towards Chapei. He kept vigil on the verandah with the hope of catching a glimpse of the returning vehicles. When Aristide, Hoboo, and I joined him there in the late afternoon, E-ling was with him. Outside there was a stillness, even for a Saturday, that was alien to the usual hubbub of the Bund. Trams did not run, the jetties were bare, and there were no rickshaws in sight. The silence was broken finally by the sound of motors coming from the north over the Garden Bridge. Crowds began to appear in the streets, and shortly the promenades and sidewalks below our building were lined with people. Slowly the lorries trundled into view. I turned to bury my face in Hoboo's shawl, but not fast enough to miss the sight in the first truck.

In the fore stood an executioner wearing the identifying scarlet sash, which looked as though it had been fashioned from a bolt of blood. He stood, legs spread apart, one hand brandishing his sword which gleamed in the last of the day's light. His other hand held aloft what seemed to be a bamboo cage no more than two feet square in which lay a severed human head. Even with my face hidden, I could still hear the roar of the people in the streets and Hoboo's repeated '*Ai yah, ai yah*'. Then Aristide was pushing his face under the shawl and hugging me very tightly. Sascha looked on, most likely to impress E-ling with his manliness, but we could tell by his voice that it was forced.

'Look! There's one of those beasts in the top of each armoured car, sticking up a head on a bamboo pole,' he was saying. Aristide screamed, and as Hoboo pushed us through the door of the verandah into the smoking-room, I glanced back. Although Sascha was pretending to watch the parade, his face was averted and his eyes were tightly closed. I looked at E-ling. A wind had come up and blown a loose strand of hair across her face. Without shifting her gaze from the scene below for a second, she deftly put the hair in place.

That evening Papa brought home the news that the strike was citywide. He said that the general opinion among the foreigners was that Nationalist agents were behind it in order to weaken the defences of the northern army now in command of those portions of the city not under extraterritorial protection. On the other hand, Nationalist sources claimed that the strike was sponsored by Communist factions. As we were to find out, there was some truth to both these reports. Immediately affected by the strike were the post office and the tramway companies, both in the International Settlement and French Concessions. Crews and labourers at the docks quit en masse, halting local shipping.

During the week of the strike, Papa stayed home most of the time or went to the Shanghai Club. In spite of the Chinese firms' being more affected than those under foreign ownership, cotton mills both inside and out of the settlement were strike-bound. Mama went to the front door daily for signs of postal delivery, but there were none.

On Monday evening, we gathered in the smoking-room to hear Papa's comments on the strike. E-ling stood discreetly in the background, but Hoboo was very much in evidence. Some of the other servants, curious for news, crowded the doorway. Papa read an account in the paper about a group of labourers who attacked northern soldiers in Siccawei. The men were armed with iron pipes and automatics. The ringleader, who was thought to be an agent for the Nationalists, had been captured and tortured. The defence commissioner had given the order for his execution. I saw Aristide look at Hoboo, whose face betrayed nothing.

'What's his name?' Aristide asked.

'Who?' Papa said.

'The leader,' Aristide said.

Papa read the item to himself this time. 'Doesn't say. Why?' Before Aristide could think up an answer, Hoboo scoffed lightly, 'Big Nose, must savee evelly thing.'

The next day an admiral aboard one of the Chinese gunboats lying in the Whangpoo gave the order to shell the Chinese territory. The admiral was announcing by this gesture his defection from the northern warlords and his alliance with the Nationalist cause. Panic was created when the arsenal situated in the Chinese territory bordering the French Concession fired back. In the exchange, shells fell into the French Concession, and shrapnel landed in Tante Tila's garden.

Papa read the account in the evening paper. The Villa Santa Tila with its eighteen *mous* of land was located on Rue Francis Garnier, in the heart of the Concession. Although Papa made light of the fact that Tante Tila had created a saint expressly for naming her home, he was aware that with its stock of antiques it was a natural objective for looting strikers or possibly troops in disorderly retreat. Clearly it was not safe for her to remain there. Mama insisted that Tante Tila move in with us at once, which she did, cramming what she could of her valuables into her Bugati La Royale, Type 41 (upholstered in ostrich skin with rosewood dashboard) and our Imperial Suburban, since no professional movers could be commissioned for the job. Characteristically, among the jewellery, Sèvres vases, and sterling were bundles of her operatic costumes, wigs, and of course her two Pekingese.

The strike ended as suddenly as it had started, and in a week it was virtually over. The General Labour Union let it be known that the workers were returning to their jobs because they believed that a Nationalist victory was imminent. Orders for executions were rescinded, and the city reverted to its normal service routines. Were it not for the increasing numbers of the Shanghai Defence Force, there wouldn't, to the casual observer, be much inkling that the Nationalist troops were already at the capital of Chekiang Province, only 160 kilometres from Shanghai.

Sascha pleaded with Papa to allow him to go to the Hongkew wharf to meet the *Megantic*, which was arriving with British Defence Force commander Major-General Duncan and two additional infantry battalions. Since the actual danger in the city seemed at least temporarily negligible and because the headmaster of the Richard Ashbury had urged attendance, Papa finally agreed.

Sascha returned from Hongkew bursting with enthusiasm over the smartness of the British regiments. He renewed his plea to be allowed to join the cadet branch of the Shanghai Volunteer Corps, but Mama put her foot down. 'Fourteen is too young to go around in uniform and carry bayonets and maybe get killed.' Since the season for pheasant hunting was not until autumn, the Winchester Model 21 that Papa bought him wasn't much consolation, and he concentrated his interests in reporting military activities. He took great delight in being able to transmit news before it was published by official sources. It was he who announced that thirteen hundred Marines had just arrived on the U.S.S. *Chaumont*, that the Japanese were sending the cruiser *Hirato* to supplement the nine men-of-war in Shanghai Harbour, that French marines were in full force along the boundary of the Concession, and that points eastward from the North Szechwan Road extension were being guarded by an Italian landing party.

Social life was keyed to the incoming forces. There were the ladies' auxiliary teas and canteens and raffles, all of which Mama and Tante Tila found woefully dreary.

Mama decided that this was as good a time as any to succumb to the blandishments of a popular Hungarian painter, and she and Tante Tila arranged for sittings. It was at one of these sessions that I discovered what was in the telegram. Mama was being painted in an evening gown and a fur pelisse. Tante Tila was posing as Charlotte in *Werther*, a black picture hat crammed over her orange wig. She insisted on Ming's and Dixie's being in the portrait with her. When the artist, whom Tante Tila called Laczi—'because all Hungarians are either Laczi or Sandor, aren't they?'—protested that to his knowledge Charlotte did not have any dogs, Tante Tila replied that this one did!

I would watch the full two hours of each session, fascinated by the progress from blank canvas to linear contours, planes of colours, and finally detail which brought the portraits to life. At one of these sittings, Mama noticed that Dixie and Ming were without their diamond collars and that certain 'standard' pieces were missing from Tila's attire. She questioned her friend.

'All gone,' said Tila cheerfully.

'What do you mean?' Mama asked.

'You know, all my assets are in stock and real estate,' Tila said. 'I needed money, so they're hocked.'

'Why didn't you come to me? How much did you need?'

'*Beaucoup*,' Tila said. Then she explained that her count had been deeply involved in an alliance with another woman and what amounted to a staggering sum was required to buy her off.

'By my life, Tila, I hope Michel marries you after this,' Mama said.

'From your mouth to God's ears,' Tila replied, borrowing one of Grandmama's expressions.

'I would *never*,' Mama said, '*never* pawn my jewels for a man.'

'Not even for Maximilian?' Tila asked.

'He's different, I meant for a *maquereau*.'

Tila winced, and I saw Mama bite her lip. Perhaps to make up for this barb, Mama confided in Tila about the telegram. It was at the final session.

'I've been going out of my mind,' Mama was saying.

'So he's coming. What can you do? It will be fun seeing Chicho again,' Tila said.

'But you don't understand,' Mama said. 'In his telegram he thanked me for *my* telegram. He thinks I've called him.'

Tila shrugged and bent to pick an imaginary flea out of Dixie. The Hungarian clucked impatiently, and Tila resumed her pose.

'I keep wondering if it's a trap. Do you think Maximilian would do such a goddam rotten thing?'

Tila shook her head.

'Then who?' Mama looked hard at Tila.

'Well,' Tila said, 'that was weeks ago, and things weren't going at all well with Michel. . . .'

'Tila!' Mama cried. 'How could you do such a thing?'

'You didn't want him and I thought why should he go to waste?'

'Why didn't you sign your own damn name?'

'He wouldn't have come. Listen, we can still pretend to Max that he's coming to me. You *don't* want him, do you? For God's sake, Regina, your mascara's running; you'll ruin the canvas, that's what you'll do.'

For the next day at least Mama didn't speak to Tante Tila, who took refuge in intense and lachrymose vocalizing of 'Les Larmes de Werther', Aristide, with his unerring ear for mimicry, was stomping around the hall with a tea cosy the same insulting orange as Tante Tila's wig pulled over his head. As usual I was Aristide's most attentive audience, and as he pantomimed and heaved his chest and growled the low notes, I applauded and shouted with laughter. As Tante Tila's voice swelled into the upper register preparatory to taking a high note, Aristide capriciously took it *before* her, holding it for all he was worth, while batting his eyes at me furiously. From opposite directions, simultaneously, Tante Tila and Mama converged on Aristide and found themselves glaring at each other like two warriors over a spoil. Suddenly Tante Tila began to laugh, and she hugged Mama and then Aristide. They had a good cry, and Tante Tila assured Mama that everything would work out all right, wait and see. And there I was, sitting in the alcove, watching.

Concurrent with the stepped-up defences of the foreign forces, the northern armies were suffering increasing setbacks at the hands of the Nationalists. Morale reached a low ebb when divisions of Marshal Sun Chuan-fang's fifty thousand men began deserting, taking with them most of the rolling stock. These troops had been deployed to a town on Hangchow Bay where the Nationalists were already stationed. Reports from foreigners who talked to the incoming Nationalists found them to be, as feared, antiforeign, but it was an antiforeignism of credo rather than a desire for violence. The northerners sent more troops to bolster Marshal Sun's forces. Although some considered this to be a last-ditch stand against Chiang Kai-shek's armies, others insisted that the new arrivals would drive the Nationalists back.

Sascha had been titillated by reports which were widely circulated, but which were nevertheless untrue, that the virgins of the Wuhan cities had paraded naked on the Hankow Bund as a protest against foreigners and the unequal treaties. For weeks he watched from the smoking-room windows hoping for a repetition of the event. E-ling scoffed at him, saying that if it were true those girls were nothing but sensation mongers. If indeed they were such patriots for the southern cause, why didn't they pick up arms and fight on a level other than sex? E-ling's opinion of the Nationalists on the whole was that they were a sorry lot.

'I cannot believe in the southerners as soldiers,' she said. 'Every rebellion has always started from the north and advanced to the south.' She went on to explain that it was a necessary geographical fact that the northerners had had to develop into fighters to keep out invaders from north of the Great Wall. She cited as an example that defence was so natural to their thinking that all the plains in that part of the country were ploughed with furrows east to west to make the advance of war vehicles impractical. She ventured that the Nationalist armies would never amount to anything. They were distrustful, as all southerners were, and they would never put their entire faith in an outsider like Chiang Kai-shek who came from Chekiang province.

On the Sunday following the strike, Hoboo set out for Siccawei Church where she attended the early mass. Since this was diametrically across town, she was bustling around our bedroom well before dawn.

I was fully awake when she returned three hours later. She complained that Annamite sentries and the French Volunteer Corps had refused to let her pass through barbed-wire barricades from the French Concession into Siccawei. Resourcefully Hoboo had her rickshaw coolie return to the International Settlement. To her complete frustration she found the boundaries on Avenue Haig in the vicinity of Siccawei heavily guarded by members of the Gloucestershire Regiment. A British patrol leader explained that the barricades had been set not so much for those leaving the Settlement as to prevent agitators from coming in.

Hoboo argued if that were the case there should be no objection to one Chinese worshipper's being allowed entrance. After lengthy discussion, Hoboo left the passport which she had required for her travelling with the family on the understanding that she would claim it on her return.

I asked Hoboo if it would be so bad if she missed one Sunday's mass.

'Velly bad,' she replied, with a cigarette dangling out of the corner of her mouth. 'Jesus velly angly.' Then, since Dah Su had not yet returned from the Hongkew Market, she said she would go to the kitchen to fix my breakfast. I don't know whether or not Hoboo realized that I was tagging along beside her; she seemed so deep in thought. When we got to the kitchen, I was surprised that she did not immediately start preparing my meal. Instead she walked out the back entrance and went straight to Lao Ni's room where she rapped loudly on the door.

Lao Ni blinked sleepily at his aunt.

'I must talk to you,' Hoboo said. Lao Ni hesitated.

'Is the northern girl in there?' The youth did not reply. 'Come into the kitchen,' Hoboo said. Lao Ni looked back into his room quickly, then he followed Hoboo into the kitchen. At that point E-ling, fully dressed, came out of his room. With her eyes averted, she slipped past us and went into the apartment.

'There is no time to waste,' Hoboo said. 'I saw Ah-ching. He leaves today to join the Nationalist forces in Chekiang.'

'He is alive.' Lao Ni looked greatly relieved.

'If he can get by Sunkiang where these northern dogs are, everything will be all right. But he says that you must go home at once and get your parents out of there. They can hide in Hongkew; the Japanese smile on poppy eaters,' she said bitterly.

'The northerners are not concerned with addicts,' Lao Ni said.

'No, not addicts, but they would like to get their hands on Ah-ching's father, you understand? Now, does the girl know where your family lives?' Lao Ni did not answer at once, but then he said, 'Old Auntie, she is a fine girl, not what you think. She is a Chinese first. . . .'

'So is the commissioner of defence, and he would have Ah-ching's head in a cage. So is Marshal Sun, and Chang Tso-lin. Go, you fool, and do not come back until I tell you to.'

Just then the door opened and Papa was standing there. His face was whiter than snow and as frozen. Beside him very calmly was E-ling. 'Go to your room,' he said to me. Then he said to Hoboo and Lao Ni, 'You had better come with me.'

16

ARISTIDE was one of those people who expended so much energy in his waking hours that he was almost impossible to rouse from sleep. I pulled at him, tugged at the baby pillow he embraced, threw off his covers, and tickled his feet, with no results. I remembered that Sascha had once awakened him with a cold wet towel.

Finally Aristide was sitting up in bed trying to make sense of my frantic ravings. 'What do you mean, they have locked up Hoboo and Lao Ni in the smoking-room? What do you mean, telephoned the police?'

How typical it was of my brother that in a moment of such crisis, with me standing on a chair so that I might be able to reach the hanging pole of the wardrobe, he would insist on a specific outfit. Getting him dressed was even more difficult, and after a third try at pulling his velvet jumper over his head back to front, we stared at each other solemnly. It was a trenchant fact that we were completely dependent on Hoboo. I watched his face for breakage. At the tiniest signal I would have burst into tears. But Aristide was not wasteful in that direction. Tears were meant to produce action and results, and we both knew that I couldn't provide either. Finally the jumper was on, with its lace collar resembling more a crumpled party napkin than anything else. Shorts were an easy matter, particularly if one didn't bother to button them. We raced for the hall with the straps of Aristide's Betsy Janes flapping against his ankles.

The door of the smoking-room was forbiddingly closed. Once Sascha came out, and when Aristide questioned him, his reply was civil enough to cause us real concern. The bell rang and Police Inspector Burnham arrived with the same Chinese army officer who had come before to question Hoboo about Ah-ching. As they were ushered into the smoking-room, I saw Mama sitting in her leather armchair, but she was an unknown tense person. In fact the only one who gave even the semblance of being entirely herself was Grandmama, who turned up shortly after the police. She shooed us, as though Aristide and I were a brace of ducks, into the drawing-room.

Mama followed us. She looked very disturbed. 'Grandmama is going to take you boys to the pictures,' she said. I applauded happily, but Aristide said, 'No, thanks, I don't want to go.' Mama seized him by the shoulders. 'Don't make me give you what's in my heart,' she said.

'Why can Sascha stay?' Aristide insisted.

'I'll give you why!' Mama said.

Outside the day was a cool calmness. The promenades and jetties were active with people. Trams clanged noisily down the centre of the Bund, and rickshaw coolies raced to beat each other out of fares. It was hard to remember the stillness of less than a week before. It was impossible, by glancing at the smiles of the Chinese pedestrians and the hawkers who passed, to recall the close suffocating aura of hate. Papa's crippled flower vendor gave Grandmama a small bouquet of lilies of the valley.

Since Aristide had been bullied into coming with us and because it really made no difference, Grandmama indulged him in his choice of the film. Pao-shing drove us to the Capital Theatre where *The Three Musketeers* was showing.

I truly enjoyed attending movies with Grandmama, because the theatre was one place where she felt no need to restrain herself. While I admit to inheriting some of Grandmama's tendency to identify with any drama that is unfolding before me, I must add quickly that I lack her ability to identify *totally*. This, in her case, went as far as the action of the play and usually one or two chosen members of the cast. She would for instance point to Adolphe Menjou and say, 'Him? I knew him very well in Alexandria.' Then Adolphe Menjou had best mind his *P*'s and *Q*'s, for Grandmama was watching each move.

Douglas Fairbanks was playing D'Artagnan in this vehicle, and of course Grandmama was playing everybody, but without her usual zest. She was having trouble placing the athletic actor. Milady de Winter was another matter. 'I know dot von fin Odessa.' As things went from bad to worse due to Milady, I could sense Grandmama's patience dwindling. The scene in which the villainess bares her shoulder to reveal the brand of a convict before the golden-curled and cowering heroine was too much for the old lady. She jumped to her feet. '*Kourva—bed gerrl!*' she cried. Aristide and I tried as best as we were able to quiet her, for we were getting complaints from all around. Between trying to suppress Grandmama's antics and watching Mr. Fairbanks' prowess, Aristide and I were kept pretty active. D'Artagnan won the last point, however, since neither of us was aware that Grandmama had marched out of the theatre.

Happily, Pao-shing, standing outside, noticed the old lady using her umbrella to direct traffic as she attempted to cross Museum Road. The chauffeur went into the theatre to bring us out, and when we got to the car, Grandmama was sitting straight as a rod, but her hand was clutching the car strap and she was twisting it mercilessly. Nobody said anything for a while, and then I said, 'You didn't like the picture, huh, Grandmama?'

She looked at me for a moment as though I were out of my mind. Then, patting my arm gently, she said, 'It's vot you call it—shit.'

'I liked it,' Aristide said. Grandmama ignored him; then she said to me, 'You like?'

'Not much,' I lied. Grandmama freed the car strap and grabbing my hand squeezed it hard. 'You're a *good* boy,' she said. With the film over, I was anticipating going to my Grandmother's for tea, envisioning a plate of *hamantaschen*, the prune-filled pastry pockets traditionally served at Purim. That was the charm of eating at my grandparents'. Since Grandpapa might have a craving for latkes or matzoth at any time of the year, their table was, so to speak, a continual out-of-season delight. With every meal and throughout each visit there was Grandmama's tea.

Because of Grandmama's nostalgic references to the gold samovar which Miriam had left to the temple, Mama had years before given Grandmama a handsome replica made of Russian silver. 'You vant a glass real Rossian tea, like Grandmama make?' the old lady would say. And one replied instantly in the affirmative since it would have been unthinkable to deny her this ritual. Never have I seen anyone prepare tea in quite the same manner as Grandmama. First water was brought to a rolling boil, then removed from the fire. This was important, she would tell you, the water must never be old or re-boiled. The leaves and water were then steeped in the samovar for a few minutes—she would never say exactly for how long but seemed to have her own inner timing device. Next, glasses in silver holders which she called *stahkans* were carefully rinsed out with the infusion. I have never quite understood this step of the procedure either; was it to heat the glasses through while at the same time imparting the bouquet of the beverage? Or was it a cleansing ritual? In either case, Grandmama held to it faithfully, and I had seen her do the same with vintage champagne. Into each glass went half a lemon and a liberal spoonful of the treacly cherry jam she put up herself. Finally the brew was released from the spigot, and there was your tea, strong, fragrant, with richly violet shadows.

Aristide too had always enjoyed going to our grandparents' home, even though upon our arrival Grandpapa would seize us in a bear-like hug, grazing our cheeks with his brush moustache, and then pushing us aside, would admonish loudly, 'Don't touch!' He didn't mean this injunction to be applied to anything in particular, it was simply to be observed as the all-inclusive order of the day. Over the years, Grandmama had had a series of pet cockatoos, each called Ivan. The current bird was a handsome creature who preened or spread his wings like great pastel shells as he squawked ill-naturedly. Aristide was fascinated by Ivan and could spend hours by his tall brass cage. He seemed to enjoy this almost as much as watching our grandparents playing Twenty-One. Invariably, if Grandmama came anywhere near winning, Grandpapa would overtly cheat, thereby provoking a scene, whereupon, insulted, he could retire from the game without having lost. While he studiously turned his attention to passages of the Torah, Grandmama in high dudgeon would thrust morsels of food through the bars of Ivan's cage. Narrowing her upper lip over those startling teeth and tossing her head in the direction of her husband, she would mutter in a mixture of momentary hatred and pride, 'A proper gonif, a robber.'

Now, in the car with these prospects at hand, I was surprised to hear Aristide say, 'I feel sick. I want to go home.'

'*Tsipinkoo*,' Grandmama said. 'You come to my house. . . .'

'No, I'm sick. I feel terrible,' Aristide said hugging his stomach. Grandmama appraised him coldly, waiting for an outburst of tears. But Aristide was too smart for that. He knew that to our grandmother crying was a sign of wilfulness, a challenge that had to be met and defeated with authority. He rolled down the car window and stuck his head out of it. Then he really began to vomit.

'Orright, go big missy house,' Grandmama said to Pao-shing. Mama came out of the smoking-room and looked questioningly at her mother.

'He's sick,' Grandmama said, indicating Aristide.

'What's the matter?' Mama asked, kneeling beside him.

'I want Hoboo,' Aristide said.

Mama hugged Aristide closely to her and said, 'Darling, you mustn't feel bad if Hoboo has to go away for a little time.' Aristide pulled away from her.

Mama said, 'Whatever happens, I'm here. I'm your Mama.' Aristide ran to the door of the smoking-room. Then he turned, and looking at our mother he said, 'No, Hoboo's my mama.' He flung the door open.

Aristide walked into the room, closely followed by Mama and Grandmama. Although my reaction, as it has always been in times of embarrassing confrontation, was to run, I made myself enter.

At the far right of the room, before an incongruously cheerful fireplace, Hoboo stood with Lao Ni's mother and the child, Didi. Lao Ni, his hands behind him, was in front of the verandah flanked by E-ling and the northern army officer. On Lao Ni's forehead a welt made an X with his eyebrow. The officer's mauser was an ugly blue-black shine in the air as it swung towards Lao Ni's head.

'Stop!' Papa commanded. He was seated at the escritoire with his back to the door. A Tiffany lamp on the desk played its carnival colours on him. Sascha was standing by his side. Papa turned to the British police officer: 'Inspector, I cannot permit this type of brutality. As a French citizen, my home and those in it are protected by the laws of extraterritoriality.'

The Chinese officer pointed to E-ling. 'According to our agent, Miss Han,' he said, 'these people have been in contact with the traitor and are guilty of collusion. They have even hidden the father, a known addict who could be made to talk.'

'You have made a number of charges,' Inspector Burnham said, 'amounting to nothing specific.'

'They belong to the same family and are Nationalist traitors,' E-ling insisted.

Lao Ni looked at E-ling with the same empty expression he had when Papa's cane had struck him a month earlier. 'It is you who are the traitor to China,' he said. The northern officer reached behind Lao Ni and twisted the rope which bound the servant's hands. Lao Ni winced but did not make a sound.

'I am afraid that we cannot accept the fact that they may be related to the suspect Ah-ching as evidence of their treason,' Burnham said.

'They are Chinese and should be dealt with by us,' E-ling said.

'Since you consider yourselves allies of the foreigners in China, you must respect the laws which permit us in the Settlement and the French Concession to try suspected criminals in our own courts,' the inspector replied.

'What grounds do *you* have for arresting these people?' E-ling challenged.

'Our own investigation has enabled us to turn up fairly substantial proof of theft,' Burnham said.

I saw Aristide staring at the inspector as the Britisher went up to the fireplace where Didi was clinging to his mother's knees. He pried the child away from his mother and fingered through the pockets of his padded jacket. Then he held up a pair of objects which gleamed. They were the cuff links Aristide had given Didi.

E-ling knelt quickly beside Aristide. She spoke so softly that I think only Aristide and I were able to hear her.

'You gave those buttons to Didi, didn't you? Tell the truth. If you don't, they will lock up your amah and her family.'

Aristide recoiled from her, but she repeated, 'Tell them the truth!' Aristide gulped air as though he were about to make an announcement, but he kept silent.

E-ling turned to the inspector. 'Can't you see that the foreign child is holding back? It's your duty to turn this family over to us. Only we can make them tell where Ah-ching is hiding.'

Burnham said, 'I will take these people to the central station and detain them on suspected robbery.'

He began lining up Lao Ni and his mother and brother and then he came to Hoboo.

'You see,' E-ling said to Aristide, 'they are going to jail because you lied. You will never see them again.'

'Wait!' cried Aristide. 'I gave him those cuff links——'

'Shut up, Aristide!' Sascha shouted.

'Perhaps now, Inspector, you will let us take these people,' E-ling said. Aristide looked from the inspector to E-ling and then to Sascha, and all at once he realized that he had been duped. He rushed at E-ling and pounded at her with both fists, until Sascha pulled him away, but with a solicitude that I had never seen from our oldest brother.

'*Si ning! Chaw beetz!* Die!' Aristide screamed, flailing and clawing in front of him. I waited, confident that any minute the verandah doors would blow open and E-ling would career past me and fall right into the Whangpoo. Nothing happened.

Hoboo stepped up to Papa. She arranged her shawl over her shoulders. One eye was bright and widely open, the other twitched furiously.

'Solly, Mastah,' she said. 'Alistide no give.' She made a gesture that included her family group. 'We steal.'

Papa said, 'I think, Inspector, that you must accept this woman's statement as a confession of theft.'

The northern officer slammed his revolver into its holster. 'You will have to answer to the commissioner of defence,' he said to Papa.

Papa lifted his chequebook from the desk. 'When the time comes, I shall have my answer ready,' he said.

Aristide began crying. Hoboo bent towards him, and as she spoke, for the first time her voice broke, 'No cly, *siao chiu*; Hoboo luvee you.' Then she turned to join the file of her relatives waiting at the door. As she passed E-ling, she gathered a gurgling wad of spittle in her mouth and spat directly in her face.

17

PAPA had thought that negotiation through the French minister would have seen a quick release of Hoboo and her family. But feelers put out to the northern defence commissioner as to compensation for relinquishing their claim on the servants were ignored. Papa became seriously alarmed when Inspector Burnham informed him that the defence commissioner's office was insisting that the Chinese family be turned over to them. He went on to tell Papa that in the custody of the northerners, Hoboo and Lao Ni would undoubtedly be tortured to reveal the whereabouts of Ah-ching and his father. On the other hand, he explained that if the municipal police returned the servants to Papa, they ran the risk of being murdered. He advised delaying action to see what further mediations might be made.

Papa took Aristide and me to the women's section of the central police station to visit Hoboo. 'At least they'll know she's alive,' I'd heard him tell Mama earlier. Hoboo seemed quite pleased to see us, as she dangled a cigarette from the gap made by her missing front tooth. She was most concerned, however, that Papa make no bargain with the northerners. 'Too bad man, Mastah. You no pay he one coppah!' It was evident that Papa was concerned, for as we left he patted Hoboo's arm.

'You no wolly, Mastah; Chiang Kai-shek takee me out,' Hoboo replied, her flickering eyelid closed, and in that moment she seemed to be winking.

One day early in March Sascha told of seeing hundreds of Japanese soldiers and marines march past his school on to North Szechwan Road, and that afternoon we watched from the verandahs as British Royal Marines paraded through the Settlement past the saluting base at the entrance to the British Consulate. The best, our older brother assured us, was yet to come. The much-awaited

Coldstream Guards were due in a week or so—'those splendid chaps with their scarlet coats and fuzzy helmets' was Sascha's description of them. Aristide at once petitioned to be taken along to welcome them. 'We'll see,' Sascha said, using one of Mama's reservations.

The very next day labourers suspended work for an hour in protest at the landing of foreign soldiers on Chinese soil. Meanwhile, in spite of reports that northern troops were in disorderly retreat on all fronts, the remaining northern generals gave reassuring interviews to the foreign press. When questioned about rumours concerning a battalion of White Russian troops which had supposedly joined the northern cause, the generals admitted that there were at present two thousand White Russians who had become Chinese citizens by virtue of their allegiance to them. This was done, they explained, so that no one could claim that they were being aided by foreigners.

At this point the more optimistic foreigners thought that Chiang's major objective was Nanking and that he would by-pass Shanghai altogether. As though to lend weight to this possibility, foreigners, particularly missionaries, poured into the city from all over China. In spite of hostile attitudes from occupying Nationalist forces, some religious groups protested against being evacuated and insisted on remaining with their missions.

The strikes and military pronouncements generally meant little to our family, particularly to Sascha, who was hard put to keep abreast of the debarkation times and parade schedules. He was keenly interested in weapons and on a Sunday took Aristide and me to see the arrival of the British transport *Rajula*. We witnessed the unloading of the much-touted six-inch howitzers with their tractors, ammunition wagons, and, unexpectedly, about five hundred mules. Since this hardly met with Aristide's notions of military splendour, he kicked up a terrific fuss and complained that he wanted to leave at once. But Sascha made him stand through the unloading of eight armoured cars before we started for home.

I was not surprised a few days later when Sascha flatly refused to permit Aristide to welcome the Coldstreams. Mama, who had second thoughts anyway about Sascha's and my attending, insisted that if we went at all, since it was a cold and rainy day, we would have to be warmly dressed. I cheerfully submitted to a flannel stomach band and allowed Mama to wrap a Venetian paisley muffler around my neck, which she did so many times that I looked like a mummy. I was so titillated at the idea of preempting Aristide that had Mama insisted that I wrap myself in furs, I would have consented.

Thanks to Sascha's British instinct for punctuality, Pao-shing drove us up to the gates of the Old Ningpo Wharf in Hongkew an hour before the official debarkation time. Sascha was disappointed at the small turnout, a few foreigners standing staunchly under their umbrellas. Presently the guards began trooping ashore. At the sight of them Sascha was crestfallen. Instead of the gold-faced scarlet uniforms and imposing bearskin helmets, the battalion was wearing the service khaki. The men proceeded to line up in columns of four and in spite of the sharp chill of the wind and the persistent needles of rain maintained what Sascha described as 'splendid bearing'. The officers began their patrol, a manner of stepping briskly back and forth in pairs. At that point the drums and fifes came down the gangplanks on the double and formed at the rear of the columns. Shortly they were joined by the bands of the Royal Marines, the Bedford and Hertfordshire Regiments, and the Border Regiment. A signal from the drum major called the battalion to attention and the march began.

We followed with the few other cars, proceeding at a very slow pace through the rain-swept and almost deserted streets. The shrill sound of the fifes pierced the emptiness through which the men were marching. When the lead columns turned from Kungping Road onto Broadway, we could hear a sudden rumbling which gathered in momentum and became so loud that it sounded fake, like the rattling of a tin sheet to simulate thunder in a theatre. Finally, as we followed the last of the bands turning on to Broadway we saw the streets lined on both sides with foreign and Chinese civilians and uniformed men of all nationalities. On one corner of the road leading on to the approach of the Garden Bridge stood the entire assembly of the Loretto School for girls. They were led by beaming and genderless nuns, who in their wet habits were like a cluster of great black cranes. At a signal from the nuns the girls burst into a shrill piping chorus of 'Rule, Britannia'. At this point the order was passed along the troops to tighten rifle slings; then the colours were unfurled. When the first columns had marched over Garden Bridge and reached the site of the British Consulate, the battalion was called to attention again. At the exchange of salutes, cheering and applause broke out that ran the entire length of the Bund. There was by now a great block of traffic, and cars were being detoured into side streets by the municipal police. I was all for following the battalion down Nanking Road to the racecourse, but Pao-shing was against it and even Sascha admitted that to do so would involve hours of travelling at a snail's pace.

Labour groups immediately exacted retribution for the public display of enthusiasm. The numbers of strikers increased daily, so that by the fifteenth of March one hundred and twenty-five thousand workers had walked off their jobs. To curtail the northerners from moving their troops out of the area, locomotive engineers of the Shanghai–Nanking Railway in the extreme north of the city and those of the Shanghai–Hangchow Railway in the south quit their jobs *en masse*. It was said that the labour unions acted under direct orders from the Communist faction of the Kuomintang in Hankow. It was also clear by now that the Nationalist armies would take Shanghai. The trembling question was simply whether Chiang's men would honour the terms of extraterritoriality and confine their onslaughts to the Chinese segments of the city or whether, true to their slogans of liberating China from the unfair treaties, they would attempt a total coup.

During these times Papa came home every day to tiffin. At some point Mama would inevitably ask about Hoboo. It was of course never a direct question but in the form of raised brows, a gesture, or soundlessly spelling out the name, employing all the language necessary for people attuned to each other and forgetting in the manner of parents that we children were equally aware.

During the month since Hoboo and her family had been taken into custody, our parents had made concerted efforts to divert us. After he had read the evening paper, Papa would gather Sascha, Aristide, and me by him while he read to us aloud. The smoking-room doubled as Papa's library, and the books stacked in the ceiling-to-floor shelves reflected his divergent tastes in literature. Without apparent concern for our ages or the extent of our comprehension, he would choose a book at random and commence reading, consciously or otherwise using Mama's philosophy that his children would absorb only what they needed to know. Curiously, it was Mama who objected to his reading of Flaubert's *Salammbô* and who seized a rare edition of Aristophanes' *Lysistrata* with erotic drawings by Aubrey Beardsley, complaining that they were '*trop actif*'. On some occasions we were exposed to the violet-drenched prose of Marie Corelli and Charles Garvice, and on others to Dickens, Hardy, and Defoe. My brothers yawned through Turgenev's *Fathers and Sons*, but Tolstoy's capacity for relating to women was another matter. In passages between Anna Karenina and Vronsky, Aristide was bright as a jewel with attention. There were lighter moods, the Arsène Lupin stories for instance, and Aristide was enhanced with the sloe-eyed women who breathed fiery perfume and murmured, 'Fool, you did not think that I was a German spy, *hein*?' just before shooting her witless admirer full of bullets.

Mama tried to compensate for the loss of Hoboo, and from time to time she took us to the Public Gardens. But perhaps because this had been so completely our amah's province, it served merely as a hurtful reminder that she was no longer with us. One day some children of our own age gathered in a group and repeatedly sang a ditty in pidgin English:

> Fatty bone banana
> Had a Chinese amah.
> Amah died,
> Fatty cried,
> Fatty bone banana.

This was a common enough jingle, and we had sung it ourselves to tease other children. There was no particular malice intended, and the fact that an amah was involved was in all likelihood pure coincidence. But it had a distressing effect on Aristide, who began to cry and could not be stopped. Mama never took us to the Gardens again.

Our grandparents, too, did what they could to distract us. Since the Passover season was approaching, and already their table would be laden with *farfel* puddings and honey-glazed *chremsel*, we looked forward to these visits. At our home Passover meant merely that matzo was set out along with the bread and that we could have it scrambled with eggs for breakfast. Grandmama could never get used to my parents' lack of concern over *chometz*. She made a point of telling Aristide and me that every year on the night before Passover Eve, Grandpapa would conduct his *bedikath chometz*, the ritual search of every corner of the house for leaven. Since of course she would have seen to it that her house was immaculate, there would be none. So in order to give the ritual its proper respect Grandpapa would place morsels of bread conspicuously in each room. Then armed with a wooden spoon and some feathers in one hand and a lighted candle in the other, Grandpapa would search from room to room, sweeping the bread into the spoon with the feathers. This he would follow with a short prayer nullifying any leaven he may have inadvertently overlooked. On the following morning all the *chometz* was burned and a final prayer said.

Aristide wanted to know why anyone should go to so much fuss and bother over a little bread. We were in Grandmama's kitchen. She was standing in front of her stove, where a fat hen (properly killed by a *shohet*) made golden soup in a kettle. Grandmama told us her version of the Passover story, of Moses and the burning bush, of *Moloch Homovis*, the relentless Angel of Death, as she stirred her *kneidlach* mixture, interrupting herself now and then to impart a piece of culinary advice such as: 'Always beat de vites of egg separate, oddervise you will hev matzo balls like kennon balls!'

We ate at the kitchen table with Grandpapa. He was wearing his long flannel underwear, carelessly buttoned, so that he bunched in some places and gaped in others. But we were used to this careless-ness from Grandpapa, and it really never concerned us that he might sit through an entire meal with exposed genitalia. Although he always wore his caracul cocoshnik, even when undressed as now, because he complained that his head got cold, Grandpapa never seemed to change much. Although the thick brush moustache was threaded with white, his eyebrows had remained eloquently black. And those eyes, like perfect spheres of corundum, still glittered as though they had been faceted.

To Aristide, caught up in Grandmama's story of Passover, the Angel of Death was most fascinating, and he asked a lot of ques-tions. 'Who was he? What does he look like? Do we have an Angel of Life?'

'Ve have all kind of angels. Better dan anybody,' Grandmama said, bouncing a *kneidlach* from hand to hand.

'But the Angel of Death. Is he good?'

'*Moloch Homovis?* Sure he vos good,' insisted Grandmama. 'Didn't he make dat Pharaoh let free der Jews?'

'But he killed all those babies,' I cried.

As Grandpapa bit into a dill pickle, he put his hand on mine. 'Egyptian babies,' he explained.

18

AROUND the twentieth of the month, Papa took Aristide and me for a drive to the cotton mills. It might strike some as peculiar that with a Nationalist invasion imminent, Papa should risk exposing his children and himself. But foreigners were conditioned to Chinese upheaval. Our newspapers had for so long made light of skirmishes between warlords that we were impervious to the concept of Chinese as real soldiers.

On the rare occasions that we went out with Papa, he made it worth our while. We might stop at Bianchi's, for instance, or at the shop of the newer confectioner, Marcel, whom Papa and some other French civic leaders had financed. Aristide favoured the latter, because the proprietor had from the start considered him some sort of mascot, and on his birthday or Christmas never failed to present him with a token of regard. What with Easter coming up, I expect that Aristide felt he was due. The drive to the mills was uneventful, and on our return, Papa decided to pick Sascha up at school during his lunch hour so that he might join us at Marcel's.

The Richard Ashbury School was situated off North Szechwan Road, not far from the Chinese section of Chapei. As Pao-shing drove by the many Japanese produce and gift shops on the road, we saw by the firmly shuttered windows that they were closed for business. But from the balconies of Chinese establishments a new banner was flying, the Nationalist flag of red field and a white sun with twelve rays, superimposed on a dark blue canton. In the distance we heard random firing, then the crackle retort of machine-guns. There was a resounding explosion as the sky above the buildings became a canopy of black smoke.

'Chapei,' Pao-shing said.

Ahead of us an open lorry turned onto our road and began a slow patrol in the direction we were travelling. Standing in it were several British and Chinese municipal police and one Sikh. Pao-shing turned to Papa. 'Whatting do, Mastah?'

'Just keep behind them,' Papa cautioned. As we followed the lorry at a distance of roughly a hundred feet, we saw groups of

Chinese beginning to congregate on the corners, men and women of all ages with large baskets suspended from their arms, distributing what looked like folded squares of blue material. These turned out to be Nationalist armbands. Just then three men dressed in work clothes broke from the group and sprinted behind the lorry. We heard shots, and the Sikh in the rear of the vehicle spun around and slumped over the gate; his turban soaked in blood unwound, hanging like a Chinese holiday banner. As Pao-shing stopped our car behind the lorry, we saw the Chinese policemen leap to the ground in pursuit of the attackers, thrusting after them into the crowds, but the labourers had disappeared. The police remaining in the truck did not seem to be aware of us. Two of them lifted the dead Indian back into it. Then one, a Britisher, who appeared to be in charge, saw our car. He swung his hands across and down like a conductor calling his musicians to a halt. Then he waved his hand back in the direction that we had come.

'Don't move,' Papa said to Pao-shing.

The policeman continued signalling us. Finally he cupped his mouth with his hands and shouted that we should return at once. Papa opened the car door and hoisted himself from the running board to the road. He thrust his cane forward searching for support. Then he took a step towards the lorry, and his limp, not too conspicuous ordinarily, became a gyration. Watching from the back-seat window with Aristide, I said, 'What's the matter with Papa?'

Aristide chuckled. 'The policeman can't very well dismiss a *helpless* cripple.' Papa had barely negotiated a few steps when the policeman leaped over the gate and came running to him.

'I am terribly sorry, sir,' he said.

'Sergeant, my son is at the boys' school. I have to fetch him.'

The Britisher said that they were headed for the school now. It would be all right for us to follow, but he cautioned us to stay close and remain hidden in our car. We kept behind the lorry as it trundled like a heavy animal down the remainder of North Szechwan Road extension. At an ingress from Chapei, refugees were streaming through the barricades with handcarts and rickshaws piled high with household effects. There were many Japanese among them, their brilliant kimonos and parasols giving an absurd theatrical quality to the scene. The guards on duty made a rapid check of papers and poked through the belongings.

A foreign woman dressed years behind the times in a cape and long black skirt with a straw boater on her head ran from the barricades towards the lorry. But the driver continued, ignoring her. She then approached our car. 'Don't stop,' Papa said. When the woman realized her attempts to flag us down were failing, she stepped directly in the path of our car, her arms stretched out like a semaphore. Pao-shing brought the car to a stop. The woman hurried to Papa's window. 'Sorry to do this to you, but I have got to get help immediately.' Papa told her where we were going. 'That will serve nicely,' she said, and she climbed into the back seat.

As she spoke to Papa, the woman took my hand in hers. She must have been in her fifties, and her cheeks, pink with a tracery of red veins, reminded me of maple leaves. In contrast to the starched white blouse she was wearing, her teeth looked like large ivory buttons. She told Papa that the Catholic Mission Institution of the Holy Family had been set afire. She had gone for help to the third divisional fire brigade nearby, only to find it gutted, the fire engines totally destroyed. Her own mission was in imminent danger of the flames. Both electrical and telephone wires had been cut. She spoke with misgiving of leaving her girls, but said that it was voted at the centre that they remain while she went for assistance. Papa asked her the nature of her centre's work.

'Rehabilitation of women and girls,' the missionary replied.

'Ah, yes,' Papa said. 'Fallen women and wayward girls.'

'That's an oversimplification,' she said, looking at the man's watch on her wrist, 'but I suppose at the moment it must do.' Papa then asked if the Nationalists had caused the fire.

'Indeed, if these are Nationalists, then God help China.'

'But if they are not Nationalists, who are they?' Papa asked.

The missionary stared at Papa for a moment before she replied, 'They're labourer-Communists who take their orders from Hankow and Moscow.'

'Are you sure these are not simply labourers?'

'Sir,' the Englishwoman replied, 'in the nearly twenty-five years that I have tried to do His work in China, I have seen many political changes. I have reached the point where not only can I recognize the devil, but I'm quite capable of fighting back on his terms.'

At that point Pao-shing followed the lorry into the gravelled driveway which led up to the school.

The main building of the Richard Ashbury School for boys was an immense Gothic structure with cathedral windows. Pebbles were massed into its grey stone complexion and creepers grew like stubble all over the exterior. The lorry scrunched up to the entrance and we parked directly behind it. Standing on the steps with his hands behind him was a man in a worn black robe. The few strands of carefully waxed hair arranged in a cockscomb made him look even more bald. His round outraged eyes rested on crescents of nodules. He was the headmaster, Percy Finch Benton, or Big Ben, as he was called out of earshot by the boys. The policeman in charge went up the three broad steps to where Big Ben stood. The headmaster bent his head forward attentively as the policeman explained about the dead Sikh. Then without looking up, Big Ben snapped his fingers to a passing student and instructed him to call the Red Cross. Another student, a prefect this time, was sent to fetch a sheet from the dormitory.

The missionary thanked Papa as we got out of our car. She went to the bottom of the steps on which Big Ben was standing. He bent his head again but did not come down. The headmaster directed her to the teachers' common rooms, where he said she would find a phone. He opened the door leading into the school's hallways with one hand, but he did not turn. Although Papa was known to Big Ben as a former R.A.S. boy, and as a sports enthusiast who presented trophies to the various school teams, it was clear that the headmaster was not going to come off his perch. I noticed that his face, before he nodded to hear our cause, bore a distantly benign expression. Later Aristide was to describe it as the headmaster's Mr. Kindfellow look, which, he said, 'He puts on in the morning with his cloak, but you notice it most when he's about to murder you.' Big Ben said that it would be impossible for us to return home since the entry into the Settlement had been blocked at the Isis Theatre on Jukong Road to prevent either side of the warring Chinese from coming in. What it amounted to was that we were for the time being trapped between this section of the Settlement and Chapei. The boys were in their classes, he explained. 'We've got them playing games to keep their minds off this nasty business.' He then told us that Sascha and a chum had broken school rules and had somehow smuggled themselves into Chapei during the tiffin hour.

'He's all right?'' Papa asked.

'Quite. They had a proper scare, but I imagine they're as good as new just now.'

'Boys will be boys,' Papa said, rallying weakly to Sascha's defence.

'*Not* in my school,' Big Ben replied, and with that he assigned a student to escort us to lower five. Before going through the door I chanced to look back at the lorry. The Chinese policemen were laying the Indian upon the sheet which had been spread out on the grass. The Sikh's head wobbled in my direction, and I could see the bullet hole like a bizarre *tika* in the middle of his forehead.

As we walked behind the youth along the sweating grey corridors, we could see through the windows into the lower-form classrooms. It was obvious the boys were enjoying this respite from work. In prep and lower one, they seemed to be engaged in games like Pin the Donkey and Blindman's Buff. We went up a long flight of steps past the second floor to the third, where lower and upper five and six were located. Here too were the teachers' common rooms as well as Big Ben's office. Our prefect left us outside the glass-paned door of lower five. Sascha saw us at the door and raised his hand to the teacher. As he came out, a huge smile bisected his shiny face. I could not ever before remember Sascha's being so pleased to see his brothers. He started in at once about his experiences in Chapei, but Papa cut him short, asking if he had called home.

'They won't let us chaps call out, and I don't imagine Mama has been able to get through to the school.'

Papa asked to be directed to the phones. Sascha led us to the common rooms, where some teachers not on duty were seated in easy chairs grouped around an open fire. A library table had been converted into a makeshift bar, with bottles of Scotch, rye, and gin. In charge was a young woman, a prep teacher most likely. She had a fair shape, Eton-cropped yellow hair of a startling uniformity, and a shingly complexion. She was pouring drinks according to specifications called out to her by a man in shirtsleeves and tennis shoes. He had threaded a school tie around the waist of his grey flannel bags. I knew at once by the man's cockiness, and by Sascha's earlier descriptions of him, that this was the games master, Mr. Pringle. The school captain was seated at a desk, taking phone calls. By his side were a pair of prefects who passed messages to monitors, who in turn ran in relays to summon those students being called. A prep student about Aristide's age wandered up to the blonde at the bar and threw his arms around her knees. The woman stirred the drink in her hand with a finger and patted the boy's head with her free hand as she raised her brows in a distress signal. Mr. Pringle bounced up to them and pried the boy loose, saying, 'What's this? We want to be a brave soldier, now don't we?' At the same time he glided his hand with expert unobtrusiveness over the blonde's rump.

Papa approached the school captain and told him that we would like to call home. The boy stammered something about no personal calls being allowed. Papa looked distressed but said nothing. Sascha pulled at Papa's arm. 'Tell him who you are,' he said. Papa kept silent. Sascha pushed himself between our father and the table saying, 'You might like to know—' and that's as far as he got. Papa reached over and pulled Sascha, by the ear, out of the room.

It was now half-past three and usually the hour for home time; however, monitors on each floor announced that since the barricades had not been lifted, tea was being served in the gymnasium. The gym with its panelled walls and high ceilings served as the ganglion of the school's activities. Here it was (we had on Sascha's authority) that Big Ben droned a sermon first thing every Monday morning, plays were presented, and honours awarded. That its foremost function was the inculcation of physical training could be evidenced by rungs, chinning bars, a basketball hoop, and other similar contrivances which added to the dungeon aspect of these halls. Chinese servants brought in hard metal folding seats and at the far end of the room, on the stage, tables were being set up the length of the proscenium. In charge of refreshments was the matron of the dormitories, Mrs. Butterworth. She was a jolly Cockney lady, with a face so puffed up by oedema you could scarcely see her eyes, as though she had been stung by a swarm of bees. Her functions included the management of the school tuck-shop, from where she provended wan and lardy buns, watery cocoa, tea, or lemonade. Papa bought a plateful of buns and a pot of tea and milk for Aristide and me. With the air of someone completely in his element, Sascha carried the tray and motioned us to a group of seats.

'Now, what about this business of you going into the Chinese city?' Papa said.

'Oh, it was nothing,' Sascha replied coyly, licking the sugary end of his bun.

When Papa insisted that he tell us, Sascha explained that while the sentries were busy checking the refugees pouring into the Settlement, he and a chum slipped past them into Chapei. They went to the railway station, where they hoped to see the arrival of Nationalist troops. Instead, not two hundred yards from the barricades, they found themselves spectators to an extraordinary battle. Sascha and his classmate concealed themselves in the wreckage of a wineshop behind the station. A large group of armed men dressed in workers' clothes had commandeered the station. Sascha's friend had been convinced that these were Nationalists, but Sascha insisted that he did not see how they could be. They wore no uniforms or any insignia that might identify them as such. He was certain that they were labourer-Communists.

'They were firing on the Great Wall,' Sascha said. This was the name given by the northerners to an armoured train manned entirely by their White Russian brigade. Contrary to the hopes of the northern generals, the Great Wall had been unable to thwart the Nationalist advance and for the last forty-eight hours had been retreating under fire. At first Sascha could not understand why the train crawled at almost walking pace, back and forth in front of the station, instead of continuing at full speed. Then he realized that the labourers had torn up the tracks at either end of the train, trapping the Russians between the oncoming Nationalist armies and themselves. The brigade in the Great Wall was faced with one of two choices, either to stay put, a stationary target, or to move back and forth along the length of the remaining tracks.

'You never saw such an awesome thing as that train,' Sascha said. 'It was camouflaged mostly with blue paint, and as the cars of the train trundled slowly by, we saw bursts of gunfire from the windows, although the Russians kept out of sight. We could hear the trench mortars and the machine-guns replying from the labourers. At one point, as the train was backing up, a group of guerillas scurried towards it from the rear and climbed under the cars. When the Russians leaned out of the windows to shoot down at them, small units of guerillas ran directly up to the train and fired point-blank at the soldiers.

'Still the train moved forwards then backwards, with the guerillas climbing all over it. The shooting from inside the train grew less until there was none at all. Then the labourers hoisted a huge red flag on the engine.' Aristide was leaning on his arms, agog with admiration for what he thought of as Sascha's pluck, but Papa was pale around the mouth. 'How did you get back?' he asked.

'One of the volunteers at the barricades spotted us, and a British soldier took us back to school.'

'Sascha, there's a world of difference between bravery and foolhardiness. If I didn't think that your headmaster had ample punishment in store for you, I'd give you a good licking myself.'

Sascha's jaw began to stick out.

'I don't want you to go anywhere near a troubled area again. Do you hear me, Sascha?' Papa said.

Sascha sighed but did not reply.

By the time the barricades were lifted and we got home, it was dark. Tila, wearing a grey satin peignoir banded with chinchilla, met us at the door. She wrung one hand in that scalded gesture of hers. 'At last!' she said. 'Regina is having a *crise de nerfs*.'

Mama was in her bed, propped against an embankment of lace cushions. When she saw us, she clasped her hands, looked upwards, and said, 'Thank God, thank God.' Then she flung her arms wide and we ran to her embrace. After she had kissed and hugged us enough, she burst out crying. Papa sat beside her and took her hand in his. She pressed it hard against her cheek. Then she said, 'Maximilian, the Central Police Station called. . . .' She hesitated, knowing that she should not continue in front of us, but was unable to restrain herself. 'The Chinese have taken Hoboo and her family.'

19

EARLY next morning Papa phoned the police commissioner's office from the dining-room table, but he was unable to get any information at that hour. All of us, including Tante Tila, were gathered at breakfast. She had taken the message from Inspector Burnham last evening, but had garbled it completely. Although he kept at her, Papa was unable to ferret out who had seized the servants.

While we waited for the return call from Inspector Burnham, Zee served breakfast and Papa divided the newspaper among Mama, Tante Tila, and himself. The events of yesterday were headlined. It was surmised that before nightfall the Nationalists would be in control of Shanghai's suburbs. Papa read an editorial headed 'Who Are the Agitators?' Up to this point the terms used to describe the men dressed as workers or Chinese civilians varied from labour bravoes to guerillas. The editorial spoke quite frankly of them as Communists, and a separate news article gave an account of mass attacks on branch police stations in Chapei and Nantao. It described how Communists wielding clubs, pikes, and axes had converged on the stations, released the prisoners, and taken over the buildings. Only the fifth district station had refused to surrender, resulting in the Communists besieging it, massacring the officers, and setting fire to the station with the remaining police and prisoners inside. Another article told about the White Russians who had been wiped out in the Great Wall, mentioning that the Russians had died gallantly within sight of the British forces at the boundary, while units of volunteers and patrols of regular and special police watched from the debouchments of the railway station.

'What a futile death,' Papa said, 'and just a few weeks ago we were calling those poor chaps our allies.' Sascha, forewarned not to mention his Chapei escapade in Mama's presence, went on eating. As Mama folded the sheets of newspaper, she gave a cry. She showed Papa a headline which read 'British Missionary Shot While Resisting Communists'. There was a picture of the woman to whom we had given the ride yesterday. An account of the incident described Miss Skipworth as a spinster missionary who had come to China in 1904. It told how she had gone to the Settlement to summon fire engines, but that she had been unsuccessful because the city's fire departments had decided not to enter the area where her mission was. Upon returning to the mission, she found that the Communists had installed themselves there. Miss Skipworth ordered them out, and, to show that she meant business, seized the red flag posted at the doorway and flung it into the streets. One of the Communists then shot her full in the face.

'What kind of a man is Chiang Kai-shek to permit this?' Mama said.

'They were Communists, not Chiang's men,' Papa replied.

He had not of course made any connection yesterday between the missionary and Mama's friend, nor had he mentioned the incident, so now he said nothing about having met her. Neither Aristide nor I could mistake his look commanding us to silence. Aristide had not touched his food. Zee came in to say that Inspector Burnham was in the hall. The inspector joined us at the table. He said that it was neither the northerners nor the Nationalists who had claimed the servants.

'Then who?' Papa demanded.

'I'm afraid this will come as rather a surprise to you, but it was Mr. Liu Yueh-sung,' Burnham said.

'What on earth would Pockmarked Liu want with a couple of domestics?' Papa asked.

Inspector Burnham hazarded a guess that Liu might have taken them as bargaining points with northerners still in power in nearby areas. Then Papa said he thought it was preposterous that the municipal police should have resisted both the blandishments and the threats of the northern defence commissioner only to succumb to the whim of a gangster warlord.

'I daresay you're right, Mr. Spunt,' the inspector replied, 'but we cannot discount the fact that this same gangster warlord is in possession of a fully equipped army of plainclothes men, whose numbers some believe to be in excess of fifty thousand.'

'But if my amah's nephew, this Ah-ching, is truly a Nationalist spy, as the northerners were insisting, and if Liu is supporting Chiang, why would he sell out these servants?'

Inspector Burnham threw up his hands in a gesture of helplessness. 'This would not be the first time that Liu has double-dealed. Perhaps he is acting on behalf of the Nationalists. Who knows?' The inspector left shortly afterwards. Papa at once phoned Liu Yueh-sung. A secretary took his message and said Mr. Liu would contact him.

The evening papers confirmed the fact that the Nationalists were in control of Shanghai. The commander of a small vanguard of troops had waited outside the city until the evacuation of the northerners had been completed. The Soviet Union, meanwhile, considered the victory a personal one and fired off a congratulatory telegram to the workers in Shanghai. Thus far the Nationalist takeover had respected the laws of extraterritoriality. The Settlement and French Concession were untouched. Foreign property and persons with the exception of a few unfortunates in the Chinese area were unharmed. The fact that Shanghai had not suffered the same

134

fate as Hankow, that it had not been looted by retreating northerners or overrun by the labour-Communists was clearly due to its garrison strength, provided by the Shanghai Defence Force.

'So,' Tila said, '*plus ça change. . . .*'

20

BY Wednesday relative calm had returned to the city, but when Mama suggested that Sascha be kept home for the next few days, Papa was quick to agree. There was still no reply from Liu. Grandmama came to see us. She said that Grandpapa's rheumatism was bothering him, his feet were swollen, and he complained about his daughter and grandchildren's not visiting him. That afternoon Mama packed Aristide and me with her in the big car and we called on our grandparents. Tila went to inspect her house in the Concession. Bored by the limitations put on him and frustrated by having been forbidden to participate in the activities of the Shanghai Defence Force, Sascha chose this moment to use his Winchester 21. He lined up all Aristide's dolls against the wall of our bedroom and blew them to bits. When we returned and Aristide saw his beloved collection fragmentized to sawdust and scraps of cloth, sticking to the walls with unbearable realism, he became hysterical. Mama was furious.

'*Assassino!*' she cried. 'What a time to do this to your little brother.'

Sascha was all judicial poise. 'It had to stop sooner or later. Do you want him to become a Coco Chanel? A Madame Lucille?'

Mama paused thoughtfully. She seemed on the point of discussing the merits of the two designers. Then, seeing by Sascha's expression that she had missed the point of his allusion, she said, 'You didn't have to do it now. Not when he's so upset about the A-M-A-H?—R? How *do* you spell it?' she demanded.

When Papa came home that evening and at Mama's urging reproached Sascha, our older brother's argument was to remind our parents that *they* were constantly telling him he would one day have to take his place as *chef de famille*, and to act accordingly. I don't know what Papa really thought of this, but all he said was, 'As long as I live, *I'm* the head of this family.'

Papa went to the Shanghai Club, and Mama, Sascha, and I were in the smoking-room when Tante Tila returned that evening. Aristide had been waiting for her in the hall. Tila was incensed when she learned what Sascha had done to his dolls and she upbraided Mama.

'Maximilian doesn't want him to become, you know, a hair-dresser,' Mama said.

'If I were you, I'd worry more about what Sascha is already than what Aristide will become,' Tila said.

'What do you mean?' Mama said. 'Maximilian says that Sascha is all boy.'

'He's all bully,' Tila said.

'Thank you very much,' Sascha said.

Aristide looked up at Sascha from Tila's lap, where he had buried his face. 'Maybe Hoboo's dead,' he cried, 'and I hate you!'

'You see what you've done?' Mama said to Sascha.

'Listen,' Tila said to Aristide, '*es tu mon prince?*' Aristide nodded. 'Well, princes don't cry.' She continued, 'Tante Tila is going to give you a wonderful present.'

'What?' Aristide asked.

'It's a surprise. You'll see.'

'No dolls,' Sascha said.

'*Of course* not,' Tila replied.

The next morning before breakfast, Papa broke the news that a Chinese army, presumably Nationalists, had made an all-out attack on foreigners in Nanking. Still shaken by the reports he had heard, Papa discussed the events at breakfast.

'They mobbed the British Consulate, wounded the consul general, and killed a doctor. Then they besieged both the Japanese and American consulates. A French and an Italian missionary were slaughtered for trying to hide some Catholics. The last thing I heard at the club was that a large group of foreigners are gathered on a hill overlooking the city walls and that they are trying to get to destroyers lying in the Yangtze.'

'Then this means that Chiang is going to get rid of all of us?' Sascha asked. Papa did not reply, most likely because he did not know. From all appearances the foreigners had been premature in their jubilation and now were caught frozen in the process of their backslapping like the stuttering frame of a motion picture. To them, this assault could mean finally the shattering of their world, the fullest realization of a threat so harped upon it had ceased to have validity. The notion was terrifying.

The paper was full of the attack and labelled it the Nanking Outrage. It stated that protests to the government in Hankow had been fired off by foreign representatives. From the article Papa was reading, we gathered that the British, shakier than in their early convictions, let it be known that they were sending additional troops, and the Americans announced that the U.S.S. *Richmond*, *Marblehead*, and *Cincinnati* were on their way.

When Papa had finished reading to us, we gathered about Sascha, who was listening to reports over the crystal wireless. The foreign refugees on the hill were being peppered with gunfire from the Chinese. Messages for help were relayed repeatedly by two United States Navy Signal Corpsmen. Finally an ultimatum was sent to the Chinese general in command, demanding immediate safe conduct for the foreigners. Although Sascha kept the earphones on the rest of that day, there was no more news. According to our Friday morning paper there had been no response from the Chinese headquarters, and at noon Sascha looked up from the wireless to tell us that the British and American ships had begun firing on the soldiers and that the Chinese had stopped trying to get at the foreigners on the hill and were firing back at the ships.

That same day, March 25, Chiang Kai-shek arrived in Shanghai under the protection of the Chinese navy. An interview with the foreign press was arranged at once at the general's residence in the French Concession. Chiang Kai-shek began the interview by expressing his displeasure at the defences of the Settlement and the French Concession. It was well known, he said, that the Nationalists protected foreign property. The looting of Nanking he ascribed to the work of retreating northerners. However, he would investigate the matter thoroughly and those guilty would be severely dealt with.

Meanwhile, refugees arriving from Nanking put the entire blame on the Nationalist army. Chiang's local supporters rallied to his defence. The Nanking Outrage, they said, was a premeditated scheme on the part of the Communists engineered by Hankow and Moscow to discredit Chiang once and for all with the foreign powers.

137

That night Zee, the number one boy, showed Sascha a pamphlet which had been passed to him in the streets. The labour groups, openly called Communists, were planning a mass rally for Sunday. It was to be held at the West Gate near the boundaries of the French Concession, and the purpose of the demonstration was to march on the foreign settlements. By special messengers, on the radio and in the papers, foreigners were urged at once to evacuate the French Concession and congregate in the more fortified area of the International Settlement. The French mobilized their forces at the boundaries of Nantao and Siccawei, and the Americans, British, Italians, and Japanese trained their guns on all other ingresses to the Settlement. Aunt Annie, who had continued living at the Astor House since her husband's death two years earlier, phoned to announce her intentions of moving in with us. However, Papa convinced her that she was just as safe where she was.

On Sunday we waited for news of the rally. It was Zee who brought the first word. We gathered about him in the kitchen as he described in Chinese what had taken place. 'When I got to the West Gate there were thousands of people already assembled there. Not just labourers and students like everyone thinks, but ordinary people like me. I never saw so many banners and slogans; and the shouting and chanting, it was deafening. One fellow got up on some boxes or a stand, I couldn't see that well, and he was screaming so angrily that he was all red in the face. I heard somebody say that he was a Communist, but that didn't seem to matter to anyone. He was urging the crowds to march there and then into the French Concession. Never mind the guns, he told them, we have a greater power than foreign guns. He didn't say what that was, but the mobs seemed to believe him and they cheered wildly. All at once there was a great commotion, and I saw hundreds of people with different banners proclaiming the greatness of Nationalism, and there were many who carried the new flag and huge portraits of Sun Yat-sen. Then, standing in an open car waving to the crowds was Chiang Kai-shek himself. There was such frenzy and excitement that everyone forgot about marching on the Concession.'

We heard subsequently that one of Chiang Kai-shek's generals was responsible for the turnabout. With less than twenty-four hours in which to work, he had assembled a corps of paid propagandists to sway the crowds already vacillating between the successes of the

138

Nationalists and the hate force movement inspired by the labour-Communist groups. Chiang's presence had caused the rally to turn into a mass demonstration of Nationalistic fervour.

By Monday the situation appeared well enough in hand for Sascha to return to school. Aristide and I were playing in the hall when Papa returned from work that afternoon. Again he tried to reach Pockmarked Liu. He had phoned the warlord daily, and each time the secretary, polite as ever, told Papa that Mr. Liu would be in touch with him. Aristide and I could hear as he discussed the call with Mama in the smoking-room.

'It's no use,' Papa was saying. 'He's just putting me off. I'm going to have to go to him.'

'Isn't there some other way?' Mama said.

'It may even be too late now.' We listened as Papa phoned Monsieur Barraud, his lawyer, and heard him make the arrangements to pick up the Frenchman at his office. Aristide went into the smoking-room.

'Papa, take me with you,' he said.

'No, Aristide.'

'But you remember, I won before. We played cards and I *won*.'

'Yes,' Papa sighed, 'and Mr. Liu probably also remembers. We don't want to do anything to spoil it for Hoboo, do we?'

Zee had just finished serving our dinner when Papa returned. He sank heavily into his chair, defeat written all over him. Then he told how he and his lawyer had gone first to the French Consulate to enlist their support. 'Barraud begged them to help, citing every tiny bequest that I have ever made to France. To tell the truth, I found myself getting embarrassed, but I needn't have. They flatly refused to intervene. Mr. Liu figured too importantly in their immediate plans to risk ruffling him over a couple of servants.'

'Sure,' Mama said. 'Opium, gambling, and whorehouse payoffs are very important. Those lousy French. . . .'

Papa gave her a warning look.

'The hell with it,' Mama said. 'Everybody knows.'

Papa went on to say that he had then gone to the Municipal Council where he was received by the chairman, a position equal to that of mayor. Sterling Fessenden was an American attorney extremely well thought of by Chinese political groups. He was also a longtime friend of our family, and he agreed at once to help. Mr.

Fessenden told Papa that he was, in point of fact, preparing at that very moment to visit Liu on a matter of the direst importance but that he had no hesitation in assuming a subsidiary one.

At Liu's residence in the French Concession, armed guards admitted the foreigners to a sepulchral entry hall, which Papa noted was stacked floor to ceiling with rifles and sub-machine-guns. Notwithstanding his position, the chairman was subjected along with Papa to a thorough frisking by the guards. Then they were ushered into a reception room.

He heard the sound of shuffling feet, and from a door Liu appeared in the company of the French consular official with whom Papa had lodged his plea only a couple of hours earlier. Liu, his personal guards close behind him, padded with amazing lightness to the chair at his desk where, before sitting, the warlord glanced rapidly on either side of him. He then motioned to the Frenchman to take a place beside Papa and Fessenden.

If Liu was surprised to see Papa he concealed it effectively. Leaning over his desk he extended his hand like a bishop— '*Monsieur Spunt, quel plaisir de vous voir*'—but the Frenchman looked disturbed. Papa said that he would wait in the hall while the men discussed their business. The French official had already risen to signify his approval, but Liu, for some unknown quirk, would have none of it: '*Non, non, je vous en prie*, please remain.' He turned to the American, 'Certainly a civic leader of Monsieur Spunt's standing should be witness to these negotiations, *non*?' Papa thought the compliment unctious, and it rang familiarly to him. He realized with some discomfort that he had used much the same approach to Liu when he had forced his contribution to charity. He's going to make me pay, Papa thought.

The representatives of both concessions then outlined their plan to Liu. The Northerners were gone, true; however, the national unity for which Chiang Kai-shek was striving was being jeopardized by the increasing strength of the Communists who daily were adding thousands of labourers and civilians to their masses. The two foreign officials said that they had it on the best of authority that the government in Hankow planned to use the labour element of Shanghai as an example of efficient proletarian militancy with which to sweep the remainder of China into Communism. The Frenchman said, 'They are guided by a dedicated and brilliant leader.'

140

With those bronze-stained talons, Liu picked a shred of lint from his sleeve. 'Ah, yes,' he said, 'Chou En-lai trained in *le belle France* unless I am mistaken.' The Frenchman did not reply, and Fessenden grinned. Liu held up his hands against the light shed by a Western table lamp as though he were measuring this information with the length of his nails; then he said, 'Where do you think Chiang stands?'

The American said, 'We had hoped to come to terms with Chiang concerning our extraterritorial privileges, but the Nanking picture seems to cast some doubt on his intentions.' He added that in any event, with only three thousand Nationalist troops in Shanghai and roughly ten thousand in the nearby Chekiang province, if Chiang were to split with the Red-disposed Hankow government and the local left-wingers, he would hardly stand a chance.

'And what do your municipalities propose?' Liu asked. The Frenchman said bluntly, 'I think I speak for both our councils when I say that we want, we *must have*, the support of your civilian army against *any* force which threatens either of the foreign settlements.'

Liu extracted a tiny gold paring knife from the folds of his sleeve and began to work on his nails. Then in a voice of professed wonderment he murmured, '*My* civilian army?' Both foreigners were silent; they knew that Liu was resorting to the age-old Chinese ploy of *K'e-chi*, ceremonial courtesy, and in this case, super self-effacement. Liu allowed for the full effectiveness of the pause; then he said, 'And if perchance I were able to muster up some of my guards, what are your municipalities prepared to offer me?' This time the silence between the Frenchman and the American was a fumbling one.

'Very well,' said the Chinese. 'I will tell you what I must have. A minimum of ten thousand rifles, ten thousand automatics, Mausers or Lugers, and adequate ammunition. Next, my men must have *carte blanche* to travel through both concessions at any given time.'

The council chairman frowned. No Chinese troops of any faction had ever been given freedom of passage through the International Settlement. To concede to this one stipulation might be to create a dangerous precedent. And, if Liu proved treacherous and loaned his support instead to the Communists against Chiang Kai-shek, against the foreigners. . . . But the Frenchman had already shaken hands to seal the bargain between Liu and the French Concession. Liu turned inquiringly to the American, and the chairman gave his assent. The warlord stood. 'So good of you to come to my home, *messieurs*,' he said. Then with the briefest nod to Papa he prepared to leave the room. In view of the importance of the subject which he had just overheard, Papa confessed that he felt most foolish broaching the matter of Hoboo. He knew, however, that Liu had no intention of making it easy for him, and he also knew that this was his last chance. When Papa had explained his mission, Liu gave the impression of surprise. 'I have no knowledge of this. Of course it is possible that one of my adjutants may have requested these people for his own reasons. I assure you I will look into the matter.'

Papa took out his chequebook and said, 'You are very kind to take the trouble. I am certain that your staff must have already gone to great expense to secure the safety of my servants. Naturally I have come prepared to make proper restitution.'

Liu waved aside Papa's cheque like a man brushing a fly from a cake, swiftly but without touching either the fly or the cake. All that could be heard as he hurried out of the room was the disapproving rustle of his robe.

Papa, who had barely touched his food while telling this story, began to eat slowly and without appetite.

'Eat, eat, Maximilian,' Mama urged.

'I don't like it,' Papa said.

'The food?'

'No, the fact that Liu would not accept my cheque.'

'Papa, is Hoboo going to be all right?' Aristide was speaking.

Papa did not reply at once, and Sascha said, 'I'll bet they've already done her in.'

'Papa, is that true?'

'No. No, Aristide, I'm sure that it isn't.'

'She's deader than a doornail, want to bet?' Sascha said.

'Stop that, Sascha,' Papa ordered. 'Your brother is just trying to tease you, Aristide.'

While Aristide glowered with hatred at Sascha, our older brother took up a chant under his breath, 'Deader than a doornail, deader than a doornail. . . .'

BY the beginning of April there was a noticeable change in the statements made by Chiang Kai-shek. In face of the sworn testimony by foreign missionaries and businessmen that the Nanking Outrage appeared premeditated and had been conducted by Nationalist troops, he made no more excuses but blamed the Communist faction. After having been bitterly opposed to the curfew enforced by the foreign municipalities, he now gave his endorsement to martial law and issued an order forbidding the holding of mass meetings, the stirring up of agitation, and the hampering of loyal workers returning to their jobs. At his insistence the strike came to an end. The General Labour Union now established in Chapei was the wellspring of Communist directives. From these headquarters Chou En-lai formulated his plans for the march on the Concessions. To crown the *coup d'état* Wang Ching-wei, whose career had been one of frustratingly near hits, had been summoned from Hankow to replace Chiang's authority.

Chiang and his agents worked fast. During curfew, armoured cars moved under special passes provided by the municipalities, making a caravan from the boundaries of the French Concession at Nantao, across the Bund heading north towards Chapei. Pockmarked Liu had kept his word, and the struggle against the Communist forces began. Members of the left-wing Kuomintang combined forces with the leaders of the Communist labour army to form a local provisional government. Their capitulations were listed daily in the foreign newspapers: a temple in the old city, a spinning mill in Pootung, and police stations in Nantao and Chapei. The offensives were carried out in darkness, beginning with a well-armed attack by Chiang's soldiers and Liu's civilian army, followed by an ultimatum for immediate surrender, then mass annihilation.

Finally assured that Chiang Kai-shek's intentions were not to seize their concessions, the foreign press gave great play to the suppression of the Communist party. Chiang's counter-coup had been thorough, and the papers listed a staggering number of Communist-appropriated strongholds in Hangchow and Nanking, as well as in Shanghai, which had been flushed out simultaneously. News coverage of the mass attacks credited Chiang Kai-shek's soldiers with breaking the backbone of Communism, and while Liu's civilian army was mentioned as Nationalist Labour Auxiliaries, their role in the joint operations was played down. That the Communists had intended seizure of total control was borne out by the huge caches of arms uncovered.

On Thursday Papa read us a news item of significant interest. Captioned 'Nationalist Mystery Hero', it gave an account of a certain Koo Ah-ching, intelligence officer of the Nationalist army, who had for the last two years passed himself off as a student at the Shanghai University in order to gauge the activities of the pro-Communist students. Planted as well in the General Labour Union, he had performed so convincingly that just prior to Chiang Kai-shek's takeover, he had become the most wanted enemy by the northern army. The article continued to the effect that the raids had been formulated and carried out on Koo's explicit instructions.

Easter Sunday that year fell on April 17, less than a week after the crushing of the Communists. Hoboo had always taken Aristide and me to mass, and it was from habit or the undentable faith of idiots and children that my brother and I were up, dressed, and ready very early that morning. Because they were most likely appreciative of our feelings, Mama and Papa had outdone themselves in gifts. When we came in for breakfast, we found our places at the table covered with a great assortment of holiday presents. Fat chocolate hens sat in marzipan nests filled with eggs wrapped in coloured foil, and there were giant-sized Easter eggs decorated with ornamental frosting which, when broken into, revealed another egg and then another, like carved ivory balls.

In the midst of our excitement, and the always necessary business of staving off Sascha's sequestering hand, there was a gust of Caron's Petits Pois de Senteur, and Tila came into the room, very businesslike, pulling down her iron-coloured kid gloves. She had been shopping, and she was dressed in a tailleur. The cloche on her head was pulled down so low that we could only see the bright M of lipstick that was her mouth. Two servants followed her, pushing a large trundle cart full of gifts. Tila conducted the distribution systematically. For Mama there was a combination of manicure and makeup kit in the shape of a marquetry box standing on legs. Papa's gift was a chessboard made of squares of white and black jade. The chessmen, some four inches tall, were carved out of brilliant apple green and red jade. At this time home movie projectors were almost unheard of. Sascha snorted with pleasure as he saw a sixteen-millimetre Pathé projector, complete with several reels of films. I don't know when I had revealed to Tila my recondite wish for warriors, but failing a regiment of these, Tila had done her best for me by way of a Carthaginian leather helmet with metal trim and a crest of plumes, as well as a round Numidian shield of tooled leather.

'Tila, Tila,' Mama cried, 'what largesse; this is not Christmas.'

'For me it *is*,' Tila replied. 'The trouble is over; nothing has been damaged; I can go home.' And she added that Michel, her Frenchman, had been promoted to director of his company. 'I think that I will soon be the Comtesse de Raveur,' Tila said.

Everyone laughed and cheered and talked all at the same time, except Aristide. He was slumped in his chair, silent. Tila saw his face.

'Ah, *chéri*,' she said, 'you think your Tante Tila has forgotten you?' She made a sign to the servants. The trundle cart disappeared and returned in a few minutes, the space within it devoted entirely to one enormous carton.

'*Voilà*, Aristide,' Tila said. 'The present I promised you.'

Like everything connected with Tila, this present was a masterpiece of adornment, and it took Aristide and me fully ten minutes to tear through the trinkets, bows, ribbons, and cardboard. When we had come down to the tissue paper, the guessing began.

'It's a kennel,' Sascha said.

'Nonsense,' Aristide replied. 'Where are the dogs if it is?'

'I know,' I said. 'It's a sentry box!'

Aristide said nothing, but his hands worked like claws ripping at the paper. When the last of the wrapping had been removed, we saw what must have been the most elaborate toy house in the world. It was not a house really, but a château standing about four feet high and equally as wide. There were towers and turrets and real windows with mullioned panes. In the entrance hall a grand staircase with wooden banisters swept up and through the three tiers of the building. In the grand salon the walls were covered with damask; a miniature crystal chandelier with tiny candles hung from a rococo plaster ceiling, and the floors were parquet. But what was most

145

exciting to Aristide were the figures. Perfectly proportioned in relation to the rooms, there were wax figures of men and women dressed in brocades and powdered wigs, attended by grooms and lackeys. Upstairs in the bedrooms, chambermaids turned down sheets in four-posters or heated the beds by means of long-handled warming pans. Aristide just sat and looked at the spectacle wordless, but I was crawling around on all fours examining everything.

'Isn't that lovely,' Mama said. 'It's what do you call it, architecture.'

'It's a dollhouse,' Sascha said, but Mama was ready for him.

'Rubbish, it's a historical château and those are figurines, statues,' she said.

'Show us your projector, Sascha,' Papa said.

When a call came at the tiffin hour, Tila rushed to answer it. She was expecting to hear from her count about a *thé dansant* that afternoon. It was Pockmarked Liu on the phone. He instructed Tila briefly but explicitly. If Madame Spunt wished to collect her servants, she must come with her children to his residence at precisely three o'clock. Papa thought this curious. Why did Liu not ask him to be present? Why did he simply not send Hoboo and her family back in one of his many vehicles, or ask that our car be sent to fetch them?

'Maybe he thinks you're too busy,' Mama said, 'and he knows how anxious the children are to see Hoboo. Don't worry, Maximilian, Liu will not hurt us.'

We arrived at Liu's estate ten minutes before our appointed time. Guards dressed in Chinese working clothes but wearing leather holsters opened the iron gates, after making Pao-shing get out of the car to be frisked. I noticed that the high brick walls were topped with broken glass. The driveway twisted through a beautifully tended park where additional guards were posted at regular intervals. Beyond a curve I saw a great willow weeping over zigzag painted bridges which led to what looked like a gazebo or summer house and which may or may not have been Liu's private temple. Farther up the driveway stood a gingko tree well over a hundred feet tall, its leaves rustling like a thousand tiny fans. Far up in its boughs a bird gave its trilling song.

No one had said anything since entering the grounds. I looked at Aristide; his face was grave.

'Listen, Aristide,' I said, 'the bottle bird.'

'Cretin,' he replied. 'The bottle bird never comes before summer.' The bird trilled again.

'One more bottle,' I sang out.

'It's a babbler, a thrush, I tell you,' Aristide said, but he began to laugh at my foolish insistence.

From what we could see of the main building through the moongate of the Ningpo stone wall surrounding it, Liu's home was a Eurasian composite. The house was low with a curved tiled roof supported by red lacquer columns. Wide cement steps led up to a verandah reminiscent of the porticoes in the homes built by early Western residents in the settlement. But the huge doors were carved and gold-leafed. The house faced a rectangular cement compound unadorned save for a large tripod incense burner in one corner. When we reached the wall two guards motioned to Pao-shing to stop and indicated that we should get out of the car. We fully expected to enter, but the guards barred our way at the moongate where they told us to wait. Just then a company of Nationalist soldiers marched onto the courtyard and, filing into lines of ten, stood at attention. Mama, who had Aristide and me each by hand, told Sascha to get a cigarette out of her purse. I looked at her face, and while she might have seemed calm enough to the casual observer, I knew Mama's expressions. The door to the house opened, and I felt Aristide's pull as he surged forward only to be reined in by Mama. Hoboo, Lao Ni, his mother, and Didi came out onto the verandah. A minute or so later Liu, followed by his omnipresent bodyguards, padded out and down the steps, where he too stood.

Presently the door opened again, and a slender man of medium height dressed in a belted army jacket with flap pockets and brass buttons over riding breeches and wearing a visored cap with the Nationalist emblem strode briskly down the steps. He was followed by an adjutant. As Chiang Kai-shek faced his troops, no more than fifty feet from where we stood, I could see his face. The perennial youthfulness common to Chinese was accentuated by his mild mouth. It was a face that completely belied his nearly forty years. Once, when he lifted his head and the sun flashed momentarily across them, I saw his eyes. They were dark as obsidian and resolute. The adjutant began reading from a list. As they were called, the men in line stepped forward, and the general pinned a medal on them. Presently we heard the adjutant call the name Koo Ah-ching, and Hoboo's nephew stepped forward to be decorated. Chiang talked with him for a minute or two. Then he turned and, followed by the adjutant, walked back into the house. The soldiers were dismissed. Pockmarked Liu went with Ah-ching back to the verandah. Ah-ching embraced his mother and his aunt and hugged his brothers. Liu said something then, and the Chinese family looked towards the moongate. As Liu went into the house, Hoboo and her family crossed the courtyard, coming towards us. Aristide broke Mama's grip and ran to Hoboo.

Mama had never met Ah-ching, and she was at a loss as to how to behave. His aunt and brother were our servants, and now, according to Pao-shing, Ah-ching was a colonel and a hero as well. Mama smiled and said, 'I'm glad you are well.' Ah-ching nodded while Lao Ni beamed and bowed to Mama. Ah-ching turned to Aristide and with two fingers stiffly outstretched, pretended he was firing a pistol as he said loudly, 'Gung! Gung! Gung!'

Aristide jumped, then he remembered his visit to their house and he smiled at Ah-ching over this private joke. But Hoboo looked cross. 'What's the matter with you?' she said in Chinese, smiting Ah-ching's shoulder with her hand. But he just laughed. Pockmarked Liu had arranged transportation for them, but Aristide clung to Hoboo, and she said she would come home with us. In the car Sascha, Aristide, and I talked a great deal to Hoboo, sounding her out about the prison, Liu, Chiang, everything, but she didn't talk much. Mama did not say much either. As we started out the driveway, Mama took her cigarettes out of her purse. In lighting one, she looked up and saw Hoboo staring at her. Mama extended the pack to Hoboo. As she extracted a cigarette, Hoboo grinned at Mama, the tip of her tongue poking impudently out of the gap made by her missing tooth.

22

THE servants, who had gathered in the hall, made a great jabbering commotion when they saw Hoboo. The amah merely looked from one to the other as each offered felicitations, but she made no comment, her face set in a rigid smile. When Papa did not appear after some time, Mama asked Zee where he was. 'Mastah have got flend in dlawing loom,' Zee said. Aristide, hugging Hoboo's waist, did not seem inclined to leave her, and since no one was paying me particular attention, I followed Mama and Sascha into the drawing-room. Papa was seated in front of the fireplace, his new chess set before him on a low table. The wing chair twin to the one he was sitting in was facing him, but we could not see the occupant. Mama said, 'Hoboo is home.' Papa shifted his cane in order to rise, but Mama motioned him to keep sitting.

'Papa, we saw Chiang Kai-shek,' Sascha said, 'and what do you think? He made Ah-ching a colonel.' Mama had come up to the back of the chair turned towards Papa. A very tall man in the dress uniform of an Italian navy commander got to his feet.

'I believe that Prince Volfieri is a friend of yours,' Papa said. Whatever went on in Mama's mind at that moment, I'll never know, but she simply extended her hand. Chicho bent to kiss it. He hugged Sascha and me, then asked, 'But where is *il mio tesoro*, Aristide?' Mama waved her hand in the direction of the hall. In his navy-blue uniform with golden epaulets and a blue moire sash which cut across his chest diagonally to meet a resplendent sabre, Chicho looked handsomer than ever. Mama sat on the edge of the sofa and I climbed up next to her.

'Please continue your game,' Mama said. 'I won't interrupt. Where's Tila?'

Papa said that Tila's count had come for her. He began to make a move. The prince laughed softly. 'I shall have your queen,' he said.

Papa leaned back in his chair and drew on his cigar. 'In that case I'll have to watch my moves.'

Mama looked around the room like a visitor. 'To tell the truth,' she said, 'I'm getting a little hungry.'

Chicho of course stayed for dinner, after which he regaled Sascha with stories about the Italian navy. He said that the only expedient way of coming to the Orient had been to rejoin for a two-year hitch (he had served during the Great War), and he had always wanted to come to Shanghai. While coffee and liqueurs were being served in the smoking-room, Chicho carried Aristide and me, one on each arm, out onto the balcony overlooking the river. In the maze of masts, funnels, and lights, he pointed out various Italian ships. 'There, that gunboat is the *Caboto,* and that cruiser the *Libia,* and over near Pootung side is the *Carlotto.* Now tell me which one is my ship.'

'That sampan?' Aristide said. Chicho and Sascha thought this was very funny. Inside the room I heard Papa say in a soft voice, 'He's really a nice fellow, Regina.'

The day after he decorated Ah-ching, Chiang Kai-shek proclaimed Nanking the capital of the Kuomintang. A raid earlier in the month on the Soviet Embassy in Peiping had uncovered indisputable evidence that the Russians intended complete control of the Kuomintang. As a result, the Central Executive Committee in Hankow began to lose ground with both its Chinese and its foreign supporters. In Shanghai, the General Labour Union had been disbanded for reassembling by the new government. For Chiang Kai-shek, it now seemed only a matter of the winning over the north to secure a total Nationalist victory. Clearly the new regime intended for the time being at least to observe extraterritorial possessions. Any hiatus in the disapproval of them by the Chinese was cause enough for rejoicing, and Shanghai's foreign communities responded in the way that they knew best.

Gala functions were held at each national's club with the women vying for the most opulent gowns. Officers from every country attended in their dress uniforms, so that kilts, plumes, helmets, and turbans created colourful mosaics at each gathering. Shipping had resumed, and celebrities again began to visit Shanghai.

Papa invited his British and American taipans and their wives, and Mama was able to show Chicho off to her Latin friends. The fact that Chicho was a prince would have been enough to set that self-consciously social community on its ear, but that he was as well debonair and handsome in the tradition of a matinee idol compounded his appeal. Mama's friend, Rhoda Cunningham, was dazzled. At a reception my parents were giving in honour of a Russian dancer—I think it was Pavlova—Chicho was lionized while the diminutive ballerina sat brooding, practically by herself. Leading a small regiment of determinedly curious women, Rhoda cornered Mama.

'Regina, he's unbelievable. Where did you find him?' she demanded.

When Mama replied truthfully, 'In the Adriatic,' the women thought this the wittiest of evasions.

Tila, once again ensconced in her villa, planned a costume ball. While the parties my parents gave were festive enough for those they invited, the general tone of these events was conditioned by Papa's bark-bound sense of propriety. Mama was susceptible to personality, but Papa skimmed her guest lists of any dubious characters, however colourful. Tila, on the other hand, could not resist combining worlds and colliding milieus. At one of her parties, the Chinese mayor and an aristocrat such as Lord Li Ching-mei might easily find themselves rustling silks with an underworld czar— Pockmarked Liu, perhaps. A minister of the New Administration could pretend to ignore the presence of an attractive German widow, but it was widely known that, through his connections, she had made several millions in arms contracts to the Nationalists. The bearded French attorney with his wife on his arm might be confronted by his blonde Hungarian mistress, who fancied herself a coloratura. Gossip had it that the lawyer had spent a fortune renting Town Hall for her concerts and buying up all the tickets, which he then gave to anyone he could coerce into attending.

Aristide, to whom Tila had become even more significant since her recent gift of the dollhouse, hung on every word as the two women formulated ideas for the ball. 'You will lend me your servants, silver, and china?' Tila asked. Mama nodded. 'And what decor shall we have? A Japanese garden? A Venetian piazza? A Renaissance court?'

'Why not just what you have?' Aristide interrupted.

Tila reflected on this for a moment; then she said, 'Why not? My own Petit Trianon.' Then she and Mama discussed the menu and considered the merit of sculptured ice displays. They decided on the wines and went over the guest list once more. Aristide scraped his shoe along the parquet as though something were stuck on the side of it. He kept up the scraping until Tila and Mama looked at him. Then Mama said, 'Absolutely not. Maximilian would never—'

'Please, Mama,' Aristide said.

'Impossible. The next thing the little one will want to come.'

'Please, Mama, please.' I was right on cue.

'But their father *wouldn't* in a million years—'

'Let me handle your husband,' Tila said.

How Tila got around to getting Papa's consent is a mystery to me. Certainly she must have used persuasive arguments; possibly she played up the point that we had suffered over Hoboo and should share in some rejoicing. Knowing Papa, it could just have been that he liked the way Tila nestled towards him, putting those heavily bangled arms around his shoulders; at any rate, he gave his consent with the provisos that Hoboo attend to us, that we be kept strictly in the background, and that at ten o'clock we return home.

It must have occurred to everyone but me that Aristide was not going to let this opportunity slip by without fulfilling his dream of becoming Monsieur Beaucaire. Mama's argument that Chicho had mentioned his intention of dressing as an eighteenth-century noble-man found Aristide quite willing to compromise. 'Never mind,' he insisted. 'There will be a big Beaucaire and a small Beaucaire.' In the weeks before Tila's party, our drawing-room took on the aspect of a theatrical costumier's shop. Bolts of yardage cascaded over the furnishings. Chinese tailors and their crews came, measured, cut, and fitted, while Mama had private sessions with her Russian couturière for her special and secret costume. Papa would, as was his habit, wear a domino over his evening clothes, and Sascha was to have his first dinner suit. At no time did anyone mention how I was to be attired. I suppose the general attitude towards me was truth-fully expressed by Aristide, who said, 'A little boy not yet four should be glad he's invited at all.'

On the evening of the ball Hoboo got me dressed in my usual Viyella shirt and short pants, well ahead of time. Although she had troubled to wear her Sunday church attire and her headband was stuck with a tiny jade pin, Hoboo was in a feisty mood. Hoping to placate her, I said, 'Show me your new tooth.' To celebrate the servants' safe return. Papa had given each of them ten piculs of rice and, in addition, Hoboo had been sent to the dentist to replace her missing front tooth. She had insisted on white metal instead of gold and was inordinately proud of it. But now she refused to smile for me. 'What's the matter, Hoboo?' I pressed. Instead of replying, she took me to Mama's room to watch as she and Mama readied Aristide.

Mama was seated at her dressing-table with its lighted triple mirror. Aristide stood on her right next to the open cosmetic drawer. Although he was still in his underwear, Aristide already had on his long white hose and buckled pumps. A white linen towel wrapped around his head heightened the apricot shade of the foundation Mama had applied to his face. Now Mama dipped a feather puff in powder and held it expertly over my brother's features. Then she blew lightly on the puff and Aristide began coughing. At first he coughed in earnest, and then, for effect, he made such a business of fanning himself and clutching his throat so that his eyes bugged that Mama lost patience with him and told him to shut up if he wanted her to make up his mouth. With his lips stencilled in red like a tiny cinnamon candy, he was ready for his eye makeup. Mama opened a narrow black box which had a small brush resting in it. She spat expertly in the box and rubbed the brush over the mascara. As she started brushing his lashes, Aristide whimpered, 'It stings.'

'If I've told you once, I've told you twice, not to talk when I'm putting on Rimmel's,' said Mama as she kept on brushing. Two tiny patches, one placed on his cheek and the other on his chin, and Aristide's makeup was complete. With the towel removed from his head, Aristide's resemblance to Mama was extraordinary. While he clutched a hand mirror, staring at himself critically, Mama and Hoboo got him into a ruffled silk shirt, satin breeches, a vest, and a jacket of gold brocade. The wig, a confection of white curls fastened at the back with a black velvet ribbon, all but completed his costume. Still admiring himself in the hand mirror, Aristide said, as though he had a cold in the nose, 'My cane, if you please.' Hoboo thrust the ebony cane with its pavéed diamond knob at him. Mama, Hoboo, and I said the proper complimentary things as Aristide twirled and postured for our approval. He might have gone on for heaven knows how long, but Mama said that now she had to get ready. At once Aristide plumped himself beside me on the bed. Whenever Papa was concerned elsewhere, as he was at this moment, assisting Sascha with his boiled shirt, studs, and tie, we were allowed to watch Mama perform her *maquillage*. And what a sight it was to watch, as unguents, lotions, and tubes of every size in a palette of colourings were cast out of the drawer onto the table top. As though in a wholesale gesture of inclusion, of love even, everything was handled, opened, and examined, like the jars of cream used once, then condemned with a cigarette stab as an oblique, never a direct or final, indication of discard. In the same way she marshalled a dozen worn-to-the-nub lipsticks, like hostages in front of her, although for years she had used only Arden's Victoire. But this evening she did no more than clean her face with orange-flower water and brush her brows and lashes with vaseline. Aristide could not believe it. 'When are you going to begin?' he asked. 'I've finished,' Mama replied. Then she told us to join Papa and Sascha in the drawing-room while she dressed. This too was an innovation, since we were always allowed to watch Mama dress after she had been bodiced, corseted, and in her teddy.

'Why can't we stay?' Aristide asked.

'I told you my costume is a surprise.'

At the entrance to the drawing-room Aristide went through his whole act again for our father's benefit. Papa allowed that Aristide looked 'quite the marquis, very handsome', but he sat me on his lap and gave me a warm kiss. Chicho, who was to drive with us to Tila's, arrived. For all the elegance of his royal blue and silver tunic, for all the lace around his collar and cuffs and the ribbon tied peruke, there was to his Italianate features a warm and rascal grin, an irrefutable masculinity. He was an exquisite without being a fop, and it was Casanova rather than Monsieur Beaucaire who shook Papa's hand and bowed from the waist to Aristide. Papa must have felt in need of refreshment, because Lao Ni brought in a tray of aperitifs just then. Struggling with the hood of his domino, Sascha came into the room. Aristide clapped one hand over his mouth, for in Sascha's twisting, his studs had popped and his starched shirt front ballooned over his dinner jacket. 'You look like a fat black penguin,' Aristide said.

'Sissy,' Sascha hissed.

To a marquis en route to a château reception such insolence was unthinkable, and Aristide whacked Sascha across the legs with his cane. Sascha rushed at him, stumbling through the folds of his cloak.

Just then Mama stood in the doorway. She was dressed in the habit of a nun. The gown itself was dark blue or black and of a heavy material, possibly serge. A coif of white silk was softly fitted to her head and fell to the shoulders. From a chain around her neck a large crucifix was suspended, and she had tied a moonstone rosary at her waist. With her face censored of all artifice and brought into relief by the coif, and those Easter lily hands held delicately at her breast, as though they bloomed there, she seemed to shimmer in an aura of ineluctable beauty. By the look on his face, Aristide was clearly shocked, even betrayed, by Mama's simplicity; but Chicho, evidently unable to restrain himself, said, 'Madonna'. I glanced at Papa, who was clipping a cigar, and thought that he was taking unusually long to get it lighted.

Flaming torches illuminated the driveway through Tila's garden. From the car I could tell that the liveried bearers were not Chinese, although the faces against their snowy wigs were the brown of tobacco. Later we learned that Tila had cajoled the colonel of the French *caserne* into providing her with a unit of Annamite soldiers for the occasion. At the door to the ballroom a chamberlain took invitations, struck his cane on the floor three times, and in ringing tones announced each guest by name and the character represented. I don't know what the chamberlain would have made of a Chinese amah carrying a little boy, but he was spared the confusion by Papa's decision that we all go down the grand flight of marble stairs together. Aristide would have none of that and announced that he was making a separate entrance. This was followed immediately by a scuffle and the sound of a few imprecise slaps. We must have made a pretty sight to the guests below, the big nun, a crippled man, and the fat boy in dominoes, flapping about as they converged on Aristide. It was obvious that Aristide was prepared for a full-scale battle as he parried, thrust, and beat them off with his cane. Chicho pulled Hoboo and me to the rear of the landing, disassociating us from the fracas. Tila, waiting at the bottom of the stairs, made a flash signal to a group of White Russian musicians who struck up the opening bars of 'Pomp and Circumstance'. At once the family on the landing automated brilliant smiles, and we went down the steps without Aristide.

Tila's dress with its panniered short skirt, while reminiscent of the eighteenth century, was actually very much in keeping with the styles of 1927. Around her neck were the Golitsky amethysts. This was the first time that I remembered meeting Michel de Raveur. I had expected someone suave and romantic; certainly I had expected a younger man. Michel had a soft face with blue eyes, outlined in red, so that from a distance they looked like little pink fish. Tila had a new admirer as well. Juan Ramirez was on the Argentine consular staff. He was blond and of heroic proportions, which were enhanced this evening by his gladiator costume.

The chamberlain struck his cane and announced, 'Aristide Spunt as Monsieur Beaucaire'. Aristide stood at the top of the steps, one hand bent outwards at his waist, while the other he rested lightly on his cane. With a disregard for era, matched only by the Hollywood movies of that time, the musicians commenced playing Chopin's 'Polonaise' and Aristide began a stately march down the stairs, twirling his cane in measure to the music. Tila, enchanted, awaited him with her hand outstretched, and, as Aristide bent to kiss it, the guests burst into applause.

Champagne was being passed, and as Mama reached for a glass, an Italian baronessa dressed as a Wild West dance hostess said to her, 'Carrissima Regina, if you must be so sacrilegious as to wear the habit of the sisterhood, don't defile it further by drinking.' The baronessa had wide tight features and eyes like leather knots. It was a face of total abnegation. Mama set the glass back on the tray. Just then a lean White Russian woman passed by. She was wearing chaste white drapery, and her Arethusa profile was a work of numismatic art.

'And who are you supposed to be?' the bitchy baronessa said. 'Sappho of Lesbos?'

The Russian smiled through her like a hot knife in ice. Mama was relieved to discover that the bearded lawyer, as John the Baptist, had a drink in one hand and a cigarette in the other. She was in the process of lighting one herself when she saw the baronessa fix an eye of fiery brimstone on her. Tila and the Argentine began the dancing. The German widow wrapped in a shawl with an immense comb in her hair glided past us in the arms of a Rumanian artist, who made quite a believable clochard. His lover, a doctor, costumed as geisha, was being pushed around the floor by a determined and rather busty page-boy, whom Mama identified for us as the doctor's wife. Chicho had discovered the coloratura, who was done up as a jazz baby. Aristide, in a corner by himself, was keeping up with every dance, doing his frenetic best to steal the show. Even Sascha had been paired off with a teen-age Becky Thatcher, whom Tila had invited expressly for him. Presently it seemed that everyone, except Mama, Papa, and of course me, was on the dance floor. Hoboo had joined the servants in the kitchen. We adjourned to one of the tables set up along the peripheries of the room. My parents discussed the guests and the merits of their dancing; commented with pleasure on Sascha, who was behaving, as they said, like a grown man; marvelled at Aristide's versatility as he switched from the tango to the fox-trot and now performed a rousing Black Bottom.

The Chinese minister and an American Council member joined our table, and Papa combined with them in the sort of male confrereship which totally excludes women. I noticed that, left to herself, Mama's eyes returned every so often to Chicho, who dutifully changed partners with each dance. Hoboo came to take me to the kitchen where she had arranged for me to eat before the guests.

As we made our way there, through the tables and the dancers, it seemed to me that Hoboo was pulling my hand with unaccustomed roughness. 'What's the matter?' I said, this time quite angrily. 'Foleign man allee same, allee time pahty. Chinaman no got lice, nevah mind, pahty, pahty!'

By now the geisha was being blissfully led across the floor in the arms of her clochard, while the page boy kept downing Canadian Club straight from the bottle. The Russian lesbian, hanging on to the torn halter of her chlamys, was being pursued up the steps by the dancehall baronessa. And the Hungarian jazz baby was doing things that were considered hackneyed even then, such as performing a bead-swinging Charleston on one of the tables, while a group of men led by Tila's Argentine, toasted her in champagne out of her slippers.

I was drowsing contentedly on Hoboo's lap when the door to the kitchen opened and Mama, her coif flying in the draught she had created and a cigarette sticking from her lips like a fuse, burst in.

'Come on,' she said to Hoboo, 'we're going home.'

Tila came in, 'What did you do to Chicho?'

'None of your business,' Mama said, turning towards Hoboo and me. Then Chicho, his face lined with distress, came up to us. He was dabbing his hand with a ridiculous scrap of lace, one of Tila's hankies no doubt. I saw a round neat hole, like the burn of a cigarette in cloth, on the back of his hand.

'*Poupa,*' he implored.

Mama swung around and shook a fist under his nose. '*Mascalzone!* If you ever dare to lay a hand on me again under the same roof as my husband, I'll burn it off.'

Tila hurried after Mama, Hoboo, and me out of the kitchen. 'Regina,' she said, 'did Maximilian see?'

Mama's huffiness subsided at once. She smoothed Tila's head; it was almost a benediction. Then she smiled and said, 'Of course not, you think I'm *meshuggena*?'

23

DURING the months that followed, Chico began to earn his niche in the family. Because Sascha was so fond of anything connected with the military, Chico secured for him the type of spoils which delighted our brother: medals, naval ribbons, sailors' caps, and even souvenir cuff links of enamel and gold made expressly for the officers. And, while he encouraged Aristide to choose clothes more suitable for a boy about to enter school and succeeded in getting him to abandon his velvets for blazers and flannel shorts, he also spent considerable time in the second hallway, where Aristide's dollhouse had been set up. Together they would move furniture or change the manikins about.

Whenever Chicho called at the apartment, it was always Papa whom he asked to see, and if Papa was available, Chicho would seem genuinely delighted. They would spend long hours over the chess board or at bezique, or they might ponder the political rivalry between the Red-influenced Committee in Hankow and Chiang's government in Nanking, both of which claimed legitimacy. Conversations on this topic, begun desultorily in the drawing-room, might continue through aperitifs and resume at dinner. Although my brothers and I were spared these table discussions, whereas Mama was obliged to endure them, we would often be present at the conclusions reached over brandy snifters in the smoking-room.

I recall one such night in June. It had rained steadily for a week, and Mama, twanging idly on her mandolin, had in a fit of mild pique insisted that the verandah doors be thrown open. Papa and Chicho, in their usual friendly but no less heated ferment over politics, were oblivious to the rain splashing into the room. Chicho argued that, true, Britain had the month before recalled its representative, terminating relations with Hankow; and granted that Chiang, bolstered by recognition of the foreign powers, had begun his drive on the north; nevertheless, he maintained that Hankow would not readily give up its claims. Witness the fact that, albeit by separate routes, their armies along with Chiang's had funnelled into the province of Honan, routing the northerners. But Papa argued that at this very moment Chiang's armies were marching into Shantung Province and a Nationalist victory seemed assured. This, he wagered Chicho, would mark the end of Hankow.

It had seemed to all of us listening in on these nightly exchanges that Papa had won his bet, when the next evening Chico arrived with the news that Chiang's men had been repulsed at Tsinan, the capital of Shantung, by a great force of Japanese troops. The Japanese claimed that they were preventing a recurrence of the Nanking Outrage, but both Chicho and Papa agreed that Japan's concern was solely for the protection of her own substantial interests in the north. Thus, the First Northern Expedition, as it was called, failed.

Chicho was now of the opinion that unless some sort of unity was established between Hankow and Nanking, the cause against the north would be doomed. His conviction was proved correct that July, when, at Nanking's urging, Hankow expelled its Russian advisers and in return Chiang resigned his presidency the following month. A single new body of the Kuomintang was formed in Nanking, called the September Government.

For all the latitude Chicho permitted himself when it came to general matters in his discussions with Papa, he had a developed sense of palace politics and was careful to do homage to Papa's domestic suzerainty. He wisely supported all Papa's final decisions despite the fact that he might have earlier interceded on someone's behalf. Like the time when Mama thought it would be a good idea to condition Aristide by sending him first to the parochial Sainte Jeanne D'Arc School. But Papa would have none of it, maintaining that Aristide must sooner or later learn to contend with the rougher aspects of a boy's world. So that autumn Aristide began going with Sascha to the Richard Ashbury. He ran afoul the very first day. As he stepped out of the car, one of a group of boys from his class noticed something delicate and frothy showing from under his short flannel pants. The boy pulled at it for inspection and discovered that it was the lace trimming of Aristide's underwear.

One of the traditions of the English public school system was the new boy's ragging. Although raggings were by and large a function of the older boys, something about Aristide kindled his classmates to prematurity. During playtime, the boys gathered around him in a circle, teasing and shoving. It was a strict rule that only one boy at a time could approach the candidate. It had either not occurred to Sascha that Aristide might encounter this fate, or if it did, he probably thought it would do him good. At any rate he had neglected to apprise Aristide of the proper conduct for one who is being ragged, which was to choose a likely opponent and try to beat the tar out of him. Depending on how one acquitted himself during this initiation, he could come into leadership, acceptance, or rejection to the point of even being put in Coventry. Aristide suffered the mauling and punching in frozen horror, and then when he could no longer cope, he ran away. How different was the frayed sparrow who came home that evening from the fellow who had set out in his blue blazer with the school insignia, *Juncta in Uno*, alluding to the international flags, set in an emblem on his pocket.

When Mama criticized Sascha for letting this happen, he said, 'Everybody gets ragged, especially if they've got damned lace underwear on.'

Mama placed her hands on Aristide's shoulders and said, 'Listen, darling, the next time those hooligans try to touch you, remember what that great American president said, "Walk softly, but carry a big purse!"'

Aristide, of course, did not want to go back in spite of all kinds of rewards promised by Mama, but Papa said that he would not hear of such nonsense and Aristide returned the next day, wearing a one-piece union suit under his uniform. Somehow he managed to survive a second ragging, but then he had the problem of going to the bathroom. Until now Aristide's needs had been attended to by Hoboo. He managed to get to the school lavatory all right, but once there, became hopelessly entangled in the union suit, with disastrous results. Mama had thought that it might cheer him if Hoboo and I went to pick him up after school. We saw him trudging determinedly to the car, something in his walk reminiscent of an overburdened soldier. Following him were some of his classmates, pointing and screaming with laughter and some of them holding their noses. When he came close, I could see that his face was stained and barked from rubbing at the tears with his sleeve.

At the point where Aristide learned not to run from a ragging, even if it meant clawing and scratching, and became adept with the buttons on his underwear, he was confronted with the business of physical training and sports. The entire school was divided into game houses. As soon as a student was enrolled he was assigned to Lincoln, Clarence, Pembroke, or Nance. Each house had its own colours. The cream of the school's athletes participated in the major events, and it was of some moment when your house won a game. Since Aristide, who had been automatically assigned to a house— Pembroke, I think—was a million light-years away in age and ability from making the major teams, this was of no immediate concern. But on a class level it was another matter. It became increasingly distressing to always be the duffer, the last one picked for the cricket eleven, and at that with great resignation on the part of the team captain and the star players. But to Aristide this was nothing compared to the physical training sessions held three times weekly in the gym. Besides the fact that he could not perform with the slightest nimbleness, and the bars, rings, and tumbling represented for him the most acute torture, there was the matter of the showers. Before and after every session the boys were required to race through scythes of icy water which swept out at them from pipes along both walls. Perhaps Aristide responded from the beginning as he was expected to by being the slowest to undress and then hastily draping himself in a towel. It became a subsidiary game for the boys to wait, watch, and tease him until he ran into the showers, while others waited for him to come out, shouting with the unique and crotchy laughter of unrespecting males. Aristide's inability to 'play the game' bothered Sascha, who, in spite of his bulk, competed avidly.

'He's just a slacker,' Sascha complained to Mama.

'Listen,' Mama replied, 'give him time. Rome wasn't burnt in a day!'

Although at first I relished the thought of having Hoboo all to myself, I missed Aristide and would be waiting for him when he returned from school. In the difficulty of his adjustments, Aristide turned not so much to me as to his dollhouse. Immediately upon coming home, he would cast aside his books and race along to the second hall. He always paused for a moment when he saw the dollhouse standing beside the fireplace, as though it was some mirage which could not be relied on to be there. He would squat beside it and begin a systematic examination of each room and each figure. And Hoboo would have to call him several times to come for tea. He had strictly prohibited me from touching his dollhouse. When I was unable to resist, I would first stretch out and commit to memory every detail, the exact distances between the dolls, the degree at which an arm was raised, before ever touching one of them. It was not so much Aristide's anger I was afraid of incurring, but the fact that Sascha might uncover my interest in Aristide's dolls.

Except for the teacher's comment, 'Aristide is bright, but chats too much,' his Christmas report indicated that he had done exceptionally well and would be advanced a class the next term instead of the following summer. This could be attributed to the subjects, which were elementary, and the fact that prep teachers were all women. But in January, when he entered lower one and had to contend with schoolmasters, he was less fortunate. There was the Irishman who taught singing. Mr. Brodie's head was shaped like a pear standing on its stem. His hair, which seemed to bristle with an independent rage, reminded Aristide of a clipped yew hedge. Now Aristide's impressions of singing were of necessity formed by Tante Tila, and he found such airs as 'The Harp That Once Through Tara's Halls' and 'Drink to Me Only' punctuated by Mr. Brodie with nips taken from his hip flask, both doleful and unnecessarily graphic. Mr. Brodie did not follow the accepted routine of sending a recalcitrant boy to the headmaster for punishment, nor did he waste his voice in reprimand. All the teachers of the R.A.S. were hurlers to some degree, but Mr. Brodie was exclusively a hurler, and he would stop short in the middle of a note, fixing his boiling blue eyes at his victim, and throw whatever was handy. The first time Aristide, in the middle of 'Drink to Me Only', interposed a cascade of soprano fioritura, Mr. Brodie was halfway between a chord and a nip. The next thing Aristide heard was the whistle of the hip flask past his ear and the crash of glass as the bottle hit the window pane behind him. When Mr. Brodie saw what he had done, not to the window of course but to the flask, he went berserk and began hurling everything in sight. Big Ben happened on the scene in his custom of genteel espionage, poking his brown cereal face around the door. He saw the class being rained under the reams of sheet music, blackboard dusters, and chalk. As punishment Aristide was given five hundred lines whose message was 'I shall not trill in class'.

Mr. Hunter, who taught arithmetic, was another matter. He had recently been involved in a scandal with a Eurasian girl and her stepfather, with the uncomfortable result that the stepfather had shot at him. The foreign papers had carried the story, and the school board, to show itself progressive, had stood behind Hunter and the Eurasian girl whom he subsequently married and had welcomed him back, limp and all.

Mr. Hunter was a slicer and a basher. It doesn't take much talent to bash, and a number of the teachers including some of the women were pretty good at it. If you hit a boy just hard enough with a book, the results were usually effective and the margin for error was reduced enormously as compared to hurling. But to slice without resorting to crude language, to incise all the way to the bone in one verbal slash, was a fine art.

In order to estimate attendance before a national or religious holiday, other than one celebrated by the entire school, most of the teachers would ask the boys either to pass them a note or inform them on their way out whether or not they would be coming. According to Aristide, Mr. Hunter simplified matters in this manner: 'British boys please stand.' While among these there were naturally some who came from the British Isles, the majority were Eurasians who had either been born in Hongkong or whose fathers were British. There were also some boys from South Africa and the West Indies. Mr. Hunter would look over the lot with glittering appraisal. 'Well now,' he'd murmur, 'so many *British* boys to preserve the Empire.' Then, feigning sincere interest, he would ask each of the boys, concentrating particularly on the Eurasians and Africans, *exactly* what part of Great Britain he came from. Most of the lads mumbled a reply, but one, a Jamaican with the unfortunate name of Barley Butt, refused to answer.

'Come, come, Barley Butt,' Mr. Hunter pared away at him. 'Certainly there is a scrap of land *somewhere* which you can claim is forever a part of England?'

'Fuck you, sir,' said Barley Butt, who was seven years old.

Getting Barley expelled must have honed Mr. Hunter's edges considerably, and at his next opportunity, which was the Passover holiday, he asked all Jewish boys to stand. Now while Aristide might engage me with fantasies to cast doubt on our heritage, something obdurately atavistic prevented him from denying his religion at a public accounting. So because of Mr. Hunter, Aristide was forced to acquire the practice of self-declaration, that compulsive premium paid by most Jews for insurance against hurt. Aristide stood up and looked around at the half a dozen or so Jewish boys, who by this singling out became at once knotted into compatriots. He had known without being conscious of it that Isaac Tuttleman and Lazar Levy were Jews. But in spite of himself the very fair Manuel Mendoza from Seville and Peter Stone from Soho were a surprise to him. The Jewish boys standing had just the opposite effect of a holy ascension on the others, and as Aristide listened to whispered rumblings of disbelief and speculation, he began to feel uncomfortable.

Mr. Hunter called upon Peter Stone first. 'But didn't you stand up when I checked British boys for the Saint George's holiday?'

'Yes, sir,' Peter replied.

'Well, don't you find this ambivalence rather tiring?'

'Sir?'

'All this bobbing up and down; I mean shouldn't you decide?' Mr. Hunter said.

'Well, you might say it's been decided for me. I'm an English *Jew*,' Peter insisted.

Mr. Hunter asked Aristide and Lazar Levy if they knew that they were different Jews. Each said that he didn't. Mr. Hunter explained that Jews from Central Europe like Aristide were called *Ashkenazim* and that Jews like Levy from the near East, such as Iraq, were *Sephardim*. 'You might say,' said Mr. Hunter, 'there are white Jews and black Jews.' This was an absurd premise of course, shaped to Mr. Hunter's requirements. For he was certainly aware that the Jews of Spain and Italy, as well as those from the Arab countries, were *Sephardim*.

'Now, Spunt, given your choice, would you rather be a white or a black?'

Aristide looked at Lazar, who was watching him with a put-on smile, and he thought for a while; then he said, 'I like to be a *good* Jew.'

It could have been his own fears which prevented Aristide from fighting Mr. Hunter on more violent terms. I know that Sascha would not have tolerated abuse from either teachers or schoolmates. There was something total about Sascha which bespoke his capability of doing battle, and as a result he seldom had to. He approached a social illness with the same detached practicality as he would the extraction of a painful tooth or the removal of a festering appendix. He wasted no energy on either prophylactic or even therapeutic measures, but relied as a surgeon does on excision. In his own much-repeated words, he believed in 'having things out'. It was undoubtedly these instincts which prompted his action against Mr. Llewellyn, the one person from whom Aristide was developing security.

Mr. Llewellyn, the scoutmaster, taught nature study and in this capacity arranged field trips to the countryside, where the boys of Aristide's class could bird-watch and make plant cuttings. Aristide, who had not known a pheasant from a groundhog, suddenly developed a whole bag of orphan facts, which he scattered around to anyone at hand. It particularly pleased him to be able to inform Sascha on the migratory habits of indigenous birds.

'Did you know that spring snipe go north in the middle of May?' he asked.

'Of course,' said Sascha.

'Oh, yes, and when do they come back?'

'Next year?' Sascha said.

'They return at the end of August on their way south, and then they're called autumn snipe,' Aristide replied.

'I knew that, I just forgot.'

When Aristide explained to Mama and Papa that a pintail snipe weighed between four and five ounces, while a Gallinago Megola, a great spring, or Swinhoe could weigh up to half a pound, they were enchanted. But Sascha, contentious at this poaching on his preserves, said, 'You're so smart, how do you tell the difference?'

'Size for one thing, you fathead, and the tail feathers for another,' said Aristide.

I first saw Mr. Llewellyn on one of the occasions when I went to fetch my brothers. He was in his scoutmaster's uniform, and I thought that he was a student. He was walking Aristide to the car, one hand holding onto my brother's. They were in rapt unselfconscious conversation. When they reached the car, Aristide said I was his brother, and Mr. Llewellyn scooped me up in one blond and hairy arm and grinned at me as though he knew a secret I'd rather he didn't. I watched his face as he kept on talking to Aristide. He was not handsome in the popular style of Rod La Roque, and he lacked the stern-jawed and clear-eyed self-denial of William Hart. With his scout hat pushed back over silvery birch hair, his forehead jutted like a German helmet. Lozenge-shaped eyes, the vivid blue-green of water reflected on coloured tiles, seemed to play their lights on the tan of his face. He smelled of Prince Albert and Yardley and that recognizable and unifying scent which made me rest my head against his.

Until early summer, Aristide's interests were divided between his nature study field trips and now to a lesser degree his dollhouse. Just before school closed for the holidays, Aristide returned from an outing in a thoughtful mood. One of the boys had come across an Indian cuckoo and wounded it with his slingshot. Ever since we could remember, the resonant cry of the two double notes had meant the beginning of warm weather, and in September, when the skies were silent, you could expect it to get cooler. To foreigners the cuckoo's call sounded like a thirsty plea, 'One more bottle!' So we called it the bottle bird. Aristide told us that Mr. Llewellyn had been obliged to kill the wounded bird. He had then given the group a dissertation of his views on hunting.

'According to Mr. Llewellyn,' Aristide said, 'the only ones worth killing are sharks and men, because of all animals they are the ones who kill for other reasons than survival.' Having imparted what he most certainly now believed to be an unassailable truth, Aristide looked Sascha over appraisingly.

'Bosh!' said Sascha, who could scarcely wait for autumn to try out his Winchester on the pheasants which abounded in the countryside. 'There's something wrong with a Britisher and a *scout*master at that who doesn't like hunting.'

'Mr. Llewellyn is Welsh,' Aristide said, as though that should explain everything.

'Which means,' Sascha replied, 'all he likes to do when he's not mining for coal is sing, drink, and chase women.'

It was not until the next school term that we discovered just how wrong Sascha's estimation was.

24

ONCE during that summer of 1928, when I came into the kitchen on an errand for Mama, the servants were all talking and there were a lot of emphatic pronouncements and thumping of fists against palms. Hoboo told me that Chang Tso-lin, the tiger of Manchuria, was dead. As I look back on it, for certainly the name meant nothing to me at the time, I can understand the kitchen revelry. The Japanese, displeased with the manner in which he was handling their substantial interests in Manchuria, had placed a bomb under his train. The servants interpreted this as the much-needed breakthrough for Chiang Kai-shek. Now, with the north virtually leaderless and before the Japanese could install a new puppet, Chiang had seized control. The United States had recognized the Nanking government. Finally it seemed to be Chiang's hour.

The end of warfare and the cessation of strikes in the treaty ports caused a boom in commerce, and Papa's cotton business flourished. He had become a member of the Share Brokers Association and had turned his zeal for gambling to speculation in stocks. We saw little of him that summer, for when he was at home he spent most of his time at the ticker tape set up in the smoking-room, and when he wasn't watching the market, he was on the phone either buying or selling. He did so well that news of his gains spread through the city and he was constantly belaboured by friends for tips. Aunt Annie was among those who felt that she should be encompassed in Papa's good fortune. She came prepared to invest all her assets. The sum amounted to a hundred thousand dollars.

'But it's a gamble, Annie,' Papa protested. 'You could lose everything.'

'Have you lost? So what isn't a risk? Didn't I take the clops in the face from our father, he should rot in hell, when you ran away from Japan?' Papa had long since stopped correcting her on this lie, which she herself probably believed by now.

'Tell you what, Annie, I'll only agree to invest for you on condition that you let me guarantee your losses,' Papa said.

'Hah,' Aunt Annie replied predictably, 'if you make an offer like that it means you *know* you're going to be in clover.'

'In that case I will open an account in your name so that everything will be on the up and up,' Papa said.

'What do you mean up and up?' Annie asked.

'The Board of Governors require it, Annie; it's a technicality.'

'Listen,' she said, 'then I'll have papers to sign and authorizations. It will take time. Do we need headaches? Enough, put it in your account. I'm satisfied you'll not lose my money.'

And he didn't; by late summer he had doubled Annie's investment, and on his advice she let it ride.

The summers in Shanghai were so hot and humid that the wives and children of most foreign families vacationed in Japan or in the north of China. But this year, with the struggle for the north still going on, Papa thought it wisest for our family to stay put. For the adults there were the interminable rounds of garden parties. To them summer seemed to mean merely a change in attire, sheer dresses for the women and white monkey jackets, as they were called, for the men. But for us children the tar-melting heat in the city was wretchedly boring. The Public Gardens were too hot during the day, cinemas were not yet air-conditioned, and except for the *piscine* at the Cercle Sportif Français there was nothing to do. With its colonnaded terraces and sweeping view of bowling greens and tennis courts, its bars, grills, and ballrooms, the Cercle was by far the most popular social club in Shanghai. It was an international purlieu which, for the adults at least, served as a substitute vacation. Chicho, who had become as much a part of the family as Tila, tried to convince Papa that he should relax and join us there. 'Not only because I miss our chess games, but for your family's sake, for your health, Max,' he said. But Papa replied that this was an unparalleled opportunity and that once he'd made enough so that he was sure of his family's security, there would be plenty of time for recreation.

He encouraged Chicho's companionship and sponsored his membership in the club.

We were unself-conscious frolicking in the great enclosed pool and being attended to by Hoboo in the ladies' dressing-room. It was quite a different thing for Aristide and me from parading nude in the hostile male camp of the Y.M.C.A. where Sascha had taken us once earlier in the summer. But at the Cercle we had to compete for Chicho's attention with Sascha, who was forever urging him to abandon us for the tennis courts. Then Mama began to show up in the afternoons, and Chicho would escort her to the terrace.

Sometimes on Sundays Chicho would take the three of us to the racecourse, where we had a member's box. I recall one game he taught us. We each got a slip of paper with a number on it which we picked from a hat. As the winning horse was led back to its stall at the end of the race, whoever had the slip with the corresponding number won that many silver dollars, multiplied by the number on the slip. Somehow Aristide always seemed to hold the winning slip, usually in the higher numbers, and he would come waddling back home like a dwarf burro, his pockets stuffed and bulging.

Even with these diversions I could tell that Aristide was anxious to get back to school. He spent so much time fussing over his appearance that morning in September when school reassembled that Sascha threatened to leave without him. But when he returned he seemed crestfallen and went straight into the second hall to his toy house. He even declined an invitation from Chicho to go for a drive with Sascha and me. A day or so later I discovered what the problem was. With the autumn promotions he had found himself in upper one, where nature study classes had been reduced from weekly to bi-monthly sessions. Aristide would not see Mr. Llewellyn until the following Monday.

It was still warm, and Sascha manfully persisted in his swimming at the Y.M.C.A. At the close of the week he came home quite tight-lipped and firm of jaw, which always spelled trouble, but he did not tender any information and we had learned from experience not to probe when he was of this mind. We just dawdled at a safe distance from him in the hall, where he had posted himself to wait for Papa.

They were in the study together, Papa and Sascha, for a long time. Aristide tried to listen at the door, but when I looked at him questioningly, he gave me a Gallic shrug, implying that he knew as much as I did. Finally Sascha came out, leaving the door open. 'Papa wants you,' he said to Aristide. Papa must have been very absorbed by whatever it was that Sascha had told him, because he did not tell either of my brothers to shut the door. From where I stood I could clearly see him seated at his desk. He looked very old, his face white and sagging like a partly-filled flour sack. He seemed to be doing things with his mouth to make it stay up in a smile, but his lips were dark and flaccid, like the cut and flattened end of a rubber hose. Although he held his cigar with an air of detachment, much, I imagine, as he did in consummating an investment, almost an inch of ash trembled from its tip. He told Aristide to sit in the chair facing him, while Sascha stood behind Papa. Zee brought him a glass of water, and Papa swallowed some pills from his silver cylinder. 'Aristide, I don't want you to be frightened. But I want you to tell me the truth.' Aristide said nothing. He looked at Sascha.

'Don't be frightened,' Papa said again. 'You understand?'

'Yes.'

'You have a teacher, Mr. Llewellyn. Is that right?' Aristide nodded. 'And you like him very much.' Aristide nodded again.

'Has Mr. Llewellyn ever played with you?'

Aristide, who could be as calculatedly obtuse as Mama when the occasion warranted, shook his head negatively. 'Mr. Pringle plays with me,' he said.

'Mr. Pringle?' Papa said.

'He's lying—' Sascha began, but Papa raised a hand without turning. 'Go on, Aristide.'

Aristide put on a face of purely Chinese patience. 'Mr. Pringle is the games master,' Aristide explained.

'What about Mr. Llewellyn?' Papa said.

'He teaches nature study.'

'But does he, has he, ever *played* with you?' Papa asked.

'Aristide!' Sascha cut in. 'Tell Papa about Mr. Llewellyn touching you.'

'No—he never touched me!' Aristide cried.

'You better tell,' Sascha threatened.

'No! No! It's not true!' Aristide began to yell.

'Aristide,' Papa said gently, 'don't be afraid. Nobody is going to hurt you.'

'No!' Aristide cried.

'You see, the little bugger is trying to shield him,' Sascha said, pressing his hand on Papa's shoulder. Papa pulled away from his touch.

'I told you what I saw in the lockers, Llewellyn and the upper five student. I *know* what I saw,' Sascha said.

'Did anyone else see them? You realize, Sascha, it's your word against theirs. You would be asked for proof.'

'That's just what Big Ben said,' Sascha replied.

'Do you mean to tell me that you've already reported this?'

'Of course,' Sascha said. 'You don't want a man like Llewellyn free to go around ruining small boys, do you?'

'He never touched me!' Aristide screamed.

Mama had come in from the club, and seeing me cowered at the door of the smoking-room, she hurried in. 'What's the matter?' she asked.

'Your son,' Sascha said, pointing to Aristide, 'refuses to testify against that pederast!'

When Mama heard that Aristide had not been involved but that Sascha required testimony to substantiate his charge, she turned on Papa.

'How *dare* you do this to my child?' she cried.

'He's my child too, and I'm trying to protect him.'

'And this is how you protect? Putting ideas into his head, for God's sake.'

'If you spent more time with your children, I wouldn't have to,' Papa said.

Mama leaned against the door. 'You'll eat those words,' she said.

The circumstances under which Mr. Llewellyn left the school were never revealed. It was not known whether he had been dismissed or whether, upon being confronted with Sascha's accusation, he had resigned. All that Aristide knew or cared about was that he would never see the Welshman again, and he was desolate. Somehow the word got around school that Sascha had been instrumental in Mr. Llewellyn's termination. The boys were properly awed by this jurisdiction in reverse. Of necessity Sascha basked in the cool glow of their respect, for at home something had happened. Papa was more than ever involved in his transactions and Mama, genuinely put out with Sascha, was unwilling to forgive him. It might have been that she subconsciously blamed him for Papa's accusation. She tried doing the things she knew best to humour Aristide, but going shopping or for a drive with her no longer held the appeal it once had, and she was at a loss. Chicho, siding with Mama, was noticeably distant to Sascha; Aristide openly ignored our older brother and would not even reply when spoken to. I avoided these situations by simply hiding. If I heard Sascha in one room, I went to another. But if he found me and spoke, I replied.

As Christmas drew close, Aristide's war of mute disapproval began to get to Sascha. When Chicho set a date for only Aristide and me to attend a military presentation at the Italian Club, Sascha began trying to make up with Aristide. He was too shrewd to bribe openly, but knowing that Aristide was intrigued with films and such, he hinted that he had a fine new roll for his Pathé projector. It was a cold day, and Aristide was sitting on the floor playing with the figures in his toy house. In the fireplace a great fire crackled and blazed. Sascha, directing his remarks to me, said the film dealt with the early life of Napoleon and his meeting with Josephine. There was, he added, a marvellous scene at the temple, where the bewigged 'aristos', including de Beauharnais, were assembled awaiting execution. Not a nibble from Aristide. Sascha went on to describe the trials and the guillotine and mentioned names he hoped might incite a reaction from our brother: Saint-Just, Danton, Robespierre— nothing. Aristide yawned once. 'Who'd like to sit on the bus, while I drive?' Sascha said, making an unprecedented offer.

'Me,' I said.

'What about you, Aristide?' Sascha said.

Aristide turned his attention to one of the figures in the house. I saw a look of anger mounting in our older brother's face, but he controlled it. He lowered himself to the floor beside Aristide and attempted to sit cross-legged, but this proved too uncomfortable, so he raised himself to what turned out to be a kneeling position.

'Aristide, you must understand that what I did was for your own good. Really, when you are older you'll thank me.'

Aristide looked at Sascha, expressionless.

'Aristide, I did it because you're my brother, and I love you.' Sascha's face was close to Aristide's. My middle brother continued to stare at Sascha for a while, then he said very matter-of-factly, 'What do you want?'

Sascha hesitated. 'Well, you know how much I like parades and things like that—' Aristide did not help him, so Sascha went on, 'I just wonder why Chicho didn't invite me to the presentation at the Casa D'Italia. I mean, did you tell him not to invite me?' Sascha persisted. Aristide shook his head without replying. This incensed Sascha to the point that he grabbed Aristide's shoulders and shook them. 'You did, admit it!' he cried.

'Mama told him not to,' Aristide said calmly.

'I don't believe you,' Sascha said.

'I don't care,' Aristide replied.

Sascha was so enraged by now that, fearing what might happen, I scrambled to my feet and stood by the swinging doors so that I could escape if it became necessary. Sascha lumbered over to Aristide and seized the figure he was holding.

'Will you ask Chicho to invite me?' Aristide sat rigidly, watching the figure clenched in Sascha's fist. From where I stood, it looked like a bone in the paw of a huge animal. 'Will you? Or I'll throw it in the fire.' Sascha made a threatening motion towards the flames. Aristide swallowed, but still he said nothing. Sascha threw the figure into the fire. Aristide watched the doll as it caught fire, watched until jets of flame spurted from all over it, avidly consuming the cloth, the hair, and finally the body, which curled and writhed and blackened. As Sascha moved again, Aristide got on all fours and quickly selected a pair of the figures. He thrust them at Sascha. 'Here,' he said, 'they're yours, I want you to have them. I mean it, truly.'

'Give me the rest of them,' Sascha said.

'All?'

Sascha nodded.

Aristide quickly scooped up the remaining dolls, handing them to Sascha, two at a time. Then with his arms full of the figures, Sascha moved towards Aristide, towering over him like Kwanti, the god of war, about to make a sacrificial offering.

'Aristide,' he said, 'these are dolls.'

'No, no, they're *figures*,' Aristide said.

'They are dolls, and if you don't want me to burn them——'

'And they're *yours*, now.'

'One——'

'Just toys.'

'Two——'

173

'Please don't,' Aristide begged.

'Three.'

From the fireplace came a surprised roar of energy as the revitalized flames leaped to consume the tumbling figures. Then Sascha lifted his foot and brought it down on the spine of the house. There was the crashing of plaster and wood and the tinkle of miniature glass splintering, the fizzling crackle of the fire, and the thundering scream of Aristide's silence.

I waited by the doors, razed by the enormity of my own uselessness, until Sascha had gone. Then I went up to Aristide and I put my arms around him, and we held each other tightly. Until this moment, sobbing in concert had been our mutual identification. We had discovered its power to make things happen, and better yet, to make them stop. It was the only workable divinity we had ever known. Until now, when I realized that mine was a voice alone. I looked at Aristide and saw that his eyes, still fixed on the fire, were dry.

25

BY next spring, true to his credo of always buying on a rising market, Papa had pruned his portfolio and poured his capital into a couple of spectacular-performing stocks, thereby negating his second ethic of not putting all of one's eggs into the same basket. He believed so fervently in his choice that he was prepared to mortgage his cotton business for additional funds. To discourage this, Mama turned over her personal account to him. Nevertheless, he advised Aunt Annie, whose investment had swelled to five times its original amount, to cash in on her profits.

'They say at the exchange that you're loading up on Sino-European Radio,' Annie said.

Papa laughed. 'What a bunch of gasbags brokers are.'

'Well, are you?' Annie demanded. Papa admitted that he was.

'Why should I sell them if you are buying?' Annie said.

'Annie, it's my business to take risks. I have to make it for three young sons and my wife.'

174

'But you must believe that they're going up.'

'It's just a hunch, that's all,' Papa said.

'What do you think they can go to?'

'I don't know.'

'Ten? Fifteen? You must have some idea,' Annie persisted.

'They say there's a chance they'll jump to thirty,' Papa said.

'And you want me, your sister, to get out now?'

'It's just a gamble, Annie. They could go back down to a dollar. Maybe less.'

'I'm staying in,' his sister said.

'All right,' Papa agreed. 'But remember, I'm only guaranteeing your original capital. If you lose, don't cry.'

'Listen, Max,' Annie said, 'how you'll treat me, I should not lose sleep.'

Early that summer—it must have been some time in May, for I remember Ah-ching, splendid in his light uniform, coming to the apartment—Sun Yat-sen was to be interred in a mausoleum by the Purple Mountain. As part of the entourage Ah-ching was permitted to invite his relatives to the ceremonial services. This was a high honour, and of course Papa said that Lao Ni and Hoboo could go to Nanking for that week. We had lunched in the smoking-room where the ceiling lamp had already been replaced by the overhead fan. It was a muggy day, and the heat seemed to rise up from the river in pillows, pervading the apartment with dampness. Papa was at his ticker tape in fine spirits. Since spring Sino-European shares had risen steadily. They now stood at fifteen. Mama urged Papa to sell out.

'Why do you fret, Regina? I'll leave you a very rich widow.'

'Don't talk like that, Maximilian. I'm thinking of your health and the boys' future.'

Papa smiled at her. 'I promise, Regina, I'll leave you and each boy five million taels.'

Before Mama could reply, Papa doubled over, swinging his arms tightly across his chest and stomach, so that he looked strait-jacketed.

'Quick,' Mama said to Sascha. 'Help me get him into a chair.' Aristide was sent to fetch water.

'It's nothing,' Papa said. 'Just my indigestion.'

'Sure, sure,' Mama soothed, but she called Dr. Jarvis, and when he came out of the bedroom an hour or so later, he said, 'There's no immediate danger, Regina. I've advised Max to take a rest.'

'The children and I are planning to holiday in Tsingtao. Maybe you can make him come with us,' Mama said. The situation in the north had calmed down enough for foreigners to vacation there again.

Jarvis said that he would try to influence Papa and then he left. A few days after this, Papa said that he had decided to take a trip to the United States. Mama replied at once that we would go with him. But Papa said no, that the trip was to be a combination rest cure and business and that Dr. Jarvis had assured him that he was up to it. As part of his tapering-off plans, he intended to close his branches in New York and Washington. He figured that this would take no longer than a month. We were to proceed to Tsingtao as planned, and would meet him in Shanghai at the end of August.

I don't suppose it occurred to anyone that for a person who treated financial matters as casually as he did, Papa was being scrupulously thorough. In the days before his departure he spent hours closeted with his attorney and with the general manager of his cotton business, Mr. Isaacs, who was a naturalized American of Russian Jewish origin. He was a small man whose face was furrowed and crowded with worries like a tenement, but his eyes were tiny phials of bright liquid blue. He had a soft, almost oleaginous voice. Attending these conferences with Mr. Isaacs were two Chinese; one was Papa's purchasing agent, the other his chief accountant. Papa had grown to favour the idea that his children be present during his business dealings. Mr. Isaacs was left explicit instructions on all matters pertaining to Papa's investments. He was to notify Papa by wire of all price fluctuations. In regard to Sino-European Radio shares, if they went to twenty, he was at once to contact Mama, who had authorization to sell.

Early in June we saw Papa aboard the *President McKinley*. We were to leave a few days later, as soon as Hoboo returned from Nanking. As was their habit when we were travelling, our grandparents had agreed to stay in the apartment on the Bund. A day or so before our departure for Tsingtao, Aristide and I were sent to fetch them. Grandmama had their things packed in suitcases and cartons. Ivan, in an ugly mood, squawked and ruffled his feathers in his tall brass cage. Grandmama had made certain that her own house was immaculate. 'So you ken eat from de floor,' was the way she put it. The place smelled astringently of yellow soap and carnauba wax, and even the door knobs seemed to squeak with brightness. That she had no use for false modesty can be attested to by the fact that when Aristide commented on the crispness of her kitchen curtains, Grandmama replied, 'Hah! A *balabusta* like me, try to find anodder.'

Even though it was getting quite warm, Grandpapa still wore his cocoshnik and the erratically buttoned long johns. After tea Grandpapa went to dress, and we sat by Grandmama while she sewed. Aristide's curiosity was piqued by the characterless shape and substance of the apparel on which she was working.

'What is it?' he asked.

Grandmama lifted the garments, which were of the coarsest white fabric, like cheesecloth. There were what seemed to be a shirt, a pair of pantaloons, and a jacket somewhat like a tunic.

'*Tachrichim* for de *todt*, vod you call it?' she said.

'Shrouds?' suggested Aristide.

'Yoh, shrouds,' Grandmama said.

'Who are they for?'

Grandmama put her sewing aside and went to Ivan's cage, where she fussed over the bird, chattering with it in a private language.

'Who are they for?' Aristide repeated.

'Who dey for? For me,' Grandmama replied.

Aristide looked dubious.

'Sure,' Grandmama said. 'I show you.' She put her hand in the pocket of the tunic and brought out a dollar bill. 'Ven I go heaven, maybe I need car money.'

'But these have pants,' Aristide argued. 'Chinese women wear pants. I never saw a Jewish lady wearing pants.'

'Orright. Orright,' Grandmama conceded. She held up the tunic. 'You see, de *kittel* is for Grandpapa.'

Just then Grandpapa, looking resplendent, although he must have been sweltering in his black woollen coat with astrakhan collar, came into the room.

'Is he going to die?' Aristide asked in hushed and saddened cabal with Grandmama. Grandpapa spat three times rapidly, and Grandmama looked down the left side of her nose to dispel the evil eye.

'God fabbid,' she cried. 'He should live a hundred more goldene

177

years, but a good Jew must always be ready to go to the Lord. Any time.' She snapped her fingers. 'You onderstand?'

Aristide nodded, but he looked at me and even I could tell the *kittel* was much too big for Grandpapa.

Tila had planned to leave with us, but at the last moment she postponed her trip. For the first time since their friendship began, there was the slightest rift between Mama and Tila. While she could not explain it, Mama had taken a dislike to the Argentine diplomat with whom Tila had been dallying. When Mama learned that Ramirez supplied information to a local American scandal sheet, she felt her instincts had been justified and tried to warn Tila.

'Ouf,' Tila said. 'I don't believe it and I don't care anyway.'

'I'm only telling you to be careful, Tila,' Mama said.

'What about you and Chicho?' Tila had countered.

'What about us?'

'Don't try and pull wool over my eyes, Regina.'

'We are not having an affair, if that's what you mean.'

'Not even a tiny one, *très discrète*?' Tila measured an inch with her fingers.

'I'm not going to fight with you, Tila, but if Michel finds out about Ramirez he'll never marry you,' Mama said.

'Michel will never leave me; I have him in the palm of my hand,' Tila said. So we sailed for Tsingtao without her.

Americans said they thought of their Pacific coast when they came to Tsingtao, and the French said that with its tourmaline and lapis sea and golden sands it reminded them of the Côte d'Azur. But the British said nothing, preferring to water at Weihaiwei, the British-leased territory on the northern tip of the peninsula. Actually Tsingtao, which means green island, resembled her first foreign parents. From the hills of Iltis Huk, where pink, white, and yellow villas blossomed, down to one particular stretch of beach with its former Prince Heinrich Hotel, there was something stodgily German (*they* said Bavarian) about this city. Following the murder of two German missionaries in 1897, Kiaochow Bay, on which the port of Tsingtao rests, was leased to Germany for ninety-nine years. During the First World War, Japan defeated the German forces there and held it until the early twenties, when it was reluctantly returned to China. When you saw the Japanese civilians transacting business or watched as families consorted on the beach in their butterfly hues and listened to their tinkling invitational voices, it was hard to believe that their troops had stopped the Nationalist advance north the year before.

There was a smell to Tsingtao not quite like that of any other place. It was of foam and sand and the special air of mountains carried down perhaps from nearby Laoshan. In its essence was the suggestion of the very old East, of fraying ceremonial robes into which packets of herbs have been sewn, of buried offerings, oracular bones, and fossils. And always in the air was the cooling spray of salt mingled with the odour of a great abundance of fresh fish and some decaying ones. (The British who *did* come to the hotel made a blunt olfactory judgment. The smell, they said, came directly from the badly preserved great whale in the nearby aquarium.)

We had always stayed at the hotel on the eastern shore of the outer harbour, now called the Grand. The beach was also called that—if you can accept the idea of the Grand being grander than the Prince Heinrich; but that's the way it is in wars: names are always changed first. The building itself had an ornate wooden frame painted white, which stuck out in spires here and there, looking very starched and lacy, as though hands were lifting a wedding veil from beneath. There was a gloomy hall with round-topped marble tables and plush chairs and a big sanitary dining-room. In the mornings and evenings we ate on the terrace which crescented a shiny stone dance floor bordered with coloured glass slats under which were electric bulbs. There was always a slat or two missing and an embarrassed white bulb flickering in the gaps. Aristide and I would breakfast with Hoboo, so that we could get to the beach early. Soon Sascha was joining us on the terrace, and Aristide teased him about it. Entertainment was provided by a dozen or so chorus girls, coached in their routines by a roughly handsome Hungarian by the name of 'Joe' Farren. The girls rehearsed their numbers wearing swim suits and tap shoes with great bows on them. They did lots of arm movements, breast jiggling, and high kicks in chorus line, while Joe shouted his contempt at them. 'Camman, camman, you lazy cows, you drunk pigs!' Sometimes the girls sang in shrieky breathless discord accompanied with pointing gestures: '*You're* the cream in my co-o-o-ffee,' and '*Yes*, we have no bananas.' But they were a comely mixture of Russians, Eurasians, and Filipinos, and Sascha, watching them, at times was dazzled to the point where he was un-aware that the juice of the Chefoo pear he was munching was dribbling onto his chin, until Hoboo would slap a napkin at him. The girls all had admirers, mostly griffins who came up from Shanghai for their vacations. They were a gallant lot, who showered the girls with flowers and gifts, arriving in the morning to wait while they got through Farren's arduous coaching. Sascha, in his state of unreconciled puberty, looked on jealously as the girls went off with their suitors. After Mama had reassured herself that the dancers were husband-bent and not interested in Sascha, she warned Aristide to keep out of their way. 'I don't want you on that dance floor, making an arse of yourself, you understand?' But of course it was only a matter of days before Aristide was there, in his orange and black striped bathing suit, prancing, kicking, and shrilling with the rest. Farren didn't seem to mind, and the girls adored Aristide. They let him try on their costumes in the privacy of their dressing-rooms and shared their candy and even some confidences with him. Sascha kept his mouth shut for once, because he knew that Aristide was his avenue to the girls. But while they were pleasant to Sascha, he was too old to cuddle innocently and too young to cultivate seriously, so he remained in his walled-off estate of desire.

The sun and sea agreed with Mama, and she seemed to enjoy spending her time with us. She tried taking us for taxi drives, but the Shantungese drivers spun around the narrow mountain roads at too rapid a clip to suit her, and she screamed at them in what little she had mastered of Shanghai dialect—to no avail, since of course the drivers spoke only Mandarin. I remember one such occasion, when the driver swerved, missing a precipitous drop by a few feet. Mama made him stop by stamping on the floor of the car and open-ing the door. He must have thought she was crazy, but he let us out and we walked for hours in the heat until we came to flat roads, where we hailed a carriage. This was a means of conveyance Mama appreciated, for she never felt entirely at ease in a car, not even when Pao-shing was at the wheel. Carriages brought back her youth, and there was something totally alive about the way she held herself when seated in one. The horrible green bean flies with their iridescent bodies and bulging red eyes like stop signs, which pestered the ponies, the driver, and us, did not bother her, and she could be counted on to tell some uknown anecdote of her girlhood.

I liked the evening drives best when the carriage jogged along beach roads fenced in on one side by cypresses and on the other by stretches of sand and water. It was on one of these drives that Mama told us about the Moslem wedding she'd been to in Alexandria. I don't know what made her think of it, whether it was the northern pine tree on a distant promontory, white and bent by the wind like an anguished woman; perhaps it was the moon, determinedly virginal as it pried itself away from the horizon. Certainly it couldn't have been the bottle bird's single-minded refrain.

'It was to be a grand affair given at the palace of the khedive's mother. We got to Ramleh early, before *subh*, the prayer at dawn. Right away the bride is prepared for the Zeffet et Hammâm——'

'What's that?' Aristide asked.

'It's a procession to the baths.'

'Baths?'

'Yes, you know, like what we have, the Jewish *mikvah*,' Mama said.

Aristide was no more informed about Jewish ritual baths than he was about the Moslem traditions, but he let Mama continue.

'What a thing they make of that promenade. In front are musicians playing hautbois, banging on drums, and blowing horns. Next, the bride's relatives and attendants in pairs and after them many young girls. In a first-class wedding like this one the girls are not supposed to shriek from happiness, but I suppose it was too much for them and you could hear their *zaghârît* all the way along the beach to the Khedivial Baths. The bride walks alone very slowly, her face covered, of course. She is wrapped from foot to head in a richly coloured cashmere shawl. On her head is a small gold crown made of? how is it called, cardboard?'

Aristide looked disappointed. 'What about him, the husband?'

'Oh, she does not see him until the ceremony. Not until she is brought back to the palace.'

'You mean she didn't know who she was marrying?' Aristide asked.

'Oh, yes, she knew, but most of the time weddings are arranged by parents. It's not so different from our orthodox customs.'

'And then?' Aristide pursued.

'A simple ceremony and the reception. You have never seen such tables of delicacies in your life. No hard spirits, but wine like the Red Sea, and champagne too.'

'Was there a wedding cake?'

Mama shook her head. 'But every other kind of sweetmeat.'

But Aristide was not to be won over. 'It doesn't sound like much of a wedding to me. No wedding cake, no white gown and veil for the bride——'

'But she did. She had a white gown under the shawl, and when the photographers came she put on a long veil and a coronet of fresh orange blossoms.' Mama's eyes were closed, and she said, 'Strange, what I remember best is the smell of the orange blossoms.' Then smiling at us, she said, 'Have you ever smelled real fleurs d'oranger?'

Aristide and I sniffed deeply, but all that came to us was the resinous scent of pine, the cheek-brushing fragrance of cypresses, and the astringent smell of salt from the blown spray. And in the stillness by the beach the only sounds were the clop-clopping of the ponies and the silly repetitions of the bottle bird.

Tila arrived in July but did not stop at the hotel. Instead she had rented a bungalow on the German beach some considerable distance away. She did not come to visit us, and pretty soon the hotel was buzzing with reports about Tila and a young man with whom she'd been seen bathing in the nude. Aristide and I knew that the rumours were true, not about the nude bathing—we would have no way of knowing that—but that Ramirez was with Tila.

One day Mama had heard reports that the waves were fifteen feet high, and she forbade us to go in swimming. Hoboo was busy with ironing or some such duty, and Sascha was in the lobby pouring out his heart to one of the dancers, who was manicuring her nails and chewing gum, making loud snaps with it at intervals. Aristide and I hailed a carriage and set out to go swimming at the German beach. The waves came up like a wall of sheet glass, green and murderous, fragmenting into chips of water and bubbling surf when they crashed. The whole scheme seemed suddenly like a misadventure, but Aristide was determined to keep face and kept repeating, 'We'll go in if the next one is not so high. Does your life belt have enough air in it?' I was spared from finding out fortunately, because Tila came upon us waving that bangled arm like a flashing train signal. Aristide begged her not to reveal us to Mama, and Tila agreed on the condition that we return with her to her bunga-

low for a snack. We never got to see the inside of the place because
Tila brought a platter of roast goose and some muskmelon out onto
the porch. We were halfway through the goose, enjoying it immensely, for even the prospect of swimming had the effect of making
us ravenous, when a man's voice called from inside. It was a somno-
lent voice, the voice of an owner rather than a tenant, assured of its
own right to nakedness. And when Ramirez flung aside the curtains
to grin at us, that's just what he was—naked. I've no idea how long
Aristide, munching on a drumstick, would have continued to stare
back. But Tila quickly wrapped some of the melon for us to eat on
the way and peremptorily told us to go home.

Later that month, as we were sunbathing, Chicho appeared. He
was on leave and had decided to spend it in Tsingtao with us.
Instantly Mama put on her beach cape and that serene Madonna
smile, as though it was rather nice that he had come but that she
had in no way been party to the idea. Maybe she hadn't, but things
looked up from that moment. It had become rather boring for
Aristide and me just to sit around the beach and swim when the tide
was low enough to satisfy Mama. Chicho took us on expeditions.
We went to the Iltis Forts, hidden among the shrubberies and trees
which the Germans had planted early in the century, where Sascha
had a fine time examining the different-calibred guns now covered
with rust and mounted in turtleback turrets of concrete and steel.
And we explored the caves of red rock where German soldiers had
holed up in their resistance against the Japanese. Chicho translated
the less erotic graffiti carved on the walls and was able to evoke
from what had seemed to us a prehistoric past the image of
frightened youths, bolstering their courage by inscribing what might
very well have been their own memorials.

Unlike most Old China hands, who chose to disregard native
culture, Chicho had a genuine interest in the country, and he tried
to invest in Mama his keenness to make a journey to T'ai Shan, the
holy mountain, and to visit the burial place of Confucius at Küfow.
But Mama vetoed the idea of travelling to the interior of the province, her refusal based on fears of banditry, the recent political
uncertainty at the capital, and most of all, she said, because much
of the journey would have to be made in lightweight sedan chairs,
and, as she pointed out, she had had enough of those in the early
days of her marriage.

So instead he took us boys for long hikes—past fields of tall Kaoliang grain, down paths by steep ravines where pueraria clothed the slopes in a bewildering blue, and up mountains to breathtaking summits, where you could see the sharp peaks of the Pearl Mountains beyond Kiaochow Bay. Since these treks were far too strenuous for Mama, she became restless by herself, and so we had to become content with just going to the beach again.

About the beginning of August Tila came unexpectedly to see us. She kissed Mama and said hadn't they been foolish to squabble after all these years, and over a man who meant nothing to her. And of course Mama had been right: Ramirez was a loafer. I suppose that Mama would have felt pretty silly lecturing Tila, what with Chicho acting for all he was worth like the *pater familias*.

We had known from his letters that Papa had trimmed his stay in America, but he had insisted that we remain in Tsingtao as originally planned until the end of August. So, when in the middle of the month the hotel boy came running to the beach with the telegram which said simply, 'Come home', signed *M.*, Mama was concerned. Tila went back with her to the hotel at once. They booked passage for the following day, and Mama gave orders to Hoboo to start packing. That night, after we children had gone to bed, I could hear her and Chicho out on the verandah. I don't know whether it was the stuffiness of the mosquito net pitched over my bed like a tent or just the excitement of going home, but I could not sleep. There was something about this moment that I knew very well, like when you go somewhere that you have never been before and you know exactly what it will look like, or that feeling in a conversation where you know for *sure* what the next person will say. Is it prescience? Or was it that their voices, muted, sad, and final, recalled that other time in the past when we had to leave.

26

PAPA was waiting for us when the ship docked at the Hongkew wharf. We did not recognize him at first. His white duck suit hung so loosely that the slightest breeze caused it to fold, and I thought of a poplar I had seen one winter. A sheet from a nearby laundry line had blown onto the naked tree, causing the branches and twigs to poke through skeletally as though insisting on their right to live. On the way home in the car, Papa explained that he had been dieting rigorously for his health.

When the dishes had been cleared, Papa gave us our presents. Not very impressive gifts this time. Candy mostly, I remember. Louis Sherry chocolates in lavender and gold metal boxes. Mama made some comment about the shape of the containers. She had an aversion to anything even faintly resembling a casket. Papa lit a cigar and puffed on it, the way he always did when he was about to make a statement. A few quick short puffs until the tip glowed, then he said that he would like Sascha to come with him to the office that day. He felt it was time for Sascha to learn the workings of his business.

'But I've got two years more of school before I matriculate,' Sascha said.

'I know,' Papa replied, 'but I want you to start now. After school, weekends, all your spare time.'

'What's wrong, Maximilian?' Mama said.

Papa told her that while he had been in the States, Sino-European Radio had nosedived. It had gone up to seventeen, back to fifteen, twelve, ten, and then plummeted to its issuance price of one dollar per share.

'But didn't Isaacs let you know what was happening?' Mama asked.

'Only when they reached the dollar mark. He says that at first he was sure they would rise again. I suppose he panicked.'

'That *schlemiel*,' Mama said.

'We know that Isaacs is no brain,' Papa said, 'but what's wrong with me? Why didn't I keep after him for quotes? And why didn't I get out at a dollar; at least we'd have been even.'

'You are telling me it's less than a dollar?' Mama said. Papa explained that during the three-day voyage from Hongkong to Shanghai, the shares had dropped to twenty-five cents, which was where they stood at the moment.

'Oh, Maximilian.'

'After I've paid off Annie her hundred thousand, there won't be too much left,' Papa said.

'To hell with Annie. Let her take her loss, like you're taking yours.'

'If I can just hold on there's a chance that they'll go up again,' Papa said.

Sascha wanted to know what caused the drop. Papa conjectured that the vicissitudes of the Nationalist government might have been a factor. All through spring Chiang Kai-shek had been at war with various elements. There had been nagging flareups from Communists in eastern Kwantung, Hunan, and Kiangsi, and a struggle with Russia for control of the railways in northern Manchuria, aggravated by what became known as the Kwangsi incident. Three generals headquartered in Hankow quarrelled with Chiang over the question of national supervision of provincial resources. The generals insisted that disposition of monies in their regions should remain under their own control. To this end a campaign was started against Chiang in February which resulted in defeat of the Kwangsi faction in April. As Papa understood it, foreign backers of Sino-European Radio had grown increasingly uneasy. There had been talk of their withdrawing. And that, he assured Sascha, was enough to cause any stock to drop.

'But you say it may rise again,' Sascha said.

'If Chiang maintains his leadership, and by every indication he appears to.'

At that moment Aunt Annie brushed past Zee, who was attempting to announce her visit. She had just returned from Weihaiwei, and everything in her bearing, the way she clutched her black cotton lace shawl with one hand while the other dabbed at perspiration from her face, indicated that she knew about Sino-European.

'I want you to sell out,' she said to Papa.

'Annie, if I sell out now I'll be ruined,' Papa said.

'And if you don't, I'll be ruined,' Annie replied.

'You have nothing to worry about, Annie, your hundred thousand is guaranteed,' Papa said.

'My *what*?' Annie's window-pane eyes attached to the ribbon flashed at Papa.

'I promised that I would protect your investment,' Papa said very precisely, 'and I intend to honour that.'

'You guaranteed my losses,' Annie said, 'and figuring my profits

186

at fifteen to one, you owe me one million five hundred thousand dollars.'

'You're insane, Annie.'

'Did I tell you to wait until it reached twenty? No, that was your decision. The trouble with you is greed. That's what you are, a *chazzer*.'

'Annie, I told you to sell at five. I begged you to sell.'

'Yes, while you were buying. All right, all right. I'm not one to be an after three o'clock trader——'

'That's big of you, Annie.'

'Just give me what is due. You told me to sell at five. All right, so give me my five hundred thousand and I'll lose the million. I'll show you, Mr. Finance, who can be a sport.'

'If I sold out now and gave you what you ask, my wife and children would be penniless.'

'Why should they have half a million and I go begging?'

'It's ridiculous. Legally you are not entitled to one cent.' You could always tell when Papa was getting furious by the way the back of his neck turned red as his face got whiter.

'Oh, we are talking legal now, are we?' Annie said. 'Well you just try to back out of your commitment and see where you stand *legally*.'

'What do you mean by that?'

'If the board of governors ever found out that you used my money to speculate, you'd never transact another deal in the stock market.'

'You gave your endorsement; you begged me to do it for you,' Papa said.

'Where's your proof? Where is the separate account you should have opened for me? All I know is that I put my money into your hands for safekeeping and when I ask for it you tell me it's invested in your name. Squeeze out of that one, *wunderkind*.'

'Annie, you are a goddamn bitch,' Mama burst out.

'Don't you open your mouth to me. Better my brother should have married a Kiangsi Road whore than to have legalized you.'

'Annie!' Papa shouted.

'No,' Mama said, 'let her go on.'

'Don't you think I know about you and that Italian? The whole of Weihaiwei was laughing about Mrs. Maximilian and her naked bathing.'

'Oh, my God,' Mama cried, as though the idea of a large woman cavorting nude was more of an affront than this outright lie.

Annie went to the door. 'I'm sorry, Max, that you should have had to hear this from me, but one thing about your sisters—we may not have had style or spoken six languages, but we were always ladies——'

'Annie, get out!' Papa pounded his fist on the table.

But Mama wasn't through with Annie.

'If you were respectable, Annie, it's because you had no choice. What man in his right mind would ever drop his pants to you?'

Annie turned to Papa. 'Are you going to phone the order to sell or do I call the board of governors?'

'Go ahead and call them,' Papa said. Annie started towards the phone, but Mama beat her to it.

'Maximilian, please call Isaacs.'

'I'm not going to let her do this to us, Regina.'

'It's nothing, Maximilian. You will make another fortune, and you still have your cotton business. Please, I beg of you, call Isaacs.'

Papa phoned his office and said three words. 'Liquidate Sino-European.' He turned to Annie. 'You will receive your cheque. Now get out.'

After Annie had left, Papa asked Sascha to bring a chair to his ticker tape. It was one o'clock. By one-thirty Papa's sale showed its effect. Sino-European had dropped to ten cents a share.

'Maybe it's lucky you got out,' Mama said.

Papa's mouth twisted like tracks on a tank. 'That means nothing. Wait for the overcorrection; then we'll see if others believe in the stock. We'll see if my hunch was right.' The ticker was the only sound in the smoking-room as we all sat around and waited. At two o'clock it registered an increase up to thirty-five cents a share.

'Papa,' Sascha said, 'you promised to take me to the office today, remember?'

'I could have paid off Annie and still had a quarter of a million,' Papa said.

'Who knows what it would have done, Maximilian? Don't watch it any more, please. Take Sascha like you said,' Mama pleaded.

At closing Sino-European had reached a dollar. Papa stood up, leaning on his cane. 'Sascha, get my hat; it's time you learned how to run the cotton business.' He whirled suddenly and grabbed his chest.

'Maximilian, what is it?' Mama cried. Papa twisted and sank into his chair.

'Quick,' Mama said to Sascha. 'Run! Get Dr. Jarvis.'

Hoboo took Aristide and me out of the room, and we waited in the hall, where in a little while all the servants gathered. Jarvis arrived, and he and Sascha carried Papa to his bedroom. Sascha came out after a while, and his face was blotchy with tears.

'Papa wants to see you both,' he said.

I remember pulling back. I did not want to see Papa disabled. I had felt the same way on our return from Tsingtao when we had passed some ships which had sunk and only a few reminders of their former vigour, masts and funnels, stuck up out of the water. I had wept at seeing them, at their unwillingness to give up even after being submerged. I knew that Papa would be like that. But it was a tranquil scene in his bedroom, with Mama kneeling by his side while he stroked her hands.

Mama was saying, 'Maximilian, what Annie said about Chicho and me was not true.' Papa did not seem to hear and Mama repeated the remark adding, 'I want you to know there has been nothing between Chicho and me.'

It looked for a moment as though Papa had still not heard, then he said, 'Regina? Regina, it doesn't matter.'

'But Maximilian——'

'It doesn't matter, because I love you,' he said. Then his head fell back on the pillow.

Mama looked at Jarvis in alarm, but the doctor said, 'He's asleep.' So we left the room and Papa never spoke to us.

I woke up hardly able to breathe and wet with perspiration. It was dark in the room, and for a while my eyes could not focus beyond the musty-smelling tent of my mosquito net. I pulled up the weighted sides of it for air and saw that the spiral of punk with its tip glowing like silver was only half burned out. Aristide was still asleep but Hoboo was missing from her bed. All at once I was taken by that feeling of another presence in the room. I tried without moving my head to see beyond the netting. There was a dark shape with a pale almost glowing head standing by the dresser. I felt my throat tighten and crazily I thought of *Moloch Homovis*. But it was Grandpapa, dressed in a black suit, and when he saw that I was awake, he said, 'Come.' Aristide, hearing his voice, woke. 'Come,' Grandpapa repeated extending one hand to each.

'What is it, Grandpapa?' Aristide asked.

But Grandpapa did not answer, and we walked with him towards our parents' bedroom. All I could think of was that something had happened to Mama during the night. Papa was sick, but Papa had been sick many times. I was conditioned to that. The fact that Grandpapa, who never left his house, was here seemed to confirm my fears.

'Is Mama all right?'

'You come,' Grandpapa said, pulling at my hand.

The bedroom we had left early that evening in relative order was now crowded, hot, and filled with the sound of babbling. Papa still lay on his bed, his face the colour of ashes. The only sign that he was still alive was the rise and fall of his chest. All around him like a charmed amulet, stood a *minyan*, the required quorum of ten pious Jews, chanting in a protective wall of prayers. I had never seen men such as these, enveloped, it seemed, in uniform and total shabbiness. They were very old and each had a scraggly beard and the *payess*, side curls like corkscrews, and I thought of lithographs I had seen of Fagin when Papa had read to us from *Oliver Twist*. Each wore a *yarmulke* on his head and a *tallith* over his shoulders, and while I might have thought that they were reading from the open black books in their hands, their eyes were turned as one upon the ceiling, as if so many hard-boiled eggs were looking upwards. I looked up too, and when I saw nothing I searched for Mama. She was standing behind them, outside the circle, wearing only a nightgown, but Tila and Grandmama had their arms around her. Sascha stood just in front of her. At one side of the room Dr. Jarvis, gaunt and helpless, was seated. Hoboo came forward to take Aristide and me from Grandpapa.

The ring of men huddled closer around the bed as though to fend off any evil spirits which might try to invade and injure the dying one. They chanted in the strange gargling sound I knew to be Hebrew, but could not associate with being Jewish or, for that matter, with anything related to my family. In an attempt to counter the decree brought by the Messenger of Death, the *minyan* began to recite all of the twenty-two verses of the hundred and nineteenth Psalm. Since the verses are arranged in seriatim, each beginning with a Hebrew letter to form an acrostic, the old men rearranged the verses so that the formed acrostic became Papa's proper name, or the closest approximation to it. When it was obvious that Papa was not responding to this psalmomancy, the *minyan* conferred for a moment. Then one of them flipped open the Torah, searching at random for a passage which included the name of any of the three Patriarchs, Abraham, Isaac, or Jacob. It was with great excitement that the old man came upon the passage of Jacob, who, frightened at the prospect of meeting his brother Esau, wrestles with the angel who changed his name to Israel and thus helped him cheat death. The *minyan* must have considered the finding of this particular passage both propitious and significant of God's will, for they took up their chanting with renewed vigour. Surely now, the Angel of Death, whose warrant was made out in the name of Maximilian, would be confounded.

Papa sat up, his eyes wide open but his face twisted grotesquely to the left. The old men looked at each other for a second, then moved over to Papa, saying softly in Hebrew, 'Go! Since the Lord sends you. Go! And the Lord will be with you! The Lord God is with him and he will ascend.'

Mama wrenched herself away from Tila and Grandmama and broke through the ring of men. 'No!' she cried, flinging herself over Papa's body. 'No, Maximilian! Don't die.'

The old men stood back and intoned, 'Hear O Israel, the Lord our God, the Lord is One.' They did this seven times.

Sascha's face was hidden in the crook of his arm, but his body was shaking. Grandpapa guided him to the bed and said something in his ear, so Sascha very gently closed Papa's eyes. Then Grandmama came up. She untied a large handkerchief and took a piece of the wine glass that Papa had crushed with his foot on his wedding day, placing a fragment on each of his eyelids. When Mama saw this she began to sob and wail, and Aristide began to cry. Grandmama made a sign to Hoboo, who took Aristide and me from the room.

Hoboo woke us up still saying her rosary. It was mid-morning, and when she did not insist that we wash and brush our teeth, neither Aristide nor I made any comment. Soon Sascha came to take us to Mama. His eyes were very red and he sniffled rather showily, to let us know that he was controlling his grief. He warned us not to cry and that we must be little men and help Mama. Mama was all in black, barefoot and squatted on a mattress in the drawing-room. When she saw us she seemed to lose all control of her limbs and writhed around on the mattress, banging her feet against it and slamming her hands together. We ran to her, and Sascha said, 'Mama, please, your children are here.'

She sat up and gave a terrible sobbing wail. Then she spread her arms and drew Aristide and me within them to her breast, hugging us tightly, tightly, as she rocked and swayed and wailed in a manner which I had never witnessed.

'He's dead. Your father is dead,' she said over and over again until Aristide and I were crying unrestrainedly, but Grandpapa said, 'Tcha! Tcha! God does not like too much wailing. You have three sons. Don't tempt Him!'

'He was so good,' Mama cried. 'Why? Why didn't He take me?'

Grandmama came into the room. She had been pouring out all the water in the house, and she was carrying an empty vase. She had overheard Mama's outburst, and her glance travelled quickly to the mirrors to see that they were properly covered so that the soul of the dead might not glimpse at the living reflected in them and take them with it. To further forestall the evil eye, she took the precaution of looking down the left side of her nose before she said, 'If God would have wanted you, He would have taken you. Don't give yourself an *ayin harah*!'

Grandpapa told Sascha to see if the old men who had been conducting the rites of washing and purification of Papa's body were done.

When we got to the bedroom Papa's body was resting on the floor, feet towards the door in front of the bed. A single candle flickered at the back of his head, and a black velvet cape lined in ermine, which I recognized at once as Mama's, served to cover his body from just below the chest. When we got close I saw that his skin had turned the greenish colour of fuller's earth and that although his chin had been bound with strips of cloth, his mouth was still twisted, as though leering, to the left side of his face. He was wearing a *kittel*, just like the one Grandmama had been working on—or was it the same one?

The old men nodded as we each went up to Papa's body. Mama,

sobbing softly, was supported by her parents. Then one of the men came up to Mama with a knife in his hand. I got frightened and began to make a noise, but Grandmama hushed me.

'It's notting, he make a *Kreah* so Papa can go to heaven.' The man made a cut at the right of the neckline of Mama's dress, then he ripped it about four inches, intoning at the same time in Hebrew, 'Blessed art thou, O Lord our God, King of the Universe, Righteous Judge.' He then made a similar cut on the left side of Sascha's suit and repeated the benediction. Then Mama brought Aristide and me to the man, and we submitted to the *Kreah* and received the blessing.

So that no defilement can come to the body before its resurrection and so that the soul can do no mischief to the living, the Jews bury their dead as soon as possible. Since he had died on a Saturday, Papa's funeral was set for the next day. At once everything became attuned to the machines of death. Rack upon rack of Mama's clothes were sent to the dyers, among them the chrome yellow she had worn on our return—a dress of life, which seemed, as it dangled and swayed from its hanger, almost to protest. The casket manufacturer's representative came, pale and hushed by force of habit, and assured Mama that the best would be done for Papa. Mama ordered a fine metal coffin, overriding Grandpapa's insistence that it be of unpainted pine to show the humility of the deceased. Mama argued that, since Shanghai was built on water, she wanted one that would resist decay as long as possible. To which Grandpapa replied, 'All of life ends in worms and maggots.' But Mama got her way. Nor was she keen for Aristide and me to attend the funeral. This time Grandpapa insisted. 'For what does a man beget sons?' he asked.

Since all Jewish services require that the head be covered to show proper reverence, early on the morning of the funeral Sascha distributed Papa's headgear to us. Our own hats, he said, were not suitable, sailor hats with ribbons being too frivolous and pith helmets out of place. Besides, what would do Papa more honour than for each of his sons to wear one of his hats? For himself Sascha had chosen a Texan-style Stetson that none of us had seen before. Certainly it was not a hat that Papa had ever worn; it might possibly have been a prize of some sort. Since Sascha knew that I shared his enthusiasm for Tom Mix and loved it when Papa had read a Zane

Grey yarn, I hoped that he would let me have the Stetson, but I should have known better. There were some panamas, a homburg or two, and a black bowler. After trying on the panamas and hearing Sascha's verdict that he looked like Arnold Rothstein, Aristide chose a homburg. That left me with the bowler. Because we could not see our reflections in the covered-up mirrors, we had only the others' expressions to tell us what we looked like. Although he was clearly making an effort to control himself, Sascha burst out laughing. 'Three Jewish midgets,' he said. Whereupon Aristide hooked his thumbs into the lapels of his jacket and twaddled the rest of his fingers while he performed the steps of a nimble *fraylach*. In the midst of the hilarity Sascha stopped short. 'How can we—how can we laugh, when poor Papa is dead?' he said. At once I began to cry and Aristide stopped dancing.

From behind the folds of her cypress veiling Mama did not seem to notice anything out of order in our appearance. She just wanted to be sure that we were together and ready to leave.

'Your heads are covered, that's good,' she said. But Tila, who had come to escort her, pushed aside her veil as though she couldn't believe her eyes.

I remember the long ride to the Jewish cemetery on Baikal Road in the endless cortège. And I can still recollect the crowds of strangers, so many uniforms among them, gathered by the grave-side. When it was time for each of the relatives to throw a handful of earth on the coffin, Tila and Grandmama helped Mama to the open grave. Grandpapa came to lead my brothers and me to the pit, and when he noticed our absurd hats, his mouth dropped open. Just as he was about to say something, there was a loud disturbance from the opposite side. Aunt Annie, wearing a crêpe veil almost twice as long as Mama's, pushed to the front of the mourners and sank heavily to her knees. While she had resisted the *Kreah* for her sister Rose, she now bared the neckline of her dress for the rabbi to cut and without waiting for him to make the necessary tear, ripped it herself almost to the waist. Then she swayed back and forth, wailing at the top of her voice.

'Oh, my poor brother. He was so good. So young. Why did it have to be him? Why didn't God take me?'

The rabbi who had come to her assistance was momentarily speechless, then he said, 'God moves in strange ways.'

Mama had lifted the veil from her face to see what the fuss was about. When she saw Annie prostrating herself, she said, 'Get that hypocrite out of here or I'll push her in myself.'

The rabbi motioned to some of the *minyan*, and Aunt Annie was led away protesting, burbling last farewells and drawing out her exit to its fullest possibilities.

The rabbi made the supplication, *El Moleh Rachmin*, which he followed with a psalm. All that was left of the service was for the closest of male kin to recite the prayer of sanctification, the *Kaddish*. This, we discovered, entailed the rabbi's announcing the name of each of us in Hebrew. We had never heard our names in Hebrew. Grandpapa pushed Sascha forwards. The rabbi sang out Sascha's given names, which, since they were Alexander Douglas, came out as 'Sandor Duvit'. Then, telling Sascha to repeat after him, he began intoning the Aramaic words, '*Yis-gad-dal v'yis-kad-dash sh'meh rabbo*', and Sascha, red-faced and sweating under his Stetson, attempted to repeat the lines of prayer. All the while Grandpapa, who stood close by him, kept nudging Sascha to bend and sway, for every bone must show its respect to God. 'Bent,' he kept saying, 'bent, bent!'

Next it was Aristide's turn, and he walked with considerable poise for a boy of eight who couldn't see without tilting back his head since his homburg was well below his eyes. He stumbled once, which drew a gasp from the crowd, but picked himself up quickly and gave a great reassuring smile to his audience as he groped his way blindly towards the *minyan*. The rabbi was about to intone Aristide's name. Then he stared at the paper on which it was written. He handed the paper to one of the old men, who stared, shrugged, and threw his hands out helplessly. The note passed from the hands of one man to another, all of whom shrugged, splayed their fingers, and murmured in Yiddish, 'Aristide, *vus is dus? A nomen?*' The paper was finally handed back to the rabbi, who cleared his throat weakly and sang out in very positive tones, 'Aristi-i-i-i-de.'

When my second brother had done the shaking and bending prompted by Grandpapa, it was time for my solo. To forestall any further mortification to our family, Grandpapa swept me up in a sudden strong armful so that I had to clutch my bowler with both hands to prevent it from falling off. The rabbi had no trouble with

195

my name, none at all, and I heard 'Gershon Chaya' ring out over the assembly. It was too much for me, and to my eternal embarrassment I could not repeat one word of the *Kaddish*.

When we got home Grandpapa wanted to thrash me. But Mama said, 'For God's sake, what does he know, Papa? He's only a baby.'

Grandpapa's reply was that babies must grow to be men, and to do so, they must begin by honouring their father. To emphasize his intent, he picked up Papa's fruitwood cane and brandished it above his shoulders.

'Put that down,' Mama said. 'It belonged to their father.'

27

GRANDPAPA left before Tila and the rabbi returned from the cemetery. He had taken the implication of Mama's remark as she meant it, that he was not to equate Papa's death with the reemergence of his own control. Before departing, Grandpapa had made some nasty Yiddish maledictions tailored to filial disobedience and in which were enfolded guaranteed results of doom. Mama wept and finally Grandmama had shooed him out. Grandmama had prepared the *seudat havrach*, the mourners' ritual first meal consisting of hard-boiled eggs and bread. But Tila brought a hamper containing pheasants in aspic and a wonderful *pashtet* of calves' liver.

When she saw that Mama had returned to the mattress on the floor, she declared quite within earshot of the rabbi and Grandmama that the idea of Mama sitting *shivah*, the seven days of deepest mourning when the bereaved, according to tradition, sit on stools or low boxes, was preposterous. She reminded Mama that when Rose had died, Papa and Uncle Jeremiah had tried to sit *shivah*, but being contrary to their real and personal feelings of loss, the archaic tradition had embarrassed them to laughter and they had discontinued it.

'You're no hypocrite, Regina. Why do it?'

'Tcha!' Grandmama said, 'she must sit for her *mon*. You vant he should go *gehinnom*?'

'She's right,' Mama said firmly. 'Maximilian was a fine man but not a religious one. Now I want to be sure he goes to the best place. So if I sit and do everything right maybe he'll go to heaven.'

'Ouf,' Tila said, 'if there *is* a heaven, they'll be begging for him.'

'Just the same,' Mama said, 'I don't want him to get stuck at, what do you call it, purgative, on my account.'

The rabbi who had come primarily to console the family said that there was no doubt in his mind that Papa would ascend directly. He made it sound somehow like the journey was a bus route and Papa was on an express. The rabbi left after promising to arrange for the *minyan* to come to the house during *Shloshim*, the thirty days of deep mourning following death.

The next day the shabby old men trooped into the apartment, where they headquartered in the smoking-room. Aristide and I watched from the hall while they chanted their prayers, ending each verse with *omane*. Sascha joined them there to recite the *Kaddish*. Although, as sons, Aristide and I were expected to say the prayer for our father as well, we were exempted because of our youth, Mama said. But I think that the way we had behaved at the cemetery had something to do with her decision.

According to orthodox dictates the *shivah* period is broken down to three days for weeping and the remainder for general and more restrained mourning. Whether it was the continued presence of the old Jews who shuffled in every day and their lachrymal incantations, or the sight of Sascha's honest Celtic face somehow corrupted by his unkempt appearance and stubby beard growth, whether it was a deeply realized sense of loss for Papa, or the feeling that in her shoe-less and dishevelled state she was being dewomanized, grief was contained in Mama as if it was a fluid to pour and she merely a lipped human pitcher. Aristide and I seemed only to provide very temporary surcease, and Grandmama began to worry. She urged Grandpapa to go to his daughter. I was with her when Grandmama made a special trip in the car to fetch him.

Grandpapa, in his usual dishabille, was seated at the kitchen table. He made a great show of reading from a slender volume, which, when we approached him, I could see was written in both Hebrew and English and titled the *Book of Life*. The fact that he could read and write not just in Russian and Hebrew but in English as well served usefully when he wanted to intimidate Grandmama. While she pleaded with him to visit their daughter, Grandpapa concentrated on the lines of his book, following them pointer fashion with his index finger and flipping the pages from right to left so fast that he really could not have been reading. Finally he closed the book and placed it reverently in front of him. By then Grandmama was reduced to the most humble of supplicants.

'Abram, she's your own flesh and blood. Forgive her and console her in this sorrow,' Grandmama said in Yiddish.

'When she learns that a child owes its spiritual existence to God but its entire physical being to its parents, that's when I'll see her. Tell her I don't say this, the rabbis do; and whose word do they preach? God's, that's who.'

Grandmama cupped her chin, her fingers resting across her lips as though to censor what she really felt like saying. Grandpapa stared in front of him obdurately. The judgment had been made. There was nothing more to be said as far as he was concerned. We drove directly to the synagogue, and the rabbi agreed to come at once.

Mama sat in the darkened room on the edge of her mattress. Sascha was supposed to be sitting with her, but already he was in an armchair reading a *Chum's Annual*. And Aristide, with a large tortoiseshell comb, was trying to arrange Mama's hair.

The rabbi chided Mama gently and said the usual rabbinical things like 'the soul of man inhabits a tabernacle of clay, my child'. Mama responded to these maxims with the usual stubbornness of the bereaved, as if consolation had to make sense.

'You speak of the Lord's justice. Where was a better man than Maximilian?'

In reply the rabbi quoted Job, saying, 'What, shall we receive good at the hand of God and shall we not receive evil? Is not the hope that your husband is enjoying rewards in heaven good?'

'Not for *me*,' Mama said.

'It is His will; we are His vessels,' and he quoted Job again: 'Hast thou not poured me out as milk and curdled me as cheese?'

Naturally Mama could take scant comfort from imagining these processes, and she said as much. The rabbi's parchment face creased like a much-folded document, and he nodded and smiled as if he were thinking that argument, inimical as it is to faith, represented at least the human will. He said, 'Sit *shivah* only if you want to, my child.'

198

But Mama was still on the mattress the next day when Chicho came to visit. He had just returned from Tsingtao and upon hearing about Papa had come at once. Mama had given instructions that no one but the family or close Jewish friends were to see her during this time. It was truly as Aunt Annie had put it, that only in birth and death were we Jews, and as such it became something which required the maximum of ourselves. With no religious force of habit there was no spiritual complacency. It was a matter of being genetically Jewish, of conscience and feelings and taste, perhaps even logic, but it was not a matter of faith. The public sharing of these rites was inconceivable. They were at once far too interior and too remote.

Chicho could not know this, naturally, and I doubt if it would have stopped him anyway. He pushed past Zee and went in search of Mama. I had been dozing in the wing chair and was awakened by Mama's strange cry when Chicho came into the drawing-room. It was as though she had been caught in a private ablution. Then her hands went to her face and her hair, and in a smoothing gesture up her bare legs, as though she were straightening hose. She looked from one covered mirror to the other in a vain hope of confirming the wish that she was somewhat presentable. Chicho fell on his knees and kissed her hands. When he looked up, his face was tightened and his eyes were full of tears. '*Pauvera, pauvera* Regina,' he said.

Mama looked away. '*Per favore*, Chicho, *vai e non rittorno piu.*'

Chicho looked astonished. '*Ma perche?*'

'*Perche son tutti dui disonorevole.*'

Evidently Chicho did not think they had behaved dishonestly, and the fact that he at once placed his head in Mama's lap and began to stroke her legs and speak to her endearingly would incline me to believe that if he felt any culpability it was overwhelmed by his love. But Mama pulled herself away and her voice became very harsh. '*Vai! Vai al diavolo!*' she cried. Then she burst into tears and covered her face with her hands sobbing, '*Disonorevole! Disonorevole!*'

Chicho got to his feet in the clumsy manner of a man with erotic ambitions finding himself the target of ridicule. He made a last gentle gesture towards Mama, but she screamed '*Vai!*' so loudly that the mirror behind the piano trembled its coverings off and the whole scene was reflected guiltily back to them.

Aunt Annie came on the seventh day. As a means of diversion Aristide and I had taken to rushing to the front door whenever the bell rang. We had been told by Mama that under no circumstances were we ever to speak to Aunt Annie. Now as Aristide flung the door open there she stood, buttressed by two women friends as if to imply that by only the greatest measure of support had she managed to come at all. Her eyes were closed, and when Aristide, who was standing frozen, said nothing, she blinked them and said, 'Well, get out of the way and let me in.' But Grandmama had come out to see who it was.

'Aha!' she cried, 'der gonif.' Of course she knew about Annie's coercion.

'I've come to see my brother's widow and his children,' Aunt Annie said.

'I thought maybe you came to return the money you stole from them,' Grandmama replied in Yiddish.

'Are you going to let me in?' Aunt Annie said, very British.

'Ova mine ded boddy,' Grandmama replied. Then she wished aloud that Aunt Annie would get cholera and spend her every ill-gotten cent on doctors. She prayed that a plague should strike her father's head (it didn't faze Grandmama in the least that our paternal grandfather had been dead for years) and that she, Annie, should burn in hell. But before all that, she should have a black year. Grandmama was most impressive during this rhetoric. The wattles of her neck shook with rage and her voice rose until it became a shrill scream. Aristide loved every second of this, and he nodded with each imprecation. When Grandmama had finished, Aristide ran in front of her.

'Yes,' he cried. 'A black year, a schvarz, schvarz, schvarz yur!' He slammed the door in Aunt Annie's face and turned triumphantly to Grandmama.

After shivah, Mama made an abrupt decision to terminate the orthodox ceremonies. The minyan was dispensed with, and Sascha no longer had to recite the Kaddish daily and was allowed to bathe and shave. I don't really know what prompted the change, for the thirty days of mourning to follow, while not as intensely rigid, still required prayers and the son's daily devotion. No entertainment was to be enjoyed, no music, no business transactions. All of these were simple enough for Mama to abide by with the exception of the last.

Shortly after, Papa's will was read. He had left everything to Mama, and Mr. Isaacs came weighted down with report files. While we were quite low in liquid assets, there were realty and utility shares which brought in a substantial dividend and Papa's cotton business which fluctuated between profit and loss months. Mr. Isaacs pledged his continued loyalty to Mama, citing as an example the fact that he had lost his American citizenship so that Papa might make this last journey to the United States. They both could not leave Shanghai at the same time, and, according to the naturalization laws, Mr. Isaacs was obliged to reestablish residence in the United States every five years. While Mama thanked him profoundly she did not remind him of the occasion when his son, whom Papa had employed as a favour to him, had looted the office safe of ten thousand dollars and Papa had dismissed the incident, refusing to press charges.

There were many callers during this period, so many in fact that the servants were kept in a dither preparing and serving refreshments or meals. While most of these visits were in the spirit of condolence, not all were so well intentioned. A number of strangers appeared with claims that Papa had borrowed sums of money, or that he had lost such and thus amount in gambling debts. At first Mama blindly wrote cheques honouring the demands, until her attorney counselled her to pay nothing unsubstantiated with Papa's signature.

From Dr. Jarvis we learned at last the nature of Papa's illness. The high blood pressure which he had suffered for a long time had advanced to malignant hypertension. In the last year or so he had become increasingly beset by stomach disorders. When the pains associated with these became severe, Jarvis had suspected abdominal carcinoma. The real purpose of Papa's journey to the States had been to undergo an exploratory operation, but upon arriving there his condition had deteriorated to such an extent that surgery would most certainly have proved fatal. This was of course the reason Papa had cut his trip short. Ironically, Papa was spared the lingering agony of terminal cancer. His death had been caused by a stroke.

He had made Jarvis conceal the gravity of his illness from Mama. We were all in the smoking-room as Jarvis explained the details. He was obviously still very distressed over the loss of his friend, and he clasped his great fronds of hands which crackled when he twisted them.

'Such a fine fellow, Regina, and to go at forty-five, so very young.'

Even though we were in the middle of *Shloshim* when the autumn term began, Mama thought it best that Sascha and Aristide return to school. Since I was nearly six, she decided to send me along with them. My only equipment for school life was the fleeting glimpses I had had as a visitor and a prefabricated conception created by Mama and my brothers. Since this fable was not in the least true to the austere, code-filled world of the Richard Ashbury School, it took me quite a while to adjust. Happily, I was spared Aristide's humiliation in the matters of toilet since Mama had taken the trouble to train me and I was unencumbered by either union suits or lace-trimmed panties. Trembling inwardly at the memory of Aristide's raggings and bolstered with advice from both my brothers, I acquitted myself not too badly on the first day. The one injunction that stuck in my head was: No matter how much you want to, don't run away. I didn't, not because of all the sound counselling, but because I couldn't. As the circle of boys around me pressed close, I stood rooted, feeling quite certain that I must drop dead at any moment because my heart, which felt enormous in my chest, would pound and then stop for what seemed like forever. Finally I struck out, landing a solid punch in the mouth of a boy named Ruby. I'm sure that this was only accomplished because, like myself, Ruby was terrified, and probably his being within my striking distance was a measure of his own need to prove himself. I was left pretty much alone after that.

In spite of the rabbi's assurance that Papa was going to heaven, Mama was determined to wear her widow's weeds for the full year and to avoid public places or conviviality of any sort. Tila came often during the month when the memorial candle burned, and she and Mama would reminisce or go for drives when the nights were cool.

In late September suitors began to call. They came ostensibly to offer condolences, to report on current gossip, and generally to lift

202

her spirits. But each let it be known that when she emerged from her mourning, he would be waiting. We children would listen at the end of the day while Mama and Tila discussed the men, Mama laughing not unkindly at the obvious ones and Tila discounting those she considered hopeless. Sometimes we would catch a glimpse of one of them leaving as we returned from school. There was the American colonel in charge of the Marines, a childless widower with silver hair and black brows which curled like tendrils. There was the splintery-thin English architect, who stuttered and whose wife, Brangwynne, was quite a close friend of Mama's. When Mama as delicately as possible suggested that since the architect was already married, two wives might prove burdensome if not downright embarrassing, the Englishman said, 'I d-d-daresay I can get rid of d-d-dear old B-B-B-Brangwynne.' And the Italian baron, who wore a uniform and a short fur cap with a gold fasces and boasted about some party called I Fascisti who he declared would make Italy the world's greatest power. Some of the courters were clearly motivated by the notion that Mama was a very rich widow. The most touching and perhaps the most sincere of the wooers was Dr. Jarvis.

Tila was present the Saturday Michel de Raveur came to call. He had refused to see her since her return from Tsingtao, although she had phoned and written to him several times to explain that Ramirez had meant nothing to her. An episode, she had said, calculated to make him, Michel, jealous. At first the two women were quite excited, guessing that Michel was using this as a pretext to encounter Tila. But Michel made it plain at once that it was Mama whom he had come to see.

I had made the joyful discovery that whenever possible Mama liked to have her sons around when these men called. So, when Tila left the drawing-room, I sat firm in my corner by the fireplace. It began to look as if Michel's call was one of those based on gratitude when he said, 'You know of course, Regina, that I got my start in business from Maximilian.'

Whether she was telling the truth or not I don't know, but Mama said she didn't. But when Michel began to draw a clear picture of his financial assets, his standing in the community, and his loneliness as a single man, it became obvious that he was about to propose.

'You are a fine and beautiful woman, Regina, and you must not live alone. I know that given a chance I could make you happy.'

Mama smiled. 'How can you make me happy, Michel?'

'I have the means to keep you as you are accustomed. I would be a good father to your sons and I would offer you companionship.'

'And what about Tila?'

'Tila was never the woman you are.'

'In some ways I think she's much better,' Mama replied. 'For instance, if right this moment you asked her to marry you, I'm sure that she would.'

'And you won't?'

Mama shook her head. 'Never. I would never marry you, Michel.'

Michel drew something out of his pocket, and as he laid it on the table, I heard it clink. Mama picked it up. It was a single gold key. She looked questioningly at the Frenchman.

'If it's because you think that I'm still involved with Tila, let that key be my answer. Ramirez sent it to me. It's the key to her bungalow in Tsingtao.'

'So you are finished with Tila?'

'*Complètement foutu*,' Michel said. Then he added, 'I will wait. Perhaps in time you'll change your mind.' He started for the door.

'Michel,' Mama said, 'if you ever propose to a woman again, while you are itemizing your assets, you might remember to throw in the fact that you love her.' Then Mama tossed the key into the fireplace. Mama told Tila that Michel had come to discuss an investment, and Tila pretended to believe her.

It was November before Chicho returned. I remember that for two reasons. The first was because my birthday fell then. The other reason that makes me able to pinpoint the time with reasonable accuracy is the funny remark that Mr. Isaacs made. He had come on some routine matter of signing papers, and he told of a great stock market crash in America which, he said, had world-reaching effects. He had heard that Aunt Annie had been wiped out.

'Isn't it odd,' he said, 'that Max should have been killed by a bull movement in a bear year?'

Aristide and I were on the drawing-room verandah looking out on the river. It seemed ages since the harbour had been dense with the gunboats of all nations; now there were just a few. Zee ushered Chicho into the room. At once I wanted to rush out to him, but Aristide grabbed my arm. 'Don't, you might spoil things.' I didn't know what he was talking about, but I obeyed him. We could both see and hear Mama and Chicho through the French windows. He was dressed in a grey suit and he carried gloves; his manner towards Mama, and hers towards him for that matter, was formal. They were speaking in Italian. He was explaining that his tour of duty was over and that he would be returning to Italy. Mama had been arranging carnations in a large crystal bowl. It was a lovely feminine avocation, and I had never seen her do it before. She took nature for granted as a rule, and I had seen her shove bouquets, box and all, in any receptacle handy, leaving the arrangements to someone else. Now she took each long-stemmed flower and placed it with a sprig of asparagus fern, just so. She made no comment about Chicho's plans to return home. There was a silence, then Chicho said he had heard that men were already paying her court, adding that it was of course none of his business. Mama's smile seemed to agree that it wasn't.

'Have you wondered,' he said, 'why I have not come forward to ask you to marry me?' The carnation Mama was holding stopped in mid-air momentarily, then she placed it in the bowl.

'No, I've not thought about it.'

'I'm married,' Chicho said.

Mama reflectively pushed the flowers aside on the table and sat back on the sofa. After a while she said, 'It's funny, Chico, but all I can think about is, what a well-kept secret.'

'You don't care?'

'Oh, I care. When I think of what a fool you've made of me, I care to the point that I want to give you two slaps in the face, *due sciafe in figura*,' she said.

'And I would deserve them,' Chicho replied, 'but hear me out and then I will go.' He explained that he had been married as a youth. His bride had gone insane after the birth of their son and had been in and out of institutions since then. As Mama turned her head from Chicho I saw her face. It was tortured.

'Did you love her?' she asked finally.

Chicho explained that the marriage had been arranged by their families and that although they had not lived together for years, in her lucid moments his wife was extremely devout and would not countenance an annulment.

'Then it's hopeless,' Mama said.

'No, if you love me it's not hopeless,' Chicho replied. He said that while annulments were difficult to obtain under normal circumstances, the prospects of one were lessened when insanity was concerned. But he had valuable connections; his brother was a cardinal, and in view of the family name and position there was a chance. Chicho had not tried for an annulment before, and even now, he told Mama, he would have no heart for it unless she told him to fight, unless he could be sure that she would be waiting. He was kneeling by her and put his arms around her waist and pressed his face against her breast. Mama drew his head up to hers and kissed his lips and they held together in a long embrace. Then she pulled away and the sound she made was like a sob. 'Yes, get the annulment,' she cried. 'I'll wait, I swear—*ti Juro!*'

Aristide cautioned me to silence. Then he led me by the hand across the verandah to the doors which opened into another room.

28

CHICHO was gone for nearly a year, during which time he wrote to Mama constantly. Sometimes, when she had read the morning mail, Mama was encouraged and she would tell us enviable trifles such as Chicho's taking his son to Pompeii or show us pictures that he sent of the occasion when he was summoned to Rome to be decorated for some service by the king. Mama confided the personal aspects of Chicho's correspondence to Sascha when she thought that Aristide and I were not within hearing distance. First his wife was out of the institution and seemed tractable, and the cardinal was willing to petition for him. Then came letters which depressed Mama and made her irascible. Chicho's wife had been confined again; his brother had misgivings about approaching the council; his son depended entirely on him. He would keep trying. . . .

Meanwhile we continued to live very quietly at home and were required to reduce the household staff. Mama found it difficult to sack anyone even though those she was obliged to let go were assistant servants, such as the cook's number three helper. Of his own initiative Pao-shing decided to quit. He had been offered ten dollars more monthly to chauffeur an American lawyer. Pao-shing decided to give Mama the chance of raising the bid. This was an unprecedented action, for Chinese servants were as sensitive to employer prestige as they were to the needs of preserving their own 'face'. The accepted tactic for a servant who wanted to leave for whatever reason was to pretend that a relative was dying. 'Must go country,' he would say. If the employer asked the location of the country, the reply was invariable, 'Ningpo more far'. That Pao-shing had not troubled to put a province between him and his need to depart, indeed that he had not bothered with any pretext, Mama took as a bad augury. 'To think we trained him from a *mafoo*,' she said. 'It's that damned Nationalism.' So Lao Ni became our chauffeur, and we did not fill his old position of number two houseboy.

The suitors kept calling with varying degrees of regularity, and of all, undoubtedly the most persistent was the American colonel. As the months passed his Marine-driven Packard in front of our entrance became a frequent sight. In spring (it was 1930 now) Chicho's letters became even more desperate. The annulment had been under consideration for some time, but his wife's family was bringing pressure to bear on the Vatican. The less hopeful Chicho's cause appeared, the more attractive the suitors became to everyone except Mama. No doubt wound up by her husband, Grandmama reverted comfortably to her old position as Mama's marital counsellor. She had from the start considered Chicho anathema.

'Listen, my child—a man with a *messhugena* wife and a child to support, do you need such *tsouris* from a goy?' Mama's rejoinder that the other suitors were Christian as well didn't faze Grandmama one bit.

'But they're not married goyim,' she argued.

Tila also tried to influence Mama. 'Give him up, Regina. Don't waste your opportunities. Few women have second chances.'

Mama checked an impatient reply when she saw by Tila's expression that her friend was thinking of the mess she had made of her own affair. Even Sascha, who had got wind of the news that the colonel was up for promotion and a Washington post, put in his pitch. 'You're used to a certain social standing, Mama. What if Chicho *can't* marry you? What then? Would you be content to be his mistress?'

'We'll see,' Mama said firmly. It was only Aristide who silently but unequivocally supported Mama. He made no pro and con arguments, but once when Sascha tried to persuade him to lend his voice in favour of the American, Aristide shook his head. 'She *loves* Chicho,' he said.

For a while there was no news from Italy, and towards the end of summer Sascha began to get hopeful that Mama might capitulate to the colonel's ardour. Chicho's letter arrived on the anniversary of Papa's death. As though to be brightened by his memory, Mama had brought Papa's *yahrtzeit* candle into the main hall where she was unpacking the winter clothing. Stacked along one length of the room were the carpets which had returned from storage, and the musty camphor smell from open trunks pervaded the entire apartment. In his letter Chicho said that the Vatican council had upheld its policy on mental case annulments *ipso facto*. He had no choice now but to leave the course of action up to Mama. He was prepared to return at once to Shanghai and would take any employment just to be with her. But if under the circumstances she preferred to forget him, he would understand and would continue to love her always. The letter floated from Mama's hands to an open suitcase. Sascha, Aristide, and I, who were on our summer holidays and had been assisting Mama, watched her for some comment, but she made none. She simply wiped the palms of her hands along the sides of her dress, along her torso. Then she continued unpacking. Aristide picked up the letter and made a rather elaborate show of pretending to be able to read Italian. I could tell by Sascha's jaw that he was vexed by this, and so was I, until I realized that Aristide was attempting to conceal his distress for Mama. But he caught Sascha's expression and for once, rather than cause a scene, put the letter down. In doing so, he noticed a number of photographs tucked among the clothing in the suitcase. The one he picked up showed Mama in a kneeling position. The pose was in profile and although she could not have been more than twelve or so at the time, she was already quite mature in figure. On her head was a cluster of blossoms from which a long veil flowed into diffusion at one corner of the photograph. Her face was unspeakably sorrowful. At once Aristide questioned Mama about the picture.

'Oh that,' she said. 'That was my communion photo.'

A few years earlier, with our family's ambivalent approach towards religion, Aristide might have accepted that answer, but now he said, 'Mama, Jewish girls don't have communions.'

'Well, the convent wanted me to, so I did,' Mama said, taking the picture out of his hands and tossing it into another trunk. This might have ended the matter, however unsatisfactorily, but for the fact that Aristide came up with a companion photograph. In this one, Mama in the same veil and gown is standing stiffly by a chair in which is seated a portly, middle-aged man. The handlebar moustache does not conceal a thick lower lip, a groove which gives his mouth the appearance of a cipher. He looks constricted in his Edwardian suit, and on his head he wears a fez. In this one, too, Mama's face is that of a chastised child.

'And I suppose he is a choirboy?' Aristide said.

Instantly it was as though all the components to the puzzle of that missing year in Mama's girlhood—the visits of the khedive's kinsman told with such quips, pride, and merriment; the loss of the finery we had seen in other photographs; the glossed-over *skandal*—became fitted into an immutable, ugly design. Aristide drew in his breath sharply, and I too at once remembered the Moslem wedding Mama had described on that carriage ride in Tsingtao. 'Have you ever smelled real fleurs d'oranger?' she had said.

'They sold you, didn't they?' Aristide cried.

'No, no!' Mama replied. 'You don't understand.'

Normally it would have been the easiest thing in the world for Mama to exercise her authority. A hard slap would have shut Aristide up. But knowing that she could not curtail our thoughts, she determined to clear this issue. Maybe, as I look back on it, her greatest need was to reaffirm her own concept. She told us that at the age of twelve she had been married to Sherif Pasha, the man in the photograph. The idea, she insisted, had been her own. 'You see, I loved the thought of a party for me and all the fuss—' But when the time had come for the groom to claim her, Mama had barred herself in her room and would not let anyone enter. 'Nobody told me that I would have to live with him.' Mama turned to Sascha in the middle of her account. 'I told you how it was when I married your father. I was ignorant, I didn't know *anything*.'

'What about the man—was he angry?' Aristide asked.

'Oh yes, very angry.' Then Mama described how the Pasha had come repeatedly to the shop demanding his bride, but Mama had threatened to kill herself rather than go with him, and Grandpapa had turned the man away. After that, for almost a year the irate husband sent lawyers to discuss, to prevail, to threaten, but Mama would not budge. Although according to Moslem tradition the bride keeps all her gifts in a divorce, since there was hardly a marriage, let alone a divorce, the emissaries came to the shop and stripped Mama and her parents of everything they had been given. But it was only when the Pasha, watching from his carriage, sent a band of thugs to smash the shop windows and destroy every piece of furniture in the place that Grandpapa knew they must act fast. And that was really why they had left Alexandria.

'If you were married to this Moslem, how could you get married again?' Sascha asked.

'Your father had to pay him for the divorce. He had to buy him off to get me,' Mama said, a note of pride edging into her voice.

'But what about Barrometti—didn't you love him?' Aristide asked.

'Who knows? I thought I did then. Yes, I think I loved Barrometti.'

'Mama,' Sascha said, 'write to Chicho. Write to him today and tell him to come.'

So that autumn Mama and Chicho became lovers, married in all but legal fact. There was a bedroom adjoining Mama's, a guest room I suppose it would have been called in anyone else's home, but in a family as personal as ours it had never functioned as such. Chicho used it as a combined dressing-room and depot for belongings he wished to have close at hand. For the sake of circumspection, however, Chicho took a small apartment in the same building, and, as far as we children knew, that is where he slept. He got a job in the Italian Bank, and Mama thought at first that he had been engaged in a managerial capacity, but when she discovered he was an accountant, it seemed all the more to signify his desire to remain with her. Certainly, she reasoned, with his name, connections, and to all outward appearances his solvency, he could have done far better in Italy.

During her year of mourning, Mama had become, either through grief or anticipation, much slenderer. Now in a sally of extravagance, she ordered an entirely new wardrobe, as if by casting aside her weeds she was ensuring her new life. She discovered a few grey hairs.

Her coiffeur came to the apartment, and Mama submitted to having her hair slathered with a brown and odoriferous paste which she called a henna pack, after which her hair was fashioned into a new crenellated style called the marcel wave. She spent hours between her Russian manicurist, who lacquered her nails a deep crimson, skilfully shaping white half-moons at the tips, and her Chinese pedicurist, who scraped and pumiced and polished her feet. Most noitceable in Mama was an absence of her former reticence. One had the feeling that if she were caught naked when the front door opened, she would not falter.

Of course the suitors had stopped coming, and so had many of Papa's longtime British friends. When Mama entertained now, it was mostly for the Latins she had always admired and for Americans, because, as she said, they were so 'absorbent'. Parties were somewhat smaller but no less lavish and certainly far more spirited. Quite often after dinner the guests would join in dancing the tarentellas of southern Italy. Mama's sense of not faltering obviously did not include the buttock-bumping, joyous vulgarity of the tarentella but she sanctioned the performances led by Chicho.

Chicho liked to have a hand in the preparations for the parties, and he took us boys shopping with him. We went to Venturi's, a fine Italian grocer, where dry sausages hung in ropes from the ceiling and black wheels of aged Parmesan were stacked by the counters like rubber tyres. Vichy water gave way to Pellegrino, Veuve Clicquot and Moët Chandon to Asti spumante, and for table wines Chicho was partial to a rare Tuscan chianti, which had to be ordered through the Italian consulate. On these outings Chicho never forgot to include a bar or two of jaw-cracking nougat or a box of Perugina chocolates. But best of all we children liked the evenings Mama and Chicho spent quietly at home, when Chicho likely as not had rustled up some Neapolitan specialty. Since Papa's death Mama had rescinded the ruling that we eat in the alcove, and now all our meals were family affairs. After dining we would assemble in the smoking-room to hear Mama sing as she strummed on her mandolin. She no longer favoured the tormented arias of Puccini's women, but popular and very romantic pieces like 'Parla Mi D'amore Mariu' and 'Chittara Romana', which she sang in a growling gypsy voice: 'Sotto un manto di stelle, Roma bella mi appare. . . .'

For Sascha, Chicho's position presented no conflict. He thought of him as a close friend, and one who had been dear to Papa. Above all Sascha admired the fact that Chicho was truly *ben trovato*. He could pore over Winan's treatise on the handling of duelling pistols and was knowledgeable about the difference between sixteenth-century European and Oriental matchlocks, pointing out that in the Italian models the serpentine points towards the stock, whereas in all Oriental arms of that epoch the serpentine is reversed. He gave Sascha a beautifully embossed and inlaid snaphance, attributed to Cellini, from Chicho's own family collection.

Nor did he neglect Aristide, and he would sit hours at a stretch while this brother, who had finally graduated from 'Für Elise' to 'Loin de Bal', would pound away at the piano. His suggestions were made as tactfully as possible, since Aristide played only for approval.

As for me, I was content to welcome Chicho as a special 'uncle' who hoisted me on his shoulders and called me pet names. It only mattered that he seemed to love me and that I was not frightened of him. I never would have given a second thought to his relation-ship with Mama if it hadn't been for Ronald Frothinger. This English boy and I had gone from prep to lower one together, and while I, still longing for Aristide's companionship, tried to shape myself into a typical Richard Ashbury boy, Ronald permitted my attachment to him. He was quite ordinary-looking except for the pupils of his eyes which, whenever he was getting an inspiration, seemed to clang shut like drawers on a tiny cash register. Although by no means the brightest boy in our class, Ronald was the most opportunistic. He functioned like a collective mass, now and then adsorbing a new human cell which at once had to produce materially for him. He sat next to one of the top students, from whom he cribbed shamelessly, and his homework was mapped out if not done entirely for him by another. In return Ronald exchanged benefits within his considerable powers. His strength lay in that he seemed to know everything that was going on. He was attentive and polite in class rather than sedulous, and he spent hours analysing the teachers and catering to their needs. His influence was such that although he himself was not physically strong, he could call off a ragging. As captain of the Rounders Team he could, by choosing you, spare you the ignominy of being rejected as a 'feeble'. And it was Ronald who made out the list for outings to Jessfield Park. I was never quite sure what my friendship offered him besides an occasional invitation to the pictures or perhaps, since he rode a bicycle to and from school, he might have liked the idea that I had been able to persuade Sascha to let us pick him up and return him by car. Our friendship was initiated by Ronald's insistence that I expose myself to him in the school outhouse. After briefly resisting, I agreed, and from then on participated whenever he felt inclined. Although it was Ronald who first explained the role that sexual organs perform, giving a graphic description of intercourse as the means by which babies were born, there was nothing personal in our exhibitions to each other. Sometimes he conducted the sessions with groups of two or three, always displaying the same peremptory manner towards the act. 'Now then show, and let's get done with it.' Never did I associate the quick, button-fumbling, and viewing process with either the least vestige of affection or even carnal thralldom.

Ronald's mother, Dora, was like no other British woman I had encountered, in what certainly must have been the broadest spectrum of types possible. There were the redoubtable matriarchs with picture hats and dotted veiling, whose throats were cinched with black velvet dog collars. And I had seen the cropped horsey types at Mama's 'levenses, drinking straight gin and making loud music hall palaver reminiscent of Cicely Courtneidge. I remember ethereal, determinedly sad women, who probably thought of themselves as Iris March, as well as chic, flowing creatures who prattled about Mayfair and Old Bond Street and adored it when someone likened them to Gertrude Lawrence. But Dora Frothinger, with her precisely ill-assorted clothes, resembled none of these. She must have been in her fifties (with the extremely plain, age is often harder to tell). Her black hair was forcibly pulled back, and single grey hairs spiralled at the temples like tiny springs. She had an overall hastily powdered look which gave the impression that at the very last moment she had dabbed a puff over everything—hat, features, and dress. Her upper lip was stretched into a perpetually bracelike smile, over protruding front teeth. Since she was Ronald's mother and seemed to approve of me, I not only thought of her as most proper, but even quite fetching. Mr. Frothinger worked for one of the tobacco companies, and I rarely saw him, but like most late-in-life parents with only one child, the matter of her son's progress at school was of the utmost moment to Dora, and she came to see him almost daily. Ronald didn't seem to mind her presence and was actually quite chummy with his mother. I, on the other hand, dreaded the rare occasions when Mama came to school, particularly if Ronald happened to be on hand. I recall that what led up to his telling me about Chicho and Mama had stemmed from one of these visits.

It was a month or so after Chicho had returned. Sascha had begun to stay late for S.V.C. practice, and Aristide and I were obliged to wait for him. Ronald hadn't cared to, so Dora had taken to collecting him after school. It was warm that day, and Dora had brought Ronald a thermos of barley water—'to cool his blood', she said. We were standing in the playground near the main entrance when Lao Ni drove up with Mama and Chicho in the back seat. When she saw me Mama made a wonderful display of enchantment, as if the sight of me alone was like a golden urn of water in a parched desert. As she got out of the car in a sultry gust of Molyneux Numero Cinq, I noticed to my dismay that she was stockingless and that her toenails, peeping out of open-toed shoes, glittered with red enamel. I looked at once at Dora Frothinger. Her cotton hat was identical to the one Hoboo wore to the park, and on her feet were nice white shoes, just like a nurse's. In the midst of my despising of Mama, I noticed that Ronald tugged at his mother's hand and pointed to Mama's toenails. Dora Frothinger's lips were drawn into a tight elastic band as though she were afraid that her teeth might escape if she smiled broadly.

Most likely Ronald had tired of me anyway, for the very next day he made a slurring remark about Mama and Chicho, whom he said was a gigolo. He implied that they practised those esoteric intimacies which he had earlier described. I denied this vehemently. 'My mother would never do anything like that. Never in her life!' Ronald said calmly that she would have had to at least three times to have produced Sascha, Aristide, and me. I hit him in the mouth with all my force, and he punched me a good one in the eye. From then on we did not speak to each other.

My image of Mama was such that it totally precluded Ronald's assumption, and I might not have given it another thought but for what I saw a week or so later. I was very fond of gas balloons and enjoyed nothing more than releasing them from our verandahs, watching as each red sphere sailed upwards until it became no more than a tiny speck finally disappearing. Chicho had brought me some

214

one evening, and in my eagerness to let them go, I played truant from school the following morning. Some experiences remain ever green and delicious in the memory, and my begging off classes and walking home that autumn day, all on my own initiative, is one of them. I can clearly recall the elation of being free and, so, being happy. The accounts would have to be met and straightened later, but to consider prices at that moment had seemed niggardly. Still, I wrapped my long paisley muffler around my neck as a precaution against both the chill winds and the inevitable scolding. 'At least,' Mama would say, 'he had the sense to dress warmly.'

With the clutch of balloons straining like leashed pointers from my hand, I went onto the verandah from the smoking room, where I let a pair of them sail into the sky. I raced the length of the terrace as they veered south towards Nantao and the Chinese city, then up, up, and away until I could no longer see them. Then I let loose a few more balloons, expecting them to follow their companions, but the wind swept them westwards and I ran after them with the remaining balloons tugging impatiently at my hand. I let go the rest of the balloons, and their flight was of such dizzy and un-trammelled joy that I crowed with laughter and longed suddenly to share this moment with someone. From where I was standing I could see that the heavy drapes to Mama's bedroom had been pulled open but that the sheer lace curtains had not. I proceeded carefully. A good amount of the time Mama presumably allocated to resting was in actuality devoted to surreptitious eating from the trays brought to her bedside by Zee, and, understandably, she hated to be caught. 'If there's one thing I loathe,' she would say, 'it's to be made out a liar!' I peered through the fine mesh of the Nottingham lace, searching for some sign of Zee in his long white coat; he wasn't there. Then I saw her, Regina, my mother, but not Mama.

This woman was lying on her back naked and downward as though she had been poured. Her head seemed to flower perilously at the end of a long white stem, where at the base, her breasts mounded and rose fitfully to life under a pair of great brown spiders, whose tentacles moved independent of the bolts to which they were attached. I saw Chicho's head and the dark ripple of his spine as he braced two hairy extensions from his torso around the woman's thighs. And I heard a carnival of sounds, small sounds and great ones, that belonged to no single nationality but to all tongues. Then

215

there was the fluttering, beating, bearing-down noise. My heart? No, not my heart. I looked up. The balloons were long gone, but the sky was darkened with thousands of small birds, coveys of autumn snipe returning. (Was it from Cairo? Mr. Llewellyn had told Aristide aeons ago.) I ran back down the verandah to the farthest point of it where I could look over the great stretch of city beyond the Garden Bridge and Soochow Creek, and I raised my voice in a tight scream, 'I hate you, Ronald Frothinger!'

When Mama found me I was in my room calmly playing with building blocks. Sascha had called from school to report me missing and wanted to know if I might be at home. 'What's the matter?' Mama said. 'What happened?'

'Nothing,' I replied without looking at her.

'What do you mean, nothing? How long have you been home?' I didn't reply at once.

'Look at me!' she said, grabbing my shoulder. In pulling away I was forced to look up. Mama was fully dressed, but on her neck, just below the carotid nerve, was a purple bruise, and I thought at once of a spider's bite.

'What's the matter, my *mizinik*, are you sick?' Mama asked as she knelt beside me.

I shrank away from her. 'Yes, yes, I'm sick,' I said, and began to cry.

29

AH-CHING had come to the apartment several times since Papa's death. In 1930 he had led Chiang Kai-shek's armies in the suppression of a revolt headed by an ambitious general and the governor of Shensi province. For his part in the overthrow of this clique, Ah-ching in his late twenties was promoted to the rank of general. Time and undoubtedly his associations had plated him with a certain lustre, but in his visored hat and battle jacket (with a Waterman fountain-pen clipped to his breast pocket, like the generalissimo), he still swaggered and was, as usual, notably lacking in the superficial amenities. Hoboo was natural around her nephew and not above striking him with the back of her hand and batting her good eye agitatedly when she felt he was being disrespectful. Lao Ni, on the other hand, grinned and gawked and became putty in his brother's presence.

In the spring of the following year, Ah-ching brought his young bride to meet us. Su-mei was fragile, with hands as eloquently delicate as branch coral and a heart-shaped face emphasized by spider bangs. But by contrast she had an irreverent and witty personality. It was plain from her conversation that Ah-ching's mother disapproved of her. We learned from Hoboo that Ah-ching had met her in the ranks fighting shoulder-to-shoulder with Nationalist troops.

Like Americans, the Chinese frequently entertain with the whole family in mind. So when, during the summer holidays of 1931, Mayor Wu Teh-chen invited us to a luncheon at his estate on Great Western Road, Aristide and I anticipated seeing some friends our own age. We were, nevertheless, pleasantly surprised to find Didi there; Ah-ching and Su-mei had brought him. At the age of eight Didi had lost his plumpness and, dressed in his American-style suit with long pants, he seemed older. Only the round eyes behind spectacles with narrow silver frames were the same, with the bewildered expression of a child attempting a game which goes too fast for him.

Ah-ching had just returned from another successful offensive, this time against the Communists who had been stirring up trouble in the southeast and central provinces. He was quite effortlessly the centre of attention and held forth to an impressive group consisting of the finance minister, China's ambassador to London, and a jolly Mandarin aristocrat, Marquis Li. Ah-ching was telling them of the then little-known tactic that the Communists had been using to striking advantage, which consisted of proselytizing among the peasants and recruiting them as terrorists.

'So we will again have to crush the Reds?' Lord Li asked.

'Eventually,' Ah-ching replied, 'but first it appears we may have to contend with our greedy little neighbours.' He looked towards the entrance where the mayor was greeting Japanese Consul General Murai and his entourage.

'You think they will exploit the Nakamura incident into a war

217

with us?' the marquis asked. In June a Japanese captain travelling incognito in inner Mongolia with a great sum of money on his person was suspected of being a spy and murdered by Chinese soldiers. Fed by inflammatory propaganda, feeling ran high in Japan, and a month later there had been a massacre of Chinese residents in Korea. Ah-ching did not reply to the question.

Before leaving the luncheon, Ah-ching told us that he had moved his family to a house in Chapei near our school. We promised Didi that we would come and play with him when the term began in September. In the first week of school, revelling in the luxury of having the car to ourselves since Sascha's graduation, we persuaded Hoboo to take us to Ah-ching's. While it was a great improvement over the hovel we had been to four years earlier, the Chapei house with its sparsely furnished but clean rooms was proof of Ah-ching's integrity. Unlike other generals who maintained homes in the Settlement or French Concession, Ah-ching was living on his pay without rebates and graft. His father sat in a tall blackwood chair and was so shrunken and yellow that his whiskers seemed falsely luxuriant. The old man made much of Lao Ni in his foreign chauffeur's uniform, clearly considering him to be the success among his sons. He said several times, to Ah-ching's unconcealed amusement, that Lao Ni was a good son. The mother was no less harassed than I remembered her and scolded constantly, directing most of her barbs at her daughter-in-law. Didi had not yet come home from school. Like us, he attended a municipal institution, but his was for Chinese students exclusively and while Koreans and Japanese were admitted to the Richard Ashbury, Chinese were not.

According to the Chinese calendar it was now the eighth moon and time for the annual moon festival. Su-mei set the table with round pastries decorated with rabbits or toads and filled with sugared bean paste, each of which when cut showed the hard-boiled yolk of an egg, symbol of the moon. Didi came home and we had tea. Afterwards, while the old man dozed with his opium pipe, Su-mei gathered us around her to tell the story of the moon festival. Naturally, every Chinese festival has a legend behind it, sometimes several, and the one Su-mei told us that day concerned the chieftain's wife who stole a coin of immortality and fled to the moon for sanctuary. There the queen of heaven took pity on her and transformed her into a three-legged toad, the symbol of unattainability.

On the fifteenth day of the eighth moon, the chieftain's wife rises in the sky, and just after sunset her outlines can be discerned most clearly.

Aristide, nurtured by Hoboo on Christian concepts of charity, was quite put out with the queen of heaven for changing the wife into a three-legged toad. He said it seemed to him that any fairy queen worth her salt must certainly have known kinder ways to make the poor woman unassailable. Addressing himself to Hoboo, he said, 'Would your Jesus have done a lousy thing like that?' Before Hoboo could think up an answer Su-mei said, 'That happened about two thousand five hundred years before Christ. Times change.'

Less than a fortnight after this visit, the Japanese, on a trumped-up charge that Chinese troops had destroyed a bridge on their South Manchurian Railway line, converged on and seized Mukden. Manchuria was a prize plum in an orchard zealously tended by the Japanese. Together with inner and outer Mongolia the territory itself equalled an area three times as large as the entire Japanese Empire. Since the establishment of the Nationalist regime, Chinese interests and population had been pouring into these provinces and the Chinese had begun to build railroads of their own as a measure of independence from the Japanese.

Each year since his founding of the Nationalist regime, Chiang Kai-shek had been drawn into conflict with one or another faction. Now, powerless to resist the Japanese in a full-scale war, he issued a policy of non-resistance, appealing for assistance to the League of Nations. In short order the Japanese took all key cities in Manchuria, claiming that since these measures were taken to protect Japanese lives and property, the acts could not be construed as acts of war.

While the League of Nations conferred over the Manchurian 'incident', foreign powers clucked at Japan's aggressions with mild reproval. A message from Washington immediately following the occupation of Mukden expressed the opinion of the State Department that there was no ground for invoking the Kellogg Pact in connection with the Sino-Japanese 'tiff' in Manchuria. In Britain the foreign secretary asserted that Japan had never 'withdrawn' her assurance that she would remove her troops at the earliest possible moment. France was generally noncommittal, but it was suspected that her sympathy lay with Japan, and Russia, a longtime thorn in Japan's side, did not seem prepared to antagonize her over the Soviet's interests remaining in northern Manchuria.

By and large, to the foreign residents of Shanghai and to those Chinese whose interests were intertwined with them, the problem of the northern provinces was as remote as if it belonged to another hemisphere. The foreigner's main issue, as always, was the preservation of their Western capsules, and as long as they remained unviolated, what else mattered? The neons never even blinked in the city of life on the Whangpoo River.

But there were some who translated the handwriting on the wall as a premonitory page from the book of fate. In particular, several correspondents urged their governments to take more than a passive interest. Sascha, who since his graduation had been desultorily attending Papa's office and who had never indicated much interest in local politics other than as an outlet for soldiering, was now deeply concerned. He interpreted Premier Tanaka's lengthy memorial to the Emperor as a blueprint of Japan's designs for world conquest. He read aloud from the text to Aristide and me: 'In the future if we want to control China we must first crush the United States.... *If we succeed the rest of the Asiatic ... and South Sea countries will fear us and surrender to us.... A more dangerous factor is ... that the people of China might someday wake up ...*'

The one measure of retaliation which Chiang Kai-shek had endorsed was the boycott of Japanese goods. Relieved to have any weapon, the Chinese supported the boycott, and shopkeepers even refused to sell daily necessities to their enemy. A firm resolution was passed by the League of Nations calling upon Japan to withdraw her troops from Manchuria by mid-October. But by then it was abundantly clear that the Japanese intended expansion. Within two months the whole of Manchuria from Tsitsihar in the north to Dairen and Port Arthur in the south had been taken. Ignoring a thirteen-to-one judgment passed against her by the League, Japan attacked Tientsin. Again the cry arose from China for its own military reprisals. Chiang Kai-shek had for some time been bedevilled by a southern faction in Canton who refused to recognize Nanking and who insisted on his resignation. Disregarded by Chiang, the Cantonese had set up a separate government and had actually been en route to engage Chiang's troops when the Japanese entered

Mukden. It at once became obvious to both factions that national unity was of primacy, and in view of the public clamouring for action, Chiang Kai-shek resigned the presidency in favour of Sun Fo, the sole issue of Sun Yat-sen from an earlier marriage. Accordingly, the Canton regime was dissolved, and Sun Fo, heading the Nanking and fully recognized government of China, began to organize an army for its defence.

While the League pondered on conciliation and the foreign powers sent dilatory notes, Japan was rousing her citizenry to patriotism all over China. In Shanghai a demonstration was held by four thousand Japanese residents, after which groups of them marched through the International Settlement tearing down anti-Japanese posters. Sascha, now a sergeant in the Volunteer Corps, was assigned to patrol duty near Chapei. He told about seeing a mob of Japanese civilian reservists, *ronins*, accompanied by sailors with fixed bayonets, demolish a string of Chinese shops on North Szechwan Road, battering the glass windows and smashing furniture with clubs and iron bars. As these incidents became more frequent the Shanghai Chinese bridled under the retraints of passivity and yearned to retaliate. Only the knowledge that Sun Fo's Nineteenth Route Army was in readiness kept them in check.

Conditions worsened after the New Year. The beating of five Buddhist monks by Chinese ruffians tindered the explosion leading to the attack on Shanghai. According to Japanese reports, the monks had been peaceably going about their business in front of a large towel factory when they had been set upon. When one of them died, Japanese mobs ran amuck and units of *ronins* set fire to the towel factory, stabbing to death a Chinese municipal policeman. At a mass meeting held by Japanese residents the same day, resolutions were passed demanding their government send reinforcements to Shanghai. On our way home from school Aristide and I saw the ruins of Chinese establishments along the length of North Szechwan Road. We watched as an ambulance arrived to pick up pedestrians who had been assaulted and a British municipal policeman who had been cudgelled by the Japanese mobs.

Shanghai's foreign community pondered on the foolhardiness of Chinese revenge upon innocent priests, but Sascha produced a snapshot he had taken of Japanese monks, their gowns hoisted to the waist and manning shovels, as they assisted Japanese bluejackets in the filling of sandbags. Consul General Murai, backed by the admiral of the Japanese Navy, at once issued a five-point demand to the mayor's office. The fifth point was that all anti-Japanese propaganda must cease and the ban on their products, the boycott, must be lifted at once. Mayor Wu expressed his willingness to concede to four of the points but was unwilling to retract China's only weapon against its aggressor. He said that he would have to confer with Nanking. He asked for time. Meanwhile a carrier, a cruiser, and four destroyers joined the Japanese ships anchored at Woosung. At the urging of both municipalities, foreigners conducted their affairs as usual. Our school remained open despite its propinquity to the troubled areas, and Sascha persuaded Mama to allow Aristide and me to continue. 'The Japs are being quite careful not to step on foreign toes,' was how Sascha put it. While they chose to ignore their guilt in the matters of burning, pillaging, and assaulting Chinese civilians, Mr. Murai had been quick to pen notes of contrition to the British Consulate regarding the British policeman who'd been injured.

One day late in January, we heard via the school scuttlebutt that the Japanese had served the mayor with a twenty-four-hour ultimatum regarding the lifting of the boycott. That evening when Aristide and I returned, the tea table had not been set as it usually was, and we went to the kitchen to investigate. Ah-ching's mother was in the centre of the room conferring with the servants. I gave a start when I saw her, for her face at the bridge of her nose, at the temples, and all the way down her neck was marked with narrow mulberry-coloured bruises. My first thought was that she had been beaten, but then I remembered Hoboo had once shown me how the Chinese relieve neuralgic pains by means of pinching the flesh with a copper coin. Ah-ching had gone a month earlier to join the defence army, and the woman was saying that she had received a message from him telling her to evacuate the house in Chapei. This she had done and was now living with her husband and Didi in the Settlement. But Su-mei had refused to leave; she had some notion that she might be needed in Chapei in case of trouble and she wanted to be able to help.

'But she's seven months with Ah-ching's child,' Hoboo said.

'What could I do?' the woman replied. 'Today there are no more wives and mothers; everybody is a patriot.' She added that once they were properly settled she would go back for Su-mei. The other servants ventured the opinion, somewhat bitterly, that Hoboo needn't worry, the mayor would most certainly concede to the Japanese ultimatum and the Chinese districts would be safe. A little later on, Sascha came into the kitchen with the news that the mayor had indeed given in to the Japanese demands and that Chinese troops were withdrawing. However expected, this brought about a general disquiet among the servants. Zee, who had lost a relative in Tientsin, surmised that China would go on honouring Japan's demands until the entire country was swallowed. And Dah Su, the Cantonese, brought his cleavers down on the chopping block where he was mincing meat as though they were Japanese carcases. But Lao Ni said to his mother, 'Maybe now Su-mei will come out.'

We were awakened that night by the sound of shellfire from the river. Looking from our windows towards Woosung we could see flashes from the Japanese ships. Around midnight we heard over the radio that the Japanese had entered Chapei, where Sascha was on night patrol, and Mama became frantic. We were all up when Sascha came home in the early morning hours. He was tired but exhilarated, for at last he was being able to participate in a conflict that involved men and guns. Mama wanted him to resign from the S.V.C. at once. 'I didn't raise you to the age of nineteen to be killed by the Japanese,' she said with her usual habit of adding or subtracting six months to our ages when it suited her purposes. Sascha argued that it would be a disgrace to resign when appeals were being made for new recruits, and Chicho, who had just signed up with the Italian unit of the corps, supported him in this.

We listened as Sascha told how bluejackets had stormed Chapei only hours after the mayor had accepted the Japanese ultimatum. According to Sascha, the Japanese admiral, acting on his own, had given the order for the attack. From his patrol car Sascha had seen the Japanese marines assemble at their headquarters on Dixwell Road in the northern part of the Settlement. Then in a procession of trucks led by armoured cars and followed by marines and *ronins* on foot, the caravan headed for the Chinese city. As they pressed through the boundaries at Chapei the armoured cars beamed great naked lights over the deserted streets, while the trucks behind cast flares about them. Sascha's patrol car followed, and at first it seemed to those in it that the occupation of Chapei had been a *fait accompli,*

223

when all at once from out of windows and from the rooftops came bursts of rifle fire from Chinese snipers. At once the Japanese forces divided into columns, the trucks making for diverse points of the area as beams from the armoured cars continued to poke and search while machine-gunners attempted to flush out the snipers' nests. With his lust for the artifacts of war, Sascha proudly exhibited a purloined Japanese helmet and fragments of trench mortar shells, prompting Aristide to wonder aloud if Sascha would ever grow up, to which Sascha replied that *he* wondered if Aristide would ever become a man.

But during the next couple of days, when the Japanese, infuriated at even the token resistance, pounded the Chinese with cannons, set fires indiscriminately, and began to rain bombs upon them, Sascha's attitude changed. The actual confrontation with blood sports in which men were the quarry began to dull his enthusiasm. He described scenes of methodical but mindless carnage: a peasant woman held by *ronins* forced to watch as they slashed the throats of her three children; a boy singled out of a line of fleeing natives, made to hop first on one foot and then the other while a Japanese officer shot at his feet, the boy sweating in terror but grinning, determined to prove his understanding that this was a game. And when at last he was hit and fell to the ground, the officer made a design down the length of the boy's back with bullets. A building was emptied of its occupants, who were lined up row upon row, then systematically clubbed, bayoneted, or shot, the bodies carted away in waiting vans. Those who remained lying in the streets, some not quite dead, were set upon by packs of starving mongrels, who tore and gnawed the flesh from the screaming wounded and could not be driven off either by sticks or even pistol shots. Sascha compared this with the war he had witnessed five years earlier when labourers and Communists had joined Nationalist troops against the northern armies. Then it had all been for a purpose, in the principles and name of war. He had seen men killed before, but they had been soldiers. Whether in uniform or out, they were men of a party who died aggressively or defensively, and that was different from murder for the sheer joy of its partaking. He remembered that the buildings taken then by either side had been requisitioned for military use, not merely for the purpose of razing them. Now churches, hospitals, public buildings, and private homes were all the objects of incendiarism. Those civilian reservists, the *ronins*, whom we had known as bank clerks, shipping agents, merchants, or grocers, had now become the most inspired arsonists, laying their torches to everything in their paths, including humans. When Sascha finished his account he wept, covering his face with both his hands and making no sounds, and even though, judging by Mama's expression, we knew she was numb with pity, we also knew that she would not again ask Sascha to resign.

Early on the third morning of the fighting, I woke up as Hoboo was tiptoeing out of the bedroom.

'Are you going to church?' I asked sleepily. Hoboo said that she was. Hearing us talk, Aristide woke up. 'She's going to church,' I explained.

'Numskull, of course she isn't. It's not Sunday.' Under Aristide's persistence Hoboo finally admitted that she was off to Chapei to try to bring Su-mei out.

'But Ah-ching's mother said that she would go back for her,' Aristide said.

'She will not go,' Hoboo replied.

'Then we're going with you,' Aristide said, throwing aside his bedcovers.

'No.' Hoboo was very definite.

'Sure,' Aristide insisted, 'the Japanese wouldn't dare touch us; we're foreigners.' It was a point which Aristide was stretching somewhat; on the day before, we had read that an American boy of fifteen had been picked up by the Japanese military for having firearms in his possession, and in spite of his claims that these were war souvenirs, the boy was being detained. Hoboo was adamant, and we realized that we had no choice but to let her go.

That afternoon we heard over the radio that the Commercial Press buildings had been destroyed. Those not razed by bombs had been set afire. I saw Aristide become very pale and remembered that Ah-ching's family lived off Paoshan Road where the press complex was situated. Mama did not appear to notice Hoboo's absence. If she did, she more than likely thought the amah had gone on some shopping errand downtown. Our school had remained open, but Mama would not let Aristide and me attend, and that evening one of my brother's classmates phoned. He told Aristide how their teacher in Mandarin, Dr. Chen, had addressed the boys

225

upon hearing the news of the burning of the National Oriental Library. We knew this to be perhaps the largest and most complete library of ancient manuscripts in China. Among over a million priceless volumes destroyed were the entire Heng Fen Lau classics. Dr. Chen asked his class to bow their heads in a moment's silence, then he told them to be seated; but he remained on his feet wordless for the duration of the lesson.

By late that evening there was still no sign of Hoboo. Mama could tell that something was amiss and pried the truth from Aristide. Sascha's reports, when he returned from his long day's stint at patrolling, did not add to our comfort. Besides the total destruction in the Paoshan area, the Russian Orthodox Church and the Church of Strangers had been razed, and the Odeon Theatre and adjoining buildings, shops, and residences along North Szechwan Road had been set afire by *ronins*. The Japanese, incensed by Chinese sniping, had fanned out their activities into the Settlement roads where they were systematically emptying the buildings and dispatching hostages by the vanload. Dinner had been kept hot for our Volunteer brother, and while he ate, Mama told him that Hoboo had gone to Chapei and had not yet returned.

'That damned old turnip!' Sascha exploded.

'Will you get her, please?' Aristide said.

Before Sascha could reply, Mama interjected, 'No! Listen, you two. I really hope to God that nothing has happened to Hoboo, but she knew what she was doing. You must not, you *cannot*, ask your brother to risk his life.'

'I'll go,' Aristide said.

'Are you out of your mind? Hoboo wouldn't have wanted you to go.'

'There, you see. You think she's dead!' Aristide cried.

'I only know that you are not going; it's out of the question. And, Sascha, I forbid you to go, do you hear me?'

'Don't worry, Mama,' he replied. 'I'm not crazy.' Mama was more than usually overwrought, for Chicho, now stationed with the Italian unit at the borders of the French Concession, had been away the past two nights. Assured that Sascha was in full control, Mama retired to her room. We watched as Sascha kept on eating until all that was left in front of him was a platter of clean-picked chicken bones. Finally he rinsed his fingers delicately in the finger bowls and dried his hands on a napkin. He looked at Aristide. 'Can you draw a map?' Aristide stared back at him for a few seconds before he understood, then he jumped out of his chair and ran to Sascha and began to kiss his hands.

'Never mind that,' Sascha said. 'Make as exact a diagram as you can of the location of Ah-ching's house.' Sascha then phoned the S.V.C. headquarters and asked to be added on night duty. While he waited downstairs for the patrol car, Aristide and I, bundled in our overcoats, began a vigil by the drawing-room windows. It was too cold to stand on the verandahs.

I don't know how long Aristide and I had been huddled together asleep on the divan when Mama found us. She knew at once that Sascha had defied her orders, and I rather suspect that her feelings about this were mixed. She was not angry nor did she scold, but it was obvious that she was extremely nervous. She began to chain-smoke, letting the ashes fall on her peignoir, on the carpet, anywhere it seemed but in the ashtray which she had carefully placed on the arm of her chair. The sky became light on the Pootung side, grey-blue and sheer, like chalcedony. Outside we could hear the river life awaken and the sound of streetcars. Then there was the grind of brakes and the hard snap of a car door. My brother and I ran on to the verandah.

'Come back at once,' Mama cried. 'You'll catch pneumonia.' But she followed us out, clutching at the neck of her thin robe. Below we saw a Red Cross ambulance and Sascha walking towards the back of it. The rear doors opened, and two orderlies emerged carrying a stretcher on which lay a blanket-covered body. Aristide raced through the drawing-room into the hall where he flung open the front door. As Mama and I reached him, we heard the elevator begin to rise.

Sascha came out, followed by the two bearers and the stretcher. We could see by her black satin headband that it was Hoboo in the stretcher, but her face was matted with blood. Aristide cried out and made a hovering step towards her.

'It's O.K.,' Sascha said. 'She's not dead.'

Sascha said that they had tried to gain admission at both St. Luke's and St. Elizabeth's hospitals but that there had been waiting lines of wounded the entire length of a block at each. One of the orderlies said that Hoboo had lost a lot of blood but that he didn't think her condition was critical. Mama directed the men to the drawing-room, where they carefully laid Hoboo on the divan, propping her head up with cushions. As Aristide and I went to her, I noticed a deep slash from her left eyebrow to the corner of her mouth. I took one of her hands in mine and saw that her wrist was barked almost to the bone. Hoboo moaned then and indicated that she was thirsty. Mama went to the dining-room and returned with a decanter of brandy. Sascha gently levered Hoboo as she sipped, coughed, and then downed a small glassful. Leaning back on the cushions, Hoboo emitted a long, almost whistling sigh and closed her eyes.

'Mama,' Aristide cried.

'Sascha, try Jarvis' office,' Mama said. One of the orderlies took Hoboo's pulse. 'She's just resting,' he said. After a while Hoboo opened her eyes and, without moving her head, looked around the room, her eyes taking in each of us; all at once she grinned widely. I had already seen many manifestations of this purely Oriental reaction. Fury and grief were expressed in imprecation and loud lamenting, but the response to near death, to a holocaust evaded, was laughter. Meanwhile Sascha had been able to locate Dr. Jarvis, and he arrived minutes later with Inspector Burnham and a Chinese constable. It was apparent that the doctor had been up all night; he was unshaven and irritable. He explained that Burnham was there to make a report.

'Sorry to intrude,' Burnham said, 'but we have to get as much factual evidence as possible. There's been so much hysteria about Japanese atrocities.'

Jarvis, who had wasted no time in examining Hoboo, looked up in fury. 'Hysteria?' he said. 'Do you call shooting women and children with dumdum bullets hysteria? I suppose, in that case, what this sabre cut in an old woman's face amounts to is protection of Japanese interests.' He told us, with the exception of Mama, to leave while he dressed and stitched Hoboo's wound. The Red Cross men departed and the rest of us waited outside the drawing-room. The servants were standing at the end of the hallway, and someone had gone to fetch Lao Ni, who appeared still fumbling with his sleepwear over which he had thrown a cook's apron. Presently Jarvis came out and said that Hoboo would require transfusions and that he would see about getting her into a hospital. He had given her a sedative, but she wanted to talk to Lao Ni; he said that Burnham and the constable could get their information now; then he left.

We went back into the room, and Lao Ni approached his aunt diffidently, his eyes fearful and shiny in a face that still refused to wake up. Hoboo pulled at her nephew's hand. 'Lao Ni, she's dead. They killed Su-mei.' The constable began taking notes as, in Chinese, Hoboo described what had happened. She had not experienced any difficulty getting into Chapei after she told the Chinese municipal sentries that she was General Koo Ah-ching's aunt. Just as she reached Paoshan Road, Japanese planes began to bomb the Commercial Press complex. Ducking the flying shrapnel, she was finally able to reach the house where Su-mei was living.

'The girl was frightened, I could see that, and she didn't give me an argument. For a couple of days, maybe more, she had had nothing to eat. We got her things together quickly, but as we were going to the door we heard them coming, the Japanese. Su-mei told me to hide under the bed. She said that they wouldn't hurt her because she was so far pregnant, but that they might kill me. I tried to reason with her; I told her those monsters would attack her pregnant or not and that after all I was old. She struck me very hard then, and as I fell to the floor the Japanese burst into the room. I crawled under the bed. I could hear them, those drunken *ronins* and marines; even their voices were hot and rapine. Pushing myself back against the wall and curled inwards like a snail, I saw those ugly boots, ten, maybe fifteen pairs of them. I watched as they poked their sabres through the drapes, behind doors, into closets. One of them knelt on the floor by the bed. He was so close I could smell him. He began slashing under the bed, with each swipe his blade drawing closer to me. I began to pinch my breasts as hard as I could so that if pain came suddenly it would not be a surprise, just added pain. And so, when the tip of the Japanese's blade sliced my face I did not make a sound. The bed above me sagged heavily, and I knew what was happening. I listened hard to hear if Su-mei was crying or screaming invectives. I prayed for her to cry out anything. But she didn't, not once. I don't know how long it went on, I only know that one of them was standing guard in front of the bed, his boots disembodied and dancing with restlessness. I could see the sword which he pointed towards the bed and which he lowered from time to time. Then I heard a struggle, like someone wrenching away, and there were Su-mei's legs, rigid in front of the guard's. I heard the cheated howl of anger from the Japanese and the sucking of a blade pulled from flesh, as Su-mei's legs buckled and she collapsed. They left her there, lying on the floor facing me, her eyes wide open.'

'Did the victim say anything before dying?' Inspector Burnham asked. Hoboo did not reply, and the constable repeated the question in Chinese.

'No,' Hoboo said, closing her eyes. Mama, thinking that she wanted to rest, motioned to the inspector that it was time to leave, but Hoboo continued talking. 'I don't know for how long I stayed there, under the bed, but I realized that I'd better go. That it would be better to risk the bombs and the shooting in the streets than another raiding party. As I wandered along trying to make my way back to the barriers, I saw the sky above darken with the big birds, and in the next second they were dropping their eggs. I huddled for shelter in the entranceway of a large building. Before long a truck of Japanese pulled up, and the marines went into the building and began to comb each floor. As they brought out the occupants, they herded me along with them. They tied our hands with rope, then one of them went around with a writing brush and made the ideo-graph for sniper on some of our faces. The truck was not big enough for everyone, so they made the rest of us march behind. Somebody said that we were going to an open field where the Japanese would shoot us. I remember thinking that I didn't care anymore. Then some soldiers or snipers, anyway Chinese, started shooting from a window, and all of us who were marching ran for cover even though the Japs kept shouting for us to remain where we were. They fired on us, but I managed to get away. In a side street I found an abandoned garage and hid there. I could see out from where the garage door was hinged, and I waited until I saw foreign soldiers in squad cars, and I shouted at them but they would not stop for me. I lay in the street, ready to give up now, ready to die. One of the foreign cars stopped and I saw Sascha.. ..'

Dr. Jarvis phoned back later to say that the Paulun, a German hospital, could take Hoboo but that no ambulances were available. So Lao Ni and Sascha drove her there in our car. That night we read in the papers that the Japanese had shot one hundred and fifty suspected snipers rounded up in the streets of Chapei. The victims were described as being of all ages, men, women, and children, most of whom were thought to be peasant refugees.

Unable to cope with Japan's territorial encroachments, the new regime under Sun Fo soon found that they were no more prepared for a full-scale war with Japan than Chiang had been. In January, the same month that the Japanese attacked Shanghai, Sun Fo resigned and Chiang Kai-shek was reinstated. Chiang at once sent two divisions to bolster the Nineteenth Route Army who were defending the city. The world at large and the foreign population of China in particular, who cherished their opéra-bouffe image of the Chinese as soldiers, found themselves bemused by the fury with which these armies held their lines against overwhelming odds. Certainly no nation was more stunned than Japan, who countered by rushing reinforcements to the Shanghai zone. By the end of February more than half of Japan's standing army was in China. Peace mediations continued and temporary truces were even set up until the Chinese discovered that their enemy was using these cease-fires to make fresh landings and ship in arms and supplies. The matter of the Japanese headquartering in the International Settlement and their open use of it as a base for their operations was one of concern to the Chinese. Complaints penned by the mayor to the Municipal Council proved ineffective. Sascha saw through the veiled excuses made by the foreign body in the Settlement. 'It's very simple,' he said. 'For a council member to be re-elected, he must have the Japanese vote.'

Although Ah-ching headed one of the divisions that Chiang sent to Shanghai, it was not before March that he was able to visit Hoboo. I know that it had to be around that time, because there had been a lot of talk about the Japanese creating an independent state of Manchuria, calling it Manchukuo. I remember thinking it all very romantic how they had spirited away the last of the Manchu rulers, the boy emperor P'u-i, from Tientsin, and now he was regent of Manchukuo. But Sascha said, 'Poppycock,' and that P'u-i was no more than a puppet for the Japanese and their designs. It was Ah-ching who arrived with the news that the League of Nations had appointed Lord Lytton to make a full and unbiased report of Japan's actions in China.

But for the fact that he wore a black armband on the sleeve of his uniform, there was little change in either Ah-ching's appearance or his manner. He gave Hoboo a sackful of silver dollars. 'To donate to your favourite saint, of course,' Ah-ching said. Hoboo, her good eye fixed on her nephew, took the money without a word. Lifting her jacket she looped the sack through the cord which kept her trousers up. Hoboo seemed to have recovered from her injury of two months ago, and though she had wasted somewhat and the scar across her cheek was still a livid weal, she was feistier than ever. Ah-ching had brought Didi with him, and anxious to play the host, Aristide invited them into the parlour, but Ah-ching declined the offer. Since he gave no indication that he wanted privacy with his aunt and since the other servants were present, Aristide and I remained in the kitchen during his visit. We listened as Ah-ching made a prognosis of the war. He believed that the Chinese would retreat from their lines at Shanghai towards Nanking, but that a truce was in the offing. In a half-deriding reference to his father, Ah-ching said the old man could scarcely wait to return to Chapei, where opium stores and dens and gambling parlours were flourishing in the Japanese-administered suburb.

Ah-ching did not mention Su-mei except once, just before leaving. He had said his good-byes to Lao Ni and the other servants and had even kissed his aunt, a gesture awkwardly but touchingly made. He was standing by the door to the kitchen. Didi was propped in his arms. With his back to his aunt, Ah-ching said, 'Did she say anything?' Hoboo did not reply at once. 'You heard me, old aunt,' Ah-ching said.

'She said only one thing before she died,' Hoboo answered. 'She said, "Pao-ziu!"'

Ah-ching nodded, still not turning. Then he looked at Didi and stroked his cheek with a finger. 'Did you hear that, Didi? Pao-ziu!'

We went onto the verandah of the smoking-room to wave them off, Aristide being particularly curious to see a Chinese general's staff car. But it was a vaguely familiar car which drew up to the kerb, a black Pierce-Arrow which I was having difficulty placing in my memory until one of the occupants, a Chinese civilian in a flashy foreign suit, got out. My thoughts were diverted by Didi, who was waving a huge white handkerchief, like a flag of truce. He kept waving it out of the car window until the vehicle turned on Nanking Road and we could no longer see it.

'Hoboo,' I said, 'what does pao-ziu mean?' Hoboo drew her

shawl closer about her shoulders, shuddering slightly against the wind, and started to go inside.

'*Pao-ziu* is Chinese for revenge, you numskull,' Aristide said.

The next day all Chinese banks and a preponderance of stores in the International Settlement shut down as a protest against the foreigners for permitting Japanese planes to fly over the Settlement. Besides the serious financial consequences of this measure, leaders of the foreign communities were becoming increasingly aware that Japan's onslaughts were not limited to wholly Chinese targets. Raiding bombers had hit the Wing On cotton mill which served as the post of command for the Third Battalion of the United States Marines. Incidents of foreign residents being manhandled and humiliated by the Japanese were reported daily. Ministers of America, Britain, and France realized that the time had come for them to join the League Commission in an attempt to stop the hostilities.

30

UPON the Lytton Commission's decision that Japan was the culpable party and at their urging that members withhold recognition of Manchukuo, Japan resigned from the League. On New Year's Day of 1933, Japanese troops attacked the Chinese garrison at Jehol, a province which but for one area of the border separates Manchuria from China. Within a matter of days they occupied it. Chiang Kai-shek again fell victim to abuse from every faction, and each spoke up for concerted war against Japan. In spite of the fact that he had been steadily building military reserves and now had a fairly respect-able squadron of bombers, Chiang protested that he was not yet ready to take on Japan. He could not, he felt, consolidate a drive against them so long as the Communists continued to multiply. In May, when another one of those shaky and self-advantageous truces was signed by Japan, a group of long-standing dissenters, generals, and politicians, based in Fukien province, threatened to raise the standard against Chiang. Telegrams of denunciation and demands for Chiang's resignation were fired off. Chiang had by now reached the point where he was thoroughly fed up with the whole repetitious business of resigning his position, to be recalled, only to be asked to resign once more. Still he sent his emissaries and made attempts to placate the Fukien clique.

But in Shanghai that summer the hostilities were a forgotten matter. Chinese troops had long since evacuated, and the Japanese had entrenched three thousand men in a fortresslike barracks within a block of Hongkew Park. With the insouciance of a waterfront harlot, the city had shrugged off her minor rape, patched her sores with fresh paint, and eagerly resumed her extraterritorial liaison. Upon first returning to school, we had toured the ruins of Chapei, examining the gutted buildings with that peculiar detachment of witnessing history. Classes were taken up where they had been left off, and gradually most of the old routines were rerailed. Finally the Richard Ashbury drama department was sufficiently organized to cast for a term-end production. Since the plays of the department were reviewed by the leading British daily, Aristide was ecstatic when he received a summons to appear for one of the top roles in *Little Lord Fauntleroy*. But Sascha was aghast. He stated his objections to Mama while we were having breakfast one morning before Aristide appeared.

'What's wrong with that?' Mama was saying. 'I saw it years ago with Mary Pickford. It's all about a nice boy and a widow who's eating up her capital instead of living on her income—' Mama began reading herself into the story.

'Mama, what part do you think they want Arsie for?' Sascha insisted.

'There's that darling little boy,' Mama reflected, 'with all those long curls—'

Sascha shook his head negatively.

'I remember an old gentleman,' Mama continued, '—very gruff but most distingué.'

'It's not the grandfather,' Sascha said.

'I've got to dress. I'm meeting Chicho and Tila in town,' Mama said.

'Mama,' Sascha persisted, 'remember Billie Dove?'

Even though this episode had taken place a couple of summers before, the reminder of it never failed to bring about a jelling effect on Mama. One evening at the height of the monsoon rains, Aristide

234

had taken it upon himself to recreate for me the last scene from Waterloo Bridge. Wrapped in a Spanish shawl snatched from the piano, with me in tow to hold an umbrella over him, Aristide had proceeded to Garden Bridge. As I and crowds of Chinese passers-by stood enthralled, he capered and staggered through a protracted suicide. It had all ended in complete humiliation when the municipal police, mistaking Aristide for a noisy prostitute—he had done himself up with rouge, patches, and spit curls—took us to the Central Station. After Aristide had shrieked his explanations and finally thrown open his shawl as indisputable proof that he was not female, Sascha was contacted to fetch us.

Shaken by the recollection, I thought I'd better speak up. 'It's Mrs. Errol, that's the part.'

Before Mama could reply, Aristide entered the dining-room. At twelve, he stood a little over five feet and, while not altogether plump, seemed to have managed a certain gracious roundness where it was least expected. His hair had become curly, and he brushed the ringlets down so that they shielded his brows and stressed those great tragedienne eyes.

'The widow Aristide,' Sascha snorted.

True enough, implicit in Aristide's manner was the forbearance of loss, at once resigned but courageous. Status seemed uppermost in his bearing, as though, if he were obliged to walk in dirt, which his glance at Sascha suggested, he needn't rub his hands in it.

Later that day Mama admitted her defeat. 'It's no good. Nothing I say helps. I told him, what do you want to be an actress for, when you can be a great pianist like Uncle Benno?' Mama was referring to Benno Moiseiwitsch whom she had persuaded to listen to Aristide's laboured rendition of the *Moonlight Sonata*.

'Very nice,' Uncle Benno had said.

'Anyway,' Mama went on, 'the widow what's-her-name is a nice respectable part. It's not like he was playing Sadie Thompson. And after all, if Mary Pickford could play a boy. . . .'

Aristide plunged into rehearsals. On the assumption that if not too much was made over the issue it would resolve itself and be forgotten by the next term, Mama and Sascha left him to his own devices. This might well have been the case but for the review the play received from the North China *Daily News*. It was the habit of the Richard Ashbury teaching staff occasionally to include one of its

235

members in the school plays, especially if a role required more dramatic capabilities than could be expected from students. In the programme the cast was listed by surnames preceded by the initial. Since it was a boys' school the question of gender never came up and, not wishing to steal their pupils' thunder, the faculty made no exception in the case of a teacher's playing the part. The *News* reviewer praised the play generally, lauded the near-expert timing and precision of the cast, mentioned the settings as acceptable and the lighting as competent, and devoted two paragraphs to Aristide's performance. Mama read it aloud the morning after: 'A. Spunt, obviously a member of the R.A.S.' teaching staff, gave a performance of gem-like brilliance. In the role of Mrs. Errol, so often played to the mellifluous hilt, Miss Spunt scored by innate restraint. In her interpretation of the widow there was dignity as well as fire. In a scene of exceptional lustre between Cedric and his mother—' Mama smashed the paper on her lap. The wings of her chiffon peignoir fluttered in nervous surprise as they settled warily beside her.

'When grass grows here,' Mama said, indicating the palm of her hand, 'will you act again. *Ever* again.'

'Mei Lang-fang, that's what he is,' Sascha said. Mei Lang-fang was an internationally famous actor-impersonator best known for his interpretations of Chinese opera heroines.

'He couldn't play a nice part in a fine drama, like what was that lovely man we saw the other night in the pictures?' Mama asked.

'Peter Lorre in *Crime and Punishment*,' Sascha replied. Actually Mama had been ill after the film and had had to take a sedative.

Throughout all this Aristide remained Mrs. Errol. After all, an American widow of breeding, regardless of her financial situation, did not shout back. He sighed, carefully wiped his mouth with his napkin, and rose from the table. Apologetically I followed the star from the room.

Of the many books in Papa's library that Sascha had digested, none had a more profound influence on him than one modest-looking red-bound volume. This was a 1911 edition of *What a Young Boy Should Know*. At the least opportunity he was exhorting Aristide and me to its contents, and Aristide began to refer to it as The Book. The admonitions to plentiful exercise and fresh air were easy enough to obey, being part of the formula prescribed by Mr. Pringle in school P.T. But the harped-on allusions to the irreparable damage caused by masturbation, which I had just discovered, unnerved me. As these harangues from Sascha grew more persistent (did he know something?), I became more and more apprehensive. Aristide, on the other hand, remained imperturbable, and were it not for the shuffling about and irregular breathing which came from his corner of the room, I might have believed that he was uninvolved. Sascha maintained that the only effective therapies against the evils of tea, coffee, and masturbation were cold showers and rigorous exercise, and he persuaded Mama to enrol us in an athletic group for the summer. By then, convinced that my path led directly to acne, blindness, and fits of imbecility I was prepared to do penance, but Aristide demurred. It was only after, sitting on the toilet, he discovered stretch marks on his abdomen and began yelling for everyone to come at once because he took the striae to mean that he was bursting that he consented to the physical health programme. Originally Sascha intended for us to accompany him to the Y.M.C.A., but after some consideration he opted against it, since too many of that organization's activities involved masculine nudity. Both he and Mama agreed that there was no telling how our well-bred widow would respond to such an ambience. Instead, we were enrolled at the Cercle Sportif Français for a curriculum that included tennis, badminton, and swimming. Once the programme was under way and I discovered that my mediocrity in these sports served the cause of inconspicuousness, it turned out to be relatively enjoyable. I could with a free conscience indulge in all the peripheral benefits such as grenadine milk shakes and Saratoga chips with the serene conviction that no matter what my transgressions amounted to at night they could be exercised away the next morning.

Aristide still retained a certain amount of locker room shyness. I had observed him dexterously wrapping a towel around his waist before removing his trousers, and I noticed a tendency he had of cupping his hands over his chest when he ran to the showers. But the racing, tumbling, and plunging of the sports at which he fared quite well caused the emergence of a new dimension, a tougher, more male Aristide, and he began to abandon his Mrs. Errol demeanour.

Didi had taken to coming by several times a week, ostensibly for our assistance with his studies in English. Aristide had wanted Mama to enrol Didi with us for the summer session at the Cercle, but Mama was uncertain. While Japanese, who were considered foreigners, could become members of the club, Chinese could not and they were only permitted as guests. I recollect on one of Didi's visits that he was struggling over a poem called 'The Eagle'. Aristide was trying to help him overcome the Chinese tendency of substituting *r*'s for *l*'s and vice versa, a failing which Lao Ni for all his industriousness was never able to surmount. Time and again Didi repeated the first line of the poem: 'He crasps the clooked clags——'

'Cl-l-lasps the cr-r-rooked cr-r-rags!' Aristide repeated.

Sascha came upon us at the point where Didi had just mastered the correct pronunciation, and we were all in high spirits. I noticed that in spite of a friendly greeting Sascha seemed inordinately interested in Didi's face, where there were a few blemishes, probably insect bites. But I did not realize that Sascha had attached the direst significance to these until I overheard him telling Mama that he suspected Didi's condition was a result of poor circulation aggravated by self-indulgence and, more likely than not, at the very least a forerunner of venereal disease. Rather than cope with the ruckus she would have stirred up by banishing Didi, Mama yielded to the idea of his salvation. When all was said and done, exercise and cold showers, given a fair chance, should certainly work the same type of miracle on a Chinese boy as on a foreign one. So Didi was issued a summer membership card and began going with us to the Cercle. I can still recall his first day there, the wonderment of those round eyes as he saw the glass-enclosed pool, the chute with its highly polished mahogany ramp, and the high-dive stand. Not yet twelve, Didi stood taller than either Aristide or I. He moved with such natural litheness and coordination that he was soon at home in the pool. But he did not seem inclined towards playing tennis. A week or so after he had begun to come to the club we toured the red earth courts in front of the colonnaded terrace and Aristide urged him to take a stab at the game. Watching the players, Didi's eyes darkened and that special sweetness around his lips, a look he had of continual appreciation, was missing.

'Who are those men in the white and blue uniforms?' he asked.

'The Chinese? They're markers; they play with the members.'

'Whether they want to or not?'

'Of course, that's what they're paid for,' Aristide said.

238

'I do not want to play tennis,' Didi said.

'You don't have to play with the markers.'

'I wouldn't play with them,' Didi said. Then seeing that his sharpness had hurt Aristide, he added, 'Everywhere I look there is some evidence of Chinese bondage.'

'But they're paid,' Aristide insisted.

'You don't understand. I cannot pretend to be one of you by using my people.'

'Well, you swim, and there are towel boys in the locker room,' Aristide said.

Didi was thoughtful; then he said, 'A towel boy is different from a man who must run and jump when you say and not stop until you want to.' He smiled then at Aristide, the sweetness returning to his face. 'At Sunday school we learned that in spite of great sufferings, the Jews consider themselves the chosen people.'

'So, so,' Aristide said, his voice suspicious with folk remembrance.

'I think maybe we Chinese are the chosen people,' Didi said. The three of us laughed at that, but Didi never went near the courts again.

Because of the club's popularity as an international gathering place we were not surprised to find the poolside thronged with many of the youngsters whom we knew either from school or from parties or simply by that arcane process by which children multiply their acquaintances. I was distressed to find Ronald Frothinger was a member. He had just returned from a couple of years' schooling in England and although he was careful to assume a courteous, even a welcoming, manner, the pupils of his eyes still seemed to me to click with cash-register precision. He was taller and skinnier now, with that peculiar paunchiness which predicted exactly the type of physique he would have in maturity. He did not, as I feared he might, offend Didi, and I was sufficiently grateful so that I didn't object to his sponging milk shakes and chips from us whenever he could.

Ronald had soon established a coterie of friends; among them was a slender French boy named Jean Pierre. From his soft voice and the impeccable English achieved by Europeans, one might have expected gentleness from Jean Pierre. But he was fond of collecting butterflies, which he stored in glass jars, and he would sit at a table in the viewers' balcony alongside the pool by the hour pinning the struggling creatures to corks. On one occasion he brought a brown paper bag with him to the pool and held it out to me. Thinking that I was being offered a sweet I reached into the bag only to find my fingers in contact with something cool and slimy. I withdrew my hand as though it had been bitten. Jean Pierre then pulled out a pair of frog's legs which he had skinned and dangled them in front of my face. I stood petrified unable either to move or to take my eyes off those dancing tiny legs which looked unbearably human. Without a change of expression the French boy swung the legs like a pendulum closer and closer to my face until I began to scream, and Aristide came up from behind and pushed Jean Pierre into the pool, frog's legs and all.

The other of Ronald's chief cohorts was a tubby ginger-haired boy whom they called, for some reason, Squid. There was nothing in the least refined about Squid's cruelty. He thought it the merriest of larks to place a mango skin in the path of a serving boy and then roar with laughter as the Chinese slipped and fell, struggling under the burden of a heavily-laden tray. Another caper in which Ronald joined him was to urinate in the fresh towel bins in the men's dressing-room, both boys taking great pains not to disturb the folded linen, so that when the unsuspecting towel boy handed one to a swimmer with which to dry himself, the servant became the object of the member's abuse.

Without teachers upon whom to fawn and extract favours, Ronald might not have succeeded in his cherished position as gang leader but for the fact that he would undertake feats of outrageous daring against which he made wagers. He alone would dive from the viewers' balcony into the pool, which was quite some distance and required clearing the tiled walkway, and which was of course against club regulations. And it was he who dreamed up the innovation of sliding down the chute headfirst and backwards. Nothing pleased Ronald more than when someone was foolish or fearless enough to put up money against his challenge. He had managed to lure one or another of the boys into some of these antics, but only for reasonably safe ventures such as seeing who could swim the length of the pool longer without coming up for air or jack-knife blindfolded from the diving stand. There wasn't much money forthcoming from either of these feats, but no one seemed interested in sharing in Ronald's more bravura stunts.

Aristide began to weary of Ronald's pencil-shyness which had become so blatant that he and his cronies had taken to ordering their refreshments in advance and sending the chits to our table to be signed. It was after Aristide flatly refused to honour any more of these that Ronald made an unsuccessful proposition to me that I slide down the chute backwards. I panicked at even the idea of going down the chute in the frontwards sitting position. Once, at Aristide's urging, I had climbed the metal steps to the narrow standing platform at the top of it. But the ramp, which seemed to drop in an almost vertical line until the end of it which curved upwards, made me lose my nerve. Then Ronald began to work on Didi. While Didi was a reasonably strong swimmer and had fine style on the diving board, my brother and I knew he felt insecure without his spectacles. Didi had from the first avoided both the chute and the high-dive stand. He did his best to resist Ronald's repeated overtures and made pleasant but firm evasions. For a while it looked as though Ronald had given up until one day, when Didi had preceded us to the pool, we found him surrounded by Ronald and company. Perhaps it was the fact that his parents had come to the pool that day which made Ronald so zealous in his determination. Mr. Frothinger, in trunks with a towel over his shoulders and a pipe clenched between his teeth, the replica of Ronald to be, was leaning on the railings of the viewers' balcony.

'Come along, Didi,' Ronald was saying. 'It's ripping good fun and you can win a whole dollar.'

'But I don't have a dollar to bet,' Didi replied.

'Oh your friends will pay up—if you lose; you're their guest, you know.'

'No,' said Didi.

'What's that?' Ronald said.

'I won't do it.'

Squid spoke up. 'It seems that our littee Chinee is velly yellow.'

'Velly, *velly* yellow,' Jean Pierre echoed.

'He's nothing of the sort,' I said. 'It's just that he can't see without his glasses.'

'What about you then? You don't have bad eyesight.'

'I'm not allowed to bet,' I said lamely.

'Mummy doesn't allow us to bet,' Squid chortled. 'Then do it for *fun.*'

241

I kept silent, and Ronald made a clearing with his hands as he addressed his friends oratorially: 'Gentlemen, we have one yellow-belly and one in a blue funk—' He turned and bowed to Aristide. 'Would the pink lady care to make the palette complete?' The gesticulating circle of Ronald's group had attracted the attention of others, and they began to gather around us. Even Mr. Frothinger came down by the chute to see what all the sport was about.

Aristide turned to Ronald. 'One dollar if I do it?'

'Upon my word as an Englishman,' Ronald said gravely.

'O.K.'

'No!' Didi grabbed Aristide by the arm, attempting to pull him away. 'You must not. You will fall.'

'Don't let him, Didi,' I cried.

'I will do it. He asked me first,' Didi said.

'You don't have a dollar,' Aristide smiled.

I appealed to Mr. Frothinger. 'Sir, that is a very dangerous stunt Ronald is making my brother do. Please stop him.'

Mr. Frothinger removed the pipe from his mouth and said, 'It won't do to meddle you know, poor show.' Then in went the stem of the pipe as though to dam up any doubts he might have had on that score.

As Aristide climbed the twenty feet or so to the top of the chute, Didi and I went up along the viewers' balcony as close as we could get to him. Aristide made a quick wave of salutation to us from the standing platform, but I could see that he was very nervous. After a moment of deliberation he turned his back to us and grasped the chrome handrails on either side of him. Then he gradually lowered himself into a sitting position, the legs stiff and spread slightly, the weight of his body telling at his back muscles. The next instant he had released the rungs and was being borne swiftly down the length of the ramp. A cheer rang out from the watchers. Just as Aristide was about to clear the lower curve before landing in the pool, Squid shouted his name loudly. Instinctively Aristide turned and in so doing upset his balance. I watched frozen as he flipped back down, off the ramp, with a thudding smack on the tile of the walkway. Didi climbed through the railings and raced like a whippet to where Aristide lay. By the time I got to him a tight circle had closed around my brother. When I pushed through I saw that Aristide's face was white and that his eyes were closed. I knelt beside him and began to bawl shamelessly. Mr. Frothinger had sent someone to the first aid room for help. He was chafing Aristide's hands but there was no sign of life. I pleaded between sobs for Aristide to talk to me, and I kept asking Mr. Frothinger if he would be all right. Even though Mr. Frothinger looked quite grim, he uttered those unbelievable British platitudes: 'Keep a stiff upper lip, there's a pukka chap!' But Didi put his arms around me and made unintelligible consoling sounds the way Hoboo did when I had hurt myself. As the orderlies from first aid appeared, Aristide began to show some signs of life. He opened his eyes, looked around, and found Ronald. 'I did it,' Aristide said. 'I won!'

'Not quite, old cock—' said Ronald.

'I went down the chute like you said. I won the dollar.'

'I daresay you went down the chute but you *missed* the pool.' Ronald held this gem of evidence to the light of his friends' approval.

Mr. Frothinger said then, 'Ronald, fetch this boy a dollar at once!'

The first aid station was located in the men's dressing-room. Didi and I waited outside while a French doctor attended to Aristide. Before long he came out and told us that there was nothing to worry about. Aristide had merely jarred himself, but the doctor did not think that he had broken anything. Had Aristide fallen from higher he might very well have damaged his spine or suffered a severe concussion. As it happened, the doctor said, it was a miracle. I knew that for months I would have to listen while Aristide described the details of his near brush with death, but I was so relieved to hear that he was all right that I let out a cheer of joy as Didi and I ran back to the lockers. Ronald, Jean Pierre, and Squid had just come back from the showers and were glumly drying themselves. Didi had gotten out of his trunks and was going towards the showers when Ronald flicked the wet edge of his towel against Didi's buttocks. Although he winced at the pain he kept on walking. Ronald flicked at him again, then Squid and Jean Pierre began to lash out with their towels.

'Coolie,' Ronald taunted. 'Fetch me a dry towel.'

'How dare you speak to him like that?' I shouted. 'Didi's a guest member.'

'He's a Chink, isn't he?' Squid said. 'And Chink members are not allowed in foreign clubs.' Then Jean Pierre gave me a stinging

243

flick from his towel and said, 'First you bring your coolie to pee in our pool, and next I suppose you'll bring your amah?'

Ronald sniffed about him as though he smelled something unsavoury. 'I do believe I detect a Chink in his amah—' Ronald's pun had a pulverizing effect on his cronies, and they collapsed on the benches and writhed on the floor with uncontainable mirth. At that point Didi seized their towels and began flogging the boys with all his might. Taken so by surprise in the midst of their hilarity, and weakened from the laughter, the boys began by jeering at Didi, then by protesting and then howling in pain as they cowered and scrambled for cover; but Didi did not let up. Applauding this turn, I stood on the benches and egged Didi on, and all might have gone well but for the fact that Mr. Frothinger arrived with the news that Aristide was ready to go home. I saw him, but Didi was in such a frenzy that his legs were trembling and he began shouting in Chinese. 'Foreign pigs! Parasitic turtles! Fornicators of your mothers!'

Mr. Frothinger's mouth opened like a crane's and he said, 'See here now, you little devil, you're in a foreigners' club y'know——'

Didi turned on him. 'You are the devils, *yang kwei tze*. Wait— one day this and every club, every building in China, will be taken from you. I, a Chinese, will be the member and you, all of you, will be my towel boys!'

With the assistance of some other foreign members, Mr. Frothinger soon put an end to Didi's rebellion and we were sent packing with Aristide who, as it turned out, had only one small bandage on his brow to show for his misadventure.

I don't know whether it was Mr. Frothinger or one of the other members who reported Didi's outburst, but a couple of days later the Cercle secretary sent a letter rescinding Didi's privileges, giving the details of his scene in the dressing-room as the cause. To Mama this was a point brought sharply home. Like all foreigners, she felt threatened by eventual Chinese reprisal. In spite of that, her reaction was what it would have been if either Aristide or I had committed an infraction. Didi was brought before her in the smoking-room by Hoboo and Lao Ni, and Mama began automatically listing the blessings heaped upon the Chinese by the foreigners, upbraiding Didi for his ingratitude. 'It was a foreign missy who paid for your summer membership too. You shouldn't forget that,' Mama said. Then she told Didi that he could no longer play with us every day. At that Didi began to cry and Aristide, unable to endure it any longer, shouted, 'It's not fair. It wasn't his fault.' Mama gave Aristide an ultimate silencing look and then amended her sentence. 'All right, you can come on weekends, mind you, only if you behave yourself.'

While Hoboo had stood expressionless during Mama's censure of her nephew, Lao Ni had been smiling deprecatingly. Once outside the smoking-room, he seized Didi by the arm. 'Come with me. I will teach you to make your family lose face.' But Hoboo wrenched Didi away with sudden violence and thrust her fist at Lao Ni. 'What? What would you know of face to teach this child?' she said.

31

IN his senior school year, Sascha had been assigned, along with the rest of his class, the task of corresponding with a student in England, the purpose being the exchange of sociocultural and political views. After graduation Sascha had sporadically kept in touch with his pen pal, a girl who was now attending the London School of Economics. Early in 1934, Aristide showed me a carbon copy he had found of a recent letter.

After a summary of the political developments, in which Sascha described how, at the end of the year, Chiang had been compelled to suppress the Fukienese and how he had then renewed his campaign against the Communist stronghold in Kiangsi Province, the letter continued:

Now that you are abreast (ahem!) of our China mishmash, I must tell you about the New Life Movement. You'll never believe it! This is Chiang's private stew of Confucian precepts and Y.M.C.A. strictures. The masses, bless their uncomprehending hearts, are being led to social reforms in the best circus and bread traditions. Parades are held at the drop of a hat, where civic leaders, professors, students and labourers attend in full force and carry lanterns bearing these messages: be prompt, button your collar, brush your teeth, kill rats and flies and of course attend your house of worship. (The Methodist Church in particular, if Madame

Chiang had her way.) Meanwhile our little friends in the north (the Japs) have been keeping Chiang hopping by inciting border clashes. This in order to distract the Chinese government from their more nefarious (don't you love nefarious?) ventures, primarily the cultivation and sale of opium to the Chinese masses. . . .

The remainder of Sascha's letter dealt with his own doings, S.V.C. activities, and his aspirations of becoming a voluntary member of the French Special Police. As I handed the copy back to Aristide, I can recall my admiration for what I then considered to be Sascha's informed and masculine-paced tract. Only years later was I to realize how his views reflected the impertinence with which foreigners generally responded to any Chinese endeavour. True, the 'chin chin Chinaman' quality was present in the more fatuous commandments evolving from the New Life Movement. But its objectives were really calculated by Chiang Kai-shek to make the vast masses cognizant of a central government. Early in his campaigns against them, Chiang had discovered that the Communists succeeded in unifying the people by working in terms and projects which they could comprehend and in which they could participate. The Movement, Chiang's counterweapon, began as a provincial experiment and became nationwide. Plans for highways, bridges, and buildings were instituted and self-sustaining communities organized.

Sascha had been correct in his reference to the Japanese. By playing their puppets against Chiang and creating incidents at the boundaries of their occupied provinces, Japan was handily provided with the excuse that Nanking could not keep order. More troops— more territory taken. And opium provided Japan with a double-edged sword. Its sale provided enormous revenues, and the proliferation of its use among the Chinese army and civilians made them easy to manipulate. Since the time that the Japanese had occupied Manchukuo, poppy acreage there had doubled. Opium dens outnumbered rice shops three to one. In spite of that, addiction did not grow at the rate of production, and the Japanese began manufacturing the more addictive narcotics, heroin and morphine. Having flooded the regions under their control with narcotics, the Japanese began mass distribution. Korean peddlers were imported by the thousands. Chinese authorities who attempted to curb sales by arresting the peddlers found themselves stymied. Under extraterritorial laws, the Koreans as Japanese subjects had to be tried in

246

their own courts, where of course they were acquitted at once. Almost as frustrating to Chiang as Japan's narcotic activities was the fact that in the far west, in Szechwan province, poppy cultivation was the major industry, the lifeline of both the residing warlords and the peasants. Chiang made a decisive move. Since his hands were tied as far as punishing Japanese producers and sellers was concerned, the best he could achieve was to forbid Chinese purchase. Szechwan was ordered to reduce production gradually, and stringent rules were laid down under the Six-Year Opium Suppression Plan. A first offender was to be sent to a health clinic for cure and rehabilitation. A two-time offender who lived under the protection of the foreign settlements was to receive twelve years in jail, but if he lived in a Chinese-governed area the sentence was death by firing squad.

To our family that spring, the New Life Movement meant no more than the mayor's invitation inaugurating the recently built civic centre. We were hardly concerned with Chiang's hinterland squabbles, and to all outwards appearances the Japanese seemed bent only on gaining recognition for Manchukuo where they were in the process of having P'u-i proclaimed its emperor. But in an oblique way we found ourselves impinged upon by the new antiopium rulings. Since Mama's decree the summer before that Didi could only visit Aristide and me on weekends, we had done our best to make it up to him by planning special treats. But Mama was on one of her erratic financial cutbacks and had begun to limit what she called our wasteful extravagance. To us, weekly trips to the pictures and a foray into Marcel's constituted neither waste nor extravagance, particularly in the light of a pair of Fiats, presented one to Sascha and the other to Chicho. Although Mama went to elaborate pains to conceal it from us, we also knew that she and Chicho patronized the newly opened gambling dens which operated immune from municipal laws in the extrasettlement roads (areas belonging to the Chinese but policed by the foreign municipalities). Mama's sudden penury was the result of a recent visit from Mr. Isaacs when he had rendered a profit-and-loss accounting. Since Papa's death five years earlier, his business had been running mostly in the red, and Mama had kept it going out of her capital. When, as on this occasion, she threatened to close the office, Mr. Isaacs and the two Chinese officials came scurrying with armloads of statistics.

They pointed out that of the nearly sixty million tonnage of powered vessels that had entered and cleared the China ports that year, twenty-seven percent had been to or from Shanghai. There were at the moment a total of one hundred and forty-three cotton mills and five million spindles in the city. Next to the United States and India, China was the world's largest cotton producer. It was merely a matter of time before the political situation was straightened out; then the boom was inevitable. Mr. Isaacs swore to that; the Chinese swore to it; and Sascha, who had been going to the office still on his limited-hours basis, supported them.

When Aristide heard that the famous Hagenbeck Circus was on tour from Germany, he implored that we be allowed to take Didi to it. Mama was willing on condition that we buy cheap seats—'For two of you I'll pay for the best, but for three, the worst.' As it turned out she paid for four, since Sascha wanted to come along too. On a crisp Saturday in March we crammed into Sascha's Fiat and headed for the circus. (Lao Ni had asked for the day off and there would have been no room for him to drive anyway.) Beyond the impressive amount of wild animals, marvellous buffoonery from the clowns, and some dazzling trapeze acts, I fear the Hagenbeck performance falls into that bulging file in the memory lost among Hollywood epics and visits to the zoo at Jessfield Park. But I do recall we returned, very elated, to find Mama and Chicho in the drawing-room trying to comfort Didi's mother. Hoboo was sitting next to the woman and the other servants were standing about. Hoboo explained that Didi's mother had come to fetch him. The boy went to his mother, and though she spoke calmly, her agitation was obvious. Lao Ni had been arrested in Chapei for buying opium from an agent of the Suppression Bureau.

The mother went on to say that Lao Ni, taken into custody, had tried to pass himself off as the addict, but he had been unable to fool the medical examiners. Pretending to go along with his story they asked Lao Ni questions—where he lived, where he worked, how he had become addicted, how long? Meanwhile a bureau wagon had been dispatched to Ah-ching's house (they had moved back to Chapei), where the old man had been seized.

'Listen, don't worry,' Mama said. 'Ah-ching has influence; he'll fix everything.'

No one said anything. In these early days of the opium suppression, laws were being strictly enforced. Chiang had permitted none of the familiar latitude which we had come to expect of Chinese ordinances. Besides which, Ah-ching was fighting Communists in Kiangsi.

'It's a first offence,' Sascha said. 'He will have to submit to a cure, that's all.'

Again there was silence, for the adults in the room knew the father could no more abstain from his pipe than he could cease breathing. Lao Ni returned at that point. Upon his release he had gone to see his father at the health clinic. It was a fine place, very clean, and the old man would be made well there, once and for all. Probably it was the best thing that could have happened. I saw that Didi was missing. I found him at the back door to the kitchen. Earlier in the day Hoboo had given him a singing cricket. Now he was dangling the tiny bamboo cage from its string. I touched his shoulder, but he did not move, he seemed totally absorbed in the singing of the cricket.

Around that time something happened to Aristide's voice. That it was more or less due for a change was one thing, but the manner in which the change occurred was another. Unlike the majority of boys who undergo this transition and whose voices seesaw between squeaking and braying, Aristide had developed a complete range of voices over each of which he had perfect control. Tila, who discovered it first, became very excited and said that Aristide was a vocal phenomenon. When Mama ascertained that phenomenon generally meant good, she gave the subject no more thought. For that matter, none of us did. The sight and sound of Aristide horsing around with Tila, screeching arias, was old hat, and he had always been able to hit a piercing falsetto. But Tila assured us that this was very different. One day, still in March, she ushered Mama, Sascha, and me into the drawing-room where Aristide stood in front of the grand piano. As Tila accompanied him Aristide sang the most crystalline casta diva from *Norma* that I have ever heard.

'I tell you, it's pure coloratura,' Tila cried. 'Now listen to this.' She then joined Aristide in the flower duet from *Madame Butterfly*, allowing him to sing the mezzo role. Presumably to give life to the performance, Aristide insisted on acting out the part by sprinkling the petals from a vase of overblown roses around the room. Occasionally during the aria, when he thought that Tila was upstaging

249

him, he'd cast a handful of petals into her open mouth. Spitting out the petals, Tila claimed to be thunderstruck. 'Never, never have there been such chest tones since Emma Calvé.'

'If you ask me,' said Sascha, 'he sounds like pure *castrati*.'

'Isn't that lovely?' Mama said.

Sascha was convinced that whatever talent Aristide had stemmed from his ability to mime, so later that afternoon, when Mama and Tila had gone, Sascha closeted us up in the smoking-room, where he put some Marcel Journet, Lawrence Tibbet, and Rabbi Rosenblatt recordings on the Victrola.

'Oh, that's easy,' Aristide said when Journet had finished singing from the *Barber of Seville*. Aristide then proceeded to give a muscularly basso rendition of '*Largo al factotum della citta largo*', until the very last note, where he capriciously ended with a high C.

Even when Sascha explained to her who the *castrati* were, Mama did not make an issue of Aristide's vocal idiosyncrasies. Perhaps she hoped that like his other pain-giving foibles this too would pass, but she was wrong. Aristide began to spend a lot of time on the telephone when nobody was around. It wasn't long before I was able to make a connection between Aristide's checking on me to ensure that I was fully occupied and his secretive telephone conversations. One day I surprised him in the smoking-room. Without a nod in my direction and in a mellow and unselfconsciously feminine voice, strongly reminiscent of Claudette Colbert, Aristide said, 'Excuse for a moment; I'm being disturbed.' A brief pause followed, with Aristide listening at the receiver, then he said, 'Just my sister.' Another interrogative pause while Aristide looked me over from head to toe and said decisively, 'Myrtle.'

Of course I had no doubt at this point who Myrtle was and threatened Aristide that if he didn't stop talking at once and explain the whole business to me, I'd let on. So Aristide admitted that under the name and voice of Laverne, he had been conversing with the operators at the United States Marine barracks. He had discovered that upon a few suggestive comments he could get the Marines, bored with their long stints at the switchboard, to make heady and risqué conversation with him. Any shock I might have felt initially at these revelations was immediately squelched by Aristide's promise that I might listen in on subsequent calls. The phone discussions resumed, now with my listening in on the extension in Mama's bedroom. On one of these occasions, as I was marvelling at the smooth-ness by which Aristide caused the operators to cast aside their inhibitions and court with breathtaking candour on the telephone, Mama came upon me in her room.

'Who are you talking to?' she said, taking off her hat.

Had I not been so taken by surprise I might have had the presence of mind to say something in casual warning like, 'Good-*bye*, Laverne.' But as it happened I could only stare at Mama, my mouth a noiseless chasm as I struggled in terror with her over the receiver. I reached the smoking-room as Laverne was saying, 'I can't imagine what's causing all the static, unless it's that *ghastly* Myrtle——'

'N-n-not M-m-myrtle,' I stammered. 'M-m-mamma!'

There was a long discussion in the smoking-room that night after dinner. Only Chicho had shown some sign of affection towards Aristide and me, when he waved to us before going in to join Mama and Sascha. Aristide, who seemed to have become inured to the trauma he was continually causing, was playing Patience on the floor of the front hall. I sat beside him, resentful that I should once again be lumped with him in disaster. 'What do you think they'll do?' I said.

'Oh, they'll probably send us away.'

'Away, where?'

'I dunno; Europe might be nice.'

'I don't want to go to Europe,' I said, fighting tears.

'Well, there's always Minghong.'

I stared at Aristide to see if he was joking. Minghong was a shabby little beach town several miles from Shanghai. The only insane asylum I'd ever heard of was located there.

'You really think Minghong?' I asked.

'P'raps,' Aristide said, laying a red queen on a black king.

Naturally we were sent neither to Europe nor to Minghong. Sascha informed us loftily that he had been of the frank opinion that Mama should dispatch us to a military academy in the United States, but Mama had vetoed that. Since there was nothing even closely resembling a military school in Shanghai, Chicho had come up with the idea that we be enrolled at the Casa D'Italia.

While most of the foreign children in Shanghai had at least one school of their own nationality to attend, Italians did not and were sent to the British-operated municipal institutions or to French,

American, or German schools. Weekly sessions at the Italian Club were initiated to remedy that situation. Indeed, most of the youngsters we met there were already friends and no more familiar with the language and customs of their native country than were Aristide and I. I can clearly recall my brother asking a school chum who was present what the classes would be about.

'Deuced if I know,' said the Italian boy. 'Probably to teach us the Wop lingo.'

As we soon discovered, a fairly general curriculum was presented. Classes in catechism, grammar, and dictation were presided over by Franciscan priests. Signorina Monticelli, a sonorous ungirdled maiden who in her fleecy knits reminded me of a Christmas stocking, was responsible for history, which, to believe the Signorina, began at the Battle of Piave; and geography, which dealt mainly with Trieste and Fiume and extended to the conquest of Libya. Then we had *Conoscenza d'Italia Moderne*, supposedly a general-knowledge course on modern Italy, but which was, as treated, an all-out plumping for the Fascist regime. 'What is the name of our glorious Il Duce? What do we call our youth movement?' In charge of this was a pike-faced woman, wife of a physician and head of the Ballila Youth Movement. *Ginnastica* was taught by young officers, every week a different one, and proved to be deliciously unstrenuous when compared to the rigours of physical training at the Richard Ashbury. Though group singing was listed last on the Casa's programme, it seemed that beginning and ending every class we were expected to burst into song. Any notion Mama might have entertained that we would return inculcated with joyous serenades to the sun and moon and rhapsodies over Roman fountains and such was shattered when Aristide and I blasted out with '*Salve Popolo d'Italia*', from the Fascist youth theme *Giovenezza*. Mercifully, Aristide kept a tight reign over his vocal ranges and did not make himself conspicuous in these singing paeans. But it was soon evident that he was the Casa's star pupil and for once I could draw comfort from the knowledge that an entire class shared my frustration over his spectacular aptitude not only for language but for his ability to assume national colorization.

By early summer, while the bulk of the class and I were struggling over the simplest conjugations and thought it a worthy milestone that we had at last mastered such dubiously useful phrases as '*Io non ho tante mele quante pere*' (I have not so many apples as pears), Aristide was creating a meteoric splash in the firmament of the general knowledge course. He could advance the principles behind, to say nothing of the date and year of, the march on Rome, whereas I had fallen into a pit of ignominy by asking, 'Which march on Rome?' He informed the class, in Italian naturally, of the time and place of the concordat signed between Mussolini and the Vatican, and his hand was the first one up when the doctor's wife asked for a showing of those boys who wished to be measured for a Ballila uniform. Characteristically, I withheld my decision until I'd had a chance to discuss the matter at home. Sascha had just become a member of the French Police Specials and was dead set against the idea.

He reminded Mama that we were after all French subjects and said that he thought it was pretty sneaky of the Casa to try and suck his brothers into the Fascist Youth Movement. Mama, however, saw nothing wrong with Aristide in a black shirt. 'It's a boy's uniform, isn't it? And black shirts are quite chic.' By now Mama had several fur versions of Il Duce's cap with the fasces insignia. To prevent the virulence of Fascism from engulfing me as well, Sascha gave me long dissertations on the values of Liberty, Fraternity, and Equality and made me swear that I would never abandon my allegiance to France.

The Casa planned a pre-summer vacation party in conjunction with prize-giving. There seemed to be no doubt that Aristide would walk away with the majority of the awards. Mama and Chicho were among the parents and friends who came to the presentation that Saturday. After a serving of tepid tea and stale panettone, Signorina Monticelli announced that the minister's wife, Edda Ciano, had come down from Peiping to bestow the gifts. We waited in our rows of metal fold-up seats for Mussolini's daughter to show up. When she did, an hour late, things were delayed further by a heated argument between Signorina Monticelli and the doctor's wife. At first Edda appeared amused by the fracas and smiled and shrugged with charming helplessness at the watching crowd. Then, unable to resist the goings on, she entered the imbroglio. There they were, the three Italian ladies, now totally unconcerned with their audience as they gesticulated, smote their brows, and even, in the case of the doctor's wife, shoved. Signorina Monticelli, like a large ball of yarn, seemed to be getting the worst of it as the leader of the Fascist Youth scythed through her fluffy protestations. Edda, taking one side and then the other, had the presence of mind to smile occasionally at the watching children, parents, and friends. When the dispute was finally settled the Signorina looked completely un-ravelled, the doctor's wife sternly vindicated; and Edda got on with the prize-giving.

After all of them had been handed out and Aristide had not been singled out for one, it was clear what the ruckus had been about. Obviously, since this was an Italian institution supported wholly by their own community, with the prime purpose of encouraging Italian Ballilas, no outsider was going to walk away with the honours. On the way home Mama ranted furiously, while Aristide, huddled in a corner of the car, faked elaborate interest in the street scenes.

During the next couple of weeks, while Countess Ciano remained in Shanghai preparing to leave for Italy, everyone at our house seemed to have forgotten the prize-giving incident. Chicho came home one evening with the news that Edda was being made the victim of an outrageous prank. The Italian car agencies were in an uproar over the fact that two Rolls Royces had been delivered to the consulate in the name of Countess Ciano. Edda had at once denied placing the orders and the automobiles had been returned. On the following day we heard that the city's leading jewellers had been summoned to present themselves with their finest in gems. Next it was furs, then furnishings and household appliances. Chicho confided that although the incidents were being kept out of the press, Edda was beside herself with anger and embarrassment because questions were now being raised when she placed a legitimate order.

'Serves her right,' said Sascha when we were at dinner one night and Chicho had filled us in on the latest concerning the countess.

'But think of those poor dealers who think that they are making a sale to Contessa Ciano,' Mama said.

'Oh, I dunno,' Aristide spoke up. 'I mean look at it this way: it's good publicity, and cars and diamonds don't spoil. I mean it's not like food or cakes or anything perishable like that, you know.'

In the ensuing lull, while Mama looked at Chicho and Sascha and they in turn looked at me like I was some fat sphinx with the answers to all the world's riddles, Aristide helped himself to another serving of dessert.

'Well, they'll catch the culprit sooner or later, and then bang!' Sascha smashed his fist on the table and ground it into the cloth.

Aristide looked up from his plate. 'What would they do to him?'

'There'd be a proper scandal, a fine stink, you can be sure. Headlines in the paper and all that.'

'And maybe radio appearances, too?' Aristide asked.

But Chicho, who realized this was taking the wrong direction, said, 'Of course not. No notoriety but a severe penalty, fines, maybe jail.'

As he looked at Mama, Aristide appeared to be having difficulty swallowing.

'Well, what do you want,' Mama said, 'from Fascisti?'

Early the next morning Aristide was missing from his bed. At the door of the smoking-room I could hear a woman's voice on the telephone. It was not Laverne-Claudette Colbert, yet someone distinctly familiar with an authoritative Italian accent.

'*Pronto. Sono Contessa Ciano.* About those gowns I ordered, cancel them!'

32

ON his twenty-first birthday that summer, Sascha came into a modest inheritance. The policy, which paid ten thousand dollars, was in all likelihood purchased by Papa from some neophyte broker for whom he had felt compassion. Sascha was the only one of us for whom this provision had been made, and in the autumn he felt generous enough to announce that he had arranged riding lessons for Aristide and me. Like any gift from Sascha, this one was made conditionally. The first string attached to it was that we attend the academy with him in the early hours of morning when most businessmen did their riding; the second and for us more onerous stipulation was that we engage with him in something he called Playing Strategy. From the very sound of it Aristide and I knew that this game, or whatever, must in some way be connected with Sascha's obsession with the military. Nevertheless we agreed and one September morning waited for him in his room. By his specific orders and our own disinterest in it, Sascha's quarters had remained alien territory. It was an austere room with the minimum of furbelows and made me think somehow of a file cabinet. His effects were arranged with a sense of well-ordered clutter as though the stacks of periodicals pertaining to arms and hunting, cheek by jowl with comic books and Ballyhoo magazines, could at once be distinguished apart by the person who had arranged them. Over Sascha's bed (he had insisted on retaining the brass cot of his childhood) were his war trophies. The steel bayonets gleamed with polish, the wood shone from buffing, and there was the smell of saddle soap and Kiwi polish. But in their precise alignment they were no less chillingly instruments of death. At one end of the room stood a large table upon which Sascha had kept his electric trains. Because he had grown tired of them, we knew that Sascha had some time before dismantled and put away the elaborate collection of locomotives, tunnels, and tracks. What had been set up in its place was now covered with a sheet, and while waiting for our older brother, Aristide and I speculated on what it might be. Aristide scoffed away my first guess that it was the reproduction of some ancient city. 'Strategy, remember? It must have something to do with war.'

Sascha turned up just then and put an end to our curiosity. When he lifted the sheet we saw that the green baize surface of the table was laid out in a terrain with papiermâché hills, building block fortresses, and trenches fashioned out of modelling clay. What we saw, Sascha said, was a replica of the campaign being waged at the moment between Chiang's armies and the Communists. The lead soldiers he had painted blue were Chiang's men and those painted khaki were the enemy. Key provinces were indicated by miniature Nationalist flags while Communist-occupied strongholds were marked by red pennants. In this, our first session, Sascha showed how the Nationalists had built a concrete girdle of fortifications around the enemy and how, by tightening the girdle, they had forced the Reds out of Hunan, Fukien, and Hupei.

Sascha made the moves on his terrain strictly according to news supplied by an obscure paper which he went to some trouble to secure. On a subsequent session early in October, Sascha brought up large contingents of Nationalist soldiers towards the girdle which by now encircled the province of Kiangsi. 'The commies are trapped like sitting ducks,' he said. But Aristide did not have much faith in

Sascha's predictions and was beginning to rebel. 'You know this war could last forever.' I reminded him that we had made a bargain and that if we reneged on it, Sascha could as well, since our riding courses were to begin in winter.

We did not have another gathering until the middle of the month, at which time Sascha summoned us with the briskness of a military genius towards lacklustre adjutants. At the table Sascha described how the Communists had broken through the Nationalist strangle-hold in a cunning ploy. As Chiang's troops had converged on Jui-chin, the seat of the Communist government, the Red soldiers had replaced their lines with local partisans—men, women, and children. Then with all the force of their arms, they had moved to the least defended point of the girdle. As he was telling us this, Sascha made me help him move the khaki-covered soldiers to the southwest of the terrain where indeed the fortifications were less dense. There, in a surprise attack, the Red army hurled itself upon the Nationalists and broke through the girdle out of Kiangsi. Sascha concluded that at the last radio report the Communist exodus was headed northwest. He then draped the sheet over the table. Aristide and I exchanged hopeful looks. 'Why are you covering the campaign?' Aristide asked.

'That's it. No more Communists, nor more campaigns.'

'But what about this trek they're on? What did you call it, Long March?'

'Pshaw,' Sascha said. 'We'll never hear from them again.'

Sascha did not bother us again with strategy, and finally in November we began our riding courses. I had approached the idea of riding with my usual quotient of buoyant optimism. The rude fact was that I was extremely maladroit with horses, and after six weeks of training, while Aristide was already learning to fence, I had barely gone beyond the English trot. The head of our academy, Colonel Vouroffsky, was an ex-Czarist officer and quite sternly dedicated to the teaching of horsemanship. Everything about my riding, my seat, the way in which I tugged at the snaffle, my mis-conception of handiness, were wellsprings of genuine dismay to him. From the first, Aristide in his tailor-made habit and Russian leather boots had been at ease on his mount and able to grasp fundamental techniques, while Sascha, who had ridden before, made up for the clumsiness of his bulk by flambuoyance and kept the colonel in a dither by his infractions of riding etiquette on the country roads. Towards Christmas, so many hours had been consumed attempting to teach me the canter that, either in exasperation or out of fairness to Aristide, Colonel Vouroffsky agreed to let us join Sascha in the countryside. He expressed the thought somewhat glumly that I must have at least digested the theoretical principles of the canter. But to ensure my safety, and over Sascha's grumbling, either the colonel himself or one of his assistants accompanied us on the rides. While Aristide rode the spirited mount on which he had trained and Sascha bragged of one with an easy mouth, my emergence on the bridle paths was upon a feckless horse, a sluggard who Sascha said should long have been put out to pasture.

Horseback riding in any of its forms—racing, the paperchases, and gymkhanas—was perhaps the most favoured activity of Shanghai society, and many of our friends who had homes in the extra-Settlement area of Hungjao maintained their own stables. Naturally, and in my case literally, we were always bumping into each other. As with skiers, there is a special camaraderie among horsemen, manifested by warm greetings and jubilant 'halloos' as one or another cleared a fence and galloped away. Among those who came to Vouroffsky's Academy to rent mounts were a number of young British and American girls. Sascha knew some of these casually, and judging by the speed in which he learned their time schedules and customary bridle routes, I surmised that he'd like to have known them better. The minute any of the girls appeared, there was Sascha thrashing about, laying the crop to his horse and jumping over every fence, hedge, and grave mount in sight. Colonel Vouroffsky would become choleric. 'Vot I tell it you? Not to jumping over unnecessary fences. Not fair to farmers, tiring to horses!'

The great number of foreign businessmen who rode in the early hours made the countryside fair game for the city's more energetic adventuresses. Most of these women had a certain degree of status. Some were married but indulged in extramarital episodes for fun or profit or both. The majority had the added protection of nationality and its concurrent fringe benefits. Alone among them rode Kiki.

The emigration of the first White Russians to Shanghai following the revolution had been attended to with enormous compassion and much fund raising. As a result many of the earlier refugees were able to establish businesses which were now flourishing. Single women not fortunate enough to entrench themselves as either wives or mistresses found a showcase for their charms in a cabaret called Del Monte's. On the premise that if their wives saw how innocent it all was they would not protest at Del Monte's existence, it became fashionable for taipans and their wives to wind up a night's socializing there with early morning breakfasts. Many of the husbands returned on their own, as did the eager griffins; marriages were broken, made, and remade.

With the more recent troubles in Manchuria vast new waves of émigrés from Dairen, Harbin, and Mukden poured into Shanghai, but they found no welcoming committees, no fund-raising banquets, and very little sympathy from either their own or other foreign nationals.

The French Concession, which continued to license prostitution, permit gambling sports, and wink an eye at narcotics empires, became the haven for the White Russians from Manchuria. They settled mainly on a long tree-lined avenue which served as the spinal cord of the Concession. In short order Avenue Joffre and its arteries became known as Little Moscow and the now well-grounded jewellery, yard goods, and dress salons found themselves threaded with a network of sleazy bars and cafés pandering to servicemen. Since sheer volume had done in the White Russian woman as an enigma, the only recourse left to many was simply prostitution.

All the sporting ladies were careful to camouflage their lives as much as they were able. All, that is, except Kiki. There were, of course, other prostitutes of comparable diligence, but none had quite the audacity, the verve, the special pride in scoring, that marked Kiki. In common with her sisters, Kiki would be the first to tell you of her high birth but, to give her credit, she wisely eschewed the nobility angle. Kiki's grandfather had merely been governor of Vladivostok.

Discretion to Kiki was an abomination. If a man was worth an hour of her talent she was certainly worth his public approval, and her greatest diversion seemed to be parading up and down Avenue Joffre clinging to some embarrassed if determined male. As categorical as Kiki was in attitude, she was catholic in her tastes. Class was what she preferred, and she looked for it in the ranks of men with position, most of whom were married, of course. Occasionally she had been known to fall in with some young man who in her estimation was worthy though unmarried. Then she was inclined to get careless, allowing her emotions the upper hand, and would disappear temporarily from circulation.

I suppose after all he'd heard about her that it was fairly natural for Sascha to have taken mild leave of his senses when he saw Kiki come bouncing up to us on the country road one morning. In her tight Sunkist-orange sweater Kiki revealed a bosom that was definitely nonflapper, and from a bottleneck waist she was encased like a Spanish wine vessel in seam-splitting jodhpurs. Kiki was nothing if not friendly, and as she brought her mount up I saw that her teeth were tiny and pointed in a baby smile that was surprisingly agreeable. I expect the fact that Kiki directed her attention to Aristide rather than Sascha was a device calculated to inflame our older brother. In all fairness, though, I must admit that the calisthenics at the Cercle had had, in spite of himself, a salutary effect on Aristide's physique. He was taller, and the subtly feminine protuberances had been hardened away. Perhaps because of Sascha's eagerness, perhaps because of his own snobbery, Aristide was briefly formal with Kiki and she was quick to sense rebuff.

'Well, well,' she said in accents that were free from any trace of Russian. 'Mister High Society.'

'You should learn that society cannot be measured by either height or breadth. One is simply *in*'—and with this Aristide eyed Kiki appraisingly—'or one is not.'

'What a bitch,' Kiki said, nodding good-naturedly. Aristide smiled.

'Listen, do you know that my grandfather was——'

'The governor of Vladivostok,' Aristide finished for her.

This exchange, brief as it was, must have seemed an eternity to Sascha idling by on his horse, and while Kiki mused on Aristide's remark, he came up from the rear. Simultaneously I heard and felt the reaction to a smart slap on my horse's rump. Before I could collect my wits, we were off, my sluggard and I, at a brisk canter. I heard Aristide's outburst of anger, and Colonel Vouroffsky, who at Kiki's approach had discreetly lingered behind us, was shouting instructions: 'Sit straight! Knees in, press thighs,' which sounded to me like 'press ties'. The only thing that I could remember at that point was to relax my grip on the reins, which my much maligned mount took as a sign of encouragement as he picked up speed. I could hear someone cantering close behind and saw in a frantic sidelong glance that it was Sascha. It was he of course who had instigated this chase, presumably so that he could rescue me and show up Aristide. In spite of my rage at this thought, I could hardly wait for him to accomplish his purpose. I have no idea from where it appeared, but there, twenty feet or so in front of me, was a bristling hedge as green and monolithic as any of the breakers we hadn't dared face in Tsingtao. Desperately I tried to recall the instructions I had heard Colonel Vouroffsky giving my brothers. Over and over the phrases spun around in my mind and all the while the horse drew closer to the hedge. Lean slightly forward... or was it lean slightly backward? I remembered to close my legs, bearing my weight on my thighs and knees, and automatically I leaned forward, rising in my saddle as my mount raised his fore-hand for the jump. I all but let loose of the reins as we sailed into the air, cleared the top of the hedge, and landed together on the other side. It took me a few seconds to realize that I had indeed accomplished the jump, and I turned anxiously to see if the others had witnessed my skilful horsemanship and if they were coming to praise me. They were, that is to say Sascha was, all by himself, separated from his horse. Like a great blimp in his white turtleneck, Sascha came flying over the hedge and landed with a thud on the earth. I trotted up to him where he sat covered with mud, the most stunned expression on his face. 'My damned horse baulked,' he said.

'The thing to remember in jumping,' I said, 'is a light hand at the mouth.'

Kiki, Aristide, and the colonel had come up by then. At the sight of Sascha still squatted on the ground, now feeling his back tenderly, prodding at his ribs, and nursing his elbows, they burst into laughter.

'Such a Humpty Dumpty,' Kiki said, shaking her head in merriment. Then Aristide leaned towards Sascha and extended his hand. 'Come on,' he said.

We saw Kiki again that same week. Mama and Chicho were taking my brothers and me to the Cathay Theatre on Avenue Joffre. We were to see a silent-film star, Betty Compson, doing a collection of skits on stage. It was a particularly exciting prospect because Mama had invited the actress to a forthcoming luncheon. As we came to a stop on the corner of Rue Cardinal Mercier, who should cross in front of the car but Kiki in a furry jacket and persimmon-coloured boots. She had looped herself like a purse strap around the arm of her escort, whom we all recognized at once as Ramirez, Tila's Tsingtao paramour. While Kiki capered and giggled, Ramirez was composed and amiable with her. Then Kiki saw the Imperial Suburban and you could plainly see her flipping her memory index of models, years, and licence plates as she correctly pegged the car to us. Unhooking herself from Ramirez, Kiki sashayed up to the hood and pointing through the windshield at Sascha, squealed, 'Hello-o-o, Humpty Dumpty.'

I shan't ever forget Mama's remark when she had recovered from her surprise: 'What any man sees in that chippy beats me.'

But Chicho gave Sascha a secretive and knowing wink.

33

TO Orientals, the New Year is a time for settling accounts. 1935 had barely turned the corner when the Japanese punctiliously bit off another piece of Chinese territory in the north. Once again blandly explaining the action as precipitated by Chinese hostility, Japanese troops went across the Great Wall, neatly annexing the province of Chahar, adjoining Jehol. It was plain now to even those most indulgent foreigners in Shanghai that Japan's next moves were to consume the remaining northern provinces, continuing from Chahar to Hopei, tightening like a drawstring until they had closed in on Peiping.

In the four years since the Manchurian Incident, the Japanese had become an irritant with which we had learned to live. They avoided our vital zones, and we their distant pestilence. What Chiang Kai-shek and all his noisy dissenters were up to I'm sure never entered our minds, though once while riding I heard Aristide ask Sascha what had become of the Communists and Sascha had replied, 'Would you believe it, those doughty chaps are still marching.' For Aristide and me there was still school to contend with, and our early morning sessions on horseback. Didi had stopped coming on week-ends from the time of the old man's arrest. We knew that his father had completed the required stay at the health clinic and that he was back at their house in Chapei. We also knew from Lao Ni's evasiveness when the point was touched upon that no cure had resulted. Once Aristide asked Lao Ni why Didi did not come to us any more, and the chauffeur had replied quite brusquely that Didi was too busy and that he now had to help out at home. I hardly think that Aristide was satisfied with that answer, but he accepted it. As for me, in that moment I had the picture of a twelve-year-old solemnly preparing the pipe for his father.

Sascha's riding had improved to the extent that he was now on the Columbia Country Club's polo team. Aristide and I had watched him play several times, and he was pretty fair at the game. Whether it was due to his girth or that pretence of unassailable cheer common to those who are overweight, Sascha continued to make no romantic impression on the young ladies. It was obvious they tolerated him as a pleasant buffoon suitable for running errands and supplying information about other bachelors. They came to the parties he gave but rarely invited him to theirs. When Sascha began keeping very late hours, Mama discovered that he had begun frequenting a string of tawdry bars on Rue Chu Pao San, renamed 'Blood Alley' because of its reputation for constant brawling. Here for the price of dance tickets and fake drinks Sascha had been able to while away the time with White Russian taxi dancers. Mama was displeased with this turn and most concerned about the possibility of his involvement with what she called 'those Rooskies', and she was stunned when Sascha reminded her that she was of Russian origin. Tactfully Chicho interceded for Sascha, advising Mama that our older brother was adult enough to make his own decisions.

Although Mama persisted in lamenting her finances and threatened regularly to close down Papa's business, she couldn't resist buying a Canadian beaver coat—'Such a practical fur, beaver'—remodelling her thirty-six hats for spring, and being the first to buy a block of tickets for the fiesta night ball planned by the Cercle Sportif. She maintained her secrecy about the new casino which she and Chicho had discovered, conveniently located in the Concession. Once Aristide, hankering for some frippery denied by Mama, threw her gambling in her face.

'It's none of your damned business how I spend my money,' Mama said.

'My father made that money,' Aristide replied.

'And did he leave it to you? No, he left every penny to me. Have I denied you anything? I could have been a rich woman on just the money I've spent on raising the three of you.' Then she turned despairingly to Chicho and smiting her brow said in a voice throbbing with operatic emotion, *'Essere madre e un inferno!'* Of course right after that she bought Aristide the sapphire and platinum links and studs that he had wanted to complete his first evening suit. And when she had adjudged his pleasure and surprise, she said, 'I still say it's none of your damned business, but I want you to know that I never spend more than five hundred at the tables, win or lose, five hundred, that's all.' Then she added with a nod in the direction of Chicho, 'He's the one who gambles.' Chicho was now chief accountant at his bank, and it pleased Mama enormously that he contributed to our living expenses. If she had any regrets on the score that his promotion caused him to work several nights during the week, she said nothing. He remained thoughtfully inventive towards my brothers and me, and it was hard to remember that a time before had ever existed. It was hard to remember Papa.

All in all it promised to be a normal year for our family, and it well might have been but for Tila and her strange request. It was in May, and I can recall being very excited because we were that day to attend a gala in honour of King George the Fifth's silver jubilee. For weeks the Sunday supplements had been filled with pictures of the royal family and items about the celebration with trooping the colour and fireworks to be held at the racecourse. Tila turned up on a Saturday morning when Mama was at her hairdresser and only Aristide and I were at home. Tila confided that she had planned it that way; she had wanted to see Aristide for a very special reason. Since she had thoughtfully brought a box of éclairs with her, I magnanimously prepared to leave the two of them together, but she said that I might stay if I promised secrecy. I did so at once and Tila asked Aristide if he was still her prince. And Aristide said yes, of course he was, and what did Tila want. Then she asked him if he could still do those funny things with his voice, imitations and such.

'But I promised Mama I wouldn't,' Aristide said.

'Just this once,' Tila implored, 'to help me.'

Then Tila explained that someone was holding onto a document which she needed.

'Well, why don't you ask for it yourself?'

'I have asked, of course, but the party won't give it.'

'Why not? I mean why should anyone hold onto something that's not theirs?'

'For money,' Tila said.

'Blackmail?'

Tila nodded, and it was evident by his expression that Aristide was ready to take up cudgels for her. 'Who am I supposed to be?' he asked.

'Mr. Liu,' Tila replied.

'Pockmarked Liu!' Aristide was aghast. 'I'm not sure that I can duplicate his voice. I only actually heard him speak once and it's been years, you know.'

But I knew from repeated exposure to it that the warlord was one of Aristide's most polished impersonations. Even as he was protesting, Aristide began to pad softly across the room, clutching imaginary sleeves with fingers that suddenly looked like claws. He cocked his head in that unique darting glance, and when he began to speak the expression of benign gravity on his face was exactly that of Liu.

'*Monsieur*—' Aristide began, then he said, 'Who am I talking to, Tila?'

'Do it just like that,' Tila said. 'Just begin *Monsieur*.'

'*Monsieur, je regret de vous déranger*, but my sources inform me that you have a document——'

'A letter,' Tila interrupted.

'You have a letter belonging to Baroness Golitsky——'

'No, not exactly belonging to me,' Tila said.

'Well, what then?' Aristide said, annoyed at these punctures.

'It's a letter I want, I must have.'

'All right,' Aristide resumed, 'Baroness Golitsky desires, no, is desirous of obtaining, a letter you have in your possession. As Madame's personal friend——'

'Uhm, say protector,' Tila said. 'It's stronger.'

'As Madame's protector, I urge that the letter be delivered to her within twenty-four hours——'

'Marvellous, marvellous, *cheri*,' Tila cried.

After he had gone over his lines several times, Aristide dialled the number Tila gave him. As he spoke, with each inflection, each nuance, with the interchange of French and Chinese accents,

Aristide reproduced Liu's voice exactly. Replacing the phone Aristide smiled quizzically at Tila. 'You will receive the letter no later than tomorrow,' he said.

Tila embraced Aristide. 'We will celebrate. Tomorrow, a picnic in my garden. A *fête champêtre* just for the three of us.'

For quite a while after Tila had gone, Aristide was pensive. Finally he said, 'You know who that was on the phone?'

'Sure, you masquerading as Pockmarked Liu,' I replied.

'No, you fathead. I meant at the other end.'

'Who?'

'It was that Ramirez chap,' Aristide said.

Mama was less than keen about our Sunday picnic with Tila. It was not by anything she said that we could tell. It was her hesitation, her expression like Braille to the adept blind. Since the Ramirez episode and her breakup with Michel, Tila had drifted into that peculiar limbo of the wealthy single woman whose lack of discretion makes all her actions food for scandal. She never so determined to mask her *crève-cœur* that where formerly she had been involved singly, she now had lovers in packs. She picked them, as though for amusement at diversity, from all walks of life and flaunted them. That, after his moral indictment of her, Michel had married a Chinese ex-singsong girl seemed only to whet her appetite for notoriety, and she continued to entertain lavishly. On the excuse that she preferred to retrench from party life, Mama had long stopped attending these affairs. But inevitably accounts of them were circulated. It was said that now Tila was the first to dance on the piano, holding two champagne bottles at her bare breasts, letting the corks pop as the wine exploded on her admirers. And when one of her swains challenged the authenticity of her blondness, Tila had raised her skirts in proof. No one was able to determine how she maintained her opulent existence, but rumours were rife. It was said that one of Chiang's ministers was keeping her; a Japanese admiral provided her with money for information. Her endless verve, all were agreed, indubitably came via the needle. But there was no indication of anything like this when Tila came to us. The tie between her and Mama was stronger than rumour. And Tila had been talking of leaving China. So, with that bumbling faith in our own ability to accept or discard, Mama agreed to let us go.

Aristide and I waited for Tila in her reception room off the foyer.

On her carved and gilt piano was a photograph of Tila in a silver frame. As far back as I could remember I'd heard grownups comment that Tila was not a natural beauty, not in the sense that Mama was. Her hair was overbleached, her nose was wrong, she used too much paint. There were those eyes of course. . . . In the photograph, Tila is wearing evening clothes, all white with very simple lines. Ropes of pearls are wound around her neck and fall to her lap. The eyebrows are darkly stencilled and the eyes wonderfully anguished. She is posed cupping her chin in one hand, so that the picture is predominantly of a slim trunk of bracelets supporting a blonde-capped face. The caption is a gem in itself. Tila had signed it, 'Simply me'.

She called to us then, and we could see her through the columns of the reception room as she stood waiting at the head of the lyre-shaped staircase. The decal of that remembrance is so vivid, so unmarred by the scratchings of time, I could swear that as she paused there on the landing in that flowing negligee I heard a burst of music, violins, and trumpets. Some years after this, Bette Davis made a film called *Mr. Skeffington* in which she played a professional beauty. Symbolically, whenever the actress appeared at her staircase, there was this same heroic sound of instruments. It is the most positive of memories, which are most often treacherous. I have fused the original with the film, I know, but that is how I remember Tila, always at the top, always with music. She swept down the marble stairs, both hands outstretched. 'My princes,' she said. She embraced us both, but it was Aristide whose head she wound with that long rope of pearls so that indeed he looked like a prince in his coronet.

We went to the garden, where on the grass by the fountains the servants had laid a cloth. They had earlier carried a chaise-longue from Tila's boudoir, and while she reclined upon it luncheon was served. Although we loved her ambience, meals at Tila's were something of an ordeal for Aristide and me. She was firm in her belief that our palates needed educating, and her menus consisted in the main of what Aristide referred to as adult abominations. Caviar was a familiar enemy and just the idea of *cervelle au beurre noir* made us ill. But Aristide, who basked in Tila's approval and wanted to keep it that way, made a fine show of masking his distaste except for one instant, when Tila unexpectedly popped a *moule* into his mouth and asked for his verdict. Aristide chewed, gagged, and finally swallowed the mussel whole. Then with tears of exertion he gasped, 'Tastes like an armpit!'

At dessert Aristide asked Tila in a whispery voice whether or not she had yet received the letter. Just as cryptically, as though I had not been present at the time of the phone call, Tila smiled and nodded, placing a hand at her bosom to indicate its safe deposit.

Before the luncheon things were cleared, Tila's contingent of males began to arrive. The first to show up was a sleek Georgian, who wore his light coat, cape fashion, over his shoulders and wielded an ebony cane. He kissed both the hands which Tila extended and, growling out endearments, proceeded to kiss her feet. This tickled her and she made him stop. She introduced us and we learned that he was Prince Gogo, with one of those unintelligible Caucasian last names like Dza dza dza-dza. Unlike the majority of White Russian men in Shanghai, who settled for what honest work they could find, the Georgians were a unique lot. Most had adopted some sort of title, prince usually, and they seemed to have handy a never-ending well of enterprises, legitimate or not. As though each had convinced himself that not only cream but scum rises to the top, it was from that level they liked to operate. However, contracts in munitions, chemicals, and scrap metal were, as Gogo was at the moment assuring Tila, regrettably not always available, and one had to live by more modest transactions, was that not so? Gogo's current project was a restaurant in which he hoped Tila would invest. Presumably because she found him appealing, or because he was an imaginative lover, or perhaps simply because he amused her, Tila pretended to weigh the possibilities of his proposal.

Rene, Tila's French hairdresser, arrived next. He was very young and intense, feminine rather than effeminate in manner. While still stretched out on the chaise Tila permitted him to coif her hair, which he did, using tongs and an alcohol burner, all the while reciting Verlaine's *Sagesse* through the bobby pins clenched in his teeth. Tila tired of his rambling at one point, and shielding her eyes from the sun with her hand, scanned his girl-boyish face. '*Mais dis donc, pourquoi tu mets le Peacock sur les sourcils?*' The youth flushed and stammered, almost choking on the bobby pins, and no one understood his explanation of why he used Japanese dye on his eyebrows or for that matter why Tila had asked the question. Meanwhile a Chinese gentleman, well attired in a silk gown, had joined us, and at Tila's wave of greeting placed himself in a chair some distance from the group. Aristide must have guessed my thoughts, and he had the nerve to put them into words. I overheard him whisper to Tila, 'Is that the Chinese minister?' Tila looked momentarily taken aback. It was clear that the gossipmongers had seen to it that she heard the dirt about herself. Then she laughed aloud and gave my bewildered brother a companionable shove as she announced, 'Meet the Minister Extraordinary of my foot: Mr. Chu, my chiropodist.' Mr. Chu bowed to the assembly.

It was midafternoon when Tex sauntered up to the group. I recognized him at once because Aristide and I had seen his act in a vaudeville show preceding the horror film at the Strand. He had done some clever rope tricks and had sung, accompanying himself on a guitar. On stage, astride Lone Star, his richly caparisoned horse, Tex had cut a dashing figure. But close up, still in costume, the sequins on his jacket flashing guiltily in the sun, the worn chaps and scuffed down-at-heel boots, without the charity of stage lighting and makeup, he was quite an old man. Under the ten-gallon hat, his eyes were hot blue in a seamed and pitted face shaped somewhat like a large pickle. Tex spoke in monosyllables, which to my unconditioned ear seemed to rhyme whiningly, and as he twanged on his guitar he sang, 'Ahm haid'n fer the lai-ess rain'd-up.'

Presently Tila's number one houseboy came up and, leaning towards her, whispered something. Obviously it was a message for which she had been waiting, for at once Tila sat up and with a sweep of her hand dismissed the entire party. Some business, she said, had come up, to which she must attend. As in a well-directed play with a small efficient cast, where the actors double as stagehands and the set is transformed in minutes, so it was in Tila's garden. A few servants swarmed to where we had been sitting, and within minutes linen was shaken and folded, plates, cutlery, and food were collected, and Tila, raised aloft in her chaise-longue, was being transported back to the house. Her abandoned admirers, each, as it were, with his unfinished petition dangling, exchanged sheepish smiles. Prince Gogo, with the largest stake, was the most self-possessed. As he waved his cane in the direction of Tila's retreating figure, I was reminded of an opera character making his adieus to an imaginary lover in the wings. Rene, still jabbering Verlaine, collected his tongs, burners, and assorted paraphernalia and flitted through the garden in record time. Still strumming on the guitar, Tex ambled towards the driveway, and in spite of myself, I couldn't help laughing at the thought of him in that preposterous outfit hailing a rickshaw. Only the Chinese gentleman, the minister of Tila's feet, remained seated exactly where he had been, the patient smile still on his face. Divining my thoughts precisely, Aristide said, 'Imagine, our first inscrutable Chinee!'

We were preparing to leave and Lao Ni had in fact come into the garden to tell us that Mama needed the car, when I noticed that Tila's pearls were still wound around Aristide's head. 'You can't go with those,' I said. We told Lao Ni it would take us but a minute to return the necklace to Tila.

The door to Tila's boudoir was closed, but when no one answered Aristide's gentle knock, we entered. Aristide was in the act of placing the pearls on Tila's dressing-table when, hearing voices, he paused. Tila was talking to someone in the adjoining room. It was the man's voice that caused Aristide to motion me to silence. Then, leading me by one hand, the pearls still clutched in the other, Aristide and I tiptoed to the partially open door leading to Tila's bedroom. Tila and Chicho were standing face to face. She reached into her bosom and produced an envelope, holding it proudly and high. Though we were half the distance of a room from Tila and Chicho, and the envelope was folded, we had seen enough of them with that distinct blue colour that we didn't need to be shown the crest on the back to know that it was Chicho's stationery. As he took it from her hand, Chicho held Tila in an embrace, until with a little laugh, somewhat stagey, she pushed him away.

'*Grazie*, Tila, *grazie mille volto*.'

She shrugged off his thanks. 'The important thing is that Regina never finds out, that's all.'

He said, after a moment or so of reflection, 'Do you understand? Do you forgive me, Tila?'

'You mean do I understand that indiscretion does not constitute a love affair? Of course. Appetite has really not that much to do with taste.'

'Tila, you have saved my life.'

'Ouf,' said Tila.

I could see Aristide's knuckles whitening on the string of pearls, and I touched his hand. Even in that moment, I think Aristide too realized how comically vulgar it would have been to have broken Tila's necklace. There would have to be a confrontation with Tila and Chicho, both of them estimating wildly just how much we had heard and, more difficult, both of us concealing that we had heard anything. Then like children at an Easter egg hunt, we would be compelled to crawl on all fours and join in the search for the pearls. This action could not be shared dispassionately. Aristide placed the necklace on Tila's dressing-table as we quietly left the room.

34

WHATEVER his resentment towards Chicho in the days following our visit to Tila's, Aristide concealed it masterfully. His response to the Italian was unfailing, and only to me was the blade edge of his courtesy evident. Less than a week after our discovery Mama summoned Sascha, Aristide, and me to the smoking-room for a *conseil de famille*. Since Chicho had become, in a manner of speaking, one of the household, family counsels in the old tradition had given way to informal discussions. But Chicho was not present this day, and Mama was tense in a way specifically reserved for her dealings with and about him. She came to the point at once.

'What I have to say really only concerns Chicho and me. I want you to know about it anyway. I want you to say what I am going to do is right.'

Aristide gave me a searching look, trying to gauge with it whether I had revealed anything. I responded with a perplexed raise of the brows to indicate that I hadn't.

'There's been a bad mix-up at Chicho's bank. A lot of money is missing and he is responsible.'

'What do you mean mix-up and missing?' Sascha asked.

'All right, he took it,' Mama said.

'Chicho embezzled the bank's money? Why?'

'I don't know, Sascha. Yes, I do. It's all my fault. I took him to casinos; he wanted to keep up with me, that's all.'

'You said you never spent more than five hundred, win or lose, that's what you said,' Aristide spoke for the first time.

'And I didn't. I may not have learned much, but one thing your father taught me was gambling odds. I played for fun, but Chicho——'

'How much?' Sascha asked.

Mama drew a deep breath. 'About a hundred thousand——'

'Gold?'

Mama nodded.

'You'd have to sell the last of your utilities to raise that——'

'He'll return it, every cent. I know he will.'

'When?' Sascha pursued. Mama was silent.

'Does he have collateral? Investments and holdings in Italy maybe?'

'Everything is in his wife's name. He has a small, what do you call it, stipend? And his salary, that's all.'

'So we would get Chinese dollars which are inflating on a monthly basis. We'll be ruined. I vote no!' Sascha cried.

'Wait! Before you decide I must tell you this. If Chicho cannot return the money within a week, he will do something—something very bad.' Mama did not have to elaborate on Chicho's ultimate recourse. A carefully planned suicide would probably cause the bank to hush up the matter in deference to his family name and to avoid scandal. 'What about you two?' Mama turned to Aristide and me.

Aristide said coldly, 'Once when Tila pawned some jewels to help *her* lover, you told her you would never do the same for a *maquereau*.'

'I'm surprised at you, Aristide, you who have always loved him. Could you let him die?' Mama cried.

There was a long pause, then Aristide said, 'Very well, I say give him the money.'

Mama looked at me. 'And you?'

'What Aristide says, yes.'

Sascha, who recognized his coveted *chef de famille* position slipping away from him, began to rally. Chicho's action had been rash in the extreme, but we were all agreed, were we not, that this was a basically honest and, in all measures, solid individual. Now, if Chicho would sign a note agreeing to turn over all of his income, at the rate of roughly a thousand dollars per month with interest, the loan would be paid up within. . . .

When we were alone later, I said to Aristide, 'Why did you do it?'

'You bloodthirsty little thing.'

'Do you think he would, kill himself I mean?'

'I doubt it.'

'Then why?'

'Just supposing he did. Do you think Mama would ever forgive us? Do you think that she would ever believe the truth about him?'

'Well, why didn't you tell then?'

'Because more than we owe Chicho another chance, Mama deserves to keep her illusion.'

There was no hint in Chicho's manner of either guilt or the usual lessening of affection that indebtedness incurs. Since he was required to put in less time at work in the evenings, due, he said, to summer slackness, he spent all of his time with us.

It had been easy enough for us to dodge Tila when she came to the apartment. We knew from Mama that Tila was in the process of leaving for Europe. The villa had been sold (again according to scuttlebutt) to an agent for Chiang Kai-shek. Mama announced the day of Tila's departure, and we had no alternative but to agree when Mama assumed we would want to see her off.

It was one of those hot days early in July when the humidity rises to one's eyes that we joined the group of Tila's friends at the Hong-kew wharf. A band was playing 'Madelon' on the bow of the Messagerie maritimes liner on which she was leaving. Already the wharf was littered with streamers and confetti and the crowds were imbued with that phrenetic gaiety that certain occasions, like New Years, summon. Tila, resplendent as usual, had arranged for refreshments to be served in one of the lounges. Aristide and I managed to keep our distance, but from time to time I saw her looking in our direction. Eventually she was able to detach herself from her friends, and she made her way to where we stood. 'Quick,' she said. 'We must have a moment together.'

Tila's suite was banked to the portholes with flowers and gifts. She untwisted the wire from a bottle of Dom Perignon, expertly let the cork fly out of the porthole, and poured three glassfuls. With her first sip, Tila said, 'Now, why have you been avoiding me?'

'I've not been avoiding anyone,' Aristide replied.

'*Chéri*, don't lie. We've been *copains* for a long time. I'm leaving; I may never return.'

'Good-bye then,' Aristide said.

Tila winced but did not reply. She sipped at her glass. Her silence proved unendurable to him, and Aristide cried, 'Tila, how could you be so false?'

'*Moi, fausse? Comment?*' Her eyes widened at him over the rim of her glass.

'Was it not enough to betray Mama? Did you have to use me as well?'

'What the hell are you talking about?'

'Chicho's letter!' Aristide burst out. 'The one you tricked me into getting from Ramirez.'

'Shhh,' Tila cautioned, looking nervously at the cabin door.

'Oh don't worry. I remember what you said, the main thing is that Regina should never know. . . .'

'Then you heard us? Doesn't it mean anything to you that Ramirez had the letter?'

'Certainly. He stole it and has been blackmailing you and Chicho. That's why you had to have it.'

'Oh, what a *schlemiel* you are,' Tila cried, wringing her hands exasperatedly. 'How old are you now? Fourteen? And you?' she asked me.

'Twelve in November.'

'You're both old enough to know the truth. But you must swear not to tell Regina—' At that moment we heard those silly shipboard chimes and the voice over the speaker warning all visitors to go ashore. 'Now think. Ramirez had Chicho's letter, and I have not been with Ramirez for six years—'

The door to the suite was flung open then, and there they stood, Tila's bizarre friends, faces disembodied and floating drunkenly like paper lanterns, eminently destructible. With whoops of merriment and strident fake hilarity, they surged into the cabin. One of Tila's gallants hoisted her on his shoulders and brushing past my brother and me led the chanting parade along the corridors. Just once Tila turned and cast her arms out to us imploringly, then one of her pumps fell off, and the next minute she was caught up in the jubilation and we could hear her voice hoarsely above the others singing 'Madelon'. As Aristide and I hurried along the passageway

274

to join Mama, he paused for a moment to pick up Tila's shoe, cramming it into his jacket pocket.

35

THAT October when Italy attacked Abyssinia, Mama was most vocal in her denunciation. 'Imagine the lousy Italians picking on those poor Ethiopiums,' said Mama.

'Ethiop*ians*,' Sascha said.

'Imagine that,' said Mama.

When she read that one of Mussolini's sons described the close-range bombing of Ethiopians as akin to the spreading of a rose, Mama imposed her own sanctions on Italy. She resigned from the Italian Club and sent all her Mussolini-style hats to the milliner with explicit instructions for their remodelling. At the onset, Chicho made a few lame attempts to defend his country's actions, but he was outweighed from all sides, so for the sake of family peace he kept silent. I don't remember anyone's expressing anywhere nearly the same concern over Japan, the aggressor at our doorstep.

On our first free Saturday around the middle of the month, we invited Didi to come again and in anticipation bought tickets for the Ministering Children's League Bazaar. But he showed up with Ah-ching. The general was welcomed into our midst like an old friend, and by the manner in which Didi clung to his brother, Aristide and I resigned ourselves to an afternoon at home. Ah-ching was leaner, and though he was barely thirty, there were already grey hairs at his emples. He still had the same trigger mannerisms, but that overlay of impudence was missing. We gathered in the drawing-room. Sascha asked Ah-ching about the suppression drive, from which he had just returned. With continued Japanese encroachments, student riots in Peking, and the entire country clamouring for war with Japan, Ah-ching told us that Chiang had realized the time had come for personal involvement with his peoples. Drawing to himself a small cadre of trusted officers (Ah-ching among them), Chiang travelled his country by plane, reaching remote provinces which had for centuries known nothing more direct of government than stern land-owners and crippling taxation. It was at last a blood-and-flesh leader who came to them, who explained his projects and initiated on-the-spot reforms. And those people not already sworn over to the Communists rallied to Nanking. En route, Chiang and his men ruthlessly excised his domestic problems. As Ah-ching spoke, with his hands clasped around his knee, there was an earnestness to his face reminiscent of Didi.

'What about the Japanese? Is Chiang ever going to fight them?' Sascha asked.

'Of course. But when we are ready. When we have properly drained the poison from within our own system,' Ah-ching replied.

At that moment Dah Su came in from the kitchen and stood in his tremulous manner at the doorway. He had heard in the streets that the Communists had ended their march. Mao Tse-tung, leading the First Route Army, had come together with two other armies in North Shensi.

Ah-ching jumped to his feet almost as though he had received an order. It was shock rather than surprise, the reaction to ice or fire regardless of expectation.

'What do you think now?' Sascha said. 'A united front against Japan?'

'Not so long as Chiang lives,' said Ah-ching, but his voice was thoughtful. I looked at Didi. His mouth was slightly open, his eyes bright behind the silver-framed spectacles. I wondered, was it what Ah-ching said that so commanded his attention?

Our school annually celebrated Guy Fawkes' Day on November the fifth, which fell this year on a Tuesday. I remember Aristide's annoyance at having to gear himself for school that Monday, instead, as he reasoned, of having three days off. At home time, when the car drove up to the school entrance, Sascha was in the driver's seat; Lao Ni sat beside him; and Hoboo was in the back. We knew at once something was wrong. Sascha never came to fetch us, and it had been ages since for the sake of appearances we had asked Hoboo to stop coming to school. Sascha wasted no time in greetings as he told us to get in at once. He said then that Lao Ni's father had been caught smoking and had been taken away.

Aristide touched Lao Ni on the shoulder. 'Did they trace it through you?' Lao Ni didn't reply. Hoboo explained that since he was last apprehended Lao Ni no longer dared make outside purchases. A seemingly reliable dope peddler made regular calls to the house. Agents of the Anti-Opium Bureau had finally caught up with the peddler, who under duress revealed the names of his clients. Sascha reminded us that this was the old man's second offence and he lived under Chinese jurisdiction in Chapei. It looked bad.

Since four years ago, when it had been practically razed, Chapei had undergone a change. Buildings were new and well maintained, the streets were much cleaner, and there seemed to be few or no beggars. Ah-ching's new house was in the western section of the suburb away from the Paoshan area and its scarring memories. Following Lao Ni's directions, Sascha pulled up to a foreign-style stucco house. As we entered, the mother was coming downstairs. She looked dishevelled, a feather duster in one hand. '*Nema hao*,' she said in a flat and final voice. 'I've cleaned up his room. Put away everything.' She gave an incredulous little smile. 'It's as though he was already dead.' Then she burst into tears and sank to the floor at the foot of the steps, banging her head upon it and uttering the most anguished wails.

Hoboo seized her by the arms and pulled her up so that they were face to face. 'Stop! Where is your faith? Three sons you have, yet you wail like a cur. Jesus will be angry!' Hoboo's words were familiar. She had often told me that I would incur Jesus' wrath—if I spilled my rice, if I abused anyone with whom she had no differences, particularly if I defied her. But I was reminded of something else by the tone of this threatening consolation, and I recalled that Grandpapa had expressed much the same sentiments to Mama at the time of her mourning. I realized then that the tongue of solace was as universal as it was meaningless. Nevertheless, Hoboo's words served to calm the mother some, and we went into the front room.

There was a solidarity to the parlour, a look of permanence which had been absent in their last home, though it was by no means a luxurious room, being decorated in that Eurasian composite of Chinese carved woods and overstuffed chintz pieces inspired by Metro-Goldwyn-Mayer's conception of rural English homes. Walls of cerulean blue seemed explosive in contrast to glazed celadon pottery on stands. A portrait of Sun Yat-sen, bristling with purpose,

277

shared honours with a silver-framed wedding photograph of Ah-ching and Su-mei and a few pieces of Ningpo pewter on the fire-place mantel. Neatly folded newspapers and a basket of logs were arranged on either side of the hearth. The only wall decoration was a cheap tear-off calendar featuring a vividly rouged Chinese starlet whose mouthful of teeth, retouched with glints of zinc white, resembled a pearl-packed oyster and confirmed the benefits of Darkie toothpaste. A Blaupunkt radio, probably negotiated by Ah-ching via his connections with Chiang's military advisers, stood Germanically aloof in one corner. Like the one before, this home still attested to Ah-ching's reputation for integrity. The Chinese, with their partiality for sobriquets, evinced by such titles as the Young Marshal and the Christian General (whose intrigues, masked by a show of pseudo-Christian humility, had bedevilled Chiang Kai-shek for years), had bestowed on Ah-ching the label Honest General. And while he neither sought nor was treated to the publicity accorded these others, Koo Ah-ching was known to the people, and cheering crowds attended him.

Didi had not yet returned from school, and Ah-ching was in Nanking attending a staff meeting and was not expected back until later in the week. Sascha urged Lao Ni to wire his older brother. Lao Ni's insulation, his stubborn ignorance of progress, was such that he had no idea of how to send a telegram. After having Lao Ni write out a message urging Ah-ching to return as soon as possible, Sascha said that he would arrange for its transmission.

Hoboo had prepared and served us tea when Didi came home. With one look at the gathering he seemed to understand what had happened, as though this scene had been enacted many times over in his mind. He placed his satchel in the hall and went up to his mother, putting his hand on her shoulder. The woman did not respond to his touch.

'You do not want to fret,' Hoboo said just then. 'What do they want with an old man? Besides, Ah-ching has influence with Chiang Kai-shek.'

The woman roused herself from her torpor. 'It is not Chiang I fear, but that monster Liu *Moh-bi*, who heads the Anti-Opium Bureau.'

Only a few months after instituting the Six-Year Suppression Plan, Chiang had levied a tax on opium and appointed Liu Yueh-sung chief of the bureau. Shanghailanders, Chinese and foreign, pondered on why the Generalissimo should so blatantly undercut a decree of his own advancing. It was postulated that, on reconsidering, Chiang had decided that his need for additional resources outweighed the plan's slim chance for success. Some held that he found his stand against opium had caused his position to be threatened by the narcotic combines whose funds and manpower had proven so useful in his rise to power.

To bear out his mother's statement, Lao Ni went to the hearth. Rummaging through the newspapers he found what he was looking for.

'Here, October thirty-first, the Generalissimo's birthday.' He slapped the paper, a British daily, open to the front page and smoothing its surface showed it around. We saw a picture of Pockmarked Liu and a young girl, presumably one of his four wives, standing in front of an aeroplane. Liu's arms were folded and he had that crookedly benign expression on his face. The caption read, 'Shanghai Bankers' Gift to Generalissimo'. On the side of the plane were some Chinese characters. Sascha asked Lao Ni what they were. 'It's the name,' Lao Ni said, 'Spirit of Opium Suppression'.

'He's really playing it to the hilt, isn't he?' Sascha said.

Didi, who had not been heard from up to now, said, 'Mr. Liu has taken the cure; he no longer smokes.'

'No matter,' Lao Ni said. 'Ah-ching can certainly persuade Mr. Liu. They have known each other for a long time. They are friends even.'

'It will not help,' Didi said. We turned as one to look at the usually reticent brother. 'It is the law,' Didi continued. 'One life cannot be allowed to alter the facts on which the law was founded. It would be a loss of face.'

'Blessed Mary, listen to him,' the mother cried. 'Loss of face? What about loss of life? Eight years ago when Ah-ching led Liu's men against the Communists, we risked our lives, all of us. The northerners would have had our heads in bamboo cages for the crows to peck clean. Liu will help. He must!'

'I don't think Ah-ching will intervene,' Didi said in a small voice.

'A son not plead for his father? Is that how you are? Ingrate! Parasitic turtle! Out of my sight, *Wong-pa-tong!*'

As Didi got up I saw that his legs were trembling. At the door he said: 'It is the law. Ah-ching will never ask.' Then he ran from the room.

But Didi was wrong, for when Ah-ching returned a couple of days later, he went straight to the warlord's residence. I was in the kitchen, waiting with Lao Ni and Hoboo, when he came there to tell us the outcome. Ah-ching seemed undiscouraged by his interview.

'We played Liu's usual cat-and-mouse game—I wishing him health, prosperity, and sons to bless him, though the old shitcart is too debilitated to produce a fart, and he making a mountain of my name, my skill as an officer, and my unassailable record of integrity. Back and forth we went for I don't know how long. Matters were not helped much because one of Liu's wives, a young painted thing, whom he called Butterfly in French——'

'*Papillon?*' I said.

Ah-ching nodded. 'Butterfly sat on a low chair by his side, singing and accompanying herself on a lute. I suppose my face showed I didn't like her singing because Liu made excuses for her saying, "Of all people, girls and servants are the most difficult to behave to. If you are familiar with them, they lose their humility. If you are reserved, they are discontented. Was it not the Master himself who said that?" ' Ah-ching laughed. 'You know, old Aunty, how wise I am about Confucian analects.'

'Of course,' Hoboo replied. 'You are Christian, how should you know?' As though educated Chinese Christians never studied the teachings of Confucius.

'Then Liu dismissed Butterfly and finally inquired about my family, faking great surprise over the arrest of our father. Liu said that he could promise me nothing, his word alone was but the tiniest grain of earth upon the Purple Mountain. And I said, "The Master Liu has but to roar and the rest are as lambs." Finally he agreed to put the matter before the bureau and said that the final decision was up to them. All the while we were talking, Liu sat soaking his hands in a bowl of liquid, a bleach of some kind; I could tell by the odour. He said to me, "Is it not sad that in the light of national advancement a man must cut himself off from the things most dear to him?" '

'I don't like that,' Lao Ni said nervously.

'But as I was leaving,' Ah-ching continued, 'I noticed through the door to an antechamber that Butterfly was preparing his pipe.'

Liu had told Ah-ching to come back in three days, and when he did, a message was relayed advising him to return again in a week. And so it began, the petitioning for appointments, the waiting, and the postponements, just as Liu had handled it with our family during the troubles of 1927. A couple of weeks of this and Lao Ni's nerves began to crack, but Ah-ching refused to be discouraged. The delays, he assured his brother, were a hopeful sign. Narcotic second offenders were, as a rule, tried at once, dispatched to the nearest Chinese police station, and shot. 'Liu is making a big thing of this gesture to me, from which he will expect substantial gratitude when the times comes. Wait and see,' Ah-ching said, 'and don't be surprised if, at our New Year, he grants a general amnesty.'

But Lao Ni's doubts persisted, and our whole family found itself so caught up in this Chinese maelstrom that when each of us said, 'Any news?' the others understood at once the question was in regard to the old man.

In early December the imminent death of one father was overshadowed by the actual death of another. We had not thought much about it when Grandmama phoned one day to say that her husband had caught a chill. Grandpapa frequently suffered from colds; the varying degrees of his rheumatic pains had become his way of life and had ceased to elicit much attention. The night Grandpapa died I had been left at home against my will. Mama, Chicho, Sascha, and Aristide had gone off to see the International Arts Theatre production of *Lysistrata*. I had wanted to attend too because Aristophanes' resourceful heroine was to be played by a much-discussed young writer. Emily Hahn, with her Chinese friend, her cigars, and the gibbons, to which she seemed equally partial, had—tongue in cheek, I'm sure—caused considerable ventilation of the stuffy local scene. Mama remembered the pornography of Beardsley's drawings and said if they were representative of the play, Aristide certainly could not go. But Chicho and Sascha joined forces with Aristide, maintaining it was high time he got some exposure to that sort of thing. I took scant consolation that nobody thought it time for my moral realignment.

On the night of the show, while the family went off dressed to the nines, I settled myself in the smoking-room by the new Stewart-

Warner radio. When my brothers were home there was always a battle over which station we would listen to. Aristide favoured the tango programmes on XQHB. Sascha of course insisted that we listen to Station Radiophonique Française, and I liked XMHA's variety of programmes which sometimes featured dramatic recordings called soap operas. At about nine thirty, when I was in the middle of one of these, chewing my nails nervously, the phone rang. It was Grandmama. Grandpapa was feeling bad. He needed a doctor. Where was Mama? In face of this development it seemed to me a disloyalty to say that Mama had done anything so frivolous as go to the theatre while her father was ill. I told Grandmama that Mama was out, I was not sure where. Grandmama said I should go downstairs to Dr. Jarvis' office and try to rouse someone. Because I knew for sure, I tried to tell her that no one would be there, but she said, 'Go! Bang de hell fin de door!' I ran down the steps to Jarvis' suite and rang the bell and knocked on the door, and there was no answer. Upstairs again, I listened with one ear to the programme, the other cocked for the phone which I knew would ring again. It did within an hour. Grandpapa was worse. Where was Jarvis? Well, then why hadn't I called another doctor? Was I *sure* that I didn't know where Mama was? I admitted that Mama may have gone to the theatre.

'Dommy,' shouted the old woman, 'vich tee-a-ta?' I told her the Lyceum or the Capital, I'm not sure.

'Go! Take texi. Go right avay!'

By now I was scared witless. I had no money for a taxi. And what did I do when I got there? I said as much to Grandmama, and she screamed at me to go and never mind the money. I was to tell the driver to wait outside. Then I must ask for the manager and make *him* look for Mama. The thought of myself as protagonist in this subsidiary drama to the one being enacted on stage, of being led down the aisles or, worse yet, being sent alone, the house lights turned up and every head craned in my direction, paralysed me. If only Aristide, who loved being centre stage at any price, were here. 'All right,' I said into the receiver, 'I'll go.'

But I didn't. It was after ten thirty. I reasoned that by the time a cab got to me and took me to the theatre it would be after eleven and the play would be over. I should be faced with the cab driver and no money. Then by the time I had persuaded the driver to take me back, Mama would have long been home. I would wait where I was. The phone rang again a couple of times. I didn't answer. Later, Hoboo came by to see what I was up to, and I realized sickly that the question would arise why I had not asked her for cab fare.

'You don't have any money, do you, Hoboo?'

'Wha for?'

'Taxi.'

'Wha for you wanchee taxi?' After I had blurted the story and she had said that we must go to my grandparents at once, the family returned. Mama came into the smoking-room like a bough of radiance and opened her arms to embrace me, making it that much more difficult to wreak darkness upon her lights. One by one they dimmed, turning to smoke, as I forced out what had happened.

'You idiot,' she said. 'Why didn't you have me paged?' I stared at her dumbly; I had never heard of paging anyone.

'God, what a damned fool,' Sascha said. Mama sent Chicho to stop Lao Ni from putting the car away, then she shook a fist at me, 'If my father is dead on account of you——'

'Don't do that to him,' Aristide yelled, and I began to sob.

Grandpapa was dead when we got to their house. Propped up against pillows in a sitting position, he actually seemed to be dozing, but under brows hooked into a frown, his eyes had been left open. One leg, white with a fine blue matrix like Roquefort cheese, dangled over the side of the bed. Grandmama was kneeling by him, her face hidden in his pillow.

'Mama?'

'Go! Go avay,' Grandmama sobbed without looking up.

'Mama!'

'Fer von veek der *totah* is sick. Do you come? No, you go to de tee-a-ta. Go now! Laugh, sing, dence, your *totah* is finish.'

In the other room Ivan ruffled his feathers and squawked, '*Totah, totah*.' Mama stood alone. When Chicho tried to take her hand, she wrung it away from him. But when I went to her, she hugged me tightly and I could feel her body shaking.

36

WITH Grandpapa's burial, the shock of what Mama considered her culpability changed gradually into a sense of succession. Certainly Grandpapa's funeral had been attended with orthodox rites, and the rabbi (the same one who had ministered to Papa) again intoned the *Kaddish*. But Mama firmly resisted all his efforts to make a ritual of the mourning. For a woman of Grandmama's age to sit *shivah* was out of the question. Peremptorily Mama dismissed the rabbi's suggestion of daily visits from the holy men to ensure Grandpapa's eternal salvation. A man as reverent as her father, she informed the rabbi, was predestined. It seemed as though with the last shovel of earth upon him, Mama had decided that Grandpapa must finally fend for himself; that neither Grandmama nor she be required to meet a single premium for his passage.

After the funeral Mama went to stay with her mother for a week. We made daily visits to Grandmama, but the loss of her mate of nearly fifty years had a ravaging effect upon her, and she barely noticed our comings and goings. Wraithlike and garbed in black, she sat by the hour in a high-backed chair next to Grandpapa's memorial candle. Occasionally, when Mama was vetoing one or another religious duty proposed by the visiting rabbi, the Bunsen blue would reflame in those eyes, flicker momentarily, then die as she resumed her apathetic stance. To Mama's dismay, she would take no sustenance but continued to sit, day after day, pitched forward with hands clasped, as if she longed to plunge into the chasm created by Grandpapa's passing. Clearly, Mama said, we had to take Grandmama in with us.

After her loan to Chicho and even after he had begun to make regular payments on it in autumn, we had been forced to radical economies. No longer was it enough to trim such luxuries as the open car and extra household help. Mr. Isaacs had been summoned one day and told to close the office. I was sitting in the hall alcove with them, Mr. Isaacs and the two Chinese staff members, when Mama broke the news. Mr. Isaacs' eyes, those phials of bright liquid, uncorked and streamed tributaries down the furrows of his face.

Speaking for the Chinese as well, Mr. Isaacs said that he understood Mama's situation and that he only wished they would work for nothing. But, things being what they were. . . . However, so that her years of maintaining the firm were not a total loss, and in memory of their beloved founder, Mr. Isaacs and colleagues had come prepared to offer Mama ten thousand dollars (to be paid in instalments over a two-year period of course) in return for the good will of the company.

'You mean to tell me that you plan to continue operating the business?' Mama said.

Mr. Isaacs replied that they had agreed among them to try to keep the company afloat. It was the only work for which they had been trained, and at their ages where could they start afresh? For such a bright young fellow as Sascha it would be a breeze to re-locate.

I saw Mama hesitate and could follow just by her expressions the train of her thoughts. What was the motive behind this sudden willingness of her staff to continue, albeit for themselves, without profit? Still, they offered her ten thousand dollars, even in instalments, and she would be rid once and for all of this exorbitant monthly drain. She should have done this years ago. Why hadn't she? She must have remembered then that they had spoken of a boom. 'What about the boom?' Mama said.

Mr. Isaacs spread his hands, his eyes tipped upwards searching infinity as though it alone had the answer to where the promised boom had drifted. But, he hastened to assure her, if there was even an upsurge in the cotton market, would he forget the gallant widow and her sons who had kept them going at a loss these many years? Had he, Mr. Isaacs, not proven himself, forsaking his country of naturalization, keeping his eye, as it were, on the shop when her late husband had been required to make that trip to the United States?

Because, over the years, Mama had supported her parents generously, and since, thanks to Grandpapa's thrift, there remained a tidy sum, it seemed reasonable that Grandmama should make her home with us and chip in with the expenses. Grandmama was willing enough, and when the first week of mourning was over we arranged to move her into the extra bedroom adjoining Mama's.

The change of surroundings, as Mama had presumed, restored some of Grandmama's spirit and it wasn't long before she fired the room with her touch. The delicate periwinkle and cognac scheme became submerged in a plethora of Grandmama's belongings. A love seat was removed to make room for Ivan in his brass cage. Table surfaces were concealed by mason jars of her cherry preserves, painted black canisters of Keemun tea, knitted cosies, and her silver samovar. As well, Grandmama had brought along with her every type of crate and carton imaginable. These were stacked up and along the length of an entire wall obscuring a Gobelin tapestry. Mama, to whom this clutter was frustrating, suggested that they be put out of sight, stored safely, as she explained, 'under lock and key'. But Grandmama was adamant; the boxes, she said, contained things that were indispensable to her.

A check of her health by Dr. Jarvis shortly after revealed that Grandmama was severely anaemic and required a special diet. Accordingly, a menu high in iron was prepared daily for the old woman. With as much clatter and attention-getting as she could muster, she would take the tiniest nibble and then reject the rest. She listened patiently when Mama in desperation asked Jarvis to explain the nutritional value of vegetables to Grandmama, but when he had left and the tureen of creamed spinach was served to her, Grandmama took one look at it and said, 'No tenks, grass is for horses!'

While she may have been as well aware as the rest of us that Grandmama was using her malady as a means of bringing her daughter to heel, the sight of her mother literally wasting away in front of her had its calculated effect on Mama. The positions were again juxtaposed, with Grandmama as the sage matriarchal despot and Mama her blindly obedient subject. Christmas, with its usual joys unbeckoned, passed our home, and the days clambered drearily into the New Year. Because of Grandpapa's death there were no tree and no festivities, and Mama gave us our presents in secret.

Of us all, Chicho worked hardest to make Grandmama comfortable. He had removed his gear and seen to it that the room was immaculate prior to her arrival and had personally packed and transported her myriad possessions, making countless trips in his Fiat. And of all, he was most the object of Grandmama's contempt. Originally, she had seen in him the barrier between Mama and and another profitable match, and now he served merely to divert her daughter's attentions. I am inclined to doubt that when Mama explained her finances and invited Grandmama to live with us, she had admitted anything of her loan to Chicho. However, the old woman had mentally compartmentalized him. 'Dot Italian,' she would mutter. 'A *soupnik*.'

Nor did it please her that the usually intractable Ivan could easily be handled by Chicho. Occasionally at feeding time the cockatoo would manage to get out of his cage, and if the door to Grandmama's room happened to be open, he would make his escape. As the terror-stricken servants ran for cover, Ivan would begin a stately strut along the length of the halls, squawking proudly and spreading his wings in noisy flutter as those round enraged eyes defied approach.

Once Sascha, who thought he had a way with everything, especially animals, attempted to catch Ivan, only to receive a painful nip in the belly for his trouble. Heedless of Grandmama's entreaties, Ivan retained control of the apartment until Chicho's return that evening. At the sight of him, the bird flapped his great sherbet-coloured wings and squawked, '*Soupnik! Soupnik!*' Lovingly, Chicho murmured endearments, then with the pole end of a broom he tapped the floor a few inches from Ivan. As Chicho advanced towards him, continuing to tap, the bird retreated, until they reached the door of Grandmama's room, whereupon Ivan turned and made straight for the sanctuary of his cage which Grandmama, waiting, immediately latched. Wiping the sweat from his face, Chicho asked Mama, '*Cosa v'uol' dire, soupnik?*'

'Never mind,' Mama said. 'You caught the bird; that's all that matters.'

In the little more than a month since Grandpapa's death, Ahching had been able to receive no commitment from his calls on Liu. The advent of Chinese New Year more and more seemed to contain Ah-ching's hope for a dismissal of the charges against his father. During this time Mama had not ventured out of the apartment, hewing to her mother's desire not so much for her company as her presence. Meanwhile Grandmama continued to use her lack of appetite as her personal bludgeon. At every meal, Mama would begin by cajoling, followed by reasoning, and end with threatening and an avalanche of tears. The strain of this was beginning to tell on everyone, most noticeably Mama, and it was decided that some programme of recreation was in order. Surprisingly, when it was suggested to her, Grandmama agreed to go along with the rest of us for a drive in the country.

It was a bleak Saturday afternoon when we set out for Hungjao. Melting frost scrunched under the car tyres, leaving trails of slush. The sky hung warningly low like a great black purse, as cowherders gently flicked at muddy water buffalo along plough tracks. Though Mama didn't talk much, it was evident the chill air and country sights and sounds, even the pervasive smell of excrement, were a happy change for her. She made Lao Ni stop once to buy a basket of eggs from a villager and marvelled that eggs still cost only one dollar for a hundred in this area. As we drove past the miles of rice paddies and vegetable plots near the airport, Grandmama became galvanized into attention. She tugged Mama's arm, 'Look! You see vot dey do?' Along rows of chard and cabbage, peasant women were pouring manure by means of long-handled scoops. 'You see dat? Dey put shit on de grass and you vant I should eat? So you eat!' She glared furiously at Chicho as though not Jarvis, not Mama, but only he could have conspired to wreck her principles of *shekitah*. And that took care of the drives. Grandmama refused even to consider leaving the house ('Vot will I see next time?'), and Mama would not leave her.

Beginning the last week of January, the sky at night was suffused with colour, as if all the garish neons of the city had been assembled at Pootung across the river. Chinese workers from the Texaco and British American Tobacco companies had joined with the villagers to welcome the Year of the Rat; the sky held its flush, and the crackle and explosion of fireworks could be heard until the dawn of each day. In the kitchen, Dah Su prepared two festive dinners, one for the servants at the start of the holiday, another for our family at the end. By far I preferred the servants' gathering, where toasts were downed, scarlet gift envelopes exchanged, and uninhibited views aired. Though Dah Su went to greater expense and effort with the meal he served to our family, the servants' dinner always tasted different, better, and ever since I could remember I had been welcomed as an unofficial guest. Preparations had been going on for days in advance. I had stumbled over one of the pair of live white ducklings scheduled for transmutation into that northern delicacy, Peking duck.

I thought it expedient to wait until the actual day of the feast before going back to the kitchen. I had counted on the ducks to be in the oven by midafternoon, but when I got there they were still hanging by their necks from cords, bloated and glazed with a varnish of melted rock sugar and red bean paste. Dah Su's wife welcomed me warmly and gave me a bowl of sugared lotus seeds to nibble. Hoboo and Lao Ni were already there, waiting for his mother and Didi. The decisive time had come. We all knew that. Today Liu would grant Ah-ching's father the dismissal and end what had been over two months of suspended agony.

Hope was reflected on the mother's face when she arrived with Didi shortly after and inquired at once whether or not Ah-ching had returned from the warlord. You couldn't tell much from looking at Didi what he was thinking, nor did he seem anxious, one way or another, about his oldest brother's mission. Dah Su poured the grown-ups warmed *shaoshing* and gave tea to Didi and me. Many toasts had been drunk with Dah Su and Zee saying, 'It will be today. He will be released. The Master Liu is a big man, a number one. So a little crooked, never mind. That's just why he will be able to let the old man off. . . .'

The ducks, now hanging from hooks in the oven, were turning to russet lacquer and perfuming the kitchen with their aroma. Dah Su's wife lifted the lid of a bamboo steamer and announced that the mandarin pancakes were about done. I had joined Didi in a corner by the cathedral-shaped radio (which had belonged to Aristide and me), and we listened to Chinese stations, news broadcasts mainly. Didi said that anything we heard had been ruthlessly censored by the Nationalists. To take their minds off the fact that it was drawing close to evening and Ah-ching had not yet shown up, the servants directed their conversation to the state of China's affairs. Dah Su's wife sided with Zee that Chiang Kai-shek had better heed the opinion of his people and stop baiting the Reds, had better join up with them to drive out the Japanese. But Hoboo said, 'How can we trust them, the Reds? They have no faith, no church. . . .' She stopped as the others looked at her. Buddhists, Taoists, Confucianists —her family were the only Christians.

Didi spoke up. 'I've heard Ah-ching quote Sun Yat-sen, saying that he believes in the Christ who was a revolutionary.'

'Ah-ching meant the National revolution,' Lao Ni said.

'What about Sun Yat-sen? Are you so sure he meant the Nationalist revolution? Don't you think he meant the *Chinese* revolution? The Communists are Chinese. They have proven themselves tough and courageous. Who else armed with nothing but a belief could cross eighteen mountain ranges and twenty-four rivers, all the time pursued and slaughtered? That is courage, Chinese courage,' Didi said.

'That is endurance, stubborn Chinese endurance,' Lao Ni said.

Hoboo was greatly vexed with Didi. 'Where did you hear that rubbish? The Communists are bandits; they burn churches, kill people because they own land. Stealing from one brother who has earned to give the other who hasn't. That's your idea of justice, courage?'

'Sacrifice is also courage. If one brother earns he shouldn't have to be forced to give to the brother who hasn't. Sacrifice is necessary. Chairman Mao's wife, who was badly wounded and carried on a litter, gave birth to a baby during the Long March, but she had no time for it, so she gave the infant to the peasants.'

Dah Su's wife had interrupted her work to listen. She and the cook were childless. They had several times adopted sons and had proudly brought them clad in silks and painted to ward off the devil, but each son had died. Clumsily she tried to explain to Didi the difference between courage and dedication. 'Chairman Mao's wife gave up her baby because she wanted something else more. A woman who gives up her children because she wants them to eat is brave, not one who gives them up in order to be a soldier *rather* than a mother.'

Ah-ching came to the back door at that moment. You had only to look at him to know that his news was bad. He did not greet anyone but stood where he was, the skin taut over his cheekbones, his eyes empty. With a word his mother broke the silence. 'When?' she said.

'I have been promised a month. I will get the best legal counsel,' Ah-ching replied. As though by his pronouncement of it Ah-ching himself had made the sentence immutable, the servants began to stir, to move into ordinary actions which guaranteed the fact of their own existence.

'But why? Why has he led you by the nose all this time?' the mother said. 'Is it money?'

'Liu is probably the richest man in China. It is not money; it's something else.' Then he told us what Pockmarked Liu wanted in exchange for the old man's life. As intimated in the earlier conversation between Dah Su's wife and Zee, China was at the breaking point of its patience with Chiang Kai-shek's resolution not to fight Japan. A specific movement to force Chiang into a coalition with the Communists against the Japanese was known to Liu. Ah-ching was to thwart any such conciliation. He was, if it came to that, to lead his own troops against the Generalissimo. For some reason, Liu did not want war with Japan.

'You agreed, of course,' the mother said.

'If I had agreed, our father would be kept as a hostage, and when Liu realized that I had betrayed him. . . .'

'Then you must go to Chiang. You must tell him about Liu's plot and in exchange he will dismiss the charges,' the mother said.

'What good would that do? These are precisely Chiang's sentiments at the moment. He would not believe that Liu suggested rebellion. He would only think that Liu was loyal and I the traitor.'

'If this is what the Generalissimo wants and what Liu demands, why did you not agree?'

'Because Chiang is wrong and Liu is corrupt. The time has come for change.'

'What kind of general are you? What kind of son?' the woman cried.

'All I can do is to beg Chiang's executive clemency,' Ah-ching said.

I watched Didi, expecting him to say with that maddening dispassion that the Generalissimo would have no choice but to uphold the decision of his own bureau chief. But this time the youngest son said nothing.

37

AH-CHING returned from his audience with Chiang Kai-shek early in February. Lao Ni told us the outcome of it one day when Sascha went to the office to pick up the remainder of his possessions and they later stopped by the school for Aristide and me. Chiang had firmly refused to intervene. To dismiss charges levelled at the father of one of his generals would cause his enemies to seize upon it and exploit his discrimination. Ah-ching had not mentioned Liu's proposition. In a voice woollen with fatigue, Lao Ni admitted the soundness of Chiang's decision. Had the issue concerned a street coolie, there might have been no problem. The balance of an anonymous life, one way or another, was of no great consequence in the Chinese scheme of things. Even I knew that, from the time I had found newly born babies bundled in paper and left in the streets to die.

Going up in the elevator, Sascha mused on the parallels between the Chinese brothers and ourselves. He was, of course, Ah-ching. I thought he'd say then, since we were the same age, that I was Didi. Instead Sascha likened Aristide to the youngest Chinese brother. Aristide was not displeased by the comparison until Sascha added, 'Frankly, I think Didi's a bloody little pinko.'

I didn't give Sascha's remark much thought then. I was too concerned with the remaining similarity, identifying me with Lao Ni, the safe brother, the one who never swam upstream, whose entire purpose in life was its maintenance. The thought did not make me happy. When I had in my usual way buried that bone of discontent, I pondered on Sascha's allusion to Didi. Although Aristide had staunchly defended Didi, he no more knew what a Communist really was than I did. True, Didi's was rebellious talk, full of fire-breathing terms. He spoke of unity, sacrifice, courage, but then hadn't the northerners and the Nationalists?

Sascha's opinion of Didi might have been formed because he once heard Didi railing out against Chiang's secret police, the efficient blueshirts, whose methods were subject to much unpopularity among the Chinese. But for that matter, had not Sascha himself expressed contempt for Hitler's brownshirts? And had he not finally ripped to pieces Aristide's Ballila uniform, as a protest of Fascist behaviour?

On the other hand, there were the little-known examples of Communist strategy which became, under Didi's confiding, burnished chronicles of heroism. I surmised, at first, that some of these stories might have come from Ah-ching, who had been part of the mechanized whip which followed and flogged the Communists on their trek. But the unqualified admiration was not Ah-ching's. Only now was the hero of the anti-Red purge in Shanghai beginning to accept the bald necessity of coexistence. But this by no means constituted Ah-ching's endorsement of the Communists.

The only change in our lives at home was that the groove implemented by Grandmama was fast becoming a grave for Mama. Reassured by her daughter's continued attendance, Grandmama rewarded her by being less intransigent at mealtimes. I had discovered, on what had become daily visits to her room, that Grandmama kept a cache of comestibles—Huntley and Palmer biscuits, Fry's chocolate, and other nonperishables—stashed away among her clothing in a chest of drawers. These, while they tasted of camphor and reeked of cologne, were nonetheless nutritious, and she shared them with me generously, if secretively.

My comradeship for Grandmama was applauded, even fostered, by the remainder of the family. I began to sense that I was being groomed as a bulwark against the time when Mama felt ready to make a stab for freedom. Even Aristide, who had become stuck on himself since getting his dinner clothes and going to black-tie parties with his picture in the Sunday supplement, made some remark on the fitness of the oldest and the youngest keeping each other company. As for Sascha, when I showed signs of recalcitrance, he was quick to remind me that Grandmama didn't know I had not gone to the theatre the night Grandpapa died. But they had reckoned without Grandmama. For so long as Mama gave no indication of wishing to leave her, Grandmama was the model of solicitude, scurrying several times a day to Mama's room with *stahkans* of tea. Or, because it gave Mama such pleasure when she did so, Grandmama might undertake the making of some Jewish culinary specialty.

Grandmama even extended her sociability to Aristide, listening by the hour while he practised the piano until, unable to endure his repetitions, she would smite her brow and exclaim, 'Oi, stop oreddy da drimbling!' But Grandmama made sure that none of this was to be construed as a permanent return to health. Far from it, she was merely being stoic.

'Vot's da use to complain, you'll believe me?' One and all should respect the exorbitant interest she was being called upon to pay for her tenuous mortgage on earth. Even in the midst of reminiscences, where mother and daughter would become quite merry, if my mother were to ask hopefully, 'Mama, how do you feel?' the old lady would instantly snap, 'Very bed, *zehr shlekt!*'

As with all efficient persecution, benefits derived in the name of a cause must first be made available. This done, authority is then delegated and evidence acquired through channels. . . . By virtue of the family's complicity towards me, I automatically became Grand-mama's ally. There remained the considerable force of the servants for her to win. To acquire this fealty, while Mama rested in the afternoons, Grandmama turned her room into a free bazaar. Her cartons were opened, and they spewed forth their treasures: beaded dresses and purses, feather boas and fans, brocaded cushions, un-used linens still notched by thread, mismatched porcelains, and even some silver. Everything, in fact, which Mama had over the years discarded and Grandmama diligently accumulated. Accustomed as they were to Mama's obsession for locking things, the servants found Grandmama's spilling bounty cause enough for new allegiance. A grapevine between them was easily established. So it was that Grand-mama knew well in advance who had telephoned, who was coming to the apartment, what was being ordered and from where, and, most of all, the precise time factors. When in my naïveté I expressed surprise at her ability to foretell events, she said with a little smile, 'Mine dear, ven you oil de veels, dey move.'

Throughout the month Lao Ni had asked for time off to confer with Ah-ching and the lawyers he had commissioned to handle his father's case. From what Lao Ni told us, the attorneys considered the old man's guilt a foregone conclusion but they hoped to succeed in court, using the device which had failed for Ah-ching in person. The lawyers would ask for clemency on the basis that, frail of character and degenerate as he was, the father had sired a hero for their country, and they planned to gamble on Ah-ching's popularity. To this end considerable play was given the pending case in the Chinese press, and reporters deluged the apartment, subjecting Lao Ni and Hoboo to interviews and photographs, to which they con-sented uneasily. The trial was to take place on the first of March, and an immediate judgment was expected.

On that last Friday of February, I had anticipated, upon coming to the breakfast table, to find the family engrossed in the subject of the trial. Instead I was auditor to a plot formulated by Chicho, Sascha, and Aristide to get Mama out of the house that evening. The whole business of Mama's playing nursemaid had gone much too far, Sascha was saying, and Mama must make her break now. As they made their plans, I squirmed uncomfortably, for though they openly planned to use me as a wedge against Grandmama's objections, their unquestioning faith in my discretion blackmailed me to silence. However flimsily, I managed in my own way to support Grandmama. When Mama protested that, if she went out against her mother's wishes, the old lady would starve herself, I did not console her with my knowledge of the emergency store Grandmama kept in her chest of drawers. Chicho advised Mama that if Grandmama was systematically ignored she would soon enough give in to natural instincts of self-preservation.

Mama agreed to be firm. It was a preposterous and cruel situation, she could see that, and the sooner it was resolved the better. I suppose to get my mind off Grandmama, I asked the family what they thought the chances were for the father's acquittal. Using terms like cut and dried, shut and closed, each of them assured me the acquittal was a certainty. No doubt about it.

We came home for lunch that day because Aristide said he wanted to bolster Mama's courage in the event that Grandmama had got wind of anything. 'She knows things are going to happen before they're even planned,' he said, looking at me meaningfully.

'Maybe she's got some gypsy in her,' I replied. I was just as anxious to get back, having wrangled uneasily with myself all morning over my decision not to disclose Mama's project. Grandmama appeared at the dining-room, fastidious as ever, her hair piled high in coils, a cameo fastened at the lace jabot. She had for some time taken to using a cane, which as a rule in her hands was more like a rapier or a sceptre, employed to poke, parry, or thrust, or to be raised with solemnity in greeting. But today she leaned forwards on it as a supporting guide. Taking her place, she surveyed the table with that secretive air she had of an ancient regime she could never have known. It was clear to me at once that she had found out. Zee placed a tureen in front of her, removing the lid with a flourish. Then he ladled the soup into her plate. Everyone except me became absorbed in conversation. Grandmama brought the soup spoon to her nose, sniffed it, and put the spoon down with a clatter. Seeing that this brought about no reaction, Grandmama shoved the plate away from her. While the family continued to talk to one another, those eyes sputtered fluorescently from face to face. Then, studiously wiping her lips with a napkin as though she had consumed an entire meal, Grandmama said to Zee, 'Take avay da soup.'

'What do you mean? That's gorgeous soup...' Mama capitulated. The old lady leaned back in her chair, the tip of her nose twitching from the smile she was trying to suppress. Instantly Chicho began an account in Italian about a motor trip he had once taken through the Alps. It was an exciting tale told with all the habitual Italian gestures, and I found myself, with the rest, listening intently. At the point where he was describing a particularly perilous curve in the road, Chicho brought his fingers together in a pinch so that they looked like the head of a goose pecking, and said to Mama, '*Una curva pericolosa.*' I glanced at Grandmama, whose mouth was working as if she was trying to get rid of an oversized prune pit. 'Vot? You call mine dottah a *kourva*?' she screamed. In the ensuing hubbub, while Mama attempted to explain that a *curva* in Italian was quite different from the similar-sounding word in Russian, the old lady threw down her napkin, pushed back her chair, and striking blindly for the floor with her cane, began to leave the room. But Chicho miscalculated on her exit, and she did not miss his expostulated, '*Vecchia Gallina!*' Patently, communication was faulty between Chicho and Grandmama, but not so much that when Chicho called her an old hen did Grandmama confuse it for a girl's name in Russian. She tottered back into the room. The fingers of her free hand twitched and plucked spastically while her chin bobbed as she tried to organize birdlike shrieks of fury into articulation. 'Peemp!'

'Mama!'

'And you, you tell dat peemp, old cheeken make da best soup!'

I presume it was decided after I had followed Grandmama from the room that the only intelligent thing for them to do was to proceed as arranged. It was evening, and Grandmama had soaked some thin slices of Brinza cheese in hot water, which she served me on wafers. She herself did not eat any. As I spooned cherry jam into my *stahkan* of tea, Grandmama gave me her dazzling picture-window smile.

'Vot time?' she asked.

'Uh?' I replied, taken unawares. She rapped my glass impatiently with her spoon.

'Oh, it's seven.'

'Come,' she said. As we started for the hall I noticed that Grandmama was bent over her cane, and on our way she paused a couple of times. Consummate actress throwing herself into the role, I thought.

We got to the front door just as the family was going out. Pinned by the sight of her frail and bent mother, Mama fluttered in nervous defiance. 'I'll be home before eleven, Mama—just for some air—a change. . . .' Grandmama said nothing.

'You are not alone, you have *der klaner.*'

Grandmama gave me a withering explicit look, and I, as at a signal, began an injured departure from the hall. I was not offended by what might seem to be a breach of Grandmama's estimation of my worth but understood quite well her ethics on the point of not allowing my mother to take advantage of that regard.

No sooner had they left than Grandmama sought me out in my room. We smiled at each other with the silent confidence of true champions. I suppose to signify her disapproval of the role into which the family had cast me and to cement her bond of good faith, Grandmama squeezed a couple of scented and crumpled dollar bills into my fist.

'Go, *kukala,* my doll. Go to cinema.'

I hesitated. It was clearly understood that Grandmama had been left in my care. Over and over in rehearsal for this moment, Mama had shown me where she had written Dr. Jarvis' office and home phone numbers in the telephone folder on the smoking-room desk. True, Hoboo was at Ah-ching's house, lending her moral support for the trial on Monday, but Zee was in the apartment. I could ask him to look in on Grandmama from time to time. I'd take a railless car from Nanking Road, catch the eight-thirty show at the Grand, and be home well before the family. When all was said and done, it was the weekend, no school tomorrow, and here was the old lady, practically begging me to go.

When I got home after the film, Zee opened the door. In reply to my questions about Grandmama, Zee said that she'd retired about an hour after I had left. No, she hadn't wanted anything for dinner but perhaps I'd better pop in and check on her.

The night light was on in Grandmama's room, and Ivan rustled testily in his covered cage. I noticed that Grandmama, lying on her bed, had not undressed, and I put this down to the absent-mindedness of age. As I raised her hand to pull the blanket about her, I felt that it was icy. I switched on the top light and peered into her face. It seemed to be ashen—or, I wondered, did she always look that way asleep? She was breathing loudly, and as I chafed her hands and said, 'Grandmama, Grandmama,' she issued a funny gargling

297

sound and those incredible dentures began to emerge from her mouth. With the hollowed cheeks, sunken eyes, and now the projected teeth, her face looked like a skull. The word coma came to my mind. I ran to the kitchen and told Zee to go at once to Jarvis' office. He argued, as I had only a few months earlier with Grandmama, that no one would be there, and like Grandmama, I told him to go anyway. As he reached the front door, I said to him, 'Zee, not a word about my going out tonight. You understand?' I saw him ruminate on the shining weapon I had just placed in his hands, so I added, 'Remember, I left you in charge. I'll say that you promised to take care of her.'

In the smoking-room I dialled the Cercle number, all the while trying frantically to recall what it was you were supposed to say when you wanted someone to come to the phone. The word was somehow related to book, that much I knew. Please book Madame Spunt? No. Leaf, that was it. The Cercle operator answered in French and I asked her to have my mother leafed. She didn't understand, so I tried leaf in French. '*Voulez-vous feuillez* Madame *Spunt?*'

'*Vous voulez que j'appelle Madame . . . ?*' the operator asked.

'*Oui, oui, appellez, appellez!*' I shouted.

Mama came to the phone, her voice crackling with fear. 'What is it?'

'Grandmama, she's breathing funny. I think she's in a coma.'

'We'll be home immediately. Did you call Jarvis?'

'Yes,' I half-truthed.

When Zee came back to say that no one had answered his summons, I knew that I had to call the doctor at his home, and I dreaded it. But when I reached him, Jarvis made it seem very simple, saying not to fuss with Grandmama and he would be right out.

I was with him in Grandmama's room when Mama came in, her face seeming to undulate like a parachute. Jarvis was putting away his syringe. 'Not to worry, Regina, she'd fainted from weakness, that's all. I've given her a stimulant and B-complex, and tomorrow the dear lady and I had better have a little chat.'

My mother fell to her knees by the bed and grasped Grandmama's hands. 'Mama, Mama, forgive me. I'll never leave you again for a minute.' Grandmama's eyelids flickered, and with her teeth now back in place she gave Mama a gentle and forgiving smile.

I could only think, once I knew that Grandmama was not going to die, of how rotten fate was towards me. Here I was trapped between the family who could tell Grandmama at any time about that business when Grandpapa died, and now Grandmama had exactly the same advantage over me.

38

WHEN Hoboo and Lao Ni did not return on Monday evening, Sascha took it as ill omened, but Mama said perhaps they had gone to the family home to celebrate the acquittal. That night Zee told us that the old man had been found guilty and sentenced to death. Next morning Sascha drove Aristide and me to school. After we had made certain of his departure, we left the grounds and headed towards Chapei.

From outside we heard a din of singing and the banging of pans like a Chinese opera. 'Maybe Zee was wrong,' Aristide said, 'and they are celebrating.' Hoboo opened the door for us. Once in Ah-ching's house, we knew that no mistake had been made. The mother and Didi were in the parlour. Didi, by the silent Blaupunkt, got up to welcome us. But the mother sat rigidly in her chair without moving. Watching her tired expressionless face I got the feeling that, for his wife, the old man had died some time ago, perhaps the day when she had come down the stairs after cleaning his room. Now her burden was to adjust to the finality of the fact. There was a shrill note of song in the kitchen, followed by a wail and then cackling laughter. Hoboo explained it was Lao Ni making the racket. 'Last night he went to the Great World, and now he's drunk on *Lao chiu*.' I wondered in that moment if that was the first time Lao had gone back to the amusement palace since his happy times with E-ling.

'When is it to be?' Aristide asked Hoboo.

'Today noon. Ah-ching has gone to Liu to beg him to intercede,' she said.

'You think he will?'

Hoboo shrugged. Lao Ni came in from the kitchen, waving a

small greenish-brown flask at my brother and me in greeting. Then he came up and gravely offered the flask for us to drink. When we refused he thrust the container at Hoboo, his mother and Didi. They ignored him. Lao Ni shook his head wonderingly and tilting it back poured the contents of the bottle down his throat. The liquor coarsed from his lips in a stream down his corded neck.

The mother asked the time once. It was nearly noon and still no sign of Ah-ching. 'Maybe he's gone to get his father. Maybe they'll come back together,' Hoboo said.

'Ah-ching would have telephoned,' Didi said. Hoboo silenced him with a glance. The oldest brother returned at one o'clock. He looked around at the faces turned to him. 'It's finished,' he said.

Lao Ni took a step towards him. 'No, no,' he cried. Ah-ching put out his hand in a clumsy attempt to comfort his brother, but Lao Ni brushed him aside.

'You, the almighty hero who can't save one life. And you'—he turned on Didi—'with your textbook judgments.'

'And what are you?' Didi blazed suddenly, not moving from his corner. 'Nationalists, Communists, or even Japs, you'd find your whining dog level,' Didi cried.

'Enough, enough between brothers,' their mother said. 'Your father is dead.'

At that Lao Ni, who had advanced to strike his youngest brother, stopped and covered his face with great stemlike fingers and began to sob. Ah-ching sighed and sat on a stool, his hands clasped before him.

'Now,' the mother continued in a very calm voice, 'we must make proper burial arrangements.' She spoke of her visits to the jail where she had tried to persuade her husband to convert to her faith, thinking he might take consolation from the thought that they would meet again someday in eternity. But the old man had not wanted to become a Christian.

'Who knows,' Hoboo said, 'but that if he had found our Saviour, he might have been spared this fate.'

'There are no Christian addicts?' Lao Ni said with fresh bitterness.

'The fact remains that A-pa lived and died a Buddhist, and he will have the ceremony of his religion,' Ah-ching said. 'My brothers and I will walk among the mourners.'

'Catholics participating in pagan rites?' The mother faltered.

'You and Hoboo can suit yourselves,' Ah-ching replied.

'I will march among the mourners,' Hoboo said.

'Good. Rest assured, old Aunty, my father will have a funeral like a giant firecracker. It will sound to his heaven and to ours.'

Even Grandmama wanted to attend the funeral a couple of days later, but Mama vetoed the suggestion. Since Dr. Jarvis' conversation with Grandmama the morning after her fainting spell, a remarkable change had come over the old lady. For the next day or so her meals had been brought to her with all of us in attendance. She seemed pleased by this and to Mama's great relief ate without the usual promptings. Once, when Chicho came to see her, and sitting on the bed tried to smooth her brow gently, murmuring '*Mammina mia*,' she flinched momentarily. Then she gave him that winning sweet smile, and I knew that it marked only time and truce. My guess is that Grandmama had given herself a scare, that her physical condition, independent of her mentality, had run away with the situation. But by the time of the funeral less than a week afterwards, she was sitting up and in quite good spirits.

The cortege was to begin at the Temple of the Queen of Heaven in the Northern District and progress along the Bund through the International Settlement to the ancient cemetery in the French Concession. Sascha wondered aloud at this unnecessary peregrination. There were nearer cemeteries, one close by the temple in fact. But Aristide remembered Ah-ching had promised that his father would have a spectacular funeral.

Sascha drove us over the Garden Bridge to the temple at North Honan Road. We went through the wide gate to the entrance court which was already thronged with worshippers and idlers. The temple itself had an impressive façade of diamond-shaped stonework with enamelled medallions. By each side of the great carved door rested a stone lion, which according to tradition came to life at night. A monk in grey robes led us into the central court, which was a huge chamber surrounded by galleries. At the back of the chamber was a vermilion and gold stand with a curved roof. In it were shelves containing ancestor tablets. We were about to enter the inner court when the massive doors swung open and a group of chanting and incense-carrying monks began to file out. I saw the statue of the

301

Queen of Heaven gleaming through yellow draperies high above them in the darkness of the inner court.

Behind the monks were attendants bearing a lacquer coffin covered loosely with inscribed silks, and following it came the chief mourners. We could not see them at first because of the white cloth enclosure, like three sides of a square fastened on long poles. When they came abreast of us, I recognized Ah-ching in front, followed by Lao Ni, then Didi. The mother came after the sons, and then Hoboo. All of them were garbed in caps, gowns, and shoes of the roughest white cloth. On their caps was affixed a square of rice sacking, and each wore a surplice of the same. This was a token of humility and distinguished the immediate relatives from the other mourners. Behind them were a dozen or so people, possibly distant relatives, and trailing after were at least fifty professional mourners, all clad in the same funerary attire. The paid mourners conversed calmly among themselves. Outside the temple gates a hearse drawn by four white-plumed and caparisoned horses awaited. While Ah-ching had eschewed the by now customary procedure of renting a motor hearse, Aristide drew my attention to the Rolls Phantom Coupe Ah-ching had hired for the purpose of transporting an enormous framed photograph of the old man as its solitary back-seat occupant. With the coffin installed in the hearse, the procession began to assemble. To lead it were a group of brass band musicians in smart navy-blue uniforms and tall hats with ostrich plumes. Behind them, the hearse was followed by the open Rolls, then the relatives and mourners. They were joined last of all by a hundred or so urchins in peaked caps bearing umbrellas, with red and gold boards slung over their shoulders, while others straggled into line carrying silver foil replicas of worldly goods, coins, and *sycees*, shoe-shaped ingots, to fulfil the material needs of the departed in the future life.

And so the cortege began, slowly heading back over the bridge onto the Bund. The band struck up a tinny martial version of 'Camptown Races'. At once the paid mourners threw themselves into a frenzy of grief, the wailing and lamenting both spontaneous and genuine.

Because of Ah-ching's popularity, or because so much of the trial had been recounted in the Chinese papers, the promenades and sidewalks on both sides of the broad waterfront were densely lined with spectators. The winds, still of a wintry cold, sighed in the trees, but the people fringing the road, muffled and in their padded clothes, did not seem to notice it.

At the intersection of the Bund and Nanking Road, a large number of young men and women began to march alongside the hearse, their ranks filling until they formed an alternative procession of their own. Suddenly banners were hoisted, carrying glaring black-on-white inscriptions in both Chinese and English which we could easily read. IS THIS POCKMARKED LIU'S JUSTICE? said one. ADDICT MURDERER OF THE OLD AND FEEBLE read another. DOWN WITH THE OPIUM CZAR was the legend on still another. The crowds watching and reading the banners were moved to stir, then to cry out in anger, so their voices could be heard above the brass winds and timpani, above the howling anguish of the mourners. Now at each intersection more protesters joined the cortege with more pennants and stronger-voiced slogans. Long before Sascha turned down Rue du Consulat, long before my brothers and I saw the orange walls of the temple at the Pah-sien-jao cemetery, we knew that this was Ah-ching's gauntlet to the warlord.

Pockmarked Liu struck back at once. The next day Didi came to tell us that Ah-ching had been summoned to Nanking. The next thing we heard was that Ah-ching had been transferred to Shensi province.

Around the middle of summer I came across a letter Mama had begun to Tante Tila. Since her return to Europe, Tila had written twice to Aristide, but he had not replied. Mama's letter to her was lying open on the escritoire in the smoking-room: 'Mama has been a jewel. I know she doesn't like to be alone, so we don't go out much.' While Grandmama on the surface seemed to agree that Mama must have a life of her own, she had by no means made her peace with the idea. She still collected scraps of information from the servants and had taken to eavesdropping on the telephone herself. She was quite unashamed if I happened to catch her at it and would immediately enlist my assistance by turning over the receiver to me, while she scurried in search of pencil and paper for me to record the vital facts. Grandmama had not for a minute forgiven Chicho, although she was pleasant to his face. Of all, she listened to his conversations most meticulously. Sometimes in Mama's rare absences, Chicho would use her room for resting or making calls, and of course Grandmama was at once on the extension in the smoking-room.

I don't know when it was that Chicho began to skip his monthly payments. Though Mama covered up for him, she was worried. The money represented the bulk of what we depended on as living income. Nor did it make her any happier when Chicho came home one evening with the news he'd heard from a banking colleague that Isaacs and the two Chinese had entered a million dollars in the Hongkong Shanghai Bank under the name of Papa's company. When she called him on this, Isaacs denied it at first. Then, heated by Mama's accusations, he admitted the deposit and said that it was little enough recompense for all that he'd had to endure from our family. Mama's attorney advised her that the contract she had signed with Isaacs was binding. She had no financial recourse there. As might be expected, Isaacs' prediction that Sascha would have not the least difficulty relocating was as valid as his other statements. Michel de Raveur regretted he had no openings, and a Dutch financier to whom Papa had loaned the initial capital to start his operations jested that, overweight as he was, Sascha might collapse from the strain of honest work. Chicho, presumably in an effort to bring his finances into shape, stayed at the bank more and more in the evenings. All in all, it was not the happiest of times, that summer of 1936.

The moment Grandmama was waiting for came on a day towards the end of the season or just about then, for I saw a flock of Indian cuckoos flying south purposefully, like drunkards heading for a wine fountain. The weather was still hot enough for all the verandah doors to be opened in the daytime, and the overhead fans in the smoking-room remained in place. It was a weekend, and Chicho was at the apartment. Mama and Sascha had gone downtown, and Aristide in the drawing-room was thundering away at Liszt's *Piano Concerto*. Tired of watching the flight of the birds and the river life which through waves of vapour seemed to shimmer in almost suspended motion, I went into the smoking-room. Grandmama was on the phone, listening, not speaking. When she saw me, she put one finger warningly to her lips and beckoned with the receiver. Handing it to me, she got busy in the escritoire, looking for a pen and paper, making agitated noises and slamming one drawer and another as she searched.

It was Chicho on the phone. 'No, *cara*, I don't know if it is possible today.'

The voice that replied was a woman's. It was a voice I knew but could not place. 'How will I know then?' she said.

'Eh—how can I say?' I could in my mind's eye see Chicho flinging out his hand characteristically.

'You better meet me, that's all,' the woman was saying.

Grandmama had shoved the pad and pencil in my hand. 'Write,' she hissed. Although I had no notion of how Grandmama planned to use this information, I had an unhappy premonition. Muffling the receiver, I whispered, 'What shall I write? They haven't said anything.' Grandmama pressed her face close to mine.

'Outside the Cathay Theatre, six o'clock, be there with the *bapki*,' the woman said. While Chicho was arguing the woman hung up. I could hear Chicho's long sigh as he replaced the receiver.

'Hah, *bapki*!' Grandmama muttered. I looked at her questioningly. She slid her thumb and forefinger together to indicate coin. 'Write,' she said, pointing to the pad.

'*Bapki*?'

'Dommy! Katay Tee-a-ta, seex o'gluck.'

I didn't know what it was about, but I didn't like it. Most of all, I didn't want to bear the burden of this intrigue by myself. Aristide had missed a bar in the opening of the concerto which he had begun for my benefit. He frowned at me. 'Look what you made me do,' he said. I told him about the phone call.

'You recognized the voice,' he said when I had finished.

'Yes, but not who it belongs to. Why do you suppose Grandmama made me write down their meeting place?'

Aristide thought for a moment, then he said that when Mama returned we had to keep her at home no matter what.

Around midafternoon, when Chicho had already gone, Mama returned without Sascha. She at once changed into a housecoat and said as she did every summer that she thought the heat would never end. Aristide got to her before Grandmama with a tray of muskmelons and a Cinzano and bitters. Then he sat beside her and told her how hard he had been working on the Liszt. 'I've planned a concert this evening, just for you, Mama.'

'How lovely,' Mama replied, genuinely pleased.

As Aristide settled himself at the Steinway, there was Grandmama leaning against the doorjamb of the drawing-room. Aristide started playing; Mama put down her drink. 'Wait a minute, Aristide. Mama, are you all right?'

The old lady smiled weakly, fanning herself with her hand. '*Heiss*,' she said.

'Have a Cinzano,' Aristide said briskly and began again.

Grandmama tugged at her throat. 'Air, I vant air,' she croaked.

'Open all the verandah doors,' Mama said to me. When I replied that they were already open, Mama went to her mother and guided her gently to the love seat by the verandah. 'Better?'

Grandmama inhaled deeply and the usual river stench was such that she did not have to act. Her gasp was genuine. 'I vant *frish* air!'

'Would you like to go for a drive?' Mama said.

Grandmama pretended she had not heard.

'It would do you wonders. I could send you with the little one. . . .'

'*Der klaner?*' Grandmama scowled.

'Or Aristide. I'll go too, if you want, Mama.'

Grandmama paused reflectively, then she said in tones of self-sacrifice, 'Orright, you vant to go, I go.'

Aristide looked up from the piano. 'What about my concert? I've been practising all day, just to play for you.'

'I can hear you any time. Grandmama never wants to go out. How can I refuse her?'

'But you said you would.' Aristide crashed his fingers on the keys.

'So I said I would. Listen, you're fifteen; stop acting like a child.' She turned to me. 'And you tell Lao Ni to get the car out.'

Aristide got up from his piano stool. 'Grandmama, how can you do this?' he cried. Grandmama met his eyes unflinchingly.

'What's the matter with you, Aristide?' Mama said.

'Mama, I beg you, don't go. Don't listen to that scheming old woman.'

I saw Grandmama blanch. Her fist tightened over the knob of her cane so that it was raised, and I thought she'd bring it down about his shoulders, but in that moment of decisive hesitation she bent her head and tottered slightly. Mama gripped the fringes of the shawl draped over the piano. 'How dare you speak that way to my mother?'

I thought then that Aristide would jump the old lady as he moved towards her, but Mama pulled on the shawl and brought a huge crystal vase of roses crashing to the floor. Still she held the shawl as though Aristide was some docile beast unaccountably turned savage. My brother tried to outcountenance her for a moment and then ran from the room.

'Come, *bebela*,' Grandmama said gently. 'You'll see air vill be good for you too. You'll see, you'll tenk your Mama.'

By the time we reached the French Concession Mama had forgotten her upset with Aristide. We came to the circus of life on Avenue Joffre. On one corner the inevitable cluster of Georgian traders, Gogo among them, was gesticulating grandly. The shopkeepers had come to their doors. I glimpsed the bead lady at hers. Carmencita wasn't her name really, but the one given her by the other White Russians because of her predilection for Spanish adornments. Today she was as resplendent as ever, a tall amber comb atop her masses of ringlets and kiss curls. Painted spokes to resemble lashes radiated from her eyes, but the sleek black moustache she petted with one finger was her own.

We had discovered a Russian café which made, among other things, superlative *plombières*. Grandmama confessed to a yearning for some. The shop was located catty-corner to the Cathay Theatre, and while Lao Ni was dispatched to fetch the ices, we waited in the car. I recognized Kiki by her hips, swinging like hanging chianti flasks, and the persimmon-coloured boots. As she crossed from our side to get to the theatre, I knew beyond doubt that she was going to meet Chicho. Sure enough, there he stood under the marquee, his Ballila Fiat parked for a speedy exit in the no-stopping zone. Kiki hooked her arm into his, collapsed her weight, and looked into his face. I began talking at once. I can't remember what about, but it must have been pure rubbish, because Mama stared at me, then beyond me, the spoon freezing, it seemed, to the roof of her mouth.

'Lao Ni, you see Mastah Chicho by the theatre? You drive there.' Methodically Lao Ni began to collect our dishes and was about to take them back to the café. 'Never mind those,' Mama cried. 'Get across the street.' By then Chicho had seen us, and he was shoving Kiki into the Fiat.

'Follow them!' Mama said. Chicho made a U-turn at the intersection and then headed down Rue Cardinal Mercier. We caught sight of him making a right at the first corner. Lao Ni followed.

'Faster,' Mama said. Grandmama, who had not relinquished her plate to Lao Ni, was watching between delicate spoonfuls of *plombières*. 'Faster, you hear?' Mama cried, pounding Lao Ni's shoulder. The Fiat sped up to Avenue Joffre again, then straight down. In his desperation to get away, Chicho ran red lights, and when Lao Ni attempted to heed them, Mama pounded at him again. The cars whizzed past the intersections on Avenue Joffre, veering into Route Pottier and Avenue Pétain. Mama was now standing on the running board. She had seized Grandmama's cane and was directing Lao Ni with it. It was clear that Mama would continue the chase to Siccawei Village and beyond if necessary. I had seen Mama before in rage and in grief, but never had I seen her so violent as in this pursuit of her quarry. Her hair, long before freed of its moorings, flew straight behind. I huddled towards Grandmama, who shoved me away better to see the goings on. Finally, Chicho turned into a lane with us right behind. It was a dead-end street. The chase was over. He came out of the car, both hands raised as though it were a holdup. Mama pointed the cane at him.

'I just wanted you to know that I saw you. That you could not lie and say it was someone else, that's all.' She started to get into the car and that might have been all if Kiki had not decided to participate. Chicho lost his struggle trying to keep her in his Fiat, and she flounced towards Mama.

'Say, Mrs. High Society, what are you, crazy or something? You always drive like that?'

Mama ignored her, but she said very distinctly and with much poise, 'I think I could forgive you, Chicho, if you had chosen an equal, even a friend, like Tila.'

'Whaddyou mean equal?' Kiki cried. 'Do you know who my grandfather was?'

'I don't know who your grandfather was, but I know what you are,' Mama said.

'I am Kiki. And that means something when men will take from women like you to give to girls like me.'

Grandmama, who had been watching the whole scene, relishing every minute, became galvanized into action.

'Give her a good von,' she cried to Mama. 'Give her clop vit my stick. You hear?' But Mama stood immobile.

'Listen, sweetinka,' Kiki said to Mama. 'You're getting too old to be so picky.'

Grandmama, with a sudden and startling nimbleness, pushed Mama aside, seized her cane, and brought it across Kiki's rear with such force that the girl shrieked in surprise and pain. Again and again Grandmama whacked until Kiki began to run down the lane, those chianti-bottle hips waggling furiously as she stumbled along in her kid boots.

Chicho had not moved. He stood apart, his head bowed. Mama ignored him. Helping her mother into the car, she told Lao Ni to go home.

On the way, Grandmama touched her daughter's hand, a gesture of concordance, but Mama looked at her through eyes full of tears and said, 'I don't thank you, Mama. Not at all!'

39

ON returning from the drive, Mama went directly to her room. From outside we could hear the sounds of ripping and tearing and the self-incriminating charges of her vanity, stupidity, even senility. Kiki had struck home. Later that night when she opened her door, the coals of rage had burned down to a white consuming heat, and her surface appearance was calm. In her room the tabletops and the floor were littered with torn photographs and letters. Grandmama, having deduced that Mama's anger at her would be short-lived, was waiting. 'Go, tell the servants to bring me every glass in the house,' Mama told her mother. I joined Sascha and Aristide in the smoking-room. They had of course by now heard the details of the chase from Grandmama. Mama came in and cleared the top of the game table. In relays, Zee, Hoboo, and Dah Su brought trays of stemware, with Grandmama in full charge saying, 'Bring de glasses. Bring! Bring!'

Sascha tried to reason with Mama, advising her against compounding the awkwardness of the matter by an unseemly show of violence.

'No damn fear,' Mama said. 'I controlled myself in front of that little bitch, but now he's going to get it. If he only dares to show his face here. . . .' Sascha argued that she was acting out of wounded pride, nothing more. That when all was said and done perhaps she was in a sense responsible for Chicho's dalliance with Kiki. 'You are so very possessive, Mama.'

'I don't understand *too* possessive. What does it mean? You cherish or you don't. If you do, all of you is not too much to give. All of him is not too much to ask.'

'But you grip, Mama, and you don't let go. There's such a thing as smothering.'

Mama stared at Sascha, bemused. 'If a man loves you, what is there to let go? Those who complain of overlove from you are those who want no love from you. *Accomodamento*, maybe, but not love.'

'You can bet that all he was getting from Kiki was accommodation.'

'Then let her give him love too, and money, that, that——'

'*Soupnik*,' Grandmama supplied.

Mama was an essential woman but she was also a woman of her parents' times and mores. Her husband had provided worldly goods in abundance and given her a name and children, without having neglected her in any sense. When he had philandered discreetly she had shrugged it off. 'He's a man,' she had said, because in her rearing, a single standard was the unspoken clause, as well as the tacit reward of a generous and loving husband. But love was a new luxury. To permit herself the affair, Mama had faced almost irreconcilable value adjustments. To retain her self-respect she required absoluteness from Chicho.

'What am I supposed to do, Sascha? Wish him luck, do a *bubba's* dance?'

I remembered, then, a conversation which had taken place after Michel had become engaged to his singsong girl and had taken her to Tila for her blessing. Because she knew that Tila still cared for Michel, Mama had been outraged. 'What did you say to them?' she asked her friend.

'What could I say? I wished them *bonheur*,' Tila had replied.

'I would have wished them both cancer,' Mama said.

It was close to midnight before Chicho dared face Mama. And when I saw him standing in the doorway, a dishevelled supplicant, I couldn't help feeling sorry for him. Mama sat calmly behind the table and started throwing. The glasses came at Chicho one after the other, crashing on him and tinkling to the floor. Shielding his face in the crook of his arm, Chicho tried to reach Mama.

'*Poupa*,' he implored.

Mama now stood for better aim and hurled the glasses with both hands. Aristide and I sat silently in the club chairs, but Sascha tried to grab Mama's arm. She wrenched herself free and, in doing so, nicked him. 'Mind your own business and you won't get hurt,' she cried.

'*Poupa*,' Chicho tried once more, but the glasses continued to rain on him. The bombardment eventually proved too much and Chicho retreated.

A day or so later he phoned Sascha from his apartment, saying that he wanted to confer with the three of us. Aristide had not wanted to go along, but Sascha insisted that it was the only impartial thing to do. Chicho greeted us at his door with a sad, sweet affection as though someone mutually dear had just died. When we were settled in his quarters, he explained about Kiki, admitting that they had had a brief fling the year before. Then he had written to her to say that it was over. It turned out that Kiki had teamed up with Ramirez in a profitable correspondence badger game. Kiki's function was naturally to entice and extract as much as she could for the longest time possible. When a man wanted to end the relationship, Kiki would give him no peace. She would make terrible scenes, saying that she did not believe he truly wanted to part with her. He was being pressured, his conscience was bothering him, he was victimizing both of them because of guilt feelings. At this point the men involved would become stupefied and use any means to convince her that now they were being sincere. They wanted out. More than one offered her money. This offended Kiki. 'Money? You offer me money when I gave you my love? How like a man.' Then with visible bravery, Kiki would agree to the dissolution on one condition. 'If you can write that you no longer love me, then I'll believe it.' There it was in all its transparency, yet Chicho with countless attached men fell for the ploy. Since apparently all the foolish girl really wanted was their sober decision, the men wrote to her. And because she was at heart really a decent sort (refusing money, who'd have thought it?), many of them sentimentalized her in their letters. The next step of course was for Ramirez to move in with extortion.

311

I watched Aristide as he listened to Chicho and observed the perplexed look and the frown between his brows. 'Then you and Tila never were . . .' he said.

'*Santo spirito*, Tila.' Chicho clasped his hands worshipfully. 'Tila saved my life—she forced Ramirez to give back my letter.'

Sascha, leaning on his elbow, assumed a confiding, between-us-males attitude, and said, 'Come on, Chicho, what were you doing with Kiki again when Mama caught you, huh?'

'She pestered me; said she would telephone Regina and tell her everything.' He smote his brow. 'Eh—what's the use, Sascha, I'm a *cretino*!' Sascha got up, put his hand on the older man's shoulder, and smiled, indulgently wise. 'Don't worry, old fellow, things will be patched up.'

And they were, after a time and after a fashion. I don't remember how they were reconciled exactly, but there was Chicho, a few days later, back with us as though nothing had ever been amiss. I feel sure that Mama wanted to forgive him, and I'm equally sure she would have liked very much to forget the entire episode. But the wounded cells of her pride became malignant. She had never before known uncertainty in her relationships. As a high-grade commodity, Mama had been able to function reciprocally and superbly, but she needed her brokers. She was accustomed to being in demand, not to competing. Now, if Chicho was not at home immediately after office hours she questioned it, not aloud but in her expression and in her manner, relating each occasion to the many nights that he had said he worked late at the bank.

In May, on the day that Italy occupied Addis Ababa, Chicho did not come home at all. Mama had stayed up, phoning his apartment at intervals. She had gone along the Bund in the early morning hours with a flashlight, padding in her slippers between the rows of parked cars, to see if she could find his Fiat. And when he showed up at noon the next day, saying that he had spent the night with mutual friends celebrating Italy's victory at the Casa D'Italia, Mama called him a liar and there was another row. Later, secretly and full of self-loathing, Mama checked with the Italian friends and found that Chicho's story was true. Then Mama was ashamed; she felt deceitful and ungenerous. She was also unused to these emotions. Someone had to be blamed. She said to Aristide, 'Look, look what this man has brought me to.'

That was the summer all the young women in Shanghai were imitating Deanna Durbin. They wore dirndls and organdie dresses and tied their curls with ribbons. On the radio and in every ball-room, staccato-happy Chinese sopranos trilled '*Il Bacio*'. Because Chicho's indiscretion had been with a much younger woman and possibly because of Kiki's searing remark, Mama sought youth. She had managed to keep her weight down, but still she dieted, some-thing called the Hollywood Diet, guaranteed on the subsistence of black coffee, grapefruit, and lean meat to effect a trade-in of one's own body for a Jean Harlow chassis. The diet made Mama irritable but she persisted. Dieting caused sagging, and that meant exercise. Mama could not endure exercise so she circumvented that problem with massages and facials. She applied long-handled patters to her face, whacking the offending contours as though they were Kiki's buttocks. Or she sat by the hour, her face greased and taut, literally bandaged in a brocade chin-strap. And she tweezered constantly. Plucking at offending hairs became more of a nervous habit than a necessity as she peered into a magnifying mirror and denuded her brows, upper lip, and chin.

One day, in the middle of this ordeal, Grandmama came into her room, joining me on Mama's bed to watch the operations. As she observed what she considered Mama's utterly wasted efforts, Grand-mama's lips curved into a sneer. 'Tsip, tsip, tsip der face vill not make from you a *maydl*.'

Mama stopped plucking long enough to confront Grandmama's reflection in the mirror. 'Who the hell said I want to be a *maydl*?' she replied. Grandmama shook her head but said nothing, continuing to sit there. When she had completed her makeup, Mama tossed her hair and defiantly tied a black velvet ribbon into a bow on top. Then she turned to Aristide. 'I used to wear ribbons when I was young. I have a picture——'

'It looks fine, Mama,' Aristide said.

'Say it. Your mother is a goddamn fool. I'm forty-five, Aristide.'

'Forty-six next month, God should spare your life, you should live to be a hundred,' Grandmama said.

Mama pulled off the ribbon in despair. Grandmama, offended that her good wishes were so ungraciously received, began to leave the room. We could hear her outside. 'Tsip, tsip, tsip, crrrazy.' Aristide came up to Mama. He picked up the ribbon and looped it around her hair, tying it neatly. Then he kissed Mama's cheek, and she pressed her face against his gratefully.

Who can say what element contributes most to the creation of a love affair and, equally, who can pinpoint the agents that cause its dissolution? I know for sure that coming as it did that autumn, at the lowest ebb of Mama's security, Ramirez' book was a factor. Undoubtedly using the material accumulated during his gossip legman days and writing under a pseudonym, Ramirez purported to dig into the backgrounds of Shanghai's leading foreigners. Titled something like *Shanghai! Haven of Harlots and Hoodlums*, the exposé had an astonishing international sale. Though Mama had no inkling that she had been written about, people constantly mentioned the book to her, and she could hardly wait to get her hands on a copy.

My brothers and I were in her room the morning she received it. In a chapter called 'Shanghai's Four Hundred', Mama discovered that the Wayside Saloon in which she had worked for a week upon her arrival had been converted by the author to a waterfront brothel. She was depicted as a hefty wench who stood outside and buttonholed sailors. Much harder for Mama to cope with was the description of her relationship with Chicho. Here she personified a matron scavenging lustily for sex with lean young men, who indulged her for a price. While Ramirez had been thorough in exfoliating the pasts of his subjects and, in cases where he could substantiate at least part of his claims, he had used their actual names, his thin attempt to camouflage Mama was to accord her the name of Big Bertha, while Chicho was portrayed as a simpleton gigolo renamed Tino. Mama understood why so many had been eager for her to read the book. As it tumbled from her hands, she sat in her bed dazed, and all she could think of to say was, 'Why should he call me Big Bertha? That's nothing like my name.' Sascha explained that Big Bertha was the name given by the Germans during the First World War to a massive long-range cannon. If Sascha expected Mama suddenly to rally at this dubious compliment he was mistaken. She grew despondent, her eyes filling with tears.

'To think my actions should have let this happen to your father's name,' she said.

'Not your actions, Mama,' Sascha said. 'Just that swine's lies. Everybody knows they're lies.'

'Hah,' Mama replied. 'People are willing to forget what they know in order to believe what they hear.'

Aristide got on the bed beside Mama, put his arms around her, and rocked her gently. 'Listen, what are you blubbering about? You're in the best of company. The time to cry would be if he had left you out.'

At first Mama wisely decided to ignore the scandalous reference and made a point of being seen everywhere with Chicho. Then she noticed, or thought she noticed, heads turning when they appeared together, whispers, laughter. It reached the point that she began to insist that they conduct their relationship secretly. She would go to the Cercle, then Chicho might join her there. They must leave separately. If they went to a film, she would go in first and he would look for her in the dark. Afterwards she would go out and wait in the car and he would follow.

In November Chicho told her he was returning to Italy. It was an unseasonably cold morning when we heard the news, and Mama had had a fire lit in the smoking-room fireplace. She was wearing a yellow dress, light wool, both becoming and befitting. She looked particularly beautiful in the effortless way she used to have. Often I have wondered about that, being at one's very best at the deliverance of the cruellest blows.

Aristide and I were having coffee with Mama before going on to school, and she talked about inconsequentials for a while. Then I expect because she could contain it no longer the words cascaded breathlessly. 'Chicho's going back to Italy, you know.'

'You mean soon?' Aristide said.

'He wants to be there for Christmas with his family.' Chicho had broken the news to Mama while armed with his ticket, I discovered later.

'Funny, I've never thought of Chicho as having any family but us,' Aristide said.

'Well, he has.'

'But he's coming back?'

'He says that he will come back after he's arranged the annulment. . . .'

'And that will be?'

'God knows,' Mama said.

Sascha had one of his rare job interviews that morning, and he joined us, hastily gulping down a cup of coffee. 'Chicho's going back to Italy,' I said. Sascha looked over the rim of his cup at Mama, and when she smiled as though the fact was of no particular moment to her, he said, 'Well, we'll miss him, I suppose. Mama, you will make certain to get it in writing that he continues to pay us back from abroad?'

Less than a week later, Mama, Aristide, and I saw Chicho off. Sascha, told to return for a follow-up job interview, had been unable to come. Aristide and I tried to keep a discreet distance as Chicho took his farewells, but the throngs on deck by the gangplank pressed us close, and for that matter Mama kept reaching out for her sons as though they were necessary buoys to keep her afloat. Chicho, shedding very genuine tears and clasping Mama's hands, stated his unworthiness and deplored the fact that he had kept Mama from a happier life. Mama was very poised and silent.

On the way back in the car Aristide said, 'He'll come back, I guarantee it, Mama.'

And Mama replied, 'Aristide, when a man tells you you're too good for him, that's the end. Nothing is too good for a man in love. When a man says you're too good, he really means you don't have what he wants so give it to somebody else, please.'

'Oh, Mama.' Aristide's voice broke, and he made a move to comfort her.

'No, no.' Mama shrugged away from his reach. 'Don't feel sorry for me. Have you ever felt you'd give anything to get out of your girdle?'

'Like when I eat too much? Loosen my belt, yes.'

'Yes, I feel I can loosen my belt now.'

As Lao Ni drove us back to the apartment, we sat in silence. Mama held each of us by the hand. Then she laughed, a falsely cheerful sound. 'Isn't it funny?' she said. 'The one time I didn't listen to my mother I made such a goddamn mess. I mean, isn't it?'

40

ON the day our school closed for the Christmas holiday, the second
weekend of December, we were let off early. Rather than fuss with
phoning for the car and waiting, or packing ourselves into a bus, or
haggling with rickshaw coolies, Aristide and I decided to walk home.
North Szechwan Road, normally a busy thoroughfare, was jammed
with traffic; the street corners were knotted with pedestrians. 'Wonder what's up?' Aristide said. We came to a wall where men were
pasting bulletins. The knots loosened and the people swarmed
around the wall, reading the bulletins and commenting among themselves. There was a tautness to the crowd, a communicable trepida-
tion. Then Aristide saw Didi at the outer periphery and tried to hail
him. We had seen him only rarely since his father's funeral in March.

Didi saw us and signalled that we should remain where we were,
as he thrust to the fore through the aggregate of people. Aristide
and I watched his face as he squinted to read the bulletins. The
colour rose in his cheeks, and his spectacles flashed as he tossed back
his head in unrestrained joy. But all around us the gloom was pervasive.

'Didi, tell us, what is it?' Aristide demanded.

The armies in Shensi had thrown down their arms rather than
continue fighting the Reds. Flying up to Sian to investigate, Chiang
had been made a prisoner. It was mutiny.

'Do you think Ah-ching is involved?' Aristide asked.

'Of course,' Didi replied much too quickly, too confidently, as
though prepared to answer the question he was asking of himself.

'Will they kill Chiang?' Aristide asked.

'I don't know,' Didi said. 'It doesn't matter.'

'Then one way or another this means war with Japan?'

'It means,' Didi said, 'that the moment has come at last between
the tigers and the foxes.'

When we left him, Aristide said, 'What do you suppose Didi
meant about the tigers and the foxes?'

'The Chinese against the Japs, of course,' I said.

Aristide didn't answer and he didn't look reassured.

For the next week China waited. In the streets, in shops, in tea-houses, the outcome of Chiang's kidnapping was weighed, measured, and generally deplored. The Chinese might not have approved of Chiang's propitiating policies, but he was their leader, the only one who had given cohesion to this vast mass of humanity. Nowhere, certainly not in our kitchen, was Didi's elation shared. Even Dah Su's wife spoke darkly of the mutineers.

On Christmas day Chiang was released, the kidnapping was over. Chiang reassigned those who he felt were not deeply involved in the mutiny and who were able generals. Ah-ching was one of these. But the Communists had officially agreed to put aside their aims and follow his leadership. In a sense, Chiang had negated the Communists as a threat to Nationalist security. Negotiations began discreetly between the Generalissimo and Mao Tse-tung. Something would come of the Sian incident, that much was sure. China waited, and Japan watched and waited also.

For a while after Chicho left, Grandmama was quite happy. She had her daughter almost exclusively to herself. Mama had become indifferent. She no longer had to please, so she didn't. Her moods alternated between fake jubilation and darkness. She made dreadful scenes over the most inconsequential details—that ring of keys, for instance, which she constantly misplaced, throwing the household into a frenzied search. And when the keys were discovered, usually where she herself had put them, she seemed unconsoled, as though it had finally dawned on her that the most important key on her golden ring was lost to her forever. She began to lose her sense of being a woman, taking on the incipience of genderlessness that comes to the retired.

Sascha could not have picked a worse time to tell her that he wanted to get married. No doubt Sascha was much bolstered by the security of having gotten a job. He had been hired by one of the American oil companies. It was a night early in the year and we were having dinner. At Sascha's announcement Mama looked stunned, and I could picture the scrambling around in her mind as she tried to fit her prospective daughter-in-law with the girls Sascha might have been dating.

'Who is it?' Mama asked.

'Her name is Anastasia,' Sascha replied, watching closely as the fork Mama had brought to her lips stopped.

'A Rooskie? Are you trying to tell me that you want to bring a Rooskie in my home?'

'Not necessarily.'

'What does that mean?'

'We don't have to live in your home. I'm working, you know.'

'How old is this woman?'

'Anastasia is eighteen.'

'Of course she's a princess.'

'I never said that, but her family does come from some special class in Russia.'

'Sure, the class of hookers,' Mama agreed.

'Listen, Mama, give up. You can pull the silver cord on your other sons, but it won't work with me.'

A silver cord meant only a sash to Mama. She stared at Sascha. 'What silver cord?'

'A navel cord. You're still trying to make me hang by my navel.'

Mama glanced furtively at his navel. Reassured, she said, 'Don't be disgusting.'

'I'm getting married. Now at least let me bring Stasia to meet you.'

'Over my dead body will a Rooskie ever set foot in this house.'

After Sascha left the dinner table we speculated on what she would be like. Aristide visualized someone much like the Russian we had met so long before at Tila's party. 'She'll be very svelte and mysterious, with a long cigarette holder.'

'She'll be a chippy, an Avenue Joffre chippy like Kiki,' Mama predicted. 'Wait and see what I'm telling you. She thinks she's getting a millionaire.'

'You tink maybe she's a Bolshevik?' Grandmama asked.

Sascha brought his fiancée to tea the next day. Mama had Zee serve in the drawing-room and went to so much trouble with her own appearance and the setting that one might have thought that it was she who had to pass muster.

When she arrived, with Sascha gently guiding her by the elbow, it was evident that Anastasia was unlike any of our expectations. She was very plainly dressed and, while thin, moved without appearing brittle. This lissomeness was part of her character, too, we discovered. Her features were Slavic, defined cheekbones and deeply set eyes. She had a child's complexion and wore no makeup, and her dark ash-blonde hair fell to her shoulders.

319

Mama's face had been set in a frozen dessert of formality, but at Anastasia's obvious vulnerability, the ice melted and the sweetness came through. Mama kept up the conversation throughout tea, which was a good thing, with the rest of us staring at the girl as though she were some exhibit. Anastasia spoke little English but what she said, though uttered tentatively, was precise. Sascha proudly remarked that she had studiously mastered the English pronunciation of w's. 'Go on, Stasia, say "I want water from the well." ' The girl blushed and looked pleadingly at Sascha, but their relationship had been cast. She repeated the sentence meticulously. Sascha beamed with pride at each of us. Grandmama pressed two fingers at her cheek, shook her head admiringly, and said, 'Vell, vell, vot do you tink from dat?'

Anastasia told us that she had just come from Harbin in Manchuria, where her father had been connected with the Chinese Eastern Railway.

'A railvay vorker?' Grandmama asked.

'How do you say? An accountant,' the girl replied. Mama tried to turn the subject to more general matters, but to Grandmama the business of a match between her first grandson and an unknown was of the utmost seriousness. Although Mama had warned her that Anastasia was a member of the Eastern Orthodox faith and not to bring up the matter of religion, the old lady said, 'You go to church?'

'On holidays,' the girl answered, looking up at Sascha, who stood behind her chair. Then Sascha said that they must leave and they did. But he returned within the hour to hear the family's verdict.

'She's nice,' Mama admitted. 'She needs styling, but she's nice.'

'And what do you think, Grandmama?'

'Nice,' she agreed, 'a *proste maydl*, but nice,' she echoed.

'What do you mean a common girl?' Sascha exploded.

'Onijjicated,' Grandmama explained.

Sascha told us then that Anastasia had graduated with top honours from her high school. The *gymnasium* in Harbin had awarded her a gold medal upon her graduation.

'This *gymnasium*, is it a White Russian school?' Mama asked.

'Of course not. The Russian government is Soviet. The railway and the schools are run by the government.'

'Oi, I told you a Bolshevik!' Grandmama said.

'No, she isn't. You have to apply for Soviet citizenship. Stasia is White Russian, stateless,' Sascha insisted.

Mama did not reply, but she looked worried. There had been an ugly rash of terrorism in the city recently: Nationalists cutting down Communist sympathizers; Communists murdering Nationalists, pro-Japanese, and influential White Russians. The leader of the White Russian community and his wife had been assassinated a short while back.

Sascha said, 'Listen Mama, in order for Stasia to become a French citizen, our consulate has to verify her background. They will send to Harbin for information and we'll receive a full report. There, does that satisfy you?'

'I'm still not saying yes,' Mama said. Sascha did not ask either Aristide or me our opinion, and it's just as well, for later Aristide remarked that Anastasia reminded him somehow of E-ling.

Sascha brought her to the house frequently from then on. I was the first to succumb. For though I was going on fourteen I still doted on stories. Mama and Grandmama had told me all that I was going to hear from them. On the pretext of helping me with my maths homework, Anastasia arranged to meet with me in the hall alcove, and there, in the aura of clandestine trysts, she told me fables of golden fish, beautiful czarevnas, nightingales, and the terrifying machinations of Baba Iaga.

Mama's capitulation and, for that matter, Aristide's too, came later. Anastasia could play the balalaika, and one evening she played and sang for us after dinner. Not only did she know such chestnuts as 'Dark Eyes' and 'Two Guitars', but many of the folk songs of Isa Kremer which Mama loved. And while Anastasia played, Mama shook her shoulders, snapped her fingers, and laughed and cried simultaneously. Then, as we were all gathered around her, Anastasia strummed a lively peasant dance and Sascha, carried away by the tune, attempted a gopak. With his arms crossed, and balancing himself on his haunches, he thrust out first one foot, then the other until he lost control and came crashing down on the floor. At the sight of his stunned embarrassment, the would-be gallant become the village idiot by his own ineptness, Aristide and I roared with laughter, and Mama too had a hard time deciding between motherly concern and the comedy of it. But Anastasia ran to Sascha and stroked his forehead gently, asking repeatedly if he had hurt himself. That night

Mama gave Sascha her own engagement ring to present to Anastasia. 'The girl really loves you and I suppose, today, that means everything.'

But Grandmama was not so easily won over. 'Bolsheviks can play music too,' she scowled at me over tea the next day. Early in spring when the date for the summer wedding had already been set, the investigatory report required for citizenship by the French Consulate came. It was a brief account of her father's education, position, and family status. He was described as being from the Dvorianye class of Russians. It went on to say in French that he had one daughter, and described her as '*la fille de gentilhomme*. . . .'

'The daughter of a nobleman?' Aristide said.

It took some doing to explain this to Grandmama, but there it was on a legal paper, and a document to Grandmama was forceful evidence. The day after, when Anastasia came to the apartment, Grandmama was there to greet her. Dressed in her finest black with jet bead trimming, Grandmama was Dowager Empress Maria Fedorovna come to acknowledge one of her own.

Since Chicho had continued payments on the loan Mama had advanced him, not the full amount but money nevertheless, and since Sascha was, after all, employed, Mama could see no reason why her firstborn should not have a magnificent wedding.

There was the matter of different religions. While he respected Anastasia's belief in her faith, Sascha had no intention of marrying in the Russian Orthodox Church. Equally, Anastasia did not fancy marrying under a *huppah* even if such a ceremony could be arranged without her conversion to Judaism. The practical solution seemed to be a civil ceremony at the French Consulate, followed by a reception. Then the bridal couple could enjoy the trappings of an elaborate wedding without compromise to the feelings of either.

Sascha was entitled to a week's vacation in August. For some reason, now obscure to me, it was to begin at noon on Friday the thirteenth. In order to take the fullest advantage of the week for his honeymoon, Sascha had planned the wedding for the same day. But Mama objected. 'A young couple has enough to worry about without getting married on Friday the thirteenth!' Finally, to compromise, Sascha agreed to have the civil ceremony on that day, the reception to be held the following day.

In the preparations Mama came back to life. She arranged for the hiring of the Cercle Sportif lawn for the reception, and she engaged the Argentine Tango Band from the newest and most talked-about nightclub casino. Caterers were called in to plan the menu. The wedding cake required a specialist in the art of sculpting sugar and weighed two hundred and twenty pounds. Case lots of champagne were commissioned.

Early one morning in the first week of July, while Mama was addressing envelopes, Zee came into the room very excited. There had been an exchange of shooting the night before between the Chinese and the Japanese. The skirmish had taken place on the Marco Polo Bridge a dozen miles southwest of Peiping. To the rest of us, including the servants, this clash seemed like just one more border incident, and we thought that Zee, as a native northerner, was reading into it the direst of consequences. Sascha told Zee to calm himself: the Japanese were just getting ready for another bite at the northern pie, that was all. The Japanese, at once and as usual, termed the incident an outrage, and notes were sent back and forth between them and Nanking. But this time Nanking was standing firm and demanding redress. Concurrently with the grievance notes, the Japanese had ousted the Twenty-ninth Army Garrison at Loukouchiao, replacing them with a puppet detachment under a malleable Chinese ex-bandit general, and Japanese troops began moving up from Tientsin.

Ten days or so later, Chiang Kai-shek issued a declaration from his mountaintop retreat in Kuling. The statement was a resolute commitment to his people. Chiang was not going to permit the Japanese to make Hopei province into another Manchukuo. He was not going to yield to any more Japanese transgressions. He was prepared to go all the way. He warned his countrymen, 'We are not seeking war, but we do not seek for peace at any price ... let our people realize to the full the meaning of the expression: the limit of our endurance.' Most foreigners thought that Japan was still only trying to detach the five northern provinces from Nanking's control and make them autonomous Japanese satellites. If war came, it would happen in northern China. That seemed entirely reasonable.

Meanwhile the Twenty-ninth Army had decided to resist the Japanese. In their black Mongol uniforms these soldiers had fought stunningly at Jehol when the Japanese had crossed the Great Wall. On a muggy day near the end of July, while Mama was supervising the fitting of Anastasia in the Brussels lace gown that had been her own wedding dress, Sascha poked his head through the door to say that there was war in the north. He explained that the Japanese army had the unique power of declaring war. An insult to any member of the Japanese military was a direct affront to the Son of Heaven himself. A Japanese general interpreted the stubborn resolve of the Twenty-ninth Army as insult enough. And while he did not declare war, he announced his intentions of 'freedom of action' in dealing with the Chinese, which amounted to the same thing.

Mama shooed Sascha out of her room, saying, didn't he know it was unlucky to see the bride in her gown before the wedding?

'Two weeks to go, and he bothers me with war!' she exclaimed.

That day Japanese troops marched from their military base south of Peiping, and by nightfall they had surrounded the ancient city.

While Chiang reiterated his determination and battles continued to rage in the north, the Yangtze Valley and the south were un-involved. But to contradict this, Ah-ching turned up bringing Sascha and Anastasia a fine scroll painting as a wedding gift. He told us that four divisions of the First Army Corps and an artillery brigade were moving to the Shanghai area. There were over one million men below the Yellow River. That the Japanese should start an embroglio in the Shanghai area didn't make sense, Sascha said. In the north they had only the Twenty-ninth Army and a few other Chinese divisions to contend with, whereas the naval garrison at Hongkew and the few Japanese ships off shore were scarcely a match for the vast force Ah-ching had just described.

'Why on earth would the Japanese even consider fighting in Shanghai?' asked Sascha.

'They don't,' Ah-ching grinned. It became clear shortly after that these were of course the very reasons why Chiang Kai-shek allowed the war to move into the Shanghai area.

Four days before the wedding, Mama and Anastasia were in the drawing-room unwrapping the constant stream of gifts. Aristide was helping to sort and define. While I was doing what I could to make myself useful, collecting the cartons, wrappings, and ribbons and stashing them into the fireplace, I could hear news broadcasts at top volume from the Stewart-Warner in the smoking-room.

'Tell your brother to turn that damned thing off and come in here to help,' Mama said.

324

When I got to the smoking-room, Sascha told me he had just heard that a shooting had occurred. This one had not taken place in the remote north, but near the Hungjao aerodrome. A Japanese naval officer and a sailor were driving there when some Chinese soldiers appeared and accused them of spying on a military installation. In the ensuing altercation the two Japanese were killed. By now these incidents were definable as the substitute declaration of war.

'I don't like it one bit,' Sascha said. 'It's too damned close.'

Back and forth the protests went, the Japanese demanding apologies and restitution and the Chinese authorities not backing down an inch. The mayor of Shanghai informed the Japanese that they had been warned not to spy on Chinese positions, and to lend weight to his argument the troops stationed at the aerodrome began to erect sandbag fortifications.

Within the next two days eighteen Japanese warships joined the twelve already lying upstream in the Whangpoo River. And the newspapers said that the remainder of the Third Battle Fleet was headed towards Shanghai. Meanwhile the British were sending up troops and ships from Hongkong.

The civil ceremony at the French Consulate that Friday was a staid and brief business. Attended only by the family and a pair of witnesses, Sascha and Anastasia were now legally married. An informal luncheon had been arranged at home just for the wedding party. The big to-do, the reception, was for the next day.

Just as Dr. Jarvis, who had been one of the witnesses, raised his glass in a toast, we heard the boom of cannon in the distance. The verandah doors shuddered; then we heard firing from the gunboats in the river.

'Nobody can say this wedding isn't getting started with a bang,' Jarvis quipped. We all laughed, but it was nervous laughter, too close to the surface. Another thundering explosion and we went on to the verandahs. In the northwest, the sky was black with smoke.

'Chapei again,' said Sascha.

Across the river, on the Pootung side, we saw landing parties of Japanese marines set forth from two cruisers. A shower of covering fire exploded from the gunboats.

The guests left shortly after lunch, Jarvis on the safe assumption that his services would be needed for the wounded. All afternoon we heard the volleying of cannon and the playback of shelling from the ships. As dusk settled, the sky became bright with colour through the smoke over Chapei. Lao Ni's mother and Didi arrived then, with as many of their belongings as they were able to strap to themselves and carry by hand. They told us that for the last two days the North Station had been crowded with thousands of people trying to escape by the Shanghai–Nanking Railway. Japanese blue-jackets had forced their entry into that vicinity, and the refugees had scattered, abandoning their possessions. Didi and his mother had only just managed to escape a Japanese raiding party conducting a house-to-house search for snipers.

Gathered about the radio, we learned that the Japanese marines who had landed now planned a circular march through the Settlement to their naval garrison. With mixed feelings of excitement and foreboding, we listened to the newscaster's comment that General Koo Ah-ching had warned the Japanese that attempted entry into either foreign concession would be thwarted by military force. That meant that we in the Settlement could easily find ourselves the centre knot pulled by the two fighting sides.

But when Mama expressed her alarm and wondered if perhaps the reception should be postponed, Sascha reassured her. It was just another skirmish, he said. It would have no more bearing on the concessions than had the one five years before.

Later that night, long after Sascha and Anastasia had retired, Aristide, Didi, and I watched from the verandahs. Since early noon that day the refugees had started pouring over the Garden Bridge. Still they came, thousands upon thousands cinched at the bridge over Soochow Creek into rank and file, then fanning out onto the pavements, promenades, and even the street. Though many of the homeless took refuge on the grassy walks, setting up their goods and chattels, the majority moved on like a wide conveyor belt to the Chinese Bund and Nantao. Here, where the fighting had not yet started, Didi explained, those who had the means hoped to escape by the South Station to Chekiang province. As the night deepened and dampness blew up from the river, we saw the red light on the customs building tower signal the approach of a typhoon.

41

THERE was no typhoon the next day, but threatening clouds huddled angrily over the Yellow River. The human ribbon from the north of the city was constant, predictably notching itself over the Garden Bridge, then unfurling into a spilling bolt, like fabric. The skies over Chapei were smudged blacker than thunder clouds, and the rumble of trench guns persisted. But the Whangpoo itself was a miracle of calm. Downriver off the Japanese Consulate, the flagship *Idzumo* lay anchored. It appeared, as Sascha had predicted, that this was again a fringe tug-of-war between the Japanese and Chinese.

Waiting for the reception, Anastasia, her hair in the popular Juliet style and already dressed for the photographers, made an exquisite bride. Grandmama, looking quite resplendent herself, was directing the servants. Dr. Jarvis phoned to say that he would be delayed and that he would go straight to the Cercle Sportif.

Didi watched in our bedroom as Aristide got into his tails and fastened a pearl tiepin on his grey satin stock. I had been ready for ages in my new blue suit. Hoboo came in to hurry us up. Appraising his reflection in the mirror of our dresser, Aristide said to Didi, 'Aren't you going to get ready?'

'I'm not going,' Didi said.

'But why? You're invited,' Aristide argued. Actually he had persuaded Sascha to invite Didi. Sascha had demurred only on the grounds that, except for Hoboo, the remainder of the servants were attending in a serving capacity. Ah-ching was unable to come and Didi might feel awkward. But Aristide had urged him to invite our friend anyway.

'I'll be there, Didi,' I said.

'No, I think not,' Didi replied and it was positive. There was no time to argue, for just then Sascha looked in, saying that the photographers were waiting, it was half-past three, and we'd better get a move on. I was the last to join the group assembled in front of the fireplace in the drawing-room.

Flashbulbs popped several times. Then the bride and groom were photographed alone, Sascha looking just the way Papa had in his wedding pictures, cangued but immensely proud. Next came single poses of Anastasia, Grandmama, and Mama. In her *bois de rose* gown with a matching picture hat Mama looked radiantly lovely and, as we all said, not a day over thirty-five. It was after four by then, and Sascha said that if we were to get to the Cercle by five, what with the streets jammed and all, we had to leave at once.

Outside, while Lao Ni attempted to bring the car to the kerb, we found ourselves in the midst of the Chapei refugees. Men, women, and children were crowded in the porticoes of buildings with mattresses bundled and utensils stacked, or they squatted against the walls and sat on the steps, peering at us with the vacant uncomplaining patience of a people weaned on adversity. The wind frolicked with Anastasia's veil and almost bore it away. The refugees applauded and some said it was a wind of fortune, a good omen. Sascha distributed money among them. We got into the car—Sascha and Aristide sat up front with Lao Ni and I sat behind with the women.

At the first intersection heading south, I heard the distant drone of aeroplanes and stuck my head out the window to see them better. I counted ten monoplanes almost directly above. Just as we reached the corner of Nanking Road and the Bund the planes began to head downriver. There was the regurgitating sound of anti-aircraft guns from the *Idzumo*. Mama pulled me away and rolled up the window, and Sascha said to Lao Ni, 'Drive!' Lao Ni accelerated as a rain of shrapnel and tracers fell about the street. Sascha shouted for all of us to crouch on the floor of the car—not the easiest thing to achieve with all the flowers and veiling. Meanwhile traffic ahead came to a standstill. Perhaps to make more room in front or perhaps because he could not resist the hero stance, Sascha got out, carefully closed the door behind him, and stood on the running board. Mama and Anastasia begged him to return inside the car, but Sascha was watching the planes, shielding his eyes from the glare with one hand. 'They're going up into the clouds, scared off,' he said. With that I thought it safe enough to peek out the back window. I could see only the four monoplanes which made up the rear of the squadron. I never did see the bombs fall, but I heard their thin shrill whistling. A great yellow wall of water rose up from the river and cascaded over the banks, irrigating the grassy plots of the promenades and washing in one sweep over the stalled cars. Before Sascha, who was completely drenched, had time even for an utterance, an explosion came that left in its reverberation the cracking sound of internal fracture. Buildings splintered from within. Steel ribs crumpled and sinews of forged iron were twisted by impact into hot white coils. There was another explosion. And after a moment of stunned wavering the façades crashed in large lifeless slabs into the street.

'My God, oh, my God,' Sascha cried. Still crouching, I peered out the window. As the fumes and smoke wreathed upwards I could see the crater in the street, immense and crawling with what seemed to be only partial bodies, like maggots in an open sore.

Sascha opened the door on the driver's side. 'You go on, all of you. I've got to help.' I saw Aristide hesitate for just a second, then he was out of the car, standing by Sascha.

'No, don't!' Mama cried. Anastasia seized Sascha's hand through the window and held it.

'Vot's a matter, you crrazy boys;' Grandmama shouted.

'Do as I tell you, Lao Ni. Take the women to the Cercle, you hear?'

'You'll get killed! It's dangerous!' Mama said.

'They've stopped bombing, can't you see? We've got to pitch in.'

'Let the others do it. It's your wedding day.'

'I've got to, Mama.'

I cringed in my seat miserably. No one had said anything about my either going or staying on to help. Aristide saw my face then, and he said gently, 'You go with them to the Cercle.' I knew what I should do, but already I could feel my gorge rising, and my mouth tasted rusty.

'Go on!' Sascha commanded Lao Ni.

Before the chauffeur could start the car again, I jumped out and joined my brothers. Mama rolled down her window. 'Come back, come back at once, you idiot.'

I shook my head and smiled with an all too obvious fake bravado, and we watched as the car headed for the turnoff leading to the French Concession.

At the Nanking Road intersection we trod gingerly over shattered fragments of glass, metal, plaster, and undefinable masses of torn flesh. The smell of burning was everywhere, intense and unbearably acrid. My head began to reel and I reached out for support. Aristide steadied me. Already, people were arriving to help. A crew of policemen and volunteers were untangling a mass of bodies smashed into

329

the arcade entrance of the Cathay Hotel. Their jackets off, Sascha and Aristide began at once to help. I leaned against the wall of the hotel and closed my eyes. Just then there was another explosion, not directly in the vicinity but near enough to jar us. The police, Sascha, and Aristide stopped for a moment. 'What the hell was that?' Sascha said. A British policeman looked up beyond the buildings. In the southwest the sky was turning black with smoke. 'Another bomb, I'm afraid. Looks like it might be at the juncture of the Settlement and the Concession.' Sascha turned pale.

'No,' Aristide said firmly. 'It's all right. The car could not have reached there yet.' But I could see that he was trembling. They began the digging and pulling away again. I looked around me. A car had been spun into the middle of the road and was blazing like a funeral pyre. As the flames licked it, I saw the distorted remains of the occupants. Across the road, the roof and a great portion of the Palace Hotel walls had been demolished. Swaying masonry with jagged panes of glass hung by filaments. On the fourth floor, where just a crumbled segment of outer wall remained, I saw a foreign man clinging desperately with one hand. I tried to call out to tell Sascha and the volunteers about him, but I could not speak. Now a group of firemen had brought a ladder and were testing it against the walls for soundness. The man fell, going through the glass of the entrance awning to the pavement. On the main level, along the wall of the cocktail lounge, the wounded stood looking out into the street. From the gap that had once been a window, a woman dangled, her bright floral hat still attached to her head.

Chinese Red Cross workers arrived and began sorting through the human debris like shoppers in a cabbage market. The wounded who had regained consciousness were moaning, some screaming, their agony resounding in the valley created by the tall buildings on either side.

A couple of furniture vans pulled up. The rescue workers started tossing in the mangled remains—half of a human torso, arms, legs, heads. A volunteer called out to me impatiently to help, but I could not move. Even in my fearsome ineptness I knew the systematical cleaning up had to be done. I had seen butchers' wagons with carcasses and limbs hanging from hooks, and I tried to associate the vans with them. Just then one of the workers held up a bleeding bundle. It was a disembowelled infant.

I don't know when it was that Aristide shook me by the shoulder. 'Are you all right?' he asked, his face tense with concern. I nodded sickly. Aristide smoothed my cheeks. 'Poor brud,' he said. 'Such a heart of chicken fat.'

I began to sob then, because I knew that my inability to cope with pain and so with life had nothing at all to do with kindness.

At home the glass of our windows and verandah doors on the south and west had been shattered. By the time Sascha and Aristide changed into dark suits and I got myself cleaned up and the three of us piled into Sascha's Fiat, it was nearly seven. The guests would have begun to arrive an hour before, but as Sascha said, that didn't matter since this was a cocktail and supper reception. Outside the Cercle were the long rows of parked automobiles with white-gloved chauffeurs standing about. We saw, much to our relief, the Imperial Suburban, but Lao Ni must have gone inside.

The reception that evening was attended by over a thousand foreign and Chinese guests, the women in flowing chiffons and sheer organdies, the men in monkey jackets, some beribboned with orders. Lanterns spilled delicate glowworm colour on the grounds, and everyone discussed the bombings. It was close, so very close to their city within, to themselves. Still the corks popped, the orchestra played, and the guests danced long after the bride and groom had left. I went into the garden with a champagne bottle and found a dark corner. High above the filigree of the trees, in the far north, I could see the sky blazing with life, with death, with destruction. I got drunk for the first time.

42

THE next morning's papers headlined the bombing. Four bombs had been dropped by Chinese pilots in their attempt to hit the *Idzumo*. Two had fallen into the Whangpoo, which accounted for that near tidal wave over our car. One had ploughed through the roof of the Palace Hotel, the other had ricocheted from the Cathay Hotel and struck the street with the force of a giant shovel. Over seven hundred people had died and nearly a thousand were wounded at that one intersection.

At the reception no one had remarked on Dr. Jarvis' absence. Nor for that matter had Michel de Raveur and his Chinese wife been missed. The newspapers accounted for them. The explosion we had heard only minutes after arriving at the Nanking Road intersection had been caused by two more bombs accidentally dropped by a disabled Chinese plane. Striking near the busy juncture of the French Concession and the Settlement, where only the day before a great refugee centre had been set up, the bombs had killed more than a thousand people. The paper gave a gruesome account of those who had met sudden death at the Great World Amusement Palace: a Chinese policeman dangling from his traffic crow's nest; a British doctor in tails, his head blown off by shrapnel; and, among the many trapped in burning vehicles, a French count and his Chinese wife. Even the poor Georgian, Gogo, hurrying downtown on who knows what enterprising deal, was found among the dead. In an editorial, the British paper expressed the public's resentment and dismay that the citizens of an international enclave should have been victimized by the embroilments of Sino-Japanese hostilities. For the first time, foreigners had been at once audience and sufferers of a Chinese moment. The British began the evacuation of women and children to Hong Kong.

There was no respite on the waterfront as daily bombing parties set out to strike the *Idzumo*. Our windows, those that remained intact from Saturday's mishap, shuddered constantly from the fierce shelling of anti-aircraft guns. Then, after an unsuccessful torpedo attack, the *Idzumo* moved downriver to the Yangtzepoo area and there was calm for a while.

For the next week we followed the fighting in the newspapers and on the radio. All sources agreed that the Chinese ground fighting was stunning. In Chapei, where Ah-ching and his divisions were headquartered, trains arrived every few hours debouching additional Chinese troops at the North Station. Chinese divisions formed a semicircle through Kiangwan to the Whangpoo northeast of Shanghai and began to press the Japanese forces in upper Hongkew towards the river.

Then Ah-ching's men attacked the centre of the Japanese concentration at the naval garrison in Hongkew, driving them to Wayside

Wharf. They thus succeeded in creating a wedge which held despite fighting on two fronts and being shelled from the ships in the river.

Though there was space for Didi in Lao Ni's quarters, we persuaded him to share our room. We would sit up late into the night watching the tracers and looking out in the distance where the fires burned in Chapei and Kiangwan. Didi had been learning about ancient cities in school, and he fascinated us with stories about the Ziggurat of Ur, a prototype of the Tower of Babel. He told us about the rare ivories of Nimrud, the biblical Calah, and the treasure of Priam discovered by Schliemann.

'I didn't know you cared about things like that, Didi,' said Aristide.

'To understand the workings of new cultures it is necessary to study the old,' Didi said.

Aristide looked puzzled.

'If only to understand why they became lost, why they failed,' Didi explained.

'Just think,' Aristide said, 'I've never even been to the Willow Tea House in the Old City.'

'Perhaps someday we'll go there,' Didi said.

His mother, who had moved in with Hoboo, was less content. She was used to space, a home of her own, a certain order. Before long the two sisters were quarrelling loudly and the mother announced her intention of moving to relatives in Chekiang province. She consulted with her two sons and they agreed that for the time being she might be better off there. Then the mother said Lao Ni and Didi had no use for her, were trying to get rid of her, and only Ah-ching was a proper son. She would wait until he managed to get leave, and he would decide on her course of action. But a day or so later she complained that being cooped up with Hoboo was unendurable. Ningpo would be better. She would go. Lao Ni told his mother that she had better decide while Nantao was safe and the trains still left from the South Station. So it was decided the mother would leave around the end of the month.

In a rash of bombings, the Japanese hit the American flagship *Augusta*, inflicting a score of casualties. Protests were fired off at the Japanese, and regrets were promptly forthcoming. Two days later, Sascha and his bride, shopping downtown, had a narrow escape when Japanese bombs fell on two of the largest department stores in

333

the settlement and killed six hundred people. On orders from their consulate, American women and children began to evacuate Shanghai. A second contingent of British dependants left for Hong Kong, and the French, as usual, issued a statement that any of their nationals who wanted to leave could do so entirely at their own expense. This blasted Aristide's hopes for an exciting vacation, and he was glum about it. Each day there was some news item that clearly mirrored the fact that the foreigners no longer lived in a shell of inviolability.

On the day that the mother was to leave for Ningpo, Mama told Lao Ni to take her to the South Station in the car. The woman was highly prepared for the trip with countless bundles and packages of gifts, to say nothing of two straw baskets each containing a live hen. There was a great emotional parting in the hallway between Hoboo and her sister, and the servants came out to wish her luck on her voyage. They assured her that the trouble would soon be over, Ah-ching would come home to stay, and she would be reunited with her sons before she knew it. As the mother tearfully collected her packages, Mama reminded Lao Ni that she was going to the French Concession and to please return as soon as he got his mother settled at the station.

We were at the luncheon table around one o'clock when Lao Ni returned. He said that the station was crammed with travellers, almost entirely women and little children. His mother had been quite put out by the crowds and had almost decided there and then to forget the whole venture, but finally he had got her comfortably ensconced.

As he was talking we heard the bombs. Sascha ran to the verandah. 'Where did it hit?' Mama called, but Sascha did not reply. Lao Ni ran out and in a minute he was back, his face very pale. 'Nantao,' was all he said. We followed Sascha to the smoking-room. On the radio the broadcaster told of the destruction of the South Station. Without warning Japanese bombers had struck at the Chinese suburb, which so far was not being used by the Chinese as a military depot. Hearing the explosion, Hoboo, Didi, and the other servants had come into the room. Lao Ni began to weep bitterly, chastising himself for encouraging his mother to leave. The doorbell rang then, and though we couldn't imagine who might be calling, we all went into the hall. When Zee opened the door, there stood the mother;

334

behind her was a cab driver loaded with bundles, packages, and the baskets with the two squawking hens.

'I changed my mind,' the woman announced. 'The minute after Lao Ni left, I thought, what am I doing here? My sons are in Shanghai and I'm running off to Ningpo. It's crazy. So here I am.'

Her sons ran to her and hugged her with such displays of affection that the mother was momentarily unsettled. Then Hoboo embraced her sister and told her to give thanks to whatever patron saint it was who prevented disasters and promised that she would never quarrel with her again. Lao Ni then told his mother about the bombing of the station. The woman listened wide-eyed and said, 'I thought I heard a noise.'

The Japanese, alarmed at the strategy and force of their enemy, had begun heavy landings of troops at Woosung. Occupying at first a narrow strip of river landing, the vanguards began pressing north and west against two towns held by the Chinese. To Sascha this was obvious strategy. He explained it to Aristide, Didi, and me: 'By moving northwards the Japs are consolidating their landing area. Lotien in the west makes an ideal transportation centre. Then wait and see, the Japs from Woosung will cut back south, behind the Chinese in Chapei, and press down to meet with their own troops in Hongkew.' Sascha said this was a traditional flanking tactic.

It all sounded depressingly efficient and Japanese to my brother and me, but Didi said thoughtfully, 'It's not that simple to do.' And he was right, for the fighting, though fierce along these lines, remained at a stalemate for the next few weeks.

While the Chinese struggled to hold onto their towns in the north and the west of Woosung, the Japanese attempted landings at Pootung across the river, simultaneously bombing Chinese positions there. Again our windows rattled as the sky screamed with the whistling of bombs and blazed hotly night and day. In the west of Shanghai proper, Japanese planes destroyed a bridge next to the Settlement boundary foreign defence posts. Shortly after the middle of the month, Lotien was taken by the Japanese. They had seized it once before and been driven back, but reinforcements of Japanese had arrived and they were now attempting to turn the flank of the Chapei-Kiangwan front and force a Chinese retreat.

On the night that Lotien fell, Ah-ching slipped out of Chapei through Hongkew and into the Settlement. It was late when the

335

doorbell rang and I went to the door. I was so conditioned to Ah-ching's appearance as a spruced-up general, almost ablaze with polish, that at first I didn't recognize him. He was wearing jacket and pants of coolie cloth, and on his feet were soiled tennis shoes. Then he grinned impudently and said, 'I am not so brave as to go through Hongkew in uniform.'

The women in our family had gone to bed, but my brothers and I were up, and Sascha asked Ah-ching into the smoking-room. His mother and Hoboo came in, the mother making a great to-do over his appearance and the fact that he smelled like a goat. Ah-ching listened to all this maternal babbling, although I'm sure he would have preferred to talk with his aunt. Vexed finally, Hoboo said, 'Why are you clucking over him? You say he's thin? Fix him something to eat.' The mother went off, calling excitedly for Lao Ni and Didi.

Ah-ching hugged both his brothers, then settled back in the club chair with the beer that Aristide had fetched for him. Sascha told him how the Chinese troops had inspired everyone's respect by their bravery and persistence. Ah-ching laughed but he was obviously pleased. Sascha asked him if the Chinese could keep the Japanese at Lotien, and the general replied that he had his doubts.

'Superior logistics, how can you beat that?' he said.

'But not superior men,' Didi said.

'No, not men, but manpower, and that is a different matter.'

'And what if the Japs succeed in turning your flank?' Sascha asked.

'We'd be cut off in Chapei.'

'Then you retreat?' Sascha said.

Ah-ching took a long draught of his beer and ran his finger over the rim of the glass until it made a squealing sound. '*We* retreat, but I do not retreat.'

'I don't understand,' Sascha said.

'I have been ordered to hold Chapei at any cost. Chiang Kai-shek says my battalion must fight to the end.'

'Alone?' Lao Ni cried. 'But that would be suicide.'

'Why?' Didi said. 'Why you?'

'Because I'm there, I suppose. It's all politics and I'm no good at it. Some nonsense about me being the hero of Chapei in nineteen twenty-seven.'

'Against the Reds,' Sascha remembered.

'Ah-ching,' Didi's face brightened, 'you know that Mao Tse-tung has reorganized his soldiers into the Eighth Route Army and they are standing by.'

'To kill us all,' muttered Hoboo darkly.

'Mao Tse-tung has pledged his support to Chiang Kai-shek, and they have both sworn to uphold the three party principles of Sun Yat-sen.'

Ah-ching looked fondly into his youngest brother's eyes. 'I know, I know, *hsiao* Didi.'

'I don't like this at all, this business of you and your men holding out in Chapei,' Lao Ni burst out. 'So you were the hero and now they want to make you the martyr. Saint Ah-ching of Chapei.'

Ah-ching laughed and said, 'You work for a living, so you must take orders from your bosses. I am a soldier, I must obey my superiors.' I noticed how delicately Ah-ching had skirted mentioning Lao Ni's position.

'But there is really no danger of anything happening to you, is there?' Didi said. 'I mean if it came to that and you had to defend Chapei, Chiang would never abandon you, would he?'

'No, of course not,' Ah-ching said.

'There, you see,' Didi turned to Lao Ni. 'You're such an alarmist, an old woman really.'

Ah-ching then asked Didi to go see what was taking their mother so long with the food. When the boy had left, Ah-ching pulled a white envelope from his pocket and held it towards Lao Ni. 'It's not much, but it will help a little to take care of our mother and Didi.' Lao Ni looked alarmed and Ah-ching chucked him gently under the chin. 'Nothing is going to happen. Didi is right, you know—you *are* an old woman.'

For six weeks after Ah-ching's visit, the Japanese plied their resources northwest of Chapei in an attempt to smash through the Chinese lines and turn the flank of the Chinese army. And desperately the Chinese sought to stay the Japanese at Lotien, to prevent the measure that would force their retreat from Chapei.

Toward the end of October the Japanese, hurling mammoth forces, broke through the Chinese defence positions at Kiangwan below Lotien, where the Chinese were less concentrated. From there, they succeeded in pressing down to the rear of Chapei. The Chinese had fought for seventy-six days in this area; now they retreated west across Soochow Creek. But Ah-ching and his battalion remained. Each day the press, the radio, and the people in the streets spoke of the heroes of Chapei who would not abandon it. They called it the Alamo of Shanghai. It was a stirring testimony to Chinese courage. At home we clustered by the radio where reports came on the hour. The battalion had holed up in adjoining warehouses in the Paoshan district, resisting all offers of surrender. To the Chinese people the retreat of Chiang's armies from Chapei became minor by virtue of this stubborn display of fortitude. On the third day we heard that a courier had been sent from the battalion inside Chapei. Questioned by newsmen, the officer said his only purpose was to relay General Koo's message that he and his men would fight to the last.

That same night the officer came to our apartment. He told us that the battalion could not hold out much longer: they had run out of rations and their munitions were about gone. Ah-ching had sent him, not for the purpose of that vainglorious comment, but to urge Liu Yueh-sung to send military assistance.

'Pockmarked Liu?' Sascha said.

The officer reminded Sascha that the warlord had placed his army of fifty thousand men at the disposal of the Generalissimo ten years ago.

'And what did Mr. Liu say?' Sascha asked.

The officer sank his head into his hands as he told us that Pockmarked Liu had professed surprise at the request for his aid. What he had helped accomplish in 1927 was water under the bridge. 'See, today the Communists are Chiang's allies. This war was never to my liking. I was not consulted on it. I have no idea why the Generalissimo should expect my assistance. Even if I had so strong an army as you suggest . . .'

It was typical of the warlord: the feigned astonishment, the moral lesson, the skilful evasion of mentioning Ah-ching by name—Ah-ching his enemy, over whom he exulted in this final coup of vengeance. Even the deprecating of his own power was characteristic of Pockmarked Liu.

Lao Ni said, 'Ah-ching must surrender. Obviously Liu has betrayed a promise to Chiang.' I looked at Didi, who was wall-eyed with fatigue and concern.

'I will go to Liu; I will beg him to save my brother,' Didi cried suddenly, thrashing his arms as though persuasive action could be achieved simply by movement.

The officer looked up and reached to steady Didi. 'I have a message to you from your brother,' he said. Didi waited.

'Tell Didi that to live is more important than to avenge; tell him to forget *pao-ziu.*'

Next day, when the Chinese in the warehouses did not reply to their gunfire, the Japanese entered Paoshan district. Ah-ching and his men were marched to a field. The Chinese inhabitants were summoned to witness. One of them gave an account of the mass executions to the newspapers. Before the six hundred soldiers were put to death by firing relays, Ah-ching and his officers were led into a deep trench. The people were told to line up above the trench. This they did hesitantly for if, as they presumed, the Japanese planned to shoot the general and his officers, they as the forced onlookers might easily be hit. General Koo had smiled at them and told them not to fear. Then a dozen Japanese soldiers with fixed bayonets thrust their blades again and again into the general and his officers, using their live bodies for bayonet practice.

This story was published in every paper. It was narrated several times a day on the air, accompanied by appropriately sombre music. Much play was given to the drama of the general's having died in Paoshan district where the Japanese had murdered his wife five years before. Timed as though they had been prepared well in advance, giant posters of Ah-ching appeared all over the Settlement, and immediately vendors of Japanese atrocity pictures sold millions of copies of what was purported to be a photograph of the brutal execution. Ah-ching's was a tale of unsurpassable courage at the peak of the country's national impetus. The Generalissimo sent a telegram to Ah-ching's mother, and that day Didi ran away from home.

43

TEN days after Ah-ching's death the Japanese landed at Hangchow Bay. Already routed from the north of the city, now with their rear lines threatened in the south, the Chinese were forced to withdraw from Shanghai. They straggled in retreat along the Shanghai-Nanking Railway. The skies blazed in the east over Pootung, in the west over Jessfield. Nantao in the south had been laid to the torch. And still in Chapei and Kiangwan the sacrificial blaze had not abated.

Once again Shanghai had been bruised and Nanking violated. A month later, after Chiang had moved his government to Hankow, the Japanese took the capital. Tales of the killing and rape of thousands of women and girls, the massacre of refugees, even in sanctuary zones, trickled back to us in Shanghai. Indiscriminate bombing had become a major tactic of the Japanese. In Nanking, schools, universities, hospitals, and particularly civic or historical buildings became the targets.

'To the limit of our endurance,' Chiang had warned his people, and the Japanese seemed determined to test that endurance. By summer of the next year the Japanese had swallowed most of the north, had taken key cities in the east, and were pushing towards central China. Even so, vast territory behind the Japanese lines remained in Chinese hands. Chiang had begun another exodus, this time to Chungking in the far west. That autumn Hankow fell and Canton was invaded by sea.

When the smoke had cleared and the rubble had been swept away, foreigners in Shanghai found that after all not much had been changed. True, all the former Chinese municipalities were now under Japanese control, including those extra-Settlement roads west of the city. What if the reports were true that there were twenty open gambling dens and equally as many protected opium hongs in Nantao alone? Grudgingly the foreigners conceded that the influx of Chinese refugees, some quite well-to-do, had caused a housing problem. Rents had sky-rocketed. Then there was this unsettling

340

business of the terrorists. But after nearly two years we had still managed to keep our extraterritoriality.

Since his marriage Sascha had worked at four jobs and produced one child. Discouraged by his lack of success in the business world, Sascha turned to his abiding interest, the military. He had joined the American Machine Gun Company of the S.V.C., and now in his leatherneck uniform he spent most of his time at shooting contests, where he was usually high gun. Maximilienne, his daughter, was a pretty and agreeably spoiled infant. Anastasia, completely woven into the cocoon of motherhood, with the Russian passion for diminutives, called the child Lienne.

We had not heard from Chicho for a long time, which meant naturally that he didn't send any money. Our cash reserves dwindled but we had had sufficient foresight to convert it into U.S. currency. The rate of exchange was now fifteen Shanghai dollars to one U.S. dollar. Mama called in a jewellery appraiser, one of the most eminent, at whose *atelier* Papa had spent a fortune. She dressed for the occasion since it wouldn't do for the jeweller to think that we were in financial straits.

'You understand,' she said to him, 'it's not that I *need* the money. It's just that I'm bored with these things; I never wear them.'

The jeweller removed the examining glass from his eye and sighed wearily. 'Madame Spunt, a lady never sells her jewellery unless she needs money.' He then gave her a flat figure for the lot, which so offended Mama that she packed him off.

That spring of 1939 Sascha applied to Mr. Isaacs for his old job and was turned down. But Mr. Isaacs said he might consider hiring Aristide. It had always seemed to him that of us three Aristide was the only one with the slightest vestige of Maximilian's acumen. Aristide was not due to take his Senior Cambridge exam until June and then there were six months to go before he could matriculate. But Mama said this was a golden opportunity to get a toehold in the business that had made Papa a millionaire. And on that score how much formal education had Papa had? Aristide argued that things were quite different from what they had been in Papa's youth, and anyway he wouldn't consider working for a Judas like Mr. Isaacs. Back and forth they went, and finally Aristide quit school and went to work for a transportation concern belonging to the widow of a man Papa had helped in the past. While these job arrangements were in the negotiations stage, the widow confided to Mama that her fondest wish was to acquire membership at the Cercle Sportif Français. Though lacking in money, Mama still had influence. It meant only a phone call to the director of the Cercle and the woman was proposed. Aristide had his job for the length of time it took the widow to go through the club's balloting. He was out of work at the end of June. At first Mama was properly contrite and self-admonishing. But later she wondered aloud how such an impractical and preposterous idea could have ever been hers. 'Listen,' she cautioned me, 'if you ever decide to leave school, I'm going to make you write me a letter to that effect. *You're* never going to blame me for ruining your life.' Unlike Sascha, Aristide found another job very soon. This one was with a motion picture distributor. It paid reasonably well and carried with it the bonus that we could preview the films at private showings. Aristide was able to chip in with the expenses at home, with a little to spare for his own needs. Aristide was popular as Sascha had never been. His incandescence shed its light on everyone; young and old, men and women, even children. And he didn't know how to discriminate, so he never chose nor did he reject. He waited and, when summoned, blazed away with the full intensity of his supercharged personality. He expended all his energy, and it lasted exactly until the next summons. Those left behind in the middle of their worship found themselves in a darkness of their own creation and called him insincere, superficial. The clique which had chosen him at this point was the *jeunesse doree* of Shanghai—hard, articulate, and beautiful women; vigorous but courtly men, among them the handsome officers of the Sixth Battalion, Fourth Marines. The colonel in charge was an affable bachelor. Again the chauffeured limousine waited at our entrance, not for Mama this time but for Aristide.

Shortly after the Shanghai warfare Zee had decided to return home to the north. It made not much difference now, he said, where he went—the Japanese were everywhere, and he had some family interests to look after in Tientsin. From then on, Lao Ni became more of a member of the family, much like Hoboo. He doubled as number one boy and chauffeur and filled in whatever time was left over as general factotum. As for Didi, none of us had seen him since the night he ran away two years before. Lao Ni said he had heard that Didi belonged to some school or guild and that he was probably

342

learning a craft. It was not until the day in early September when Great Britain declared war on Germany that Aristide and I ran into him.

We had gone to a rehearsal for an amateur play about Disraeli in which Aristide had a part. He was onstage when the news of war came. There and then it was decided to discontinue the production. Feelings were intense, and the British-born wife of an American admiral, who was playing the duchess, ordered champagne brought onstage for the cast. Solemnly we drank a toast to Allied victory.

It was a balmy evening and we decided to stroll home from the theatre. On Bubbling Well Road, outside the newest high-rise hotel, we saw Didi. He was taller and had an air of challenge, much like Ah-ching's expression when we had first met him. He seemed happy to see us, but restless. Aristide asked him to come for dinner, but Didi said he couldn't, he was waiting. Aristide assumed it was for a bus and said to come along with us and we'd see that he got wherever he wanted later. But Didi was firm.

'Don't you want to see Lao Ni, your mother, Hoboo?' Aristide insisted.

Didi hesitated and I thought he was about to relent when a limousine sidled up to the kerb and the driver in a foreign suit opened the door. Without a backward glance at us Didi jumped in. The men in the car were considerably older than Didi, one of them with strange eyebrows like caterpillars, quite mean-looking.

Not much happened in Shanghai immediately after the Allies declared war. Not much happened on the surface, but from the Japanese-occupied areas there was a spreading toxin. More and more the Japanese were becoming incensed at the two foreign pockets separating them from total consumption of the city and its revenues. They had already seized the Maritime Customs. The postal system, radio, railway, telephone, and telegraph lines followed.

Before evacuating Chapei the Chinese had placed their land office records with the Shanghai Municipal Council for safe-keeping. These records established ownership of all parcels of real estate belonging to the Chinese. The Japanese demanded return of the records in the name of their puppet government. The council body refused to part with them.

It became clear to the Japanese that they must establish a regime with some semblance of legality, headed by an eminent Chinese. In

343

March, 1940, the new government became official. At once the Japanese demanded jurisdiction over the Chinese courts in the foreign areas. They wanted access to the Nationalist funds banked in the Settlement. They insisted on more representation by Japanese council members. We thought it strange that they did not bother much with the French Concession. Sascha surmised it was due to the fact that the Concession was wholly French and protected by a large *caserne* of soldiers. But in June, when France fell, we understood why. Japan had simply been marking time. They would be able to deal with the Vichy government.

The Chinese press published in the Settlement flayed the regime ceaselessly. They played up the terrorist assassinations to the fullest. And the regime struck back: editors and writers were kidnapped and mutilated; their heads were placed on pikes and left in front of busy intersections as a warning. But the press continued its war. The Japanese stepped in, and under their pressure a strict censorship of the Chinese press was enforced and at least four newspapers were suspended.

But the regime's assassins were no match for the trained crew of terrorists, who were said to have a list of eighty-seven important officials who had defected from Chiang, opposed the United Front, and had betrayed China. As the shots rang out in the streets or the theatres, as a knife sliced across a throat or plunged into a body, that list of names shrank.

Early next spring there was an assassination at Farren's, a nightclub casino in the western area. Although this act of terrorism occurred in a section under their own jurisdiction, the Japanese at once put the blame on the council members of the Settlement. Proper cooperation, they said, a vigorous flushing out of the terrorist nests in the city, and this would never have occurred; another major political assassination and the Japanese would be compelled to take over the International Settlement.

After President Roosevelt's aid-to-China programme began, the Japanese reacted with outrages against foreign individuals and property in their occupied areas. Everyone contemplated the possibility of a full-scale war between the United States and Japan. The Marine colonel and his men were shipped off to Corregidor. And Aristide spent most of his time with me.

Summer came and went and the city was quiet. Too quiet. Sascha

344

had finally found a job of sorts, working for an enterprising German refugee, one of the many thousands who had poured into Shanghai since the European war. The job had to do with automobile parts, wrenches, and axle grease, and Sascha liked it. He was in charge of a group of Chinese mechanics. One day early that autumn Sascha came home with the rumour that the Japanese were recruiting for a new Chinese leader. The present one's inability to incite the local Chinese against the foreigners dismayed them. There had been talk among Sascha's workers of a more powerful individual, a man of great personal wealth who was politically resourceful as well. Obviously not a man above personal corruption. It was not too difficult to pinpoint such a person.

'Pockmarked Liu,' Aristide said. 'But why? He's got all the money he could ever use.'

'Power?' I suggested.

Sascha assumed that power might be a factor in Liu's considering the position, but his opinion was that the warlord most likely believed in an ultimate Japanese victory. 'Look, nobody's come to Chiang's aid yet and the war's been going on for four years.'

That night Aristide and I went to a film. It was raining when we came out of the Grand Theatre and even in our Burberrys and Wellingtons we were getting soaked. I was all for returning home at once, but Aristide was intoxicated by the scent of the rain and the heavy sky with its intermittent scar of lightning. He got an inspiration. 'Tell you what, let's go to the Old City.'

'What's there?'

'Everything. The old and the new. Pagodas and opium dens.'

'No, thanks.'

'You're eighteen, don't be a fig. Think of it, the original city and we've never seen it.'

'I can do without.'

'Then I'll go alone.'

Suddenly he made one of his extravagant sallies, and we were shouting with laughter and spinning around crazily when we saw Didi. He had just come out of the bar behind us, hands thrust into the pockets of a shiny black raincoat such as the Sikh policemen wore. He was grinning at us. When he came close I could see the bar sign chattering its golden neon reflection in the lenses of his dark glasses. When he learned that we were going to the Old City,

Didi said, 'I'm on my way there; I'll walk with you.' In the main it was Didi who kept up the conversation, carefully aiming it at our interests. He asked about Lao Ni casually, as though he too belonged to our world rather than his. Aristide did not question Didi concerning his activities.

Didi led us to the southern boundary of the French Concession where the ancient moat had been converted into a boulevard. Here there was an entry to the Old City. It was disappointing. Gone was the encircling black brick wall, with its four thousand archer loopholes and its twenty guardhouses, the walls Mama had wanted to inspect on her sojourns with the matchmaker, Madame Liebgold, and which I think she never did see.

Now the entrance was marked by nothing more imposing than a gateway guarded by Japanese sentries and their Central Government hirelings. They let Aristide and me through. But Didi had to bow to the sentries and show them the permit required by all Chinese traversing the occupied areas. The policemen then frisked Didi, one prodding at him with the butt end of his rifle while the other made him take off his raincoat, his jacket, and even his pants before letting him join us.

Just then the rain let up and an even light bathed the flagstones of the streets. It was quiet in the centre of the city, over the public square, and along the ivory street canopied in blue. And it was quiet on the street of birds hung with hooded cages which made me think of heads and executions. It was ghostly silent at the Willow Tea House, where we tiptoed over the crooked bridges. Aristide cast a pebble in the pool to ward off the devil, but the pebble struck one of the stone figures and lay at its base. Beggars with truncated limbs and organs swollen from elephantiasis slept against the spirit wall of the temple, as if they had been cast there, deposits of pulpy gourds.

Aristide shuddered. Spreading his arms, he took a deep sniff of the foetid air and said in perfect white-shoe tourist imitation, 'Sa-a-ay—*this* is China!'

'This *was* China,' Didi laughed.

Then he led us out of the Old City by way of Nantao suburb. Here music blared from the open hongs and Chinese civilians walked companionably with Japanese businessmen. Cars in bracelet attachment honked frustratedly while rickshaw and pedicab coolies wrangled with each other over fares. We came to the elaborate scarlet and gold entrance of what looked like an amusement palace, but that old cloying scent I remembered told me it wasn't. We went across the street and standing in front of a closed oil shop watched for a long time the traffic coming and going at the opium den. Presently, with much tooting of its horn, a large Pierce-Arrow slowly drew up to the entrance. Standing on either side of the running boards were the personal bodyguards, each still zealously attired like the gangsters in American movies. The car stopped and a big man in a brocade mandarin jacket got out, glanced quickly to the right and left, and hurried past the scraping guards, letting the women in his company trail behind.

'Didi,' Aristide said, 'remember Ah-ching's message, forget *paoziu*. They'll kill you, Didi.' But Didi did not reply.

It was very late. On the way home the three of us stopped by the banks of the Chinese Bund to watch the dawn. In the river, sampans sleepily bobbed against each other and farther out a junk was silhouetted, its masts like black church spires against a sky now turning citron. And curving northwards was the great smile of the city, where the buildings rose in perpendicular thrusts of steel and concrete, their windows hammered by the early sun into solid sheets of gold foil. Aristide jumped on a capstan and turned towards the city. 'Look, look at it, Didi.'

Didi walked to the edge of the river, shielding his eyes. After a while he said, 'It's a foreign monument.'

'So now all foreign things must be destroyed?'

'Not physically. The character of this city as it is now, the names. The symbols of foreign imposition must die in order for Shanghai to rise again as a city of its people.'

'But don't you understand, Didi? We love Shanghai; it is our home.'

'No. It is *our* home. You just rent here.'

'Then have it! Watch your stinking phoenix try to rise from our ashes and see if it can fly.'

'It will. It will fly as never before in our history. And for you, this moment in time, this place you call Shanghai, will just be a sentimental memory.'

Life was coming to the river. There was one impatient funnel blast from a tender, and along the Quai de France and the International Bund the streetlights went off.

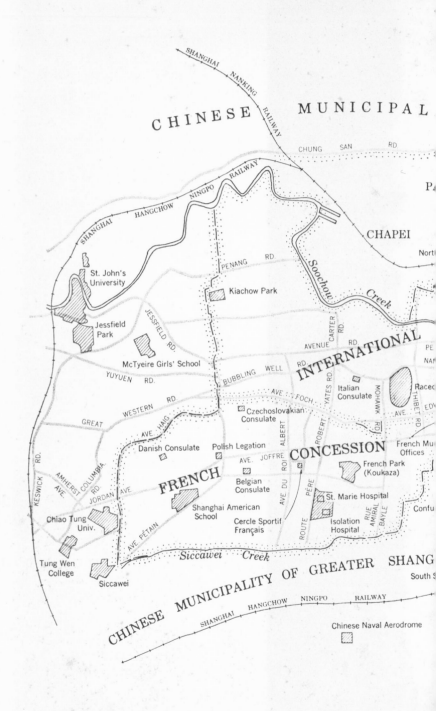

CHINESE MUNICIPAL

CHUNG SAN RD.

SHANGHAI NANKING RAILWAY

SHANGHAI HANGCHOW NINGPO RAILWAY

P

CHAPEI

Nort

PENANG RD.

Soochow Creek

St. John's University

Kiachow Park

Jessfield Park

JESSFIELD RD.

CARTER RD.

INTERNATIONAL

PE

McTyeire Girls' School

AVENUE RD.

NAN

YUYUEN RD.

BUBBLING WELL RD.

Italian Consulate

Raced

WESTERN RD.

AVE. FOCH

YATES RD.

MOHAWK AVE.

THIBET RD.

ED

GREAT

AVE. HAIG

Czechoslovakian Consulate

ROBERT RD.

Danish Consulate

Polish Legation

AVE. JOFFRE

ALBERT

CONCESSION

French Mu Offices

KESWICK RD.

AMHERST COLUMBIA RD.

AVE.

JORDAN AVE.

FRENCH

Belgian Consulate

AVE. DU ROI

French Park (Koukaza)

Chiao Tung Univ.

AVE. PÉTAIN

Shanghai American School

Cercle Sportif Français

PÈRE ROUTE

St. Marie Hospital

Isolation Hospital

RUE AMIRAL BAYLE

Confu

Tung Wen College

Siccawei Creek

Siccawei

CHINESE MUNICIPALITY OF GREATER SHANG

South S

SHANGHAI HANGCHOW NINGPO RAILWAY

Chinese Naval Aerodrome